Riot and Rebellion in Mexico

{ ANA SABAU }

Riot and Rebellion in Mexico

THE MAKING OF A RACE WAR PARADIGM

University of Texas Press   AUSTIN

Copyright © 2022 by the University of Texas Press
All rights reserved
Printed in the United States of America
First edition, 2022
First paperback printing, 2024

Requests for permission to reproduce material from this work should be sent to:
permissions@utpress.utexas.edu.

♾ The paper used in this book meets the minimum requirements of
ANSI/NISO Z39.48-1992 (R1997) (Permanence of Paper).

LIBRARY OF CONGRESS CATALOGING-IN-PUBLICATION DATA

Names: Sabau, Ana, author.
Title: Riot and rebellion in Mexico : the making of a race war paradigm /
    Ana Sabau.
Description: First edition. | Austin : University of Texas Press, 2022. | Includes
    bibliographical references and index.
Identifiers:
    LCCN 2021021114
    ISBN 978-1-4773-3079-1 (paperback)
    ISBN 978-1-4773-2423-3 (PDF)
    ISBN 978-1-4773-2424-0 (ePub)
Subjects: LCSH: Insurgency—Political aspects—Mexico—History. |
    Equality—Mexico—Philosophy—History. | Elite (Social sciences)—
    Mexico—Attitudes—History. | Mexico—Race relations—Political
    aspects—History. | Mexico—Race relations—Political aspects—Sources.
Classification: LCC F1392.A1 S23 2022 | DDC 305.800972—dc23
LC record available at https://lccn.loc.gov/2021021114

doi:10.7560/324226

Contents

Acknowledgments *vii*

INTRODUCTION 1

PART I. *The Bajío*

CHAPTER ONE. Vanishing Indianness: Pacification and the Production of Race in the 1767 Bajío Riots 31

CHAPTER TWO. "So That They May Be Free of All Those Things": Theorizing Collective Action in the Bajío Riots 53

CODA ONE. From the Country to the City: Movement, Labor, and Race at the End of the Eighteenth Century 69

PART II. *Haiti*

CHAPTER THREE. The Domino Affect: Haiti, New Spain, and the Racial Pedagogy of Distance 83

CHAPTER FOUR. Staging Fear and Freedom: Haiti's Shifting Proximities at the Time of Mexican Independence 105

CODA TWO. Haiti in Mexico's Early Republican Context 125

PART III. *Yucatán*

CHAPTER FIVE. On Criminality, Race, and Labor: Indenture and the Caste War 139

CHAPTER SIX. The Shapes of a Desert: The Racial Cartographies of the Caste War 164

CODA THREE. "Barbarous Mexico": Racialized Coercive Labor from Sonora to Yucatán 193

EPILOGUE 209

Notes 218

Bibliography 277

Index 302

Acknowledgments

This book had many previous lives, all of them traversed by the vibrant conversations and exchanges I had with colleagues and friends during the time it took to get to this, now published, version. Although it would be impossible to include in these acknowledgments everyone who played a role in this journey, I still would like to recognize some of those who did.

The first seeds of this project lay in the years I spent as a graduate student at Princeton University. I'm grateful to Gabriela Nouzeilles for her guidance during that time and for piquing my interest in the study of the nineteenth century. Susana Draper and Rachel Price also were crucial to those formative years. I thank all three of them for their support and for continuing to be my interlocutors.

I'm especially indebted to Paulina Alberto, Ivonne del Valle, David Kazanjian, and Daniel Nemser, who generously read an early draft of the manuscript and offered their insightful and helpful feedback in a workshop held in 2018. I thank my colleagues at the University of Michigan for their support. Being a part of the stimulating conversations that take place in the halls and alleys of the Modern Languages Building opened many new and exciting paths for my research. Nilo Couret, Enrique García Santo-Tomás, Michèle Hanoosh, Alejandro Herrero-Olaizola, Juli Highfill, George Hoffmann, Kate Jenckes, Annette Joseph-Gabriel, Victoria Langland, Larry Lafontaine-Stokes, Ana María León, Cristina Moreiras, Giulia Riccò, William Paulson, Gustavo Verdesio, Sergio Villalobos, and Gareth Williams all provided support, guidance, and encouragement at different stages of this process.

Before joining the University of Michigan, I spent a year at the University of California, Riverside. I'm grateful to Alessandro Fornazzari,

Benjamin Liu, Marta Hernández-Salván, Jennifer Hughes, Covadonga Lamar-Prieto, José Luis L. Reynoso, and Freya Schiwy for the many exchanges we had while I was there and that were also central to developing the book as it stands today.

A special thank-you to William Acree, Becquer Seguín, Mayra Bottaro, Juan Pablo Dabove, Daylet Domínguez, Margarita Fajardo, Laura Gandolfi, Víctor Goldgel, Natalia Brizuela, and Jorge Quintana-Navarrete, who kindly opened spaces for me to share my work and/or read through drafts of chapters and grant proposals. Their comments, questions, and suggestions were invaluable in bringing this manuscript together. Similarly, conversations I sustained with Miruna Achim, Jens Anderman, Alejandro Araujo, Erica Beckmann, Ron Briggs, Sibylle Fischer, Shelley Garrigan, Carlos Illades, Adriana C. Johnson, Brendan Lanctot, Horacio Legrás, Agnes Lugo-Ortiz, Joshua Lund, Felipe Martínez-Pinzón, Fabienne Moore, Dawn Paley, Pablo Pérez Wilson, Adela Pineda, Ignacio Sánchez-Prado, Antoine Traisnel, Emmanuel Velayos, Amy E. Wright, and Brian Whitener enriched my thinking and the pages of this book. More broadly, my work benefited greatly from feedback I received in numerous presentations I gave at different conferences. I'm grateful to my colleagues in the circuits of Mexican studies and nineteenth-century Latin American studies who made that possible.

I started my career as a young scholar surrounded by an amazing network of brilliant women academics who accompanied me in every way possible, navigating a profession that, like many others, is impacted by gender inequality. I'm forever grateful to Amanda Armstrong, Juanita Bernal Benavides, Amy Sara Carroll, Catalina Esguerra, Silvia Lindtner, Aliyah Khan, Meena Krishnamurthy, Laura Torres-Rodriguez, Judith Sierra-Rivera, Kira Thurman, Carolina Sa Carvalho, Anna Watkins Fisher, Tamara Williams, and others whom I've already mentioned for opening feminist spaces to reflect on, challenge, and escape the gendered pressures of academia. I couldn't have finished this book without you. You all inspire me.

I taught two graduate seminars on topics related to the scope of this book, one at UC Riverside and the other one at Michigan. I'd like to thank those who participated in them for the stimulating conversations we had: at UCR, Conor Harris, Bret Noble, Emily Pryor, Oscar Rivera, Seher Rowther, Jorge Sánchez Cruz, and Oscar Ulloa; at Michigan, Claudio Salvador Aguayo, Barbara Caballero, Sergio Cárdenas, Hannah Hussamy, Emmanuel Navarro, Garima Panwar, Rudy Pradenas, Matías Larramendi, and Alejo Stark. I'd also like to thank María Laura Martinelli, Paige Rafoth Andersson, and Mary Renda for inviting me to be a part of their intellectual trajectories within our graduate program.

I thank Barbara Alvarez and the staff at the library of the University of Michigan for helping me find access to the different documents and resources I needed to complete the research for this book. Similarly, I thank those working in the Archivo Histórico de la Secretaría de la Defensa Nacional (AHSDN), Archivo Histórico de la Ciudad de México (AHA), Getty Research Institute, Hemeroteca Nacional de México (HNDM), and William L. Clements Library (CLE) for their help collating materials and making them accessible to me when I visited. Thank you to Quetzil Castañeda and Edy Dzib, who taught me what I know about Yucatec Maya.

During my time at Michigan, I received the generous funding of two ADVANCE Faculty Summer Writing Grants, and participated in a first book workshop that was extremely helpful to prepare me for different aspects of the process of publishing a first manuscript. I thank Susan Scott Parrish for doing an amazing job at leading the workshop and Allison Alexy, William A. Calvo-Quiros, Charlotte Karem Albrecht, Jeremy Levine, Ana María León, Diana Louis, Ava Purkiss, and Matthew Spooner for sharing their work and for their insightful comments about mine. I also joined a Women of Color in the Academy Project Summer Writing Retreat that gave a calm space of collegiality to advance in my writing.

I extend my gratitude to Kerry Webb at the University of Texas Press for her work and for believing in this project. I also thank Andrew Hnatow and the rest of the press's team for the work they put into publishing this book. Working with them has been a wonderful experience.

Thank you to Kim Greenwell, Robin Myers, Heath Sledge, and Erna von der Walde for their help in editing the manuscript at different moments. Because I am not a native English speaker, their editing eye was vitally important.

Finally, a whole system of care and support outside the academic world was also crucial to my completing this book. Thank you to Sofia Arredondo, Paulina Campos, Mariana García, Sergio Galaz, Humberto Beck, Meena Krishnamurthy, Alejandro Reynaud, and Alejandra Foerg for the special gift of their friendship. Through uncountable texts and phone calls, their love and support was always a source of light and encouragement. Thank you to Julie Nagel for many years of collaboration working through some of my own internal obstacles to writing.

I'm forever indebted to my lovely family in both the United States and Mexico. Thank you to Michael Arnall, Brynn Arnall, Joanne Arnall, and Yolanda Espinosa for opening your hearts to me. Thank you to my grandmother María Luisa García; to my parents, Hernan Sabau and Mila Fernandez; and to my sister, Lucia Sabau, her husband, Pedro Sordo, and their three beautiful children, Maya, Emilio, and Daniel, for their unwavering love.

This book is dedicated to my love and life partner, Gavin Arnall. His heart and unique mind have always invited me to see the world anew, never taking anything for granted. He stood beside me through the intense intellectual and emotional roller-coaster that was writing this book, even when things got heavy and challenging. I could not imagine having gone through all of this without you. I'll always be grateful for all the love and support you've given me. The biggest gift of life came with the arrival of our daughter, Moira, in September 2020. The joy of having her in the world, even as the COVID-19 crisis made it all so very hard, provided me the energy I needed to get through the final stages of revising this book. I love you, Moira; thank you for being. A final note of recognition needs to go to our sweet dog, Clementine, who patiently napped under the blanket next to me for endless hours while I was sitting in front of the computer, typing away. Her tender gaze of nonjudgmental love was absolutely the most wonderful gift she could give me.

Riot and Rebellion in Mexico

Introduction

A telluric image haunted Domingo Faustino Sarmiento's writing as he dedicated his last published book, *Conflicto y armonía de las razas en América* (1883), to his dear friend Mary Mann. The book expands the analysis he had elaborated nearly forty years prior in his canonic piece *Facundo o civilización y barbarie* (1845) beyond the Argentine context to all of Spanish America, for, as the renowned politician and writer put it, there was an "evil running deeper than what the visible accidents of the American soil could let on."[1] He was referring to racial conflict (*conflicto de las razas*), an issue that, in his view, plagued the nations once under the hold of Spanish colonialism, from Mexico to Venezuela, Chile, Peru, Bolivia, and beyond, and explained the region's political immaturity and developmental lag when compared to rising US imperialism.

That Sarmiento presented racial conflict as a subterranean current, a "general tendency" that pulled events across different regions of Spanish America into the same undertow, reflects how pervasive and plastic the language of, and concern with, "race war" was throughout the nineteenth century.[2] This alarmist term was used by Sarmiento and others not only to describe tensions among the divergently racialized groups of a specific nation but also to imagine an allegedly shared threat that connected the countries of the hemisphere. In his dedication to Mann, Sarmiento detailed how the political geography of the Americas had been forged through racial conflict: "Mexico lost to racial conflict California, Texas, New Mexico, the Pueblos, Arizona, Nevada, Colorado, Idaho, all of which are now blooming states in the U.S. . . . Like Mexico, we too have lost to racial conflict, the Oriental Band and Paraguay to Guaraní uprisings, and the Alto Perú due to the serfdom of the Quichua."[3] Although Sarmiento placed Mexico first in his narrative of how the Americas' political geography came into being, few people today would think of this country when evoking the idea of race war. The term is more commonly associated with straightforwardly white settler colonial states such as the United States and Australia or even, within Latin America, Uruguay and Argentina.[4] It is also connected to places where slavery played a major role and was deeply entrenched, as in Cuba or Haiti. The common exclusion of Mexico and other countries with more analogous paths, such as Perú, from this conversation probably reflects the efficacy that *mestizaje* as a racial ideology holds in such places.[5] But as the passage from Sarmiento's piece evinces, racial conflict was hardly foreign to Mexico; indeed, it was a central, if contested, preoccupation.

In the following chapters, I show that Mexican authorities and elites shared with their counterparts in other Spanish American countries a similar concern about the dangers and impacts of what they called "racial conflicts." What is more, the variegated responses they articulated to address this concern were crucial in solidifying the foundations of a racial state and a racially stratified society that, as I further elaborate in the conclusion, still holds sway in the present.[6]

While scholars have recognized that the legal abolition of "casta," proclaimed shortly after Mexico declared its independence from Spain in 1821, did not translate into the immediate destruction of the complex racial hierarchy constructed by and inherited from Spanish colonialism, most assert that by the turn of the century, racial categorization became obsolete as class-based distinctions became more prominent and a largely mestizo population reared its head.[7] In this view, the legacies of the colonial caste system are taken for granted as anachronistic residues that are doomed to dissolve and decay.[8] I take a different approach. I track the inheritances of colonial race-making practices at both the material and symbolic levels through the processes that consolidated Mexico's racial state. I treat these residues of colonialism not as fragile relics from times past but rather as persistent governmental techniques and ideologies that were revisited, readapted, disputed, and challenged in specific regions and at specific moments of the nineteenth century.

RACE WAR IN MEXICO

In 1849, when Antonio Garay and Mariano Gálvez reminisced about the conditions that led to the founding of Mexico's Direction of Colonization and Industry, both acknowledged that avoiding race wars in the country was one of the institution's primary objectives.[9] In their yearly evaluation of the Direction's enterprises, Garay and Gálvez felt that "racial subversion" was among the most dangerous threats lurking beneath the young republic's social tissue.[10]

At the time, so-called racial uprisings were thought to be especially dangerous and flagged as such, compared to other, allegedly less risky kinds of social conflict. This sense of difference was articulated in many official documents of the time, including a proposal drafted by the secretary of war and marine in 1840 arguing that military colonies should be established along the US-Mexico border to contain raids by Apache, Comanche, and other local tribes: "The military campaigns that are waged against barbarians are very different from any other kind of conflict caused by war."[11] This view was also articulated in unofficial documents, mostly in articles that were printed and widely circulated in the press. Consider, for instance, a five-piece series that was published in *El Universal* in December 1848 on the topic of "caste wars." Although unsigned, the articles have been attributed to one of the most renowned conservative thinkers of the time, Lucas Alamán.[12] Devoted to the popular and indigenous uprisings in Yucatán and the Sierra Gorda, the series envisions a set of both military and pedagogical strategies that could be implemented to contain and pacify the conflicts. The series thus opens by highlighting the characteristically disquieting quality of "caste wars" and establishing a tacit distinction between this particular "life or death situation" and both civil wars and wars with foreign nations: "Neither the general government, nor the local state governments, or even the peaceful citizens seem to understand the importance of this present struggle. It is about life or death and a thousand times more dangerous than a war with a foreign nation. . . . Once a caste war unravels, especially if one of those castes is uncivilized, the war will have no end if not through the extermination of one caste by the other."[13]

It may seem obvious that insurgencies would have been treated as a direct challenge to the state's sovereignty. But politicians and writers of the time invested a great deal of time and ink shaping them as such and explaining the implications of the challenge posed by these rebellions. Many articles were penned in the attempt to categorize unraveling indigenous uprisings as war, and more precisely as caste wars. These attempts to frame public opinion indicate that events and state responses needed constant interpretation, framing, and legitimating.[14] From Yucatán to the Sierra Gorda, the term "caste war" resonated in local newspapers printed throughout various states of the republic, many of them also impacted by the forces of rebellion. With its strongest reverberations in Yucatán, the term traveled across the country, bringing many other indigenous revolts under its umbrella. As the widespread adoption of the term shows, despite the singularities driving these conflicts, they were all perceived as similarly interrupting governing elites' visions of a smooth path toward the consolidation of a criollo nation-state.

Another article, published on March 25, 1849, illustrates the breadth of the translocal discursive network through which alleged racial conflicts were constructed as the most important threat to the nation. First published on March 19 by the Veracruz newspaper *El Arcoiris*, the piece was reprinted a few days later in the Mexico City–based *El Monitor Republicano*. It addressed the topic of racial conflict as a general issue facing the nation and once again linked the 1847 Yucatán uprising with contemporary popular revolts in the Sierra Gorda. In the body of the text itself, the anonymous author weaves together passages from articles published in other places and by other newspapers. With its reprints and its quotations drawn from newspapers printed in different states of the republic, the text illuminates how shared meaning about local events was gradually woven together into a broadscale narrative about the impending dangers of race war.[15] Creating resonances from Campeche to Veracruz to Mexico City, the piece condensed and channeled elite anxieties over indigenous unrest, linking contemporary disturbances to the unfitness of racialized and poverty-stricken groups for citizenship.

The previous examples showcase just some of the terms used in nineteenth-century documents to refer to what were seen as racially motivated and, therefore, highly threatening social conflicts. From "fights against barbarians" to "wars of colors" to "subversion of the races" to "caste wars," all these labels charted the complicated cartography of what I call the race war paradigm in Mexico. The terms index the many forms that the fear of racial conflict acquired as well as the variegated political projects that late colonial and early national government officials attached to it. This raises some important questions that guide my discussions: How did the fear of racial uprisings become both so pervasive and so singular? How was it that struggles that sprouted from very different conjunctures and in different locations could all be lumped into the same paradigmatic specter of race war? And, most importantly, what work did the language used to name and characterize these conflicts as race wars *do*?[16]

On the ground, many of the rebellions that authorities, politicians, and intellectuals placed within the conceptual field of race war articulated desires, demands, and political imaginations that challenged contemporary racial structures. Yet the ways in which these struggles engaged with notions of race and racialization were far more complicated than the lens of the race war paradigm could recognize. Time and again, rhetoric detailing the many dangers of race war specifically insisted that the vengeful extermination of "whites" by racialized Others was the primary and ultimate motive behind this type of social upheaval.[17] Although rebels involved in the conflicts did sporadically advocate for targeted violence against whites, their struggles opened up a much wider range of possibilities beyond the violent removal of their oppressors. I thus explore not only the state rhetoric of race war and its uses but also key rebellions around which this paradigm crystallized. Documented in rich textual archives, these rebellions offer powerful insight into alternative modes of organizing social, economic, and even environmental relations.

The letters, manifestos, proclamations, and statements penned by the rebel leaders of these uprisings illuminate a shared understanding of the structural and systemic dimension of race and its shifting intersections with the exploitative conditions of the expanding global capitalist system. The texts that compose what I call the rebel archive of the race war paradigm (discussed in chapters 2 and 6), as well as the state documents and other sources I analyze alongside it, were written at different historical moments and responded to varying local, regional, and global conditions.[18] For this reason, I do not attempt to systematize these insurgent texts into a coherent unit but argue that taken together, they articulate a constellation of demands that aimed to dismantle the institutions and policies that jointly produced racial and economic stratification in Mexico.

Contrary to what both state authorities and the press constantly reported about them, these rebellions did not simply promote direct attacks on people who were racialized as white. Instead, and more prominently, the rebellions targeted the very foundations that enabled the production and reproduction of race. They sometimes called for the abolition of tribute, taxes, and prisons; they pressed to reshape social relations by changing the structures of land property; and they challenged the charting and measuring of territories that aligned with processes of accumulation and dispossession.

Crucially, many of the texts that constitute this rebel archive did not do away with racial terminology. Instead, they repurposed racial categories in their imagination of what David Kazanjian might refer to as "plural universality."[19] These documents articulated visions of freedom and equality that still relied on, yet challenged, racial difference.[20] This is the case, for example, in a brief statement from a letter sent by Maya rebels to the Yucatec government. The letter was collectively written during the Caste War and showcased how racial categories could be repurposed for emancipatory ends. The authors of this text envisioned a world in which "whites, blacks, and Indians may plant their 'milpa' wherever they want," adding that "no one will impede it."[21]

In recent years, scholars working in different fields and disciplines have pointed out the limits of the once novel contention that race is a social construct. As Patrick Wolfe suggests, this statement, although incredibly important in its time, leaves us with more questions than answers—namely, "how are races constructed, under what circumstances, and in whose interests?"[22] I build on Wolfe's approach to race not as ontology but as process in an effort to elucidate some of these questions in the context of Mexico's late colonial and early national history.[23] Like Wolfe, I understand that regimes of race are always incomplete projects that need to be continuously maintained, performed, and enacted. Racialization—that is, race in action—is the process that brings differentiated human groups into being by mobilizing a wide array of resources and drawing from the entire spectrum of social discourse, from the legal to the economic, aesthetic, and moral.[24] "Races are traces of history," writes Wolfe. He maintains that although structural, racial regimes are not inert and are therefore also far from being static or uniform. The processes through which racial regimes are continuously reproduced are always contested and, as such, bear the historic traces of dispute and resistance.[25] Building upon this work, I argue that untangling the contested meanings behind so-called racial conflicts is a way of illuminating the multilayered and palimpsestic processes of making and disputing race in Mexico.

RACE WAR AS PARADIGM

Scholarship on race both in Mexico and in other contexts commonly refers to the fear of racial uprisings among those in power.[26] It is also all too common, however, to confer a transhistorical quality to these affective discursive responses. Such an approach presupposes that the fear elite groups express when confronted by popular uprisings is not only self-evident but also constant and stable throughout time. I denaturalize this position by investigating the race war paradigm not so much as an affective response to the threat of racialized uprisings but rather as a surprisingly effective rhetorical device that facilitated the further implementation of policies and practices aimed at pacifying social conflict and sustaining racial difference. I explore the changing modalities of this rhetoric and the various ways it operated at different moments in Mexico's late colonial and early national history. State officials and elites were among the most vocal in articulating their concerns about racial conflict, to be sure, but I am less interested in *who* invoked this discourse than in *how* these claims worked and *what* they made possible and accomplished, both materially and symbolically. Appeals to the threat of racial conflict were an important piece in supporting state-led processes of pacification beyond the use of military intervention to contain insurgency. I discuss, for instance, how mobilizing the generalized fear of racial conflict enabled projects for economic development through displacement, colonization, and the expansion of networks of coercive labor.[27]

Organized in a loosely chronological order, the following chapters touch on specific conjunctures in Mexico's long nineteenth century and move through major historical inflections within this temporal arc, from the beginning of Bourbon Reform and the crumbling of the colonial order, to the political volatility that marked the early national period, up to the Díaz regime and the consolidation of plantation economies in the country's southeastern states. However, there is no claim here to an exhaustive or comprehensive history of the region or period. I offer something other than a history of every racialized conflict in Mexico. There are, indeed, other cases that could be considered under this axis. Instead, I embrace a conjunctural approach that explores how race-making operates through accretion—that is, through constantly repurposing past racializing practices and discourses into new configurations. Such an approach begs for an understanding of temporality less interested in clear beginnings and endings than in the overlapping layers of the already prior and the yet to come.

I focus on three flashpoints to sketch the general workings of the race war paradigm and to grapple with what was at stake when elites and state officials rhetorically appealed to and mobilized the affective economy of racial fear.[28] These three flashpoints include the following: first, the Bajío riots that sprouted north of Mexico City in 1767 and the racializing projects promoted by Bourbon reformers to contain them; second, the Haitian Revolution (1791–1804) and the responses to it articulated by New Spanish elites and authorities; third, Yucatán's Caste War (1847–1901) and the joint conservative and liberal projects aimed at repressing it. Again, these three cases do not exhaust the breadth of the race war paradigm, but they do stand out as pivotal moments that produced ripple effects and resonances that spanned well beyond their time. The Bajío riots were possibly the largest conflagration seen by the colonial state up to that point. The widespread uprisings altered the rhythms of life in towns, ranches, and cities in the mining heart of New Spain, leading authorities to seriously consider the potential demise of the colonial order. Similarly, the news of Haiti's revolution marked a decisive moment not only for the history of the radical abolition of slavery but also for new articulations of colonialism across the Atlantic. Although New Spain has seldom been considered a piece of this puzzle, I make a case for its inclusion. Finally, Yucatán's Caste War was the largest (and perhaps most successful) indigenous rebellion of the nineteenth century to be categorized under the language of the race war paradigm. As I show, the term "caste war" radiated from the Yucatán Peninsula to nearly all corners of the Mexican Republic, providing elites and authorities with an expansive category that could paint disparate conflicts with the same brush and legitimate extraordinary measures to contain them.

Although each flashpoint allows me to discuss a specific iteration of the race war paradigm, I also aim to highlight how these instances built on each other by tracing the past discursive contours of race as they were repurposed and reimagined to address the specificities of each new context. Together, these three flashpoints compose a constellation from which the workings of Mexico's race war paradigm can be sketched and studied. Conceptualizing these events as a constellation also allows me to take on two simultaneous tasks. First, it enables me to track connections and patterns among the various racializing practices and discourses appearing in different places and at different historical conjunctures, practices that otherwise might seem unrelated. I connect these practices and discourses without collapsing the frictions between them and between the ways in which they were concretely deployed and envisioned in each instance.[29] Second, it enables me to highlight the modes of persistence and shape-shifting continuities that stretched between colonial and postcolonial racializing ideologies and modes of governmentality in Mexico.

My intention in outlining the race war paradigm is not to abstract this framework from the myriad ways in which it operated on the ground, but to track the practices and mechanisms that continually made and remade the paradigm over time and across space. Following Giorgio Agamben, I argue that the paradigmatic relation is not one that preexists, external to the instances made intelligible through it. A paradigm arises neither from abstraction nor from an exhaustive enumeration—an accumulation—of particular cases. Rather, it emerges and becomes graspable (though always in an elusive manner) in the act of exposing itself, in the "medium of its own knowability."[30] The three flashpoints studied here and, more concretely, the different primary sources that I analyze in each chapter constitute the medium through which the race war paradigm makes itself knowable. While I sketch the general tendencies at play in how the race war paradigm operated, to fully understand its traction requires examining its concrete instantiations. This book accordingly grapples with the specific workings of race war rhetoric in different contexts while also engaging with it as a paradigm.

TWO MODES OF RACE WAR

The race war paradigm served two primary purposes, both related to mediation. On the one hand, appeals to the dangerous nature of racial conflicts were used as a tool to manage external affairs and to situate New Spain/Mexico in relation to a broader Atlantic spectrum of racial difference. At the dawn of the nineteenth century, the paradigm was invoked to differentiate New Spain from other colonial sites by arguing how unlikely it was for a "race war" to erupt there in contrast to other places. On the other hand, the race war paradigm was also mobilized as a means of managing and producing the "internal" racial difference that threatened the body politic—be it the viceroyalty or the nation—from within. In practice, of course, these two mediating modes of race war rhetoric were not neatly separated from each other; the internal management of racial proximities often impacted external ones and vice versa. However, I parse their workings here in order to more clearly analyze the paradigm's specific modes of operation.

As the threat of racial conflicts seemed to grow at the close of the eighteenth century, so too did discourses connecting visions of supposed racial harmony to notions of progress and civilization. For many state officials throughout the Atlantic world, a polity free of the threat of racial conflict was increasingly equated with moral, cultural, and even economic development and civilization. Latin American historiography has examined the importance of notions of racial harmony for nation-building but has mostly focused on the postindependence period. In contrast, I illustrate that these concerns were already present in and mobilized by New Spain's late colonial administration and that these worries were absorbed and continued even after the colonial break.[31]

Ideas about the harmonious coexistence of heterogeneously racialized groups allowed authorities to frame internal "racial disturbances" as exceptional events that were deeply discordant with the colony's (or the nation's) general disposition. But these ideas also had a transatlantic dimension. As waves of political instability hit the colonial territories of the British and French empires, the rhetoric of racial harmony became more and more prevalent in the writings of New Spanish colonial authorities. Latecomers to the so-called Age of Revolution, New Spanish colonial officials relied on discourses of racial harmony to position the colony they governed as distant from the unrest shaking other empires. In this context, ideas of racial harmony became intricately linked not only to domestic political stability but also to transatlantic imperial (dis)equilibrium more broadly.

This framing of New Spain in relation to Atlantic political (in)stability is clear in colonial officials' response to the Haitian Revolution (1791–1804). As I show, the revolution in Haiti became a measuring stick for racial conflict in the early years of the 1800s. Colonial authorities in New Spain sought to establish and manage their racial distance from Haiti not only vis-à-vis their internal affairs but also as a way of situating the polity they headed in the inter-imperial arena of the Atlantic. By presenting New Spain (then the most profitable colony of the Spanish Empire) as immune from potentially contagious racial disturbances like those in Haiti, authorities did two things. First, they responded to the circulation of ideas about Spain's colonial brutality that had crystallized in what has come to be known as the Black Legend.[32] Second, they attempted to diplomatically recover Spain's lost ground in the imperial crossings of the Atlantic.

Authorities seemed to view possible racial conflict, in its more dominant "internal" modality, as lurking primarily in border zones, prowling in the "lumpy" spaces of empire and nation where only partial sovereignty had taken root and where plans to expand it were at play. The threat of racial subversion marked its presence in spaces historically described as isolated hills or inaccessible deserts, unruly enclaves where economic and social relations were shifting and being renegotiated.[33] These potentially profitable yet liminal and allegedly dangerous spaces included the Bajío region, located north of Mexico City, where in the mid-1700s the mining industry was restructured to become the most profitable source of revenue for the Spanish Empire, and the Yucatán Peninsula, where in the mid-1800s sugar plantations began to be replaced by a booming henequen economy. The possibility of race wars was understood to haunt these "anomalous zones," where the expansion of the state and the global capitalist system was simultaneously advanced and contested.[34]

RACE WARS AND THE WORKINGS OF LEGAL EXCEPTION

As intellectuals and politicians from both the late colonial and early national periods increasingly insisted that race wars constituted the most significant threat to the economic and political stability of the states they headed, they also made increasingly urgent appeals to suppress them. Their labeling of social disturbances as various types of race war, I argue, was a way of demarcating zones where legality could be unevenly or exceptionally managed, of outlining spaces where the rule of law could be strategically suspended or differentially applied in the name of safeguarding the country, even "civilization" at large.[35]

In *The State of Exception,* Giorgio Agamben distinguishes between Western countries that have regulated the state of exception by law and those that have preferred not do so explicitly in their legislature.[36] The gap between these two positions arises from the difference between viewing the exception as a de facto situation (external to the law) and viewing the exception as one that is directly tied to the juridical order. While Agamben challenges both positions and argues that the state of exception is neither internal nor external to the law but rather exists in a "zone of indifference where inside and outside do not exclude each other but rather blur with each other," his charting of these two traditions is useful to explore Mexico's history of emergency legislature and its ties to the making of race.[37] Here, both positions coexisted. In the period that concerns me, instances of exception were at times regulated juridically and at times extra-juridically, and the line that separated one response from the other was racialized.

The discursive and affective threads that throughout the nineteenth century framed race wars as the most extreme threat to the polis were produced extralegally, delineated not explicitly by law but by what we could call a dominant "common sense," a set of shared perceptions that allowed elites and authorities to present racial conflicts as the ultimate threat within the taxonomy of social upheaval.[38] This is not to say that legal procedures were evenly followed in the context of pacifying racial uprisings. On the contrary, I track multiple instances of legal unevenness and exception. It is to say, however, that elites and authorities across the political spectrum situated race wars as singularly dangerous events and coincided in the need to suppress them by any and all means necessary, with little to no regard for how the implementation of extralegal measures in these contexts might impact the existing juridical order.

During the first two-thirds of the nineteenth century, Mexican congressmen were, at different moments, involved in long and tedious conversations about how to define the exact conditions under which both the general congress and the executive power could instate regimes of exception suspending civil liberties and granting the executive branch and the army complete power. Brian Loveman observes, for instance, that in the wake of the 1812 Cádiz constitution, both liberal and conservative legislatures in Mexico incorporated the grounds for some degree of state-sanctioned exception, even if initially only through vague terminology.[39] As legislators and statesmen attempted to reconcile the emerging languages of civil liberties with the legacies of the ancien régime, Mexico's constitutions—like many others in Spanish America—would be marked by the dependency of an emerging liberal democracy on modes of sovereign exception.[40] In Loveman's words, "Monarchists, conservatives, and liberal Mexicans had achieved at least one fundamental agreement: Mexico could not be governed unless civil rights and liberties could be suspended when circumstances required."[41] Although elites and authorities across the political spectrum agreed on this assumption, they had different views and anxieties about when exactly the use of legal exception might undermine the constitutional order instead of safeguarding it. Notably, this concern arose in a number of circumstances but not in the face of responding to so-called race wars.

While the institution of martial law was discussed from at least 1828, the parameters for calling it into effect were not officially incorporated into the Mexican legislature until 1860.[42] The legal decree that explicitly introduced martial law was instated by Benito Juárez in response to the turmoil brought on by the "Guerra de Reforma" (1858–1861).[43] His decree put multiple locations, from Veracruz to San Luis Potosí to Mexico City, in a state of siege. This was a strategic move in the struggle between conservatives and liberals. I will not explore the details of this political tactic here. Instead, I am interested in highlighting how, along the proclamation of article 29 of the 1857 Mexican constitution, this decree marked the explicit introduction of the language of emergency into the republic's legislature, where both (the article and the decree) became the center of numerous subsequent discussions attempting to determine the nature of their existence within the bounds of the country's constitutional order.[44]

One such discussion took place in relation to a series of conservative-led mutinies that were organized from Cuba in an attempt to reinstate the conservative order and/or separate the Yucatán Peninsula from the rest of the republic. Documentation surrounding what tactics would be employed to contain these mutinies suggests that congressmen understood them to be qualitatively different from rebellions that appeared to have a racial connotation.[45] The mutinies erupted in Yucatán in December 1867, months after the execution of Emperor Maximilian of Hapsburg and the so-called triumph of liberalism in Mexico. As conservatives desperately grabbed for power in the peninsula, debates in the federal congress ensued around whether and where a state of siege should be declared: Only in certain regions, or in the entire state of Yucatán? These debates revealed concerns surrounding a deeper question: Would opening a legal space for declaring martial law and suspending civil liberties erode something fundamental about the law itself?[46] Indeed, those who opposed declaring a state of siege in the Yucatán did so because they dreaded the paradoxical consequences of inscribing anomie in the juridical order and of legally sanctioning the violation of constitutional rights and liberties, such as freedom of speech and the press, freedom of movement, and freedom of domestic privacy.[47]

The very occurrence of these congressional debates made it clear that, after independence, state authorities responded quite differently when facing racial uprisings than when facing other types of armed conflict. Many places (including the Yucatán itself) experienced indigenous and popular rebellions that were categorized as race or caste wars, and although martial law and other modes of legal exception were locally declared or practiced in attempts to repress them, these responses did not become the driving force for congressional discussions about how their implementation might threaten the constitutional order.[48] The absence of such concerns in relation to "racial uprisings," I argue, points to the fact that a differential use and framing of exceptional legal measures separated this type of conflict from others. In fact, during discussions about imposing a state of siege in Yucatán to contain the threat of conservative-led mutinies in 1867, a few congressmen declined the proposal not only on the grounds that it could erode the rule of law and the political autonomy granted to each state by the federal structure, but also on the basis that declaring a state of siege would siphon economic and military resources already allocated to wage the "war against the savage Indians" of the peninsula.[49] In other words, the debates themselves accentuate that so-called race wars were perceived to be of a different order and, therefore, beyond the pale of generating anxieties about the consequences of extra-legal exception.

I suggest that these different ways of responding to social conflict were an important part of producing a racialized administration of political inclusion in the polis. Insofar as those participating in conflicts that (apparently) had little to do with matters of race were socially seen as fraternal, equal-to-all enemies—that is, as full citizens, who even in their treasonous criminality ought to be judged according to the prescriptions of the law—they were placed within its boundaries, even when the congress discussed the possibility of inscribing legal measures to suspend that law. Conversely, debating the constitutionality of employing "exceptional" measures to repress racialized groups and their acts of rebellion was not deemed necessary. On the contrary, when social upheaval was perceived to have a racial bent, rebels who participated in this type of conflict were frequently seen as disposable members who could de facto be placed either inside or outside the boundaries of legality and the body politic, depending on which was more politically convenient in a given situation. As I will demonstrate, when "extraordinary" measures were employed to suppress racial rebellions, they were not perceived as threatening to the rule of law. More often than not, they were seen as either necessary civilizing measures or, less frequently, the undesirable but inevitable results of confronting the particularly raw violence assumed to attach to so-called racial conflicts. Appealing to the rhetoric of race war effectively produced a caesura in the social body and demarcated an extralegal line between, as Michel Foucault would have it, "what must live and what must die."[50] It was, to put it differently, a way of drawing a distinction between which groups of people were to be protected "under" the law and which groups would be placed "before" it.[51]

The regions that were haunted by race wars thus became spaces where the rule of law was "commonsensically" ignored or suspended in the name of colonial/national security and civilization, where the differential deployment of state-violence was unquestioned.[52] Not coincidentally, it was in these same areas that economic expansion and development were pursued at the cost of the lives and livelihood of racialized (mostly indigenous) groups that contested assimilation to the structures of both the late colonial and burgeoning national states, challenging, among other things, the loss of their autonomy and control over communal lands. Under the guise of protecting the polity from the dangers of race war, authorities pursued new possibilities for economic development and industry, paving the way for foreign and national colonization and creating both a racially segmented workforce and a surplus population. In the forthcoming chapters, I track how the extralegal rhetoric of exception surrounding these events was used and reused in multiple contexts and conjunctures, showing how crucial the race war paradigm was for the territorialization of Mexico's racial state.

Although the invocation of the race war paradigm was particularly important in mediating the transition from colonial to republican rule, state officials relied on it throughout the entire nineteenth century. In 1869, for instance, in the southeastern state of Chiapas, Yucatán's Caste War was perceived to be extending to nearby regions as the Chamula and Tzeltal rebellion reached its highest point.[53] Desperately seeking to pacify the growing uprising, Governor José Pantaleón Domínguez appealed to the "civilized world" by claiming "that a caste war had now begun in all its horror" in the state under his command.[54] In a diplomatic communication promoting the deportation and dispersion of local indigenous inhabitants to different parts of the state in order to keep the peace, Domínguez utilized the race war paradigm to its fullest extent by announcing the futility of dealing with "Indian" rebels according to the law:

> Another means we could try is to judge them according to the law. This, however, is infeasible because one cannot jail entire populations, nor are there enough resources to support the forces that would guard them while the processes unravel. In this matter we'd have to stumble with the malice and rebelliousness of the Indians as they impede a perfect investigation. The only possible path given the current circumstances is to take them out of their burrows and transport them to other places in the state where with them we can form new settlements and towns that can be useful for the Republic.[55]

For Domínguez, Chiapas's "notable [racial] disproportion" was a crucial problem.[56] Like many others before him, he saw foreign colonization as the key to reintroducing "equilibrium" in the unsettled region, but the repopulation of the area with white settlers could be pursued only after the rebels had been dispersed and relocated to other parts of the state. Otherwise, he said, incoming settlers "would have to come prepared for battle rather than for work."[57] Intriguingly, as we see in the passage above, Domínguez's exceptional measures were determined by the governor's concern with the fragility of the state's penal infrastructure and its lack of resources. His doubts about the state's prowess to control subversion were echoed repeatedly at different moments when the race war paradigm was called upon. These cases illustrate that Mexico's relation to exception was (and continues to be) framed not as a matter of the excessive exertion of state power but rather as the only path available to a weak and impoverished state apparatus.

In the previous extended passage, Domínguez also related the necessary suspension of the law to Indianness. Insofar as Indians were presumed to be inherently malicious and rebellious, treating them as full political subjects under the law and taking them to trial was similarly discussed as infeasible. In his assumption that Indians could only offer distorted versions of the truth in their confessions, that their responses to questioning would only "impede a perfect investigation," Domínguez conjured the legacies of colonial modes of racialization that constructed Indianness as linked to unreliability and untrustworthiness.

As this example shows, the race war paradigm and the construction of Indianness were often intertwined, shaping and feeding off of each other in an ongoing cycle. Racial conflicts had to be managed and suppressed at any and all cost, by any measure, in order to save and expand "civilization." To justify this, the rebels who participated in these conflicts were marked as "burdened individuals," whose actions could be conveniently regarded as incommensurable with the law.[58] Insofar as Indians had already been constructed as incompatible with the workings of the law, their actions of resistance could always be framed as "unreasonable," conveniently placed outside the boundaries of political and legal legibility and thus vulnerable to the operations of exception.

PENALITY AND MILITARIZATION

The race war paradigm should also be understood in relation to changes in the penal system. In the late colonial period, measures deployed to punish those who participated in the 1767 Bajío riots were concomitantly designed to create profit for the colonial bureaucracy. As such, punitive measures became tied to the growing mercantilist disposition of the Spanish Empire under Bourbon Reform. Sentences of banishment and displacement to military garrisons, which were commonly used under Spanish imperial rule, were similarly repurposed in nineteenth-century Mexico and paired with budding ideologies that associated racialized convict labor with moral reform. According to this perspective, forced migration and labor promoted the moral improvement of rebels. Indigenous men and women, criminalized for their alleged involvement in racial conflicts, were often punished, uprooted and separated from their lands, making these territories available for further colonization and development. As Domínguez's interventions show, uprooting and relocating "Indian rebels" to settle and work in other areas of the nation (or even outside the country) was framed as advancing "civilization" while enabling the "rebels'" own moral progress.[59]

The race war paradigm should likewise be understood in relation to facilitating processes of militarization. Under the cloak of protecting the colony and, later, the nation from the threat of racial conflicts, authorities and elites pushed to implement changes in the structures of the army. It is not coincidental that in 1767, when New Spain's mining region became the stage for the largest wave of popular uprisings the viceroyalty had ever witnessed, the repressive response led by José de Gálvez framed the disturbances as racial uprisings that specifically targeted whites. This justified not only his forceful response to the riots but also his efforts to consolidate a permanent colonial army.[60] The colony's expansive militarization in the wake of the 1767 riots was closely tied to protecting the interests of Spanish and criollo entrepreneurs from such disturbances.

During earlier times of colonial rule, local militias were important institutions for New Spain's free Blacks and mulattos, but in the late 1700s, Bourbon policies restricted a number of rights that free colored militias had previously enjoyed. A "whitening," a creolization, of the colony's army was underway.[61] New Spain's military system was restructured in the encounter between Bourbon Reform and the 1767 riots. The consolidation of a colonial army was not only linked to protecting Spain's territories against foreign invasion, particularly after the momentary loss of Cuba in 1762 to the hands of the English, but also as a containment strategy in response to the perceived growing threat of "race wars" in one of Spain's most profitable colonies.[62]

Correspondingly, in 1848, when the conservative intellectual Lucas Alamán addressed the recent eruption of "caste wars" in the Sierra Gorda and Yucatán, he called for the reform of Mexico's army. Reflecting on the lack of resources and technology that faced the country's military forces, Alamán argued in favor of consolidating rural and urban militias, both operating under the command of the federal government. He insisted that propertied men should fill the militias to be led by government-instated officials. He thus tacitly excluded indigenous groups from the draft as he stated that the main objective of the militias was to "attend to the nation's public safety and, specifically, to contain indigenous rebellions."[63] Although Alamán's suggestions did not come to full fruition, his recommendations were illustrative of elites' fear of racial and class conflict and, subsequently, their desire to safeguard their interests in the hands of the military.[64]

Gálvez's response to the 1767 riots and Alamán's take on the Yucatán Caste War exemplify how, at different moments, the race war paradigm became enmeshed with projects to expand and reform the colony's and the nation's military forces as well as their penal systems. Militarization and punitive measures were important instruments that produced racial distinctions and protected the interests of the wealthy and the white in Mexico.

THE RISE OF PLEBEIAN SECTORS

The modalities of the race war paradigm I focus on were prominent toward the end of the eighteenth century and forward, when it emerged as a concern over the polity's security and became tied to military and punitive governmental projects. But its roots stretch deep into earlier colonial times. The 1692 riots that took over Mexico City, famously documented by Carlos de Sigüenza y Góngora, for instance, could be considered an important precedent for it. The race war paradigm is part of a broader genealogy related to paranoid narratives about the dangerous rise of racialized plebeian sectors in New Spain's political landscape.[65]

Daniel Nemser has argued that a new motor of colonial governmentality, the plebe, coalesced around the 1692 riots; colonial texts touching on these events obsessively registered the "disturbing" presence of the plebe in Mexico City. Nemser shows that the texts also mobilized narratives about the supposed breakdown of racial stratification linked to the appearance of this unruly collective body in order to support the refashioning of existing governmental mechanisms geared toward sustaining and reproducing racial distinctions in the colony.[66] The rhetorical tools of crisis and collapsing racial boundaries would mark not only the final stages of the colonial period but also the efforts to build an independent nation for the next hundred years and beyond.

Although used in a range of ways, the term "plebe" in colonial texts indexed fears of "mixture" and "impurity," pointing toward how authorities and elites feared the coming together of heterogeneously racialized bodies—those who were considered to be of different castes and those considered to be already mixed and impure in themselves (mulattos, mestizos, *lobos*, etc.).[67] But "plebe" also held connotations of class: the threatening encounter of differently racialized bodies was also a coming together of the impoverished and dispossessed lower sectors of society. "Plebe" is thus an important term in thinking about the intersections between class and race, for it is a window into how class was racialized and race was classed.[68]

While the emergence of the plebe category has often (like *mestizaje*) been read alongside colonial texts as a sign of deteriorating racial stratification and the emergence of a growing "mixed" body, Nemser warns against an all too easy embrace of this dominant narrative. He argues that the obsession with impurity and mixture that markedly took over colonial governance (and the pens of Spanish and creole intellectuals) around 1692 should not be read on its own terms as the actual undoing of racial hierarchization. This obsession should instead be read as illuminating the fact that mixture itself acted as a racializing marker.[69] Building on Nemser's work, I argue that across the span of nineteenth century, authorities and elites came to see race wars as the most extreme outcome of collapsing racial stratification, even if diverging causes were ascribed to this crisis at different moments. In the late colonial period, for instance, authorities connected racial disturbances to a governmentality that was failing in its mission to adequately police and instate racial distinctions and, therefore, desperately needed reform. In the early national period, alternatively, elites often viewed race wars as the undesired byproduct of having abolished the *casta* system and extending legal rights (in disregard of racial difference) to groups they perceived as unprepared for the responsibilities of political inclusion. In both moments, popular uprisings and riots were categorized as racially motivated upheavals made more likely when society suffered a lack of clearly defined racial boundaries. These conflicts were thus sites at which the making and unmaking of race was at stake.

As previously stated, the race war paradigm haunted the frontiers of capitalist expansion where communal indigenous lands were increasingly appropriated and a racialized workforce grew. This dynamic of subsumption was also accompanied by narratives that relocated political threat as emerging from within the body politic. As the global capitalist system became more and more encompassing, resistance and opposition to it also became more and more internal. The appearance of the dangerous figure of the plebe in colonial texts indexes a process of immanentization. It addresses the emergent suspicion that a new political threat was being created by an increasingly internalized excess—an excess that, as the cases I study show, was racialized.[70]

As I conceive it, the race war paradigm offers insight into this process of immanentization in Mexico. While state authorities and elites were drawing from the repertoires of legal exception, they were also designing a set of racial differences to manage the growing "dangerous" presence of racialized plebeian sectors within the polity. I expand on the idea that when state officials, politicians, and intellectuals racialized conflicts, they were concerned not only with directly suppressing social upheaval but also with defining the terms of (un)desirable, (un)ruly behavior for those who after the repression were to be subsumed or assimilated into the polis. This was an important way of dealing with the immanentization of the political threat and the growing body of the plebe.

In the forthcoming chapters, I also explore how processes of racialization produced what I call metonymic displacements of race.[71] These are instances in which government officials and elites implicitly unfixed racial terminology in favor of a more fluid understanding of race than what their explicit engagement with the rebellions allowed. They did so by unfixing racial terminology, associating it not with concrete or specific perceptible visual or biological markers but rather with what they described as the generally undesirable and unruly behavior of growing popular sectors. In these cases, the material practices, affective responses, representations, perceptions, and principles commonly used to construct a specific racial formation such as Indianness or Blackness seemed to overflow; they were mobilized to describe and manage patterns of allegedly dangerous social conduct associated with impoverished popular sectors within the polis. Metonymic displacements of race thus make visible the connections and overlaps stretching between and across diverging racial formations.

THE GRADATED BURDENS OF RACIALIZATION

Although the rhetorical dimension of the paradigm I trace often functioned through polarization, setting up Manichean distinctions such as whites versus Indians, Blacks versus whites, and civilization versus barbarism, I investigate how this rhetoric actually produced a kind of spectrum, a gradated set of unequal social relations. When intellectuals and state officials mobilized the polarizing rhetoric of race war, they did not (or did not only) exclude an "absolute enemy"; they also made possible the gradated inclusion of pacified individuals into the polis. Warding off deadly punitive measures, many of those who were criminalized by the race war rhetoric and the punitive practices it supported eventually entered into agreements with state officials. Often these agreements were burdensome and placed weighty caveats on the inclusion and participation of pacified subjects and citizens in both the colony's and the nation's body politic, respectively.

Examples of how these burdens were imposed can be found in both the Bajío and the Yucatán. When a series of popular rebellions hit the mining region of the Bajío, José de Gálvez's campaign to repress them levied heavy and punitive taxation on various indigenous towns. While the funds raised through these means were used to finance clothing and weaponry for emerging local militias, the penalties increased these impoverished towns' marginalization within the empire, sometimes even stripping them of their right to political representation. Similarly, in the Yucatán Caste War, some rebels negotiated unfavorable surrender agreements. These agreements, which pardoned the rebels and gave them contingent access to basic rights, often required that they join the national army as cannon fodder or become debt peons on plantations and lands abandoned in the conflict.[72] As Caren Kaplan has noted, the Yucatán's state government also racialized citizenship by making it dependent upon notions of "good" and "bad" behavior. These notions operated as euphemisms avowing select discrimination against indigenous people: rights were denied to those presumed to be unprepared to manage them appropriately. This produced a racially segmented citizenship that coexisted stealthily with constitutional bans outlawing racial differentiation.[73]

As these examples illustrate, the production of "gradated burdens" occurred largely at the local level. As such, these burdens created tensions with conceptualizations of the law as an even, abstract, generalized, and homogenous entity of the type promoted by liberal citizenship and, to a lesser extent, by Bourbon Reform. It has been a common argument that these burdens stood in contradiction to constitutional right and should therefore be critiqued as the failed actualization of law. Underlying these interpretations is the idea that burdens could be avoided if the law were to be applied to its fullest extent. This position, however, misses the point of the cocreation of gradated burdens and constitutional right (including its regimes of exception). I argue that attending to the dynamics that produced said burdens can add nuance to our ideas about Mexico's purported racial inclusivity and enrich our view of how the polarizing rhetoric of race war actually operated in tandem with it.

RACE WAR: INCLUSION AND EXCLUSION

In the short duration of his tenure as the Mexican minister of foreign relations in London, prominent liberal thinker José María Luis Mora faced a slew of diplomatic challenges. As he attempted to channel official support from the British government into Mexico's negotiations with the United States during the final stages of the Mexican-American War (1846–1848), his attention was unexpectedly redirected toward the massive indigenous rebellion that took over the Yucatán Peninsula in the southeastern region of his home country. Indeed, the rebellion, categorized in Mora's diplomatic correspondence as a "war of colors," seemed to conjure within him the fear of a political threat far greater than US invasion.[74]

Once again, the race war paradigm entered the stage. According to Mora, the uneven racial distribution of the Yucatán's population—tipped overwhelmingly in favor of indigenous inhabitants—was the main culprit behind the expanding uprising that conspired to "eradicate whites" from the region and that threatened "civilization" at large.[75] Dismissing the complexity of the demands articulated by those involved in the rebellion, Mora portrayed it as a "war of extermination" unjustly and irrationally waged against the region's criollo inhabitants. As we have already seen, his diagnosis of the situation was far from unique. In his diplomatic correspondence, Mora recommended that the Mexican government promote, by any and all means necessary, a better distribution of races within Mexico's population, one that would secure the consolidation and expansion of a criollo hegemony.

Under a banner that presented the ongoing social conflict of the peninsula as a race war, Mora legitimated his call for the suspension of state jurisprudence in the name of national security. In many of his letters, he warned fellow state officials that it was crucial for the Mexican government to define and prioritize a strong public agenda and "make sure that racial uprisings not only stop but become impossible in the future."[76] Securing this outcome was first presented as an issue of "peacefully" promoting white (particularly European) immigration and colonization in Mexico's extensive and supposedly depopulated territory, with the aim of facilitating a process of widespread miscegenation that would "whiten" and neutralize indigenous presence. In only a few months, however, Mora altered the presentation and urgency of his message. As rebels gained terrain over the peninsula with the aid of gunpowder and weapons supplied by British settlers in Belize, Mora announced the need for a *"guerra sin cuartel"* (total war) against the *indios*. He also wondered with awe about what might have prompted British settlers to reject a "white alliance" with their Yucatec neighbors, thereby betraying the "most vulgar principles of humanity and civilization."[77]

Expanding on his position, Mora insisted that the success of securing the peninsula's safety depended on banishing all indigenous prisoners immediately upon their capture. He thus urged Yucatec soldiers and officials to ignore all due legal process and disregard the age, gender, and other qualities of indigenous rebels in their custody. He also insisted that lands expropriated through these means ought to be given to white, specifically Spanish, settlers who for years to come should be exempted from state taxes and legally favored in any future dispute or disagreement that might arise between them and the remaining, pacified indigenous inhabitants.

As the most important liberal thinker of his time, Mora often argued against continuing the institutional legacies of Spanish colonialism. And yet the strategies he envisioned for dealing with the Yucatán Caste War were adaptations of governmental practices routinely implemented by New Spain's colonial state in an effort to secure a racialized stratification of the viceroyalty's social body. Indeed, the establishment of Spanish settlements as a means of securing territories within imperial sovereignty and promoting the "pacification" and subjection of "barbaric tribes," as well as the engineering of white privilege through a series of tax exemptions and legal favorings, were common governmental measures used throughout the colonial period. In a similar way, rebel prisoners who were expelled, as Mora suggested they be, from the peninsula between 1848 and 1861 and sent to Cuba as indentured servants followed the routes that had been established during colonial times for the banishment and relocation of garrison prisoners.

Although a buoyant scholarship on critical race studies in Mexico has been on the rise, few of these studies focus on the nineteenth century.

If they do, they emphasize the later part of this period and the framework of "scientific racism," which is considered to be independent and distinct from the workings of *casta* during Spanish colonization. These studies trace the consolidation of eugenic theories and the influence that figures such as Spencer, Darwin, Lamarck, and others held over politicians and intellectuals of the Porfiriato.[78] Although some recent studies have attempted to think through the continuities of race and *casta* between the colonial and postindependence period, emphasis is often placed on the strategies and discourses of assimilation and racial inclusion that led (albeit not linearly or directly) to embracing *mestizaje* as the central national ideology in the aftermath of Mexico's 1910 revolution and beyond.[79]

My intention here is not to question the degree to which assimilation and racial inclusion were legally, symbolically, and materially fundamental for the consolidation and expansion of the Mexican state. However, I sustain that focusing only on this narrative ultimately blurs and undermines the important role played by strategies and fantasies of racial exclusion such as the ones Mora proposed. It also makes it harder to understand how these strategies and projects of exclusion were connected to the production of gradated burdens.

In recent years, scholars including Christina A. Sue and Jason Oliver Chang have dedicated their efforts to denaturalizing Mexican mestizo nationalism. Both Sue and Chang convincingly show that embracing *mestizaje* as a national ideology has been an important factor in fostering deeply rooted and still-current ideas about how race and racism were and remain allegedly "non-issues" for Mexico's society.[80] Although the main focus of this book is not placed on *mestizaje*, I contend that a dual perspective that grasps the interweaving of exclusionary and inclusionary practices facilitated by *mestizaje* is crucial to tracing the continuities of the colonial-postcolonial transition and to understanding the work that the race war paradigm does in said transition. I would even suggest that dominant discursive practices of the time illustrate how racial assimilation and racial exclusion were more often than not two sides of the same coin. This is what Mora shows us. The quick shift that his correspondence articulates, from promoting foreign (white) colonization and miscegenation to the declaration of total war against Indians, renders visible the suture between both projects—their entanglement rather than their separation. Colonization, miscegenation, and war were all practices the burgeoning Mexican state would unevenly mobilize "to root out," in the words of Garay and Gálvez, "the danger of racial uprisings that lurk[ed] behind the vast majority of the Republic's population."[81]

THE CONSTRUCTION OF WHITENESS

The story of the race war paradigm is also an important part of the story of the construction of whiteness in Mexico. As is commonly stated in critical race studies, whiteness as a social construct has depended on and stemmed from the racialization of others. It is in this sense that the trajectory marking the racialization of popular and indigenous sectors coincided with the processes through which the structure of whiteness in Mexico came into being.

I trace different moments of this process, beginning with the inclusion of the term "white" in the counterinsurgent texts of the late colonial period. Scholars have written about 1692 as a moment when Spanish-descendent elites began to perceive themselves as pitted against a general coalition of "Indian" subjects and members of other "castas."[82] At this moment, however, Spanish-descendent elites did not yet describe themselves as white. By 1767, on the other hand, this category had already entered the lexicon and was used widely and specifically in the context of so-called racial conflicts.

After the Haitian Revolution, whiteness increasingly became a category that mediated the spectral relations of elites living in Atlantic colonial sites. New Spanish officials' responses to the revolution allow us to track how an intercolonial modality of whiteness was being constructed. Through their shared fear that a race war might erupt in the colonies where they lived, elites in different sites of the Atlantic began to explicitly think of themselves as mirroring each other, as occupying an equally vulnerable position within their racialized societies. During the second half of the nineteenth century, ideas about white vulnerability continued to grow roots as Mexican society increasingly absorbed the tenets of liberalism. At this moment, whiteness and the privileges tied to it were often described and defended as property.[83]

As I approach it, "whiteness" does not strictly refer to subjects and citizens who might have appeared or self-identified as white. On the contrary, my understanding of the term stretches beyond race as both identity and visual bodily marker. In the same way that I address the question of how race was constructed under the light of the race war paradigm, I also intend to parse the concomitant procedures that were involved in producing economic, affective, and legal positions of privilege that were linked to notions of whiteness. In other words, I want to show how the materials I work with point toward the fact that whiteness in Mexico, to borrow Gastón Gordillo's phrase, was "the not-fully conscious disposition, shared by people of multiple backgrounds, to desire a nation" without *indios*, without *negros*, without *chinos*.[84]

A NOTE ON METHODOLOGY

The question of riots and rebellions has been widely discussed in the scholarship on Mexican history. It is particularly central in the historiography that developed in dialogue with subaltern studies during and after the 1990s. Seminal books such as Eric Van Young's *The Other Rebellion* (2001) and Florencia Mallon's *Peasant and Nation* (1995) approached major moments of political upheaval to respectively account for the roles that subaltern groups played in shaping the uncertain processes of independence and nation formation during the nineteenth century. Riding the waves of writing "history from below," this scholarship aimed to highlight the agency of subaltern actors, attempting to recover from the archives their behaviors, ways of thinking, and modes of resistance. As Friedrich Katz puts it, these efforts were geared to presenting peasants as real people of "flesh and blood," rather than abstract sociological categories.[85]

The breadth of work that exists on popular uprisings in Mexico has certainly succeeded in painting a mosaic of narratives that highlight the complexity and heterogeneity of the issue.[86] Rebellions broke out at different times and places and for a number of reasons, and those involved in them built all sorts of local and cross-class alliances depending on location and conjuncture.[87] To offer an overarching argument about the place of rebellion in Mexican history would therefore be greatly reductive. I join the authors of the existing scholarship in emphasizing the singularity of the uprisings I discuss. Far from trying to systematize their unique logics into a single cohesive narrative, as I claim the race war paradigm attempted to do, I instead highlight their specificity while also grappling with how these events showcase efforts to engage the production of race not merely at the level of racial ideologies but also at the level of dismantling the concrete material practices that sustained them. Importantly, that I aim to address the singularity of these uprisings should not be read as narrowing the scope of the political imaginations that sprouted from them. My engagement with moments of upheaval is not centered on providing a factual reconstruction of localized events bound by their past temporality. When I offer close readings of select texts that were produced by and during rebellions (see chapters 2 and 6), I look to trace the unfinished projects of emancipation they unleashed by addressing how they might continue to speak to us today.

In these pages, I approach rebellions and riots as moments in which political (and racial) boundaries were exposed and disputed. But my analysis differs from the dominant tendencies in the scholarship in two major ways: first, by foregrounding the question of race-making (and unmaking) as a central factor of social upheaval and repression in Mexico's long nineteenth century, and second, through a methodology of examining "racial conflict" as a genealogical device. In other words, I approach the "race war paradigm" as a web of discursive practices that, when studied in conjunction, constitute a site from which it is possible to parse out the conditions of possibility for the reproduction of racial difference in Mexico, particularly during a period when race was assumed to be eroding. At the center of my study is thus a concern with the rhetorical pull that accompanied the racialization of popular uprisings, more than an emphasis on the empirical.

Through these pages, my main mode of analysis is the close reading of select primary sources that showcase a range of uses of race war rhetoric at each of the flashpoints considered. As I stated at the beginning of this introduction, processes of racialization involve the whole spectrum of social discourse. I draw from literary analysis to discuss an assembled corpus of texts including theatrical plays, novels, inquisitorial edicts, legal proclamations, political manifestos, photographs, travel journals, newspapers, and maps to account for the multifaceted dynamics through which race was produced and contested at the crossroads of representation, state policy, affect, and the material and symbolic organization of space.

Most of the texts that are at the center of this study were produced from the perspective of either the state or colonial and national elites. I therefore engage them as fragments of Mexico's colonial archive and its legacies, where the term "archive" refers not only to the material collection of files housed by state institutions but also to the repositories of practices, fantasies, and anxieties of power that were unevenly repeated through time and gave shape to the race war paradigm. While some of the documents studied in these chapters have been previously discussed in the scholarship, I here explore how reading them through the repetitious trope of the fear of racial conflict might allow us to open them to a different set of questions. An important premise of this study is that to denaturalize assumptions about the stability of the paranoid rhetoric of "racial fear" in order to parse out its variegated iterations and workings, one must carefully engage its archive. In this sense, I follow Ann Laura Stoler's invitation to read the sources that are at the center of my writing "along the grain"—that is to say, not assuming that their scripts and power effects are already known to us but rather allowing for the possibility that these might be more uncertain and unfixed than we have cared to consider. To read the texts of the race war paradigm along the grain, feeling the "pulse of the archive," is therefore also to consider the contradictions, frictions, repetitions, instabilities, and anxieties of power.[88]

{ PART I }

The Bajío

{ ONE }

Vanishing Indianness
PACIFICATION AND THE PRODUCTION OF RACE IN THE 1767 BAJÍO RIOTS

In May 1767 the silver-veined heart of the Spanish Empire was shaken to its core. The Bajío mining region that historian John Tutino has described as the engine of eighteenth-century world capitalism became the stage for the largest wave of uprisings that New Spain had witnessed to that point.[1] The riots, or *tumultos*, as colonial authorities called them, peaked shortly after the Jesuit order was expelled from Spanish territories and stretched across localities from Michoacán to San Luis Potosí.

Rioters were mostly miners, "free-mulattos," and "indios vagos," all living in ranches, cities, and towns of the area.[2] They rose to challenge the variegated local impacts of Spain's imperial restructuring in the aftermath of the Atlantic crisis that had led to the Seven Years' War (1756–1763).[3] Concerned with securing the empire's hegemony, Bourbon administrators developed policies to increase the production of silver in New Spain and to expand the economic revenues extracted there and in other colonial territories. They also joined a contemporary wave of global militarization pushing to reshape Spain's imperial army and strengthened the garrisons, or *presidios*, strategically located in important fringe zones and commercial ports of the empire such as Alta California, Florida, Habana, Acapulco, and San Juan de Ulúa.[4]

At the local level, in the Bajío, many of these policies burdened the lives of workers. Their economic activities and familial ties were disrupted by forced military levies. Free mulattos and *indios vagos* were further economically marginalized by measures designed to expand tributary and tax exactions within the colonial structure.[5] Although, historically, those not living within the dual-republic system (*repúblicas de indios* and *repúblicas de españoles*) had been in practice exempt from paying tribute, Bourbon Reform policies after the 1750s sought to incorporate these groups into the empire's income stream. As might be expected, their assimilation into the tributary system brought them many strains and little reward. They labored in precarious conditions to produce the main fuel of the global market (silver) and were excluded from the access to resources and social securities normally granted to those living in *repúblicas*.[6] Untethered as they were to the racialized spatial organization of the dual-republic system that dominated in New Spain's heartland, the increasing numbers of free mulattos and *indios vagos* built up the Bajío's floating population. In the official reports on the 1767 riots, colonial authorities frequently described these groups as unruly, nomadic vagrants whose bodies were insufficiently racialized. As such, they represented an obstacle to the region's safety and economic productivity.

The 1767 riots surprised and deeply challenged New Spain's colonial authorities. In a diplomatic letter, Viceroy Marqués de Croix described them as a "universal sedition," to which he responded by sending a repressive campaign headed by José de Gálvez.[7] The campaign was supported not only by improvised regional militias and local priests, but also by the largest military entourage ever amassed in New Spain.[8]

Born in Málaga, José de Gálvez was one of the intellectual fathers of Bourbon Reform. He was sent by Charles III to New Spain in 1765 as inspector of courts and royal houses, and put in charge of restructuring the colony's fiscal apparatus.[9] When the riots broke out, Gálvez received license from Viceroy Marqués de Croix to pacify the domestic rebellions in the Bajío and environs at any cost.[10] To carry out this directive, Gálvez initiated a military expedition, which he later documented in a report addressed to the viceroy where he explained the motives behind each of his disciplinary and punitive decisions.[11] Centered on Gálvez's *Informe sobre las rebeliones populares de 1767 y otros documentos inéditos* and other texts that documented the events, this chapter explores how Gálvez and other local authorities constructed the riots as racial conflicts. They sustained that the rebels' main objective was to target white residents in the region and to unmark themselves from racial differentiation. Figuring them in this way sutured the riots to ongoing processes of racialization: Gálvez's punitive policies aimed to (re)generate racial difference in the Bajío as he associated a neatly racialized society with economic efficiency and productivity.

Here, I invert the presumed logic between race and riot. Rather than suggesting that race was the cause of the conflicts, I look at how race was (re)produced in the process of pacification.[12] I explore how Gálvez's project for the social rearrangement of the Bajío in the aftermath of the riots centered on expanding profit extracted from the mining region. This goal seemed possible only through measures destined to redraw racial difference in a society Gálvez perceived had become dangerously de-racialized.

The campaign's focus on populational management for profit illustrates how colonialism's importance to the history of capital goes beyond the extraction of raw materials. As Onur Ilas Ince states, "Colonial sites and networks were central as social spaces providing the concrete conditions for imagining and experimenting with new ways of organizing social production for profit, which would be difficult to conceive, even harder to implement, in Europe."[13] In this vein, Gálvez's Bajío campaign tested a number of strategies, from reorganizing space and land distribution in certain locations to reimplementing strict racialized dress codes to pushing mine overseers to subtract tributary quotes from workers' salaries. At the center of many of these efforts was the attempt to make "Indians" reappear. In Gálvez's narrative and that of others who supported his punitive campaign, the problematic erasure of racial boundaries in the region—and the subsequent wave of uprisings it supposedly engendered—was primarily connected to the depletion and increasing indecipherability of Indian populations.[14] It was linked to the perception that "Indian" bodies were becoming illegible when found within the growing mixed collective body of the "plebe."

The repressive campaign placed as one of its principal goals the remarking of "Indian" bodies. In order to accomplish this objective, Gálvez insisted that a spatial rearrangement of the region's towns and *rancherías* was a necessary precondition. Although his interventions suggest that the clear racialization of bodies was tied to spatiality, Gálvez and his supporters also implemented other measures for populational management. They drew from early colonial legislature, repurposing past racializing practices and codes into the context of the 1767 riots. Gálvez's campaign has sometimes been described as nostalgic. Unlike other contemporary reformers who sought to restructure Spain's empire by imitating the English or French models, Gálvez appears to be a figure who, against the tide of his times, stubbornly sought to revitalize codes of the "golden years" of Spanish imperialism.[15] Under this light, the reformer's attempts to neatly racialize the Bajío appears as an outmoded effort propelled by a leader who could not see that matters of race were soon to be supplanted by matters of class.[16] I here resist framing Gálvez's efforts as passé. Viewing his project as anachronistic impedes a full appreciation of how racialization works through accretion. Thus, I offer a detailed reflection about how continuous race-making processes can occur, as Gálvez intended in the aftermath of the 1767 riots, through the intermittent and seemingly contradictory repurposing of past codes and practices.

RIOTS, RACIAL CONFUSION, AND THE PROBLEM OF "VANISHING INDIANS"

Only a few months after the riots broke out on October 7 of that same year, the Franciscan friar Manuel Escobar stood before a large crowd gathered in San Luis Potosí's main plaza and delivered a sermon. As they listened to his stern words, the audience was confronted by a morbid backdrop: the corpses of eight Indian men hanging from the mining city's gallows. They had been sentenced to execution under Gálvez's punitive campaign.[17]

Escobar's sermon sought to channel listeners' emotions as he justified the severity of the punishments imposed upon the rebel communities. Colonial authorities generally endeavored to pacify uprisings with a "calculated blend of punishment and mercy," but the repression overseen by Gálvez was exceptionally brutal.[18] Under his command eighty-five people, almost all "Indian" men, were executed and decapitated postmortem, their heads and other mutilated body parts exhibited in public plazas. Their families were banished from the jurisdictions, their houses burned, and their lands sown with salt. Another set of penalties, including long periods of labor in military garrisons or general banishment according to the case in question, were levied on 854 others.[19]

Escobar addressed his sermon specifically to the city's indigenous inhabitants, the "naturales," explaining that the tumults in which they had participated had "tarnished" and "defaced" San Luis Potosí's peaceful and beautiful semblance.[20] In Friar Escobar's view, the riots had unleashed a crisis, one caused by their direct attempts to blur and erode the colony's racial order. He elaborated on how rebels had deliberately muddied and confused racial distinctions, upturning the parameters that had been historically established by colonial authorities to differentiate "Indians" from members of "other castes": "A determination that freed the City from the incomparable weight of confusion, in being warned that the Indians and Plebeians were mistaking themselves for one another in the assaults and mayhem, the second group taking up the voice of Indians and the Indians asserting themselves and gaining in strength and temerity with the mixture of many other castes."[21] The passage from Escobar's sermon offers a clear glimpse into how eighteenth-century colonial authorities established connections between their concern with the breakdown of racial boundaries and ideas about the plausible collapse of the political, social, and economic structures of the colony. In presenting the rioters' deliberate blurring of racial boundaries as their central strategy and thus the cornerstone of the threat they posed, Escobar inadvertently betrayed the degree to which racial categorization seemed fundamental to the reproduction and stability of New Spain's colonial order. The erosion of racial distinctions allegedly made visible by the riots evoked the possibility that New Spain's world could, like San Luis Potosí's, be unexpectedly turned upside down: in just a few months, the mining city had been radically transformed "from an affectionate city into a harsh one; from a pleasant city into an evasive one; from a *political* city into an incommunicable one; from a civil and martial city into an unsociable one."[22]

In a letter sent by Viceroy Marqués de Croix to the Count of Aranda, back in Madrid, Croix discussed the pressing need to militarize the viceroyalty in response to the riots. Croix asserted that since the early years of the Conquest, the threat to colonial stability was no longer contained in indigenous communities but had spread to other groups. It had also spread to other geographic areas. According to Croix's letter, a general malaise now extended across the interior provinces of the viceroyalty and beyond: "These kingdoms are no longer subsumed by that crass ignorance in which they were found when Cortés conquered them. It is no longer a few Indians we must contain and subject, but the mestizos, those of two colors, and the infinite vagrant peoples who have come from Europe; these are the ones who may cause trouble at any point if there are no troops to keep them in line."[23]

Although Croix focused on the threat posed by both low class and racially mixed populations (hence the mention about the unruly behavior of "mestizos," "two colors," and "vagrant Europeans"), he singles out "Indians" as the primary category from which imperial concerns about unruliness had historically sprouted ("It is no longer a few Indians we must contain and subject"). This implied that Indians were the anchor of New Spain's racial order.

Croix, Escobar, and Gálvez all articulated variations of a concern about the fast-growing body of the plebe that was channeled through discourses on the risk of racial boundaries massively breaking down in the colony. They all registered this phenomenon when writing, albeit in different ways, about the legibility—that is the apparent presence or absence—of Indian bodies. To put it differently, all three mobilized ideas about the expansion of unruly behavior from indigenous communities into other sectors of society and located the origin of this issue at the point where Indians "vanished" and fused with other racialized bodies.[24] In the views of these three figures, undesired behaviors associated with Indianness overflowed in a metonymic displacement of race and presented in other groups.

Historically, the making of Indianness was at the crux of colonialism in the Americas. The marking of bodies as Indian was central to the economic accumulation that built Spain's empire and contributed to the consolidation of the global capitalist system.[25] Indianness was thus the cornerstone of New Spain's racial structure, and it is not surprising that eighteenth-century colonial authorities saw the process of remarking "Indian" bodies as a central step in restoring "peace," "order," and racial legibility to the Bajío. What is more, the most salient motivations for colonial officials' desire to reconstruct Indianness were productive: its erasure was thought to be linked to a risky economic deficit that affected not only New Spain but the empire itself.

TRIBUTE, RACE, AND THE ECONOMIC DEFICIT OF "UNDIFFERENTIATION"

In Gálvez's well-known *informe* addressed to viceroy Antonio María de Bucareli (1771), the Bourbon reformer touches upon the historical "extinction" of indigenous populations in colonial territories:

> The truth is that the number of Indians has so greatly diminished over the two and one-half centuries since their conquest that there are currently no terms, among the few that exist, to compare them with that prodigious multitude that the old stories and accounts have told us about these Indies. Truly, the abandonment experienced by these natives, as well as the other common causes that regularly cause the destruction of dominated Nations, has extinguished the Indians in many parts of America, as has been verified on the Isles of Barlovento, and more swiftly in the Colonies belonging to other Powers toward the North of this Continent.[26]

Although New Spain had not "diminished" its native populations as thoroughly as other colonial sites, they were, Gálvez insists, being replaced: the viceroyalty's "naturales" were gradually being supplanted by growing numbers of "blacks, mulattos, and other castes of the lowly plebe."[27] Without minimizing the deadly toll of colonization, I am interested in reading Gálvez's diagnosis of vanishing Indianness as a matter of racial (i)legibility and not as a narrative about the actual extinction of indigenous groups.

In this report, Gálvez brings up the historical "extinction" of Indians in relation to a discrepancy he perceived between the amount of tribute revenue being collected and the number of New Spain's tributary inhabitants. He sustains that tribute revenue could double and perhaps even compete with the huge revenues from gold and silver mining if it were extracted correctly, in line with legal stipulations, from all tributary populations.[28] It is true that Gálvez saw the tributary deficit as due in part to the bureaucratic inefficiency and corruption of colonial institutions, but he also saw it as caused by vanishing Indianness and the unregulated movement of bodies throughout the viceroyalty's provinces.[29] Gálvez specifically highlights the problems that arose when people from "Indian jurisdictions" migrated into "free territories": "Specially when it comes to not conceding exemptions to towns without extraordinary cause, but rather adhering to mere extensions in order to avoid the irreparable damage of natives of the immediate jurisdictions moving into free territories."[30] This brief passage from the report illustrates that, for Gálvez, tribute was not only an important source of colonial profit but also a policing mechanism useful to gain information about New Spain's populations and to regulate the movement of bodies within the viceroyalty. What Gálvez calls "free territories" were zones where tributary exaction was fragile and unevenly practiced, and "naturales" who migrated into these areas often slid off the grid of the tributary payroll.[31] Perhaps more dangerously, they became invisible: racially illegible, mixed with other castes, or, as Escobar would have it, "confused"—in other words, "de-Indianized." Indeed, colonial inhabitants creatively navigated the census, which recorded *casta* adscriptions, to their advantage, finding ways to fluidly move and adjust within the parameters of colonial racial categories. Fugitivity from tributary exaction was one among many of those strategies.[32]

Gálvez was fixed on increasing colonial revenue and reforming tributary exaction, two tasks that are symptomatic of the mercantilist rationality that grounded the Bourbon project.[33] As such, he reminded

Viceroy Bucareli of the reduced tributary exactions caused by the unregulated mobility of bodies into spaces where colonial control was feeble and where racial distinctions were easily blurred or "confused": "but I cannot omit the reminder that in Mexico the King unjustly loses nearly one hundred thousand pesos a year from Tributaries who are confused in its lowly-plebe."[34]

To reduce the income drain and maximize the empire's profit, Gálvez proposed two simultaneous legal reforms. First, he sought to effectively expand tributary exaction into "free territories" to eliminate the incentive for migration into these areas. Second, he proposed regenerating racial distinctions in those areas and rendering legible the "confused" Indian bodies that already inhabited free territories. The latter was particularly important. Although racialized groups that remained outside the structure of *repúblicas* were required to pay dues by law, historically Indian tribute was much more normalized and regularly exacted. Indian tributaries, too, were required to pay higher sums.

TRIBUTARY DEFICIT IN THE "LUMPY" SPACES OF SOVEREIGNTY

Gálvez linked his project of generalizing tributary exaction across all the provinces and castes of New Spain to the historical emergence of the money form. In his report to Bucareli, he explains that in earlier colonial times tribute had been charged in specie, leaving authorities no effective way to justly homogenize the amounts to be extracted from contributing populations. Variations in landscape and agricultural practices meant that the nonmonetary tribute was not collected evenly across various regions and that the yoke of imperial sovereignty was thus also irregular.[35] But by the time Gálvez reached New Spain, tribute payments were made exclusively in the form of money, which provided the material conditions necessary to generalize tributary exaction and reshape and homogenize the contours of Spain's imperial grasp over the colony's inhabitants and resources:[36]

> The notable inequality that can be appreciated in Tribute is, without a doubt, born from the fact that in its origin it [tribute] was imposed with the worthy mercy of Our Kings. They commanded to apportion the rights to goods and lands of contributors. And since these could not be equal amongst them, the fee to be paid in recognition of vassalage to

the Supreme Dominium and protection of the Sovereign in fruits and other effects was diverse. Now reduced to a monetary contribution, it must be uniform in all those who compose this class of vassals, so that the relief of one does not result in the affliction of others, when they are all of equal condition.[37]

Gálvez here faced a conundrum. While he thought that the money form allowed tributary exaction to be more consistent, producing a considerable increase in revenue, tribute that was evenly levied across class and racial groups could also consolidate interracial block alliances, enabling rebellions. Indeed, in other documents where he addresses the 1767 riots more directly, Gálvez explicitly asserts that the rebellion stemmed from a general cross-caste conspiracy.[38]

Gálvez thus sought to expand profit from tribute by generalizing its exaction while at the same time sustaining or even producing caste differentiation among contributors to make them more controllable. Although he explicitly connects his plans for reforming tribute to the more general project of increasing colonial profit, his standard definition of tribute as a recognition of vassalage and subordination suggests that this was not simply an economic policy; it was also a way of rethinking the grasp of imperial power over the colony's racialized subjects.[39] In addition to serving as a means of wealth extraction, tribute took on a major sociopolitical role as it shaped the reaches of imperial sovereignty and jurisdiction and mediated the relationship between viceroyalties and the metropole.[40] Tribute was also a crucial mechanism in sustaining and producing racial difference within colonial societies themselves. Although in its origins Indian status was centrally linked to it, in time, other caste distinctions were also sustained by imposing differential burdening fees to certain groups while exempting and generating privileges for others (notably Spaniards, both "peninsulares" and criollos).[41] As *visitador*, Gálvez was developing more precise strategies for the management of both New Spain's resources and its colonial population, and his visions for expanding tributary exaction were ultimately efforts to reshape imperial sovereignty from the colony, both materially and conceptually.

In *A Search for Sovereignty*, Lauren Benton argues that imperial sovereignties were imperfect, uneven, and not all-encompassing. Notably, New Spanish colonial officials seemed at times to be aware of the unevenness of Spain's imperial power, addressing it and sometimes even capitalizing on it. As we have seen, Gálvez's engagement with the 1767 riots was presented as an effort to level the patchy, semisovereign "anomalous zones" of the colony, starting with the Bajío.[42] His discursive enterprise—to advocate for a uniform colonial landscape where tributary exaction was equally generalized—was also a vision of an expanded and smoothed sovereignty and jurisdiction. Indeed, in both *informes* discussed here, Gálvez asserts that colonial institutions should operate in accordance with the law, which he describes as an abstract, level, and unchangeable entity. This, in practice, consisted of interrupting the production of legal anomalies, of eliminating the common practice of applying laws unevenly based on selective localized exemptions. Specifically, Gálvez insists that colonial authorities at all levels had to deny petitions from local leaders asking that their communities be excused from tributary payments, as was commonly done.[43] To be sure, although he advocated for the fixity, abstraction, and even application of the law, on the ground, Gálvez's repressive campaign generated other forms of anomaly and exception. In some villages that rioted, for instance, lands were confiscated; other towns lost the right to elect their governors and republican officials until further notice; and elsewhere, in places such as Tlaxcalilla, where neighbors had cooperated with the punitive expedition, no penalties at all were levied.[44]

If, as I suggest here, tribute and sovereignty were bound, generalizing the former and smoothing the latter depended on efforts aimed at producing a neat racially legible social body within the colony's anomalous zones.[45] Tributary exaction and its correlate of racial distinction could only be evenly expanded into "free territories" after these areas were physically, not only legally, rearranged. In other words, Gálvez's vision of an even application of the law, as expressed in his project to level tributary exaction, was connected to a concrete project of reorganizing space and land distribution in rioting sites of the Bajío. According to his reasoning, this spatial rearrangement was essential to create the conditions for adequate populational management and, therefore, to achieve legal regularity in these zones.

RACE, SPACE, AND THE UNREGULATED MOVEMENT OF BODIES

Shortly after reaching San Luis de la Paz to duly punish the inhabitants of the small Indian town, José de Gálvez and his troops were unexpectedly interrupted.[46] As they were preparing to depart for their next stop, San Luis Potosí, the expedition received new information about the increasingly unruly riots in Guanajuato. This information altered Gálvez's original plans for his punitive campaign, pushing him to change the predetermined route of his entourage.

Gálvez's primary concern with the news about Guanajuato was not the destruction of property caused by the unrest but the stream of people deciding to leave the mines of the area and settle elsewhere. The sudden exodus of miners and other residents was deeply concerning to him, for it could jeopardize the extraction of silver, tribute, and other taxes that Gálvez held so dear to his heart. Presiding from San Luis de la Paz, Gálvez requested the assistance of regional improvised militias traveling from Guadalajara and other sites to support the repressive response from Guanajuato's local forces. He commanded the combined groups to instate a military siege across the hills and mountains of the region. Fully surrounding the city and its mining environs, the military belt stood in place for three months.[47]

In his report on the riots, Gálvez describes the siege as a spatial tactic devised to counter the racial confusion produced by the unregulated mobility of bodies. In his view, the unrestricted flow of people that existed prior to the riots had only worsened once they erupted. His military strategy to spatially intervene in the mining region had multiple simultaneous objectives: to capture "delinquents," to keep workers in the mines, and to guarantee the social and economic security of "honorable" families and merchants in the region.[48] But Gálvez's tactic, which he would use later in other rioting sites (e.g., San Pedro), had broader or more abstract implications. The report frames the siege as a spectacular display of sovereign power, one that would make tangible the colonial state's capacity for territorial control and the technological superiority of its emerging army.[49] The siege showcased a panoptical impulse at the heart of his understanding of colonial governmentality. According to Gálvez's narrative, the siege demonstrated the monarchy's unlimited power to New Spain's entire population. (As Gálvez puts it, the siege "show[ed] this entire kingdom that nothing is humanly impossible for the King's supreme power.") It also showed that rebellion was useless, for the emerging military was powerful enough to surveil the colony's entire geography, penetrating and controlling even the most remote and inaccessible points:

> Guanajuato and the famous mountains that surround it were universally viewed as inaccessible, and this belief was the greatest cause of the continuous disagreement, audacity, and rebellions of the plebs and

the mining workers, because they believed that with no other weapons at their disposal than stones, it would be easy to close the narrow Ivory entrance or to destroy a powerful army within it; and so they have seen to the contrary, with admiration and terror, in the rigorous siege that was maintained for three and one-half months.[50]

As the passage from the *Informe sobre las rebeliones* shows, Gálvez's on-the-ground response to the riots allowed him to establish associations between the command of space (and the spectacularization of this command) and the breadth and capacity of imperial/colonial power. He thus imagined the siege as the expression of an unobstructed imperial gaze for which no cave, nook, or cranny was inaccessible. In the report, Gálvez figures the repressive military campaign as a force that had been capable of altering the Bajío's spatiality and consecutively altering the reach of imperial sovereignty over it. In this fiction of colonial power, the spectacular command of space was a necessary condition to produce racially and spatially fixed—that is, legible and orderly—subjects, who could be managed to serve the empire's economic interests.

Although they focus on different historical moments, both Joshua Lund and Daniel Nemser have argued that in Mexico, race and space have been mutually produced.[51] Racialization, Nemser asserts, "took place, in part, through physical interventions in the landscape."[52] Gálvez's visions of an expanded, far-reaching, and leveled sovereignty seem to prove the point, for he insisted that to accomplish his goals of tributary exaction, the spatial rearrangement of towns and cities in the Bajío was necessary: "The arrangement of this Capital's neighborhood and of those of the other large populations of the Kingdom is the only way to improve their internal government and to update the Crown's right over tributary castes."[53]

The 1767 riots granted Gálvez the opportunity to set in motion the project of inscribing a neatly racialized spatial grid in the Bajío. He urged local authorities to implement a series of spatial interventions that were intricately tied to ideas about how to adequately, efficiently, and productively manage the movement of bodies in the region. Framing the riots as racially motivated, Gálvez sustained the forceful implementation of these measures. The punitive campaign's spatial interventions varied from site to site. For analytical clarity, I have organized these sites under three "spatial types"—mines, ranches, and "Indian" neighborhoods—based on their populations and the physical spaces they were intended to control.

Mines

Gálvez saw the mines as sites rife with social confusion. In them, workers from different "castes" and "countries" coexisted. Like he had done before, Gálvez associated this type of mingling to an unacceptable economic deficit. Once again, he insisted that the spatial disarrangement of the mines caused racial confusion and made it nearly impossible to clearly distinguish the racial assignation of the miners, which reflected in the deficient tributary fees that were extracted from them: "The greatest difficulty on these two points regarding census and tributary exaction involved the populous guild of miners and smelters in the mines and metallurgic haciendas, because they comprise so many classes of trades and occupations, and their workers from so many different castes and countries, that it seemed initially impossible to, at first sight, reduce them to the order and method of enrollment."[54] Insofar as the miners' caste ascriptions were not readily legible "at first sight," Gálvez pressured mining administrators to incorporate two governmental strategies that could guarantee maximum tributary exaction and create more adequate conditions for controlling the mines' working populations.

The first measure was designed to make every miner pay the required amount of tribute. It required each worker to be registered in the tribute books with "uniformity" and "exactitude." Perhaps more important, it stripped miners of their historical autonomy in the matter of paying the tribute owed; instead, through this measure Gálvez allowed employers to extract tributary fees directly from the workers' salaries before paying them.[55]

The second measure attempted to control workers' movement by making relocation and, thereby, potential fluxes of racial ascription bureaucratically complicated procedures. Gálvez demanded that employers request a report of duty in their hiring processes. He also stipulated that a similar report be given to workers who were fired from a mine or who wished to leave and seek employment elsewhere. The report was intended to produce a (more) racially and geographically fixed laboring population by preventing workers from moving from one mining site to another without regulation, which had allowed them to fluctuate between *casta* categories.[56]

To justify requiring this report of duty, Gálvez's *informe* uses explicitly criminalizing rhetoric. The text frames the report as a preemptive measure that would stop workers from committing a crime in one place and then moving freely, without punishment, to another.[57] The report thus makes clear how punitive and racializing practices converged in an effort to restrict workers' movement and keep productivity high. By criminalizing and simultaneously racializing workers, these measures aimed to strip miners of their previous autonomy to circulate from place to place, job to job, as they saw fit.[58]

In the Laws of Indies, legislation restricting movement applied (nearly) exclusively to "Indians."[59] However, this does not mean that other groups were allowed to move freely within the viceroyalty without the supervision of colonial authorities. Indeed, racialized notions of vagabondage were continually invoked to manage and control "black," mulatto, and mestizo populations and their labor.[60] In response to the 1767 riots, Gálvez's campaign revisited previous concerns about idleness and unregulated mobility and displaced them onto the "delinquent" bodies of miners of the Bajío. Gálvez merged different strands of colonial legislation into new measures to racially and spatially fix workers of the region.

Ranches

In conjunction with the siege of Guanajuato and later San Pedro, Gálvez pushed spatial interventions in other communities and industries in the area. Under the justification that ranchers from La Concepción and La Soledad had, like the miners, been "detrimental and rebellious," Gálvez supported the incursion of militias into their "rancherías."[61] In addition, he required all who owned land deeds in these regions to hand them over so that he could redistribute and rearrange their territories.[62]

For years, the viceroyalty's reach over these settlements had been fragile at best, but during the eighteenth century, their scattered presence rendered the region's fertile lands a site ripe for conflict. An intense struggle over the region's natural resources ensued. Ranchers were pitted against local landowners, mining entrepreneurs, religious orders, and neighbors from the town of Tlaxcalilla in ongoing legal disputes that in some cases led to violent confrontation.[63] These groups began to encroach on the ranchers' settlements and divert the flow of water.[64] The ranchers defended their communities and, seeking to gain protection from authorities, even requested to be recognized as an Indian town.[65]

These mounting tensions drew the attention of high-ranking colonial officials. In the aftermath of the riots, Gálvez criminalized the ranchers who lived in the settlements, maintaining that their "disarranged" lifestyle ultimately allowed rioters to escape the law. He thus consolidated a new racialized geography in the region, flattening the anomalous zones represented by the *rancherías*, organizing their lands according to his vision of a smooth and evenly distributed colonial power: "But as the majority have no fixed residence and all inhabit mere shacks scattered and hidden amid the density of the many trees and cacti that cover that part of the valley, the primary leaders among the ranchers escaped, prior to the active inquiries conducted by Don Francisco Mora."[66] By arguing that the natural landscape enabled the ranchers' "delinquent" fugitivity, Gálvez justified the spatio-legal reorganization of the settlements. Under his command, the ranches were fused into a single village of 350 families. Lands that had previously remained undivided and collectively owned, even if disputed, were segmented into equal plots. From then on, inhabitants of the newly crafted village were to be considered tenants and forced to pay annual rent for the "right" to live within the now expropriated and rearranged lands.[67]

Indian Neighborhoods

Gálvez also addressed the "unruly" spatial organization of indigenous settlements as proof of Indians' secretiveness. He asserted that this secretiveness, which fueled the "political arts" of indigenous leaders, drove their deliberate attempts to remain hidden from the gaze of colonial governmentality. After the riots, Gálvez ordered that the Indian neighborhoods of San Luis Potosí also be rearranged and rebuilt.[68] Specifically, he demanded that residential spaces face the streets and be easily accessible to local authorities.[69] "And I also ordered that the houses and shacks that compose the neighborhoods of San Luis be arranged into the regular formation of streets, and with their doors facing out onto them, because all, or most, were enclosed, and their entrances were concealed so that they could continue living in superstition and with the domestic disorder to which the Indians are accustomed in every way when they hide away from the public eye."[70] This demand that domestic areas be exposed to authorities' field of vision—to the "public eye"—was itself a form of disciplinary action.[71] Rearranging indigenous neighborhoods and forcibly inserting them into the visual scope of colonial authorities was meant to instantly "correct" those who lived within them. Continually exposed to colonial surveillance, those who had been historically racialized as having an innate tendency toward "diversion" and "superstition" were expected to behave in an orderly and predictable way.

Bringing "Indian" neighborhoods into the fold of colonial surveillance sought to emphasize Indians' political subordination in the colonial structure, not to erase the racial distinctions that had been historically produced and reinforced by segregation. This is made clear by the fact that Gálvez invalidated the legal practices and codes that had allowed Indian neighborhoods, congregations, and villages to deny Spaniards the right to settle there:[72] "Those Indians who have been civilized and made parishioners had practiced the abuse of forbidding Spaniards from their congregations and villages; therefore, I declared in my final ruling that they have no capacity or right to impede them."[73] Gálvez opposed early colonial ideas about segregation, which he believed had only given the Indians private spaces that cultured their "seditious" nature. Instead, he encouraged Spaniards to freely move and settle anywhere they pleased, perhaps creating another, more intimate form of surveillance over the Indians, one carried out by their new Spanish neighbors. These differential freedoms of mobility would be intricately tied to producing both Indian difference and the privileges of whiteness for years to come.[74]

Gálvez's explanation of this policy change connects efforts to recreate Indianness during the 1767 riots to the protection of the rights of Spaniards and, more broadly speaking, of whites.[75] However, the policies intended to bring about these protections were the opposite of the racializing policies that had been employed in response to the 1692 riot in Mexico City. As Anna More shows, Carlos de Sigüenza y Góngora's report on the riot indicates the intentions behind contemporary efforts to resegregate the city along racial lines, reserving the city's center for Spaniards alone. While previous segregation policies had been instated on account of protecting Indians and facilitating their conversion to Christianity, in the midst of the 1692 riots, Indianness became coded as a marker of "innate perversity," pitting the Spanish-descendent elite against a coalition of Indian subjects and members of other *castas*.[76]

Within this new framing of Indianness, a difference in terminology separates authorities' responses to the 1692 and 1767 riots. Documents on the latter explicitly use the term "whites" when referencing the Spanish-descendent elites. In the 1692 texts, this group is referred to broadly as "Spaniards" but not yet directly named as or correlated to whiteness.[77] Consider a letter by Croix in which he suggests that if the repressive forces under Gálvez's command had taken even slightly longer to reach San Luis Potosí to contain the riots, the mining city and its surrounding areas would have been the site of the "most terrible tragedy and other Sicilian Vespers against *all the Europeans and white people*."[78] The clear use of references to whites helps illustrate that Gálvez's punitive measures were also aimed at protecting and further consolidating the historical privileges of Spaniards and criollos.

THE PROTECTION OF WHITENESS: REPURPOSING COLONIAL BANS AND DISCOURSES

The racialized reorganization of the Bajío was not limited to spatial interventions. In order to safeguard the production of both Indian difference and whiteness, Gálvez revitalized early colonial stipulations from the Laws of Indies, arguing that they had regrettably fallen into disuse. These measures went beyond Gálvez's ostensible original concern with colonial profit and, along with his use of spectacular sovereign violence to punish riot leaders, were intended to secure the political, moral, and psychological subordination of "Indians and other castes."

For example, Gálvez dictated that "Indians" could not apply to themselves the epithet "don," for he saw their use of the term reserved for distinguished Spaniards as a "leveling" gesture that promoted rebellion:

> Nor shall they be called "don" nor shall they refer to themselves this way, neither in speech nor in writing; and with respect to having assigned this distinguishing name to the Indians of the city neighborhoods in the record submitted on June 28 and 30, due to the insolent pride that characterized them at said time, I order them to be struck out and removed from my commission by the scrape, so that they will not serve as an example in the future.[79]

Gálvez also ratified codes that banned "natives" and other "castes" from bearing arms and riding horses, thus deepening the power rift between those who had rioted and emerging militias.[80] Like the other resolutions I have discussed, these two bans emphasized the subordination of *castas* in general, but they placed a special focus on Indians. Gálvez argued that members of this group specifically "grew arrogant" when they traveled on horseback.[81]

Although he referred to how the gathering of lowly classes was a dangerous practice all over the world, Gálvez insisted that this was a particularly risky endeavor in colonial spaces where populations were more prone to "debauchery," "general nudity," and "lack of modesty."[82] His assertions are good examples not only of the way in which class becomes racialized but also of the manner in which racialization was additionally marked by the layers of colonial difference. To counter the danger posed by the coming together of racialized "lowly class" bodies in colonial spaces, Gálvez reinstated legal codes that had historically prohibited Indians and other castes from gathering in public spaces. Under his revised prescription, such groups could only bypass the codes through specific bureaucratic procedures. Pertinent authorities could grant them permission to gather for fiestas and other community rituals.[83]

Gálvez also challenged the erosion of racial hierarchies tied to the riots by requiring Indian men to use traditional garments and *balcarrotas* (a particular hairstyle), markers that were meant to produce Indianness as immediately visible and to prevent Indian men from accessing privileges meant for Spaniards only.[84] For Gálvez, the racial confusion caused by the deepened erosion of Indianness during the riots enabled privilege to overflow beyond caste lines; for him, the "inadequate" (adapted) use of Spanish attire gave rise to "insolent" behaviors. "They ought to be dressed precisely, with their cloak and uncovered *balcarrota*, and not wearing Spanish garments, which they had adapted and by which they had grown insolent, passing themselves off as mulattos and mestizos, an offense that garners one hundred lashes and a month in prison for the first infraction and permanent exile from the province for the second."[85] Many of these concerns about caste-jumping, the erasure of racial boundaries, and rebellious behavior can also be appreciated in the Escobar sermon discussed in the beginning of this chapter. This sermon, which was addressed to San Luis's mostly indigenous parishioners a few months after the riots had broke out, in 1767, was a rhetorical translation of Gálvez's punitive campaign. The sermon is thus also marked by the friar's attempts to shore up and protect the structures of whiteness by reracializing his Indian audience. Escobar referred to the "curse of Ham" to position Indians as inevitably and genealogically inferior to Spaniards. In both Europe and the Americas, the curse of Ham was deployed to naturalize the enslavement of African and Afro-descendant populations.[86] In Spanish America, too, the popularity of the biblical myth was directly linked to the first importations of African slaves into Spanish American colonies.[87]

In scholarship on race in the colonial period, Blackness and Indianness are often presumed to be distinct from, sometimes even diametrically opposed to, one another. However, as María Elena Martínez has noted, the difference between racializing discourses about "Indian" and "Black" subjects began to blur toward the end of the colonial period, as anxieties about blood (im)purity were extended to indigenous groups. This shift, Martínez remarks, can be explained by a range of factors: the clergy's disillusionment with the native conversion project, emerging ideas about the "decline" of the pre-Hispanic nobility, and a growing demographic of European women in the Americas.[88] As this gap between Indianness and Blackness closed, a white, Christian, Hispanic identity was produced on the other side of this line. In contrast to the opacity, impurity, and untidiness of the "lower castes" that included both "Indians" and "Blacks," whiteness was associated with limpidity and purity.[89] Escobar used the image of this purity being violated, polluted by contact with the impurity of racialized groups, to cow his audience—a rhetorical terror that was only intensified by the rebel bodies hanging behind him.

In the sermon, Escobar revisited the early colonial version of the curse of Ham and extended it to Indians. The gesture not only created a genealogy of damnation for those so cursed but also insinuated a direct connection between Spanish lineage and God:

> And after the flood, the sons of Japheth are the sons of God, and the sons of Cam [Ham] are the sons of men. We have thus deciphered the enigma. We Spaniards have descended from Japhet through Tubal, founder of Spain; the Indians, according to the scholar Silveira, are descendants of Cam [Ham]; which convinces us with respect to the causes of the curse, with which Noah punished the vile act committed by Cam [Ham] in mocking his father: Cam [Ham] shall be cursed, and his sons shall be servants to the servants of his brothers. We have verified all of this in the Indians, who regularly serve the servants and slaves of the Spaniards themselves. And thus, were the unworthy sons of men to choose Spanish women as their own, daughters descending from Japheth through Tubal, which is how they attain the nomenclature of God, it is an evil so strong that to avoid the sun from being astonished, the chiefs among them must be hanged against him; and so that the world cannot see, even in the shadows, crimes so atrocious and deeds so foul.[90]

Escobar's mention of miscegenation at the end of this passage reactivated an important anxiety that traversed the colonial imagination, that of the threat posed to the reproduction of the colonial order by the sexual union of Spanish women with men from "impure castes." Similar fantasies reemerged at other moments of riot and rebellion that were codified as racial conspiracies. At these moments, it was common for authorities to talk about rebels' desire for "taking" Spanish women and, in turn, of usurping power from Spanish men (I discuss this in greater detail in chapter 3).

Escobar's sermon is notable for how it highlights the gendered dynamics of repressive efforts, which are much less prevalent in Gálvez's *Informe sobre las rebeliones*. As he addressed his parishioners, the friar made clear his concern with the threat posed to Spanish women not only by men but also by women from "other castes" whom Escobar blamed for having challenged the established racial hierarchy during the riots. In the same vein as Gálvez's stipulations, Escobar reminded his listeners about the requirement of specific attire for "Indian" women. Ben Vinson and Cynthia Milton state that control over clothing was an effective strategy in producing and solidifying Indianness in the Hispanic world,[91] and Gálvez's and Escobar's reinstatement of an Indian dress code was again drawing from preexisting codes and initiatives.[92] The rationale behind this dress code was that it would produce a fixed link between *casta* and the body, securing the racial order the riots were charged with attempting to subvert and confuse:

> And you, native daughters of the villages, so poorly counseled by your fathers, and brothers, did you not say that the Spanish ladies ought to serve you, and seated on the stand, did you not order, with imperious voices: Now, Spanish ladies, come serve your mistresses? But this role in the performance of the tragic comedy lasted but a short time, because a providential decree has issued forth, in which it is stipulated that you shall not wear *naguas de sarga*, because this is the garment worn by poor Spanish women, and the garment that suits you, and which ought to be used by you, so that the adage "dress yourself as you are called, call yourself as you are dressed" is verified, is the huipil, or the *quixquemel*, and the cloth that is the particular attire of servants.[93]

As Vinson and Milton have shown, tribute in the Hispanic world could be determined by the status of an individual's mother: even when she herself did not pay tribute, an indigenous woman, particularly if she was unmarried or if her marriage was illegitimate, could cast her tributary shadow onto her children and her husband, even if he did not belong to the same racial category as she did.[94] Vinson and Milton cite a 1774 decree in New Granada establishing that all illegitimate children whose mothers were "Indian" would take on their mothers' racial attribution and would therefore be subject to paying tribute.[95] Although neither Gálvez nor Escobar explicitly connected the remarking of Indian women through attire to tribute, it is possible that their concern with Indian women's bodies and clothing was also part of the plan to improve and expand tributary collection.

CONCLUSION: ON THE ECONOMIES OF PUNISHMENT

Toward the conclusion of his report on the riots, Gálvez returns to the relation between punishment and profit. The penalties levied on rioting towns intended not only to restructure tributary exaction but also to bolster other aspects of the colonial economy, intertwining penality with processes of accumulation: "I venture to offer positive assurances to your Excellency, not only that the punishment and corrections shall be long-lasting, but also that the commons of the punished villages shall improve, much to their own benefit and for the sake of the public utility of the King and the Nation."[96] Gálvez's campaign was thus at the same time directed toward reshaping the "compromised" social order of the Bajío and toward increasing the economic yield of the region's towns, settlements, and cities. Through the campaign, Gálvez instated community-specific debt amounts that had to be paid within an allotted period of time. These payments were to be used for repairing government buildings that had been damaged during the riots, restoring the money "stolen" from the tobacco shops and royal coffers, and funding the uniforms and weaponry of the emerging permanent troops and other military corps.[97] The profit extracted from the rioters as punishment was thus incorporated into the colonial yield and invested in both militarizing the viceroyalty and erecting the material colonial infrastructure of the Bourbon era.[98]

Gálvez's *informe* outlines a timeline indicating how long it would take before the expedition turned a profit—before the costs it incurred were repaid in excess. According to the Visitor's calculations, in a year of following his newly instituted measures, the Crown would collect abundant profit from rioting communities:

> I must not omit here the circumstance (very specific to New Spain) that all extraordinary costs of this expedition, which has lasted five months from the departure of the troops to their return to the capital, and which has employed nearly five thousand men, do not exceed seventy thousand pesos, even including the costs of conveying prison-

ers to Veracruz, whose sum, quite small but spent all at once, shall be swiftly reimbursed with the considerable increase boasted by the Real Hacienda from tribute collected in the three provinces of San Luis Potosí, Guanajuato, and Pátzcuaro, and with the twenty-one thousand attained annually in taxes.[99]

This passage addresses New Spain's economic vitality as singular within Spain's colonial territories. As the mining region became more profitable, it would only become more cherished, requiring a considerable amount of resources and other efforts to protect it.

Scholars of the 1767 riots have pointed out that Gálvez's punitive efforts to reorganize the Bajío were either short-lived or doomed to fail.[100] Rather than limiting my engagement with the Gálvez campaign to measuring the longevity of his policies or to determining whether they were in fact applied verbatim, I have aimed to follow the logic of its premises. To do so is to begin to think about how the erosion of race that was perceived to be tied to racial conflicts was incorporated into colonial governmentality as a productive crisis. As I have shown in this chapter, this incorporation entailed a complicated weaving of the threads of punishment, militarization, profit, and race-making.

{ TWO }

"So That They May Be Free of All Those Things"
THEORIZING COLLECTIVE ACTION IN THE BAJÍO RIOTS

On the morning of May 10, 1767, the villagers of the Cerro San Pedro in the Bajío region witnessed the oral proclamation of two official colonial bans. Commanded by Viceroy Marqués de Croix, local lieutenant Joseph Ignacio de Uresti made the public announcement in the mining town's public plaza.[1] As part of the disciplining legislative corpus of the *Reglas de Policía y Buen Gobierno*, the first decree instated a ban on bearing weapons and established stringent fees and a four- to six-year sentence in an imperial garrison for anyone who transgressed it. The second ban commanded the region's "vagrants" to find employment within the next month or face deportation as convict laborers to either San Juan de Ulúa or Havana.[2]

Uresti's announcement brought instability to the region. Although similar edicts had been proclaimed several times before, in this instance, many of San Pedro's miners expressed concern about how the restrictions would impact their daily lives.[3] Accustomed to traveling with their working tools on hand and to shifting employment seasonally, the bans threatened the villagers' dynamic living habits.[4] The *serranos* who lived in the San Pedro mountains retaliated against the measures by throwing stones at the lieutenant in the public plaza, ultimately pushing him to escape the town. Two days after his public announcement, Uresti fled to the city of San Luis Potosí.[5]

During the following weeks, friction in the region spiked. On June 6 the *serranos* and their neighboring allies took to the city. They stoned colonial buildings, released prisoners from the local jail, and barricaded the streets leading to the main plaza. From there they addressed the city's colonial authorities. Led by two San Pedro miners, José Patricio Alaniz and Antonio Orosio, the rioters presented an extensive list of written demands.[6]

The pressure that rebels exerted in San Luis Potosí after both the release of jailed prisoners and the stoning of government buildings led authorities to accept their conditions.[7] The pact, however, was short lived. A few months later, on August 19, José de Gálvez's campaign overturned local authorities' decision as he levied his heavy punitive hand on the inhabitants of the Cerro de San Pedro and their neighboring allies.[8]

Against what could be seen as the inevitable failure of the riots' first fleeting success and its foreclosure by the brutal repression that followed it, I open here on the variegated political horizons still palpitating in the insurgent textualities of the 1767 riots. I read the scattered letters, papers, and notes penned by Bajío rebels as potent and vital reflections on the multiple meanings and shapes of emancipation and freedom that emerged from this historical conjuncture and that continue to flicker beyond it as unfulfilled past hopes and promises.[9]

In my readings of these texts, I do not seek to systematize the demands that were articulated from different rioting locations or attempt to faithfully reconstruct what actually happened. Instead, I am interested in how the horizons that these insurgent textualities open up can be read beyond a search for the empirical.[10] In addition to articulating punctual or context-specific rejections of Bourbon policy, the authors of these texts perform broader interruptions on the encroaching and interconnected logics of colonialism and capitalism. They challenge the precarity of the economic, political, social, and environmental relations brought about by processes of racialized dispossession and accumulation, and instead improvise with and suggest other possible arrangements for life. Indeed, these improvisations have their own fragilities and contradictions. They appear in the archives as tentative and nonprescriptive glimpses of futurity. My attempt here is to engage them in their incompleteness.

In her book *The Allure of the Archives*, Arlette Farge calls for "a historical writing that can retain the hint of the unfinished, giving rein to freedoms even after they were scorned . . . so that we can see both crimes and desires for emancipation as they appeared in the moment, holding on to the possibility that each would be wedded later on to other dreams and other visions."[11]

In this chapter, I take Farge's invitation to experiment with more speculative forms of historical writing. I offer close readings of insurgent textualities and explore the potent theorizations of collective action that stem from them. Toward the conclusion, I turn to repressive strategies, particularly those linked to how authorities grappled with the threat of intercommunal alliances during the riots. In the conclusion I thus analyze authorities' efforts to curtail historical practices of communal negotiations with local authorities in favor of constructing a top-down sovereignty based on the epoch's absolutist trends. While chapter 1 centered on a reading of official documents that were part of the repression of the 1767 riots, I here direct the reader's gaze to the rebel archive and its insurgent textualities, and wonder what the gaps and misalignments between these two archival threads that nevertheless emerged from the same historical conjuncture might tell us about the question of race in Mexico.

"TO DO AWAY WITH THE *GACHUPINES*": THE QUESTION OF RACE IN INSURGENT TEXTUALITIES

A few weeks after the rioters descended on the city of San Luis Potosí, Atanasio de la Cruz, governor of the Indian town San Nicolás de Armadillo, sent a letter to his allies in the San Pedro mountain. Confiscated along with eight other letters during Gálvez's expedition and interrogations, de la Cruz's missive registers how the dispute over race and its making factored into insurgent imaginaries and practices.

San Nicolás was a small Indian town founded in the early 1600s and populated mostly by Chichimeca and Otomí people.[12] Originally exempt from paying tribute, by the early eighteenth century the town operated as a *república de indios*. Its inhabitants collectively elected their local leaders and also recognized vassalage to the Spanish king by paying annual dues.[13] Although initially San Nicolás's land extension was vast, its lands became litigious during the first decade of the eighteenth century. Through subsequent legal disputes with the Spanish entrepreneur Nicolás Fernando de Torres, by 1725 the town had been dispossessed of most of its territory.[14]

Entering the 1767 riots, San Nicolás had a long history of resisting encroaching colonial legislature. The townspeople had not only confronted Torres in land disputes years before but also successfully rejected the 1715 official call to have a select number of their inhabitants relocate to the northern province of Nuevo León. The call came as part of a colonial project to populate New Spain's expanding northern border with convert Indians who were already knowledgeable in the ways of Spanish bureaucracy.[15]

The participation of San Nicolás in the 1767 riots must therefore be understood in the framework of a longer history of friction and resistance. Governor de la Cruz's letter was sent to the San Pedro mountains as a material confirmation of the town's ongoing involvement in the riots. Meant to further consolidate the alliance between San Nicolás and the *serranos*, de la Cruz wrote in the name of the town's inhabitants "old and young," reiterating his community's commitment to the continuing struggle.[16]

De la Cruz's letter implies that the riots were not mainly concerned with killing whites, as was generally discussed in many of the texts penned by colonial authorities. In fact, the term "blancos" is completely absent in the text except for a reference to *gachupines*. While for Gálvez and his followers the rebels' use of this latter term was constantly invoked as proof of the contempt and desire for vengeance that Indians and other castes held and enacted against whites during the riots, the insurgent textualities analyzed here complicate these assumptions. As far as I can tell, "blancos" was not a term used in the written language of the rioters and, although in some sense overlapping, the categories *blancos* and *gachupines* should not be presumed to be directly equivalent.

John Tutino maintains, for instance, that in the areas where uprisings broke out, rioters sought to forge ties with local criollo merchants who held positions of power and had roots in the colony.[17] The lack of a racial term uniting criollos and *gachupines* (or *blancos*) in insurgent textualities might therefore not only suggest the uncommon use of such a category at this time in rural areas of the Bajío region, but also express rebels' political strategies and interests in building alliances.

It is difficult to gauge how much of the fact that colonial authorities generally overlooked the distinction between *gachupines* and criollos articulated by the riots stemmed from a genuine fear and concern over what they perceived to be a generalized racial bent to the conflicts, and how much of it was a strategy to obstruct the potential alliance between rioters and local Spanish merchants and entrepreneurs. Despite colonial authorities' generalized concern, alliances between criollos and rioters didn't really materialize. In fact, in contrasting the simultaneity and diverging outcomes of the Bajío riots and the first outbursts of violence that would lead to independence in the British American colonies, Tutino stresses that in New Spain, colonially rooted Spaniards invariably rejected allying themselves with Bajío rebels and, instead, stood with the colonial government and on the side of the repressive forces.[18]

De la Cruz's letter portrays the uprisings as mainly concerned with trying to bring an end to the "new law." Likely referring to the recently imposed bans on bearing weapons and being idle, but also to the town's longer history with impinging Bourbon policy, a passage of the letter reads as follows: "Well we are engaged in that endeavor with respect to the prevention of bearing arms so that all the town can do forces with your mercies until we see the end of the new law we are seeking and good faith or we do away with the *gachupines*."[19]

The letter can certainly be read as expressing a degree of racial tension as it entertains the possibility of "doing away with the *gachupines*." However, the location of this phrase in the text (after mentions to the "end of the new law" and a search for "good faith") suggests that direct attacks on *gachupines* were actually imagined as a last resort strategy and not an end in itself. In other words, violence that specifically targeted peninsular Spaniards was but one of many paths (and the last one at that) opened by the rioters in their efforts to obstruct the encroachments propelled by the "new law."

I mention this not in an effort to contain or accommodate rioters' actions in accordance with morally palatable models and traditions of political resistance.[20] I am uninterested in looking toward the past and recharting it according to lines of innocence and guilt. I touch upon this issue, instead, to illustrate how insurgent textualities attest to more complicated understandings of race and its making than what is generally accounted for in the documentation provided by colonial authorities.

As I developed in the previous chapter, Gálvez and his followers understood the racial aspect of the riots in terms of plainly promoting direct attacks on whites, ultimately stating that the tumults opened the door for another "Sicilian Vespers against *all the Europeans and white people*."[21] But the riots and the insurgent textualities that emerged from these struggles invite us to think about race differently and at the juncture where the structural and the discursive meet. They invite us to consider the making of race well beyond the confines of visual body traits or even identity.

Whereas it may seem logical that addressing the question of direct violence against *gachupines* would be the starting point for anyone interested in analyzing the riots' engagement with race and racialization, I believe this is not necessarily the case. Could it not be that attacks on colonial government buildings such as jails and treasuries, alongside efforts to collectively defend local geographies of exchange and intercommunal support, or demands to abolish taxes and tribute, say more of the rioters' understanding of the workings of race and its making in New

Spain? Could we not entertain the idea that insofar as rioting actions and demands unsettled the heart of colonial governmentality, they were also dismantling the very foundations that enabled the material production and reproduction of racialized precarity in the viceroyalty?

To seriously consider these questions requires us to pause and question our immediate assumptions about where racial projects are configured and expressed, but also about where they might be contested and challenged. In their renowned study on racial formation, Michael Omi and Howard Winant assert that "it is not possible to represent race discursively without simultaneously locating it, explicitly or implicitly, in a social structural (and historical) context. Nor is it possible to organize, maintain, or transform social structures without simultaneously engaging, once more either explicitly or implicitly, in racial signification."[22] Although Omi and Winant address a historical context wholly different from the one I analyze here, their reflections on the correlation that exists between discursive representations of race and social structure is relevant to the questions posed above. Redirecting the conversation toward the Bajío riots, to only follow the discursive and explicit mentions of race in the insurgent textualities of the 1767 riots or, conversely, to not consider how rioting actions might have engaged the structural dimensions of race, is to effectively silence and ignore an important aspect of both their occurrence and their potential legacies.

In order to grapple with how the riots engaged race and racialization at the material and structural levels, it is first important to understand the place that the collective politics of *tumulto* held as a mediating strategy between communities and the colonial state bureaucracy. In *Drinking, Homicide, and Rebellion*, William B. Taylor analyzes the patterns shared by popular rebellions that occurred in different points of the viceroyalty during the eighteenth century. Taylor outlines the idea that the *tumulto* was a recognized form of collective political action through which communities pressed against but also negotiated with local colonial authorities.[23] The pacification of *tumultos* thus tended to take place through a complicated mix of punishment and concessions where authorities consented to some, if not most, of the communities' demands.[24]

Situated in this context, the emphasis that the 1767 insurgent textualities place on the question of building intercommunal alliances and theorizing collective action becomes clearer. Many of the texts penned by the rioters focus on thinking about the process of the *tumulto* itself. In fact, the texts often privilege this approach over outlining a fixed blueprint for the demands and desired outcomes of the riots. It is in this sense that insurgent textualities confront us with nonprescriptive modes of articulating political struggle. The texts emphasize the *doings* of the riots and sketch yet-to-be-determined futures that remain open to being reshaped by the contingencies of what happens on the ground.

Consider, for instance, de la Cruz's letter. Although at first glance we might assume that the text sketches the "end of the new law" as a transparent and fixed goal of the alliance between San Nicolás and the San Pedro miners, what this "end" might entail and how to produce it remains to be determined in the collective process of the struggle. Expressed in gerundive form, de la Cruz's missive construes the riots as an ongoing and open search "que andamos buscando" (that we go about seeking). The "end of the new law" thus emerges in the text not so much as a static and already determined end point but rather as an unscripted futurity that shape-shifts and is punctuated by the flows of the collective search that is the riot itself.

One of the three "sacrilegious papers" that was printed, circulated, and later confiscated by Gálvez in San Luis de la Paz allows us to explore this point further and from a different perspective.[25] As the brief pamphlet shows, the Indian town that had once operated as a mission was one of the few sites where the riots were directly connected to the expulsion of the Jesuit order from Spanish territories.[26] The text has often been dismissed for its lack of clarity and cohesion, but it nevertheless is quite insightful in how it describes the destabilizing and mediating practice of *alboroto*, or rampage:

> May your majesty see that the people do not cease to be moved and to convene with others, for if the people quieten, they will see that we are surrendered, and on top of the priests leaving, punishments shall be levied upon the people. This would not happen seeing that this is all in uproar, they would seek to make peace and would not attempt to cause any upset to your mercies. Several locations have risen in name of the priests, there is no need to kill anyone, being merely unruly is enough, the document they read is old and days, years have passed since we Indians ascended [to heaven?] through the church and perhaps more swiftly than the Spaniards, and still they come to take charge considering Indians their own, and we have to do anything they want and after that "to hell with us," careful how the riot ceases, because punishment will be levied, without killing, without killing, because seeing how everything is in uproar and people are together, there will be peace and no punishment, convene with the chichime-

cos, and if you quiet we will be hanged, communicate what can happen and things will work out as I tell you, and we the Indians perish, and we the Indians perish.[27]

Reading this passage with an eye to *how* it says and not just *what* it says, one can appreciate the pamphlet unfolding its political potential. First and beyond delineating concrete parameters or demands to the struggle, the text engages *alboroto* as a constantly destabilizing force, one that unravels through the sustained creation of alliances between and across communities ("convene with the chichimecos"). Second, the text opens a rift from which it questions the site of racialized violence in the colonial setting. The text not only registers that disturbances weren't really unleashed against *gachupines* themselves but also strategically stresses the importance that rioters avoid any lethal damage ("without killing") during the upheaval. The pamphlet touches upon the colonial order's structural reliance on the production of differential vulnerabilities as it outlines how Indian bodies were deemed to be appropriable and disposable ("considering Indians their own, and we have to do anything they want and after that 'to hell with us'"). The practice of *alboroto* then emerges in the pamphlet as a strategy of intercommunal support that is being mobilized both to protect communities from harsh punitive measures by colonial authorities and to challenge the precarious conditions that rendered Indian life more vulnerable to perish.[28]

De la Cruz's letter and the confiscated paper of San Luis de la Paz highlight the importance that building intercommunal alliances had for the riots. They too shed light onto a convergence between the efforts to conceptualize collective action and the tactics that were used on the ground during the struggle. Being aware of this convergence is precisely what opens the gateway to thinking more carefully about the *doings* of the riots, both textually and practically, and how we can speculate they were also engaged in dismantling the colony's racializing structure.

"CONTRIBUTING THE NECESSARY THINGS": RECHARTING COMMUNAL BOUNDARIES

The *capitulaciones*, or demands, that the Cerro de San Pedro miners and their allies presented before colonial authorities as they occupied San Luis Potosí's plaza survive in the archives. The document is likely the most detailed that one can consult as a window into the riots and has often been summarized in the historiography. Seldom, however, have scholars engaged it as a text whose reflections on freedom and communal living might extend beyond the specificities of its context.[29]

Because it is written in present tense and in an imperative tone, to read the *capitulaciones* is to set in motion the text's political performativity. I, however, understand this performativity not to be marked by a convergence between saying and doing, but rather by what David Kazanjian would characterize as an improvisational move toward what is not yet given.[30] Through a series of textual injunctions that negate and recraft the foreseeable grasp that the Bourbon project aimed to have on the region's social relations and geography, the text opens itself to the unexpected.[31]

In tension with the increasingly extractive and burdensome demands of colonial tribute and taxes, the *capitulaciones* rechart the bounds of what is both materially and socially "necessary" for life. The document thus begins with an interesting statement that forefronts the intercommunal drive sustaining the riot: "All of us in this REAL with our neighbors and those who are contributing the necessary things the REAL needs for lacking them, request the following."[32]

From the very first phrase, the text challenges the production of a colonial geography premised on the basis of isolated social nuclei. More important, it complicates and destabilizes the expected parameters that are used to delineate the contours and limits of communities. Over ascription to a given political unit, the *miners* emphasize a logic where communal boundaries are continually drafted and lived through networks of interdependence. Taking on the crucial question of social reproduction, the text stages a dispute in which the miners and their allies aimed to show that San Pedro's contours extended beyond recognized official borders to include all local communities that were "contributing the necessary things" to support each other's lives.

Concretely, in the *capitulaciones* the miners stood against new policies that taxed the introduction of resources such as lumber, palm, firewood, and water into the *real* (mining town). The rioters stated that all these materials were necessary for sustaining the life and labor of those who worked in the mines. New taxation measures impeded access to these resources and thus rendered life in the mining town precarious. The measures, it was implied, also disrupted the long history of exchanging goods and services that the workers of San Pedro and those of the nearby towns and settlements had established and practiced for years.[33]

The new system, under which the introduction of crucial resources into the mining town would be taxed, was one of many ways in which local networks of support were gradually being eroded as the region's communities became more entrenched in the mining industry and the burgeoning global capitalist system it was a part of.

The dismantling of long-standing intercommunal bonds ultimately threatened to exacerbate the already precarious conditions of life in the region, which, as described in chapter 1, mostly burdened racialized groups such as free mulattos and *indios vagos*.[34] With their demands and rioting tactics, the miners and their allies challenged the further fragmentation of their intercommunal geographies; they rejected the spatial and social reorganization that Bourbon Reform layered on top of the region's already racialized colonial grid.[35] It is no wonder that a central point in the *capitulaciones* was a demand to revise San Pedro's land deeds. The miners stated, "We live submerged in such impediment, because what we need is constantly denied to us, and to undo these misgivings we want to know the lands that belong to this REAL. We see that rent is being charged on these mining lands, even though they are inherited, and so we demand to what end is rent being charged? giving that this is of no benefit to the REAL."[36] The miners here associate their struggle to redefine what is necessary for life with the act of challenging the erosion of local geographies. This passage of the *capitulaciones* suggests that gaining control over the town's land deeds would allow the miners and their allies to contest the fragmented racial geography that new taxing measures were creating. Against encroaching tribute, tax, and rental fees, all deployed to corrode and reorganize local networks, the miners demanded their right to the "papeles and sédulas" once granted by the Crown. In their appeal to review these official documents, rioters challenged the exaction of rent over lands they had once inherited. They also asserted that the *real*'s spatial bounds included not only the extension of land inhabited and worked by San Pedro's residents and miners, but also the areas where neighboring communities that supported life at the mining town found their home.[37]

The logic proposed by the *capitulaciones* thus established the communal networks of social reproduction as the basis of how political lines ought to be determined. Their call to redefine the boundaries of their community was a way of asserting that the recently imposed measures were unlawful and ran contrary to the "well-being of the REAL."[38] The new policies, established to extract surplus value and to control the circulation of goods across the region's communities, had to be, by this logic, terminated.[39]

Repeated in diverging formulations throughout the document, the idea that rent and tax policies were contrary to the *real*'s well-being warrants further exploration. Notably, the argument depended on presenting a contradiction between the interest of promoting these extractive policies and that of sustaining the productivity of the region's mines. San Pedro miners and their allies did not shape their struggle as an attempt to break away from Spanish sovereignty. On the contrary, they actually framed their claims as an effort to negotiate the terms of their inclusion within it, hoping that their own community and those of their allies could safeguard their historical autonomy and give them more control over defining their position within the global framework of the monarchy: "without distancing ourselves from what is Law and as loyal vassals to your majesty."[40]

The miners and their allies mobilized their loyalty to the Crown to bargain for their interests. For instance, paying lip service to the monarchy's high regard for the extraction of gold and silver in the colonies, they sustain in the *capitulaciones* that exacerbating the precarity of living conditions in the *real* and its neighboring communities would ultimately impede miners from doing their work and, thus, from being able to send the accorded royal fifths to the king.[41]

Working along the grain of the logic of colonial accumulation, the miners insightfully interjected at the site of the division between the spheres of production and reproduction and refused to naturalize this schism.[42] As such, the miners demanded that the privileges of being a mining town whose proceeds enriched the Spanish monarchy be granted and extended to them and to "all of the sons" of the *real*—that is, to all the villages and settlements that surrounded San Pedro and that shared a social and economic ecology with the town. The miners demanded, "Those who are contributing to our general sustenance [must] be free of all those things that have been imposed upon them once again."[43] This "freedom" included that neighboring communities be unburdened by racializing tribute and other taxes that, as discussed in the previous chapter, were the cornerstone of Bourbon Reform and colonial governmentality in the mid-eighteenth century. It also included quite a subversive claim to self-determination. The *capitulaciones* end with a demand that neighboring towns be granted the freedom to elect their own lieutenant mayors and to hold the prerogative of replacing them at their whim.[44]

"To be free" in this text is thus to redefine the confines of collective life, not through abstract demands but rather through multilayered efforts at building and sustaining intercommunal relations and support.

"To be free" from encroaching colonial policies, in other words, is articulated here as an active communal rejection of the breakdown of local geographies through racialized economic extraction in a way that sheds light upon interdependence and the relational networks that allow for social reproduction.

"THAT THERE BE NO JAILS": ABOLITION AND THE STRUGGLE FOR LIFE

In places such as San Nicolás de Armadillo and the Cerro de San Pedro, rioting tactics were concretely tied to local histories that challenged the layering of new colonial geographies in the region. Other towns and settlements, however, resorted to other strategies and visions as they confronted the advance of Bourbon Reform upon their communities.

In San Pedro de Guadalcázar, another mining town just north of San Luis Potosí, more than five hundred *atumultuados* (rioters) met with the lieutenant mayor of the mining town and some criollo merchants to negotiate and discuss their grievances.[45]

The riot began during a game of *chueca* that, against common practice, took place in the town's main plaza.[46] When confronted by the lieutenant mayor, who demanded that players continue the game in the fields allocated for this type of communal gathering, the *tumulto* erupted. Rioters stoned the wall of the local jail and released sixteen prisoners from it.[47] They also proceeded to loot local shops, bakeries, and tobacco stands, most of them owned and run by Spanish entrepreneurs.[48]

These attacks, along with subsequent demands that *gachupines* be expelled from the town within a period of three days, were once again interpreted by colonial authorities as expressions of rioters' hatred against whites. The testimonies of those who were later arrested and tried by Gálvez's expedition, however, complicate the simplicity of these claims.

Interrogated prisoners insisted on denouncing the racialized predatory practices sustained by business owners in the *real*. They implied that merchants and entrepreneurs—most of whom were Spanish, given the social and economic privileges involved in becoming a business owner at the time—were taking advantage of the material needs of Guadalcázar's most impoverished inhabitants. Severiano Ortiz, for instance, recalled rioters' demands that the clothes that merchants had confiscated as pawns of credit purchases be returned to their owners, the workers.[49]

Under this light, the looting actions of rioters in Guadalcázar resonate with the efforts of the San Pedro miners and their allies to challenge precarity and redefine the conditions for life. The attacks on shops and other businesses also appear less as direct threats on the bodies of peninsular Spaniards and more as actions aiming to challenge the structure of racializing predatory practices that rendered livelihood in the *real* tenuous.

In the negotiations they sustained with local authorities and merchants, rebels demanded that a series of *capitulaciones* be displayed on the frontispiece of the prison. Their written demands challenged the tobacco monopoly and pressed to eliminate recently imposed taxes on the purchase of it and other products that were important items of consumption for the miners. They also stipulated that the sentences of all prisoners freed during the *tumulto* be pardoned and that jails be abolished.[50]

Notably, the demand to eliminate prisons in Guadalcázar took regional attacks on local jails a step further than those in other towns. As we have seen, stoning jails and releasing prisoners were not isolated gestures. To the contrary, similar actions were repeated throughout rioting sites and, in fact, can be associated with a longer history of these practices as a form of resistance to the colonial state. As William B. Taylor has written, "The jail was the most frequent inanimate victim of people's wrath."[51]

Although the original *capitulaciones* haven't been recovered from the archives, the demands rioters presented were transcribed in a letter that Guadalcázar's lieutenant mayor sent to San Luis Potosí reporting the *tumultos* in the mining town.[52] The call for the general abolition of jails with the phrase "que no había de haber cárcel" (there ought to be no jail) is an expression of the textual performativity discussed previously.[53] In combination with the action of liberating prisoners from the village jail and damaging the structure of the building, the demand for abolition opened the space to create a freedom that challenged the racialized regulation of mobility within the colony as well as its growing carceral bent.

The sentence that in the *capitulaciones* called jails into nonexistence was juxtaposed with demands for the abolition of recently imposed taxes on tobacco and other products that were crucial to miners' daily lives. But what are we to make of this juxtaposition? Are we to presume that the speech act that brought together these variegated issues was merely incidental? My sense is that this is not the case. Instead, I consider this seemingly random constellation of issues to be pointing toward the powerful "improvisations of life in the face of colonialism" performed and opened up by the riots.[54] Rejecting taxes, tribute, and imprisonment were all ways of reshaping the substance of life in Guadalcázar and elsewhere.

The *capitulaciones*' juxtaposition of seemingly diverging issues also brings into relief the ways in which rioters were aware of the interconnections between the economic burdens and punitive practices imposed by the state. The joint challenge they articulated against colonial taxes and jailing measures suggests that both were understood to share certain similarities as colonial technologies of control.

Challenges to taxes, tributes, and jails were by no means narrow conjunctural demands. How could calling for the abolition of tribute be narrow if, as I argued in the previous chapter, this economic system was the cornerstone of producing and maintaining the racialized social order of the colony and of mediating the horizons of subjection and freedom of racialized subjects?[55] A similar question could be posed for the demands to reject taxes imposed on products that were crucial for the livelihood of generally impoverished and racialized groups in the Bajío, as well as for calls to eliminate jails in the region. At the onset of an increasingly carceral system, the demand to entirely eradicate jails—insisting on the liberation of all prisoners, regardless of the reason for their incarceration—entailed not only a radical call for reconfiguring the present, rejecting the logic that justified rebels' (mis)treatment and criminalization, but also the de-codification and subsequent opening up of alternative horizons for life, social relations, and justice.

Although in Guadalcázar, as in other towns and settlements, the only explicit reference to the question of race was made through the demand to expel *gachupines* from the *real*, I sustain that rioters' actions and demands to abolish jails and taxes entailed implicit yet substantial challenges to the colony's racial order.

CONCLUSION

The degree to which collective actions and negotiations threatened Bourbon Reform and its ability to grow roots in New Spain's colonial order did not go unnoticed. During the repressive campaign, José de Gálvez advocated for conceptually and materially reconfiguring colonial law as an abstract, fixed entity that was beyond the realm of localized negotiations. The visiting inspector's *informe* intended to instate structural changes that would eliminate the zones of contact and negotiation that historically came into being through the interactions that communities sustained with their local judges and magistrates. Gálvez shaped his repressive campaign as an opportune moment to expropriate local communities' historical practice of negotiating and exercising the right to propose the parameters of their participation in the colonial structure:

> A generalized practice as of the latest revolutions was the scandalous temerity that rebels would capitulate with the judges and magistrates of the villages, and even with individual persons, in offense of the sovereignty, of the legitimate authority derived from it and from public tranquility, with which, in order to abolish such pernicious examples once and for all, it was necessary to declare that under no circumstances, no matter how extraordinary, could the vassals be so bold as to propose conditions with the goal of impeding the exercise of justice or the superior orders of government, under penalty of being punished as traitors for the very fact of having opposed to the execution of the law, consequently, judges shall be deprived of their ability to concede or hear such capitulations, because it would be, in my view, less detrimental and scandalous for a magistrate to offer up his throat to the knife than to convene or accept propositions that jeopardize the high respect for his majesty or the immutable rules of his justice.[56]

In portraying the law ("justice") as an abstract, distant, and unwavering ("immutable") entity, as fixed precepts imposed from above, Gálvez sought to regulate and perhaps even dismiss the sites of friction and negotiation that emerged from the ground in the interactions between communities and local government officials, such as those that occurred in San Nicolás, San Pedro, and Guadalcázar. This approach neatly coincided with more general views about how Bourbon Reform would "simplify" imperial sovereignty, making it more homogenous, centralized, and efficient.[57] It also complemented efforts to distance the Spanish monarchy from the historical legacies of scholastic pactism, which asserted that sovereignty emerged from the people and, were it to be dissolved or abused, it could and must return to them. Instead and through the 1767 repression, Gálvez brought the colony closer the epoch's absolutist trends.[58]

A sermon delivered by the Cuban friar José Manuel Rodríguez in Mexico City on the first Sunday of September 1768 seized on the previous year's uprisings precisely as an implicit foundation for promoting absolutist ideology. Although precautions had been taken in the capital city to forbid the circulation of news on the riots and other threatening responses to the Jesuit order's expulsion, Rodriguez's doctrinal address offers evidence that debates on the matter were in fact unraveling in the city.[59]

Titled "¿Cómo deben haberse los vasallos con sus reyes?" (How must the vassals interact with their kings?), the sermon sought to justify the expulsion of the Jesuit order. It also sought to lay out the foundations for a reconfiguration of Spanish sovereignty, one that was based on negating subjects' ability to question (in)justice and to negotiate the terms of their relationship with their king.

The friar defined this relationship as one that could not be questioned and that could only be imposed from the top down. From a distance, and amid a context of censorship, the sermon expunged the social struggle underpinning it. Indeed, Rodríguez made no mention to the 1767 riots or their violent repression. On the contrary, in the doctrinal address the friar described the duty of Spain's "vassals" to pay tribute and taxes as emerging out of nowhere, and he maintained that the colony's subjects had no right to question the divine and sovereign demand that obliged them to pay.[60]

Rodríguez insisted, "It is not lawful for any vassal to judge the justice of the Prince's laws."[61] Moreover, in the context of the reconfiguration of New Spain's army, which was based on reiterating racialized bans on bearing weapons to promote the expropriation and monopolization of violence by the colonial state, Rodríguez sustained that the only legitimate means of expressing resistance to the sovereign was affectivity: more specifically, tears. Turning to a quote from Saint Ambrose and planting the seed of sacrificial affectivity for the sake of protecting the king and his order, Rodríguez uttered the following words before his audience: "Set with the obligation of suffering, I dare not object. I may feel pain, I may weep, I may moan. Against arms, against soldiers, against the very Goths themselves, the arms I may use in opposition shall be my tears, because I cannot, nor is it lawful for me to defend myself by any other means against temporal powers."[62]

Rodríguez continued, albeit implicitly, in the line of what Gálvez attempted to instate during the repression of the 1767 riots. Both he and Gálvez registered the destabilizing potential of communal negotiations and aimed to expropriate through different means this historical right. Despite their efforts, collective practices safeguarding local autonomies were never fully eroded in New Spain. In fact, the legacies of communal and intercommunal negotiations and autonomy punctuate Mexico's political landscape even today.

{ CODA ONE }

From the Country to the City
MOVEMENT, LABOR, AND RACE AT
THE END OF THE EIGHTEENTH CENTURY

Between 1785 and 1787, nearly two decades after the Bajío riots were repressed by the Gálvez campaign, the Spanish lawyer Hipólito Villarroel finished writing *Enfermedades políticas que padece la capital de esta Nueva España*. The four-volume oeuvre went unpublished until 1831, when, shortly after the proclamation of Mexico's independence, the criollo intellectual Carlos María de Bustamente printed a fragmented version of it in the newspaper *Voz de la patria*.[1] The text offers a rather critical appraisal of New Spain's society at the end of the reign of Charles III as king of the Spanish Empire. It is divided into six treatises, each touching upon different topics deemed to be crucial for the adequate and fruitful government of the viceroyalty: the clergy, political conditions, police, the state of commerce, the army, and the recent establishment of *intendencias*.[2] Evoking a common trope in political thought of the time, Villarroel conceived of his intervention as a social auscultation and referenced the functional analogy between the human body and the state.[3] Mostly, he sought to provide his readers with vignettes that could explain and render legible the various "ailments" with which he diagnosed New Spain's social body. When possible, he also outlined a series of remedies and measures that could be implemented to "cure them."[4]

Villarroel arrived in the port of Veracruz around 1761, ready to take his post as the mayor of Cuautla. He spent most of his lifetime in New Spain and occupied different positions in the colonial government structure, often moving from one post to another due to controversies of corruption and abuse of power raised against him.[5] Traveling from Cuautla to Guadalajara to Mexico City, Oaxaca, and beyond, Villarroel gained knowledge about the modes of life in different regions of the viceroyalty.[6] Although perhaps not uncommon for someone of his status, the breadth of his New Spanish experience is captured in the variegated nature of the concerns he discussed in *Enfermedades políticas*.

Gálvez's ideas on colonial governmentality were an important reference for Villarroel's diagnoses. In discussion with the work of the renowned Bourbon reformer, Villarroel offered his own take on the alleged political and social risk associated with the unregulated mobility of racialized bodies throughout New Spain's territory.[7] Like his predecessor, he correlated the uncontrolled movement of people—which he registered in the rising waves of migration from the provinces to the city— with concerns for the decrease in tax revenue. Most important, however, he condemned the flows of migration for engendering a nearly spiraling process of social degeneration that, according to him, had transformed the once rich and commendable colony along with its marvelous capital city into a "blemish on all fine culture," an "impenetrable forest" filled with "pigsties" and populated by "dirty and repulsive men and women."[8]

Villarroel's description of New Spain's moral decline presents the capital city of the viceroyalty as a filthy "repository for an untamed, audacious, insolent, shameless, and idle multitude."[9] Although he makes no explicit reference to race as a differential marker ascribed to specific bodies or people, he does resort to the language of *casta* to address the spaces where the "idle multitudes" congregated. Villarroel construes these sites as the refuge "for as many castes of vices as one can imagine," producing a slippage where common discourses about the proliferation of racial categories was now displaced onto practices that were negatively viewed and associated with traits of corruption, licentiousness, depravity, laziness, and the like.[10] The phrase thus offers a good example of how late eighteenth-century colonial discourses of social hygiene, criminality, and lack of productivity constituted a lexicon that already encoded racialization. Indeed, for Villarroel the central issue plaguing urban sites was that they had become the melting pots where the divergently racialized bodies of the destitute—those who were spatially unfixed and unemployed—met and welded into a monstrous multitude that was marked for its alleged impurity and ungovernable nature.

The remedies Villarroel proposed to curtail the unregulated movement of racialized bodies into the city and thus to produce a more hygienic and ordered urban society were not tied to a specific social uprising, as they had been for Gálvez. Nevertheless, Villarroel associated his perception of the colony's social and moral crises with the raids of native tribes in New Spain's northern border. He framed these confrontations as one of the leading causes of the concerning influx of people moving from the provinces to the city. As such, Villarroel expanded the breadth of the race war paradigm, illustrating its plasticity. In this coda I offer a reading of select passages from *Enfermedades políticas* to explore a different shape of the narrative that associated New Spain's economic and moral decline at the end of the eighteenth century with racial conflict and the alleged collapse of clear caste distinctions.

While Gálvez addressed the racial nature of the Bajío uprisings in relation to the question of political security and mobilized it in his projects to militarize the viceroyalty and expand the extraction of colonial profit from taxes and mining activities, in Villarroel's case the issue acquired a different tenor. Still connected to the broad objective of safeguarding New Spain from ruin, Villarroel's focus was less pragmatic than Gálvez's. It was placed on what in the lexicon of Spanish governmentality was called police (*policía*), an umbrella term commonly used to touch upon notions of civility, courtesy, urbanity, and good or adequate behavior while also referring to the set of measures authorities could implement to cultivate and protect these attributes in the social bodies under their command.[11]

To be sure, Villarroel did have economic preoccupations, but he seemed less willing than Gálvez to reorganize the colonial structure with the single objective of maximizing the extraction of profit. Building on the long colonial legacy of a rhetoric and practice that demonized unproductivity and "idleness," the insistence that Villarroel places in *Enfermedades políticas* on the need to implement measures that could secure the employment of New Spain's racialized idle bodies acquires moralizing hues that distinguish his ideas from Gálvez's rationality of efficiency and profit. In Villarroel's text, work is discussed in terms of it being a civilizing tool that could break down collective bodies racialized as filthy, useless, and unproductive into individualized docile subjects living in accordance to the norms of colonial police, rather than in terms that centered the economic revenue to be extracted from their labor.

SITUATING NEW SPAIN: GEOGRAPHY, RACE,
AND THE COLONIAL RELATION

To highlight the ways in which unregulated movement and its corollaries of racial undifferentiation and unemployment caused problems for the viceroyalty, Villarroel situates New Spain in a broad setting. He contrasts its social conditions with those of Spain and addresses side by side Old World "Gypsies" and New Spain's "ínfima plebe" (negligible plebes), returning to a similar comparison made by Viceroy Fernando de Alencastre, Duke of Linares, in 1716. According to Villarroel, the "castas infestas" (infested castes) of New Spain were similar to Old World Gypsies in their supposed laziness, immodesty, licentiousness, and propensity for crime and other vices.[12] Although he uses the same criminalizing rhetoric to racialize both groups, Villarroel also establishes a key distinction between them that emphasizes the colonial relation of Spain and Mexico. According to him, both sites and their governments exhibited differential capacities to achieve adequate spatial organization and territorial control, two necessary conditions for managing and shaping the behavior of racialized and impoverished groups. Government policies in Spain, Villarroel argues, had successfully restricted Gypsies in the Old World to a "particular location or area," and this adequate spatial management had rendered their bodies legible to the government's gaze, producing (when "necessary" through punishment) relatively transparent and docile subjectivities.[13] By contrast, New Spain's government had failed to accomplish such a thing. The distance that separated the viceroyalty from the metropole, along with the perceived unassertive character of the former's inhabitants, weakened the sovereign hold the king had over his most distant possessions. As a colonial space, New Spain presented deeper challenges: it was characterized by its impenetrability and abundance of natural hiding places that were inaccessible to government scrutiny and therefore populated by bodies that could not be easily rendered transparent nor legible, but rather stubbornly remained mixed, undifferentiated, opaque, impure, and in a state of constant flux and flight:

> But the people of New Spain form a monster of as many species as there are inferior castes, added to which are infinite Spaniards, Europeans, and criollos, lost and vulgarized by poverty and idleness, mothers of vile customs, of ignorance, of vices and fundamental causes of frequent changes in residence, and although the excesses and crimes of these indolent peoples are witnessed and noted, and although attempts are made to punish them, it is most difficult to apprehend a delinquent, because he seeks shelter in the deepest mineral depths, in the various internal provinces, in the mountains, gorges, and rough terrains of a vast country populated by humble ranches and abandoned huts, even in the suburbs of Mexico City, Puebla, Guadalajara, etcetera. All such refuges elude the procedures of the judges and not even

the strictest laws of a good government, nor the rigors of sanction, shall succeed in remedying the grave damage caused by the multitudes of gypsies in New Spain, if there is not a strategic method applied in doing so.[14]

This passage illustrates that for Villarroel colonial spatiality was incompatible with the structure and workings of the law. As did Gálvez and others before him, Villarroel links the supposed ungovernability and laziness of New Spain's inhabitants to the land's geographical accidents and general disposition. Indeed, for the lawyer the New World was a space that rendered people unproductive and, in turn, disposed to crime and waywardness. The quotation above also shows that in Villarroel's eyes, the ungovernable force of the colony and its unruly inhabitants had become so encompassing that it now threatened to spread beyond caste lines, affecting low-class *peninsulares* and criollos alike: Villarroel declares that if those who came to the Americas from Europe ever decided to return to the Old World, they would no longer be productive to their nation.[15] To obstruct the further expansion of the problem, Villarroel advocates for interrupting the flow of impoverished and unemployed Spaniards into New Spain. As he describes it, New Spain was a disorganized labyrinth full of twists and turns where people invariably got lost.[16] This characterization of colonial geography aligned Villarroel's thinking with other contemporary debates that affirmed and constructed the inferiority of the "torrid zones" and forged a racialized global geography based on an alleged correlation between climate, land disposition, and negative populational behavior.

"IDLE PLEBES": THE CITY AND ITS EMERGING SURPLUS POPULATION

After situating New Spain in a panoramic transatlantic perspective, Villarroel zooms closer in on the specificities of New Spain's social ailments. By the time he wrote his text, the perceived danger related to the unregulated mobility of racialized bodies that had plagued Gálvez's mind years before seemed only to have intensified. Unlike Gálvez's more localized intervention, Villarroel's fantasies of reform involved a spatial imagination of New Spain's territory as a single political unit, where all its different zones and regions were interconnected in a complicated balance. His diagnoses and remedies thus oscillated between discussions about the issues facing inland territories and those affecting Mexico City, and other urban sites, as he traced links of causation among them. The broad perspective of Villarroel's text suggests that concerns with unregulated mobility of racialized bodies, as well as caste undifferentiation and racial conflict, were perceived to be increasingly expanding, seeping deeper and deeper into all realms and regions of New Spain's life decades after the Bajío riots. Villarroel describes the colony's interior provinces as an unpopulated "horrible desert," for their inhabitants—both men and women—had moved to the city, "flooding it."

Initially, the Spanish lawyer attributed the flood of "idle plebes" inundating the capital city to the opening of a large cigarette and cigar factory that, according to his calculations, had the capacity to employ nearly eight thousand men and women. The prospect of these jobs, he states, had begun a massive migration from the countryside to the city, exceeding the number of job openings available in the factory. Villarroel's diagnosis highlights how the social imbalance of one region resonated in another: the movement of people from inland territories to the capital unraveled the order of both spaces.

Regarding the city, Villarroel was puzzled by the dynamics of a sprouting industrial economy that began to generate and rely on a surplus population.[17] He did not understand how the state could be so ill managed so as to waste its potential workforce by lack of organization. He wondered why the government would allow so many more workers to move into the capital than could be accommodated with available jobs there. Clearly, in Villarroel's mind, there was no benefit to the surplus population produced around the new factory. While he complains about the materialization of this excessive, racially undifferentiated, and "idle" population in the capital, he also protests the shortcomings of the colonial state that had created the conditions for this development by not guaranteeing work for all of its inhabitants, including those who had once populated the now deserted provinces:

> What damage has not beset the kingdom with the ruin of the villages, leading to the desertion of families and thus to the general wreckage of agriculture and other artifacts, for the sole motive of furnishing said factory, enclosing seven thousand to eight thousand persons with in it, both men and women? Would it not have been more normal that, without fearing that the factory should decline in its labors for lack of manpower, and rather than following the previous fatality, a methodical though laborious census or enrollment of the inhabitants of these

residents in the capital was conducted and to then adequately populate said factory, without any need for the others? What good does it do the state to have forty thousand idle and itinerant men and women in the capital, serving as beasts of burden to the rest, accustomed to a sedentary life, without purpose, when the entire kingdom has been left an unpopulated skeleton, without culture, without Christianity, without police, without subjection, and without other specific qualities inherent to a good government? . . . One of the attentions of the government must be its refusal to allow idleness in any people, ensuring that its entire happiness consists in making them work in their respective trades or arts, so that they may contribute to the well-being of the state. What good does it do the sovereign to have one million idle, itinerant, and badly trained men in its dominions, who fruitlessly consume the work of the laborious?[18]

Villarroel insightfully perceived the social outcome of a material transformation that would begin to engender a surplus population in the city when he addressed how authorities' fear regarding the lack of laboring hands in the factory had prompted them to stimulate the influx of people into the city, beyond the available number of job openings. Nevertheless, as the passage also shows, Villarroel seemed to be out of step with this emerging dynamic of profit and disposability that was generated by and needed to sustain an incipient industrial economy, as marked by the opening of the cigar factory. He thus calls for an alternative method of populational and labor management that could eliminate the idle multitudes of the city, for, in his eyes, they were completely useless and even harmful. Against the idea of moving toward fostering more and more enterprises like the cigar factory, Villarroel calls on the state to also promote the return of "itinerant men and women" to their towns and to nurture agriculture in the provinces, allowing it to become one of the driving forces of the colony's economy.

Villarroel's suggested methods to deal with the diagnosed crisis highlight the intricate connections that stretched between labor and racialization in late colonial New Spain. While, as I detail below, he advocates for re-territorializing policies for inland territories that could re-attach bodies to clear caste lines according to tributary exaction and the dual republic system, Villarroel also insists on the implementation of surveilling mechanisms that could reinscribe racial distinctions beyond segregationist spatial management in the cities. As the above passage shows, the census was a privileged tool for populational management. Nevertheless, the technique had its limitations and seemed much harder to implement when a "monstrous" (i.e., racially undifferentiated) and idle multitude had already taken over the city. Conscription to labor was thus crucial in Villarroel's mind not only, or even mostly, for economic reasons, but most importantly because *policía*, including the policing of caste lines, was much more easily instilled and implemented through the channels created by labor relations.[19]

CHICHIGUAS IN THE CITY: GENDER, RACE, AND THE PROBLEM OF MIGRATION

For Villarroel not all labor relations were equally capable of subjecting people to clear racial lines and decorum. The work of domestic servants in the private homes of wealthy Spaniards was particularly troubling for the lawyer, as it had been for Franciscan and Augustinian friars at the time of the 1692 riot.[20] Tapping into discourses that had become a common currency of his epoch, Villarroel describes how the spatiality of the city had been impacted by landowners reducing the size of their urban properties, creating small households that allowed racialized domestic workers to conglomerate without order and against the norms of *policía*.[21] The privilege of wealthy Spaniard landowners paradoxically created zones of legal anomaly that allowed domestic servants to carve out living spaces beyond the surveilling gaze of the state, except when there was a homicide or other type of criminal investigation that permitted the temporary breakdown of an increasingly entrenched domestic privacy.[22]

Villarroel's discussion of domestic labor is particularly illuminating regarding the interlacing of gendering dynamics and the fears of deracialization. Drawing on Gálvez's 1771 *informe*, Villarroel frames migration and the depopulation of the provinces in terms of the reduction and destabilization of tributary exaction they would bring: "What quantity of tribute will the treasury not lose, tribute that such people would pay, if, according to the rules of a well policed society, they were required to reside in their towns without permission to abandon them?"[23] But, curiously, while he touches on the large population of unemployed male laborers in the city, Villarroel mostly focuses on the "indians, mulattas, *coyotas*, *lobas*, and other castes" who were hired as wet nurses (*chichiguas*) for the city's most established families.

Villarroel viewed migrant women as directly responsible for the dismantling and depopulation of the provinces. Racialized and normatively gendered, these women were, in his eyes, the anchors of their nuclear families. Their migration to the city implied the disintegration of those nuclei, thus spelling the ruin of provincial villages. Further, Villarroel criminalizes migrant houseworkers and *chichiguas* and their support networks, framing them as birthing a "delinquent" informal economy that parasitically drained the legal colonial economy of its resources. According to his narrative, it was common for family members to follow migrant *chichiguas* and houseworkers as they moved to work in the city. "Their companions arrived with the expectation to live idly, supported not by the salary or rations the women would receive in exchange for their work but by the things they would allegedly steal from their employers."[24]

To "remedy" the situation, Villarroel first suggests that migrant *chichiguas* and other servants be expelled from the city and forced to return to their villages. In his view, the return of this population to its places of origin would reconfigure and repair the devastated agricultural economy as well as the racial geography that he claimed had been dismantled in the provinces. It would resettle racialized bodies (specifically women's bodies) in their appropriate family units while also attaching them to clear caste ascriptions, thus ultimately regularizing the exaction of tribute and reconfiguring the moral tissue that had been torn with their departure. Second, Villarroel insists on the need for an accurate census of the capital's inhabitants, one that would register categories of both caste and trade with the intention of making surveillance of workers in the city more manageable. He particularly insists on the need to establish a required system of references—similar to the one that Gálvez proposed for employment in the Bajío mines—that could help regulate the movement of *criados* (domestic servants) from one house to another. This would also help curtail the informal thieving economy he associated with the city's networks of domestic labor. Finally, fusing his remedies for New Spain's social ailments with military technique, Villarroel proposes that once the exodus of workers had been successfully implemented, the city itself be walled off to prevent future influxes of migrants into it.[25]

FROM THE PROVINCES TO THE CITY: UNREGULATED MOVEMENT AND ITS LINKS TO RACIAL CONFLICT

Villarroel also associated the incursion of people from the interior into the capital with racial conflict. As he outlines the aforementioned series of strategies that the colonial government could implement to "clean the city" from its "drones" (*zánganos*), Villarroel asserts that another factor behind the depopulation of the provinces and the overpopulation of the cities was the constant attacks of "barbaric Indians" over New Spain's northern settlements.[26] According to his logic, the raids perpetrated by northern tribes had made the colony's inland territories "uninhabitable," prompting the migration of thousands of people into urban sites. Villarroel even fantasizes a nightmarish scenario in which, if uncontained, the raids of "barbaric Indians" and their felling force would advance like an avalanche from the north into the capital city if the city had no adequate means to resist them.[27] The lawyer suggests that if the situation ever got to that extreme, the only way to protect the capital city from the racial threat would be through "blood and fire."[28]

But Villarroel tended to place more emphasis on the use of other means to contain the raids and was skeptical of the expenditure of war. He insists that, when possible, other more economic and "peaceful" measures be employed to supplement those already put in place to protect the viceroyalty.[29] Notably, however, his text highlights the continuity between practices of war and "civilizing" measures, often framed as distinct and less violent than direct military action. In a critique of the limits of the garrison reforms that had been promulgated by the king in 1772, Villarroel expands his project to dismantle the unruly idle populations of New Spain's major cities by offering his own ideas on how to improve the garrison system.[30] His central argument is that one could not expect underserved *presidios*, separated from each other by at least forty leagues, to contain the forceful and expansive raids of "barbaric Indians" on their own. He thus suggests complementing garrisons with "poblaciones intermedias," nonmilitary settlements that would break down the distances between "presidios" while also providing these military posts with food and other necessary resources. Overall, the settlements would help promote the economy and civilization of the north and more effectively obstruct the advancement of "barbarous tribes" over New Spanish inland territories.[31]

To consolidate the intermediate settlements, Villarroel resorts to a common colonial practice and calls for the displacement of nearly fourteen thousand families from Mexico City, Puebla, and other major urban sites. With support from the royal treasury, these families would be relocated to northern "depopulated" lands, where they would become involved in farming, agriculture, and mining activities for the overall betterment of themselves and the colony at large.[32] According to Villarroel, relocating strategies would not only purge the cities of their "laziest inhabitants" but also help displaced subjects become productive and avoid unpleasant encounters with the empire's disciplinary apparatus, namely, its gallows, garrisons, fortifications, and arsenals.[33] He even moves toward envisioning preventative measures and devised a pipeline of employment for "idle" children. To this effect, he suggests that every year, "unproductive" boys between the ages of eight and fourteen be rounded up from the large cities and put to work on naval ships operating between New Spain and Havana.[34]

Villarroel's text offers an example of how moralizing discourse supported the overflow of surveilling and disciplinarian practices beyond the penal and military systems.[35] His text is also helpful to shed light on the ways in which concerns about social hygiene as correlated to productivity would encode and support the reproduction of racial difference in New Spain.

At different points in *Enfermedades políticas*, Villarroel discusses the unlikelihood of his suggestions ever making it into actual colonial policy. Indeed, as stated at the beginning of this coda, the text would go unpublished until after Mexico's independence from New Spain was complete. Notably, rather than pointing toward the irrelevance of Villarroel's ideas to his own time, I would like to suggest that this fact illuminates the continuities of colonial strategies into the postindependence period.

Enfermedades políticas is a text in which the past and future of colonial racializing strategies can be parsed out. In revisiting the combination of censuses, tribute, militarization, and populational redistribution already at play in Gálvez's campaign as part of making race in New Spain, Villarroel's medico-political diagnosis of the colony's ailments attests to the continuities of these strategies. At the same time, in his turn toward a moralizing rhetoric that encoded and reproduced racial difference through ideas about efficiency, social hygiene, order, work, and productivity, Villarroel foreshadowed the repurposing of these colonial legacies after independence.

{ PART II }

Haiti

{ THREE }

The Domino Affect

HAITI, NEW SPAIN, AND
THE RACIAL PEDAGOGY OF DISTANCE

In 1806, Juan López de Cancelada introduced New Spanish readers to the most recent news about Haiti's revolution. Only two years after the French side of Hispaniola proclaimed independence and the abolition of slavery, the editor of *La Gazeta de México* was framing Haitian rebels' historic victory as a "terrifying" spectacle that nevertheless harbored valuable lessons for distant readers in New Spain. In his preface to the Spanish edition of *Vida de J. J. Dessalines*, Juan López de Cancelada uses a theatrical metaphor to describe the release of his translation for the New Spanish audience.[1] The text and its images, López de Cancelada insists, sought to "introduce readers to the *monsters* who play the lead roles in the scene."[2]

While the internationally acclaimed original French text had also been translated into English, German, and Dutch, López de Cancelada's second Spanish edition was unique. Alongside his own "note to the reader" appeared illustrations from two locally renowned artists, José Simón de la Rea and Manuel López López, both commissioned by López de Cancelada himself. The edition also included his own footnotes and an appendix with the Spanish translation of both Dessalines's coronation speech and the 1805 Haitian constitution.[3]

In representing Haiti's uprising as a spectacle of "monsters," López de Cancelada entered the slippery field of contemporary debates on monstrosity. He also produced a discursive encounter between the divergent racial formations of the French and Spanish Empires. López de Cancelada's theatrical framing, which extended the original French text's racist teratological rhetoric, presented Haiti's alleged monstrosity in terms that would be both legible and distant—nonthreatening—to his New Spanish audience.[4]

One thing was clear. For López de Cancelada, Haiti's revolution was a race war with global repercussions. The racist rhetoric of the monstrous used in the original French and then repeated in his Spanish edition was more than mere flourish: it was a tactic of international diplomacy. It aimed to undercut British support for Haiti amid the Napoleonic Wars and the French-Spanish alliance, limiting international public recognition of the new nation.[5] It also sought to neutralize the premise inscribed in Haiti's 1805 constitution, which expanded into colonial domains the reach and meaning of previous proclamations about the equality of all mankind.

Domestically, López de Cancelada's take on Haiti's "monstrosity" was also a response to expanding worldly connections. The trope allowed López de Cancelada to contrast Saint-Domingue with New Spain and begin to shape an affective racialized distance between the two colonial spaces. In the eyes of López de Cancelada, Haiti's Black rebels were monsters who were, therefore, inassimilable to New Spain's social conditions.[6] Framing it as such, he thought, would help to cement readers' sense of the distance between both colonies, keeping Haiti's revolution at bay.

In this chapter I study the process through which New Spanish colonial elites and authorities began to engage with Haiti's revolution in terms of a race war of global importance. Focused on a study of the New Spanish edition of Jean Jacques Dessalines's illustrated biography, it traces emerging uses of the printing press to manage geopolitical relations and shape local readers' sensibilities by impressing upon them racialized visions of distance and proximity. López de Cancelada, who thought that proliferating global ties created a sense that events happening in remote locations were increasingly unescapable, sought to manipulate how information about these events would circulate through the colony he inhabited. I investigate the ways in which New Spain's racial histories of Blackness and whiteness were inserted into a trans–imperial Atlantic milieu, arguing that in this complex navigation against Haiti— between the close and the distant, the local and the foreign—New Spanish elites came to view themselves as sharing the whiteness of other elite groups in nearby colonies.

HAITI: A "MONSTROUS" FIGURE OF GLOBAL "RACE WAR"

Scholars have shown that the question of monstrosity was both crucial and vexing for Enlightenment philosophers, scientists, and artists.[7]

Seldom neatly defined, the unstable category of the monstrous mediated contemporary explorations of nature and the changing limits of reason. While it may be true that through the eighteenth century the figure of the monster was naturalized by growing efforts to rationalize disorder, it is also true that in many ways the figure appeared as a disturbing "corroboration of the breakdown of objective truth."[8] So-called monsters were seen at some times as accidents or signs of contingency and chaos, at others as manifestations of a providential design that naturally produced anomalies.[9] They thus presented an ongoing and complicated puzzle for Enlightenment thinkers of all kinds, and scientists and philosophers began to perceive their appearance beyond the realms of superstition and anatomy. Monstrosity became a figure used to describe unexpected and threatening political changes in societies across the world.

In Juan López de Cancelada's work, the notion of monstrosity was channeled toward the political. As it expanded out of its original categorical home, the natural sciences, López de Cancelada's work drew from contemporary ideas on monstrosity to discursively stabilize the shaky ground of history.[10] His figuration of Haiti's rebels as monsters ultimately concealed a deep reactionary angst stemming from the threat he perceived in the rising nonwhite multitudes of neighboring colonies like Saint-Domingue and Jamaica. The figure of the monstrous mediated López de Cancelada's cavillations about whether Haiti's "race war" was part of a historical-providential order or a fortuitous occurrence that pointed toward the collapse of prior certainties and structures. He wondered whether Haiti's revolutionary events held any significance for New Spain. Could the events on the Caribbean island portend a nearing global catastrophe?

As the force of Atlantic revolutions unexpectedly reorganized historical experience, the temporality and social disposition of all the nations of the world appeared to be impacted. In his writings about Haiti, López de Cancelada records his intuitions about the proximity of events unfolding in distant nations as they marked the increasing totalization of history—intuitions he shared with European contemporaries, who only a few years prior had discussed the global shockwaves of the French Revolution: "No policy is more erroneous than that of indifference to the good or ill that befalls other nations simply because it does not affect us personally. A State is fooling itself if it believes it is uninterested in what has occurred two thousand leagues away from its own continent. The political and the physical world are alike: a first motion propels the general masses, extending its driving force from one end to the next."[11] This passage captures how López de Cancelada experienced an increasing sense of global proximity and instability. To him, the world seemed more closely interconnected than ever before. Capitalism's expansion produced new trade networks and opened the doors of economic exchange across nations and empires; it also enabled news, images, texts, people, and ideas to circulate freely from one point to another. These ideas were difficult to contain, and strict censorship laws and other similar practices were insufficient in their capacity to regulate contact among the different parts of the world. According to López de Cancelada, Haiti's revolution made visible the dangers of increasing global interconnection. He compares the realm of the political to the act of tossing a stone into a lake and producing ripples that expanded across the surface of the water. In the same way, the events that took place in a given society could potentially trigger a "domino affect," influencing people in other societies, even those that were geographically or racially distant from the center.

In the late eighteenth century, elites on both sides of the Atlantic saw the unprecedented wave of revolutions not only as a global concern that could not be ignored but also as one that would indelibly mark history itself. For example, in *The Conflict of Faculties* Immanuel Kant describes the *unforgettable* nature of the French Revolution, capturing the profound ambivalence that the events of 1789 had awakened in the German philosopher.[12] Rebecca Comay suggests in *Mourning Sickness* that the key question for Kant was one of the production and administration of distance: how to shift away from the horrified fascination produced by revolution and turn instead toward its moral exaltation.[13] According to Kant, facticity mattered little or not at all to the French Revolution's place in history: its "objective" success or failure was insignificant compared to the "sympathy" it had awakened in the disinterested spectators observing the events of 1789 from afar. This shared sympathy was, according to Kant, confirmation of a moral disposition shared by "all men" and thus evidence for the telos of human life. Kant's attempts to neutralize what Comay calls the "political actuality of terror" paradoxically entailed reinserting France's revolutionary rupture into the continuum of history, framing it as verifying the progressive arc of human morality.[14]

López de Cancelada's text shows a similar concern. His fearful engagement with Haiti's revolution aimed to absorb its force, to reduce its radical potential by co-opting its shockwaves into a moral narrative that affirmed his belief in civilization and, most importantly, secured New Spain's racialized social structure, presenting it as completely foreign— and thus immune—to Haiti's uprising. By publishing this text, López de

Cancelada sought to shape his readers' affects and instill in them ideas and feelings about the distance that separated New Spain from Haiti.

While Kant may have been the clearest example of the "moral translation" by which the French Revolution was narratively purified of its "excesses," a parallel translation of Haiti's revolution unfurled on the other side of the Atlantic. Despite the echoes that may exist between the German philosopher's and the Spanish editor's take on the two revolutions, one fundamental distance divided them: that of the colonial relation that both united and separated France from Haiti. Like Kant, López de Cancelada attempted to incorporate the Haitian Revolution into a narrative of morality that, in his case, was explicitly racializing. López de Cancelada sought to purge his own fear of the events in Haiti by assimilating them into a moral narrative that emphasized the alleged impermeability of New Spanish readers' sensibilities vis-à-vis the island's race war. While Kant saw the "sympathy" awakened in distant observers of the French Revolution as a formal, abstract, and positive expression of a moral disposition common to "all men," the "horror" that López de Cancelada communicated to his New Spanish readers was framed in a negative, subtractive manner. Kant's ideas about sympathy and the French Revolution were abstractly inclusive; the fear that López de Cancelada aimed to stoke in his readers was, instead, concretely exclusive: he underscored horror as the central affective experience that emanated from Haiti in an effort to protect and affirm the racial barriers that seemed to be collapsing from the Caribbean outward. By allowing themselves to feel the same horror he felt at the successful slave rebellion of Saint-Domingue, readers in New Spain would affirm their integration into a racially circumscribed humanity that excluded from its confines Haiti's rebels and their allies by presenting them as monsters.

Kant's and López de Cancelada's responses to revolution showed very different relations to modern temporality. According to Comay, Kant's encounter with the French Revolution introduced a sense of anachronism, marking German philosophy's entry into modernity as belated. In Kant, she suggests, modernity was registered as a traumatic missed experience.[15] In colonial spaces like New Spain, however, the Haitian Revolution—at least as it is framed in López de Cancelada's introduction to *Vida de J. J. Dessalines*—produced an opposite temporal response: an anxiety about a "monstrous" modern future that seemed to be approaching far too quickly. These two forms of anxiety, however, shared a sense that both France's and Haiti's revolutionary events were inescapable; both were inverse markers of an increasingly global modernity:[16] "If the French Revolution is the epochal marker of modernity," Comay writes, "this is not because it provides a fixed or objective (strictly speaking, ahistorical) standard of comparison, but rather because it introduces untimeliness itself as an ineluctable condition of historical experience."[17] Whereas Kant saw this untimeliness as defined by Germany's absent or lacking revolution, López de Cancelada took it to be marked by the fear of a revolutionary event in the colonies, a race war, that might arrive too soon.

In their respective narrativization of the events in France and Haiti, both the philosopher and the editor sought to insert themselves and their readers into history. In both responses—anachronism and the racialization of horror—we see observers struggling to find a place, articulating (never satisfactorily) the trauma of revolutionary rupture by fostering an exegetic moral sensibility that could either reinsert or subtract the experience of revolution, suturing it back into the allegedly progressive continuum of history.

A RACIAL AFFECTIVE PEDAGOGY

According to Antonio Negri, to trace the genealogy of the political monster is to trace the other side of the genealogy of biopower. For him, the political monster is the inverted figure of what he calls Western eugenic philosophy. It is what reason cannot recover, what interrupts it: what power fears and deems to be its Other. As capitalism has consolidated and changed, Negri tells us, the location of the political monster has also shifted. It has moved from being used as a spurious, metaphorical figure of exclusion to naming an immanent existing force that strikes (and must be repressed) from within: "The monster becomes a subject, or different subjects—he is neither excluded in principle nor reduced to a metaphor. No, he's there, he exists, he's really there. . . . The wider the world becomes, the more widespread monstrosity becomes. We encounter the monster everywhere, and he truly scares the masters of the world."[18]

The trope of monstrosity in López de Cancelada's text registers a historical shift parallel to the one described by Negri. According to the editor, Haiti, a paradigmatic figure of race war, obliterated political monstrosity as mere metaphor: the island's revolution was a real, material, and embodied irruption, an insubordination in the immanent field of existence. The island, which in his view had been taken over by a disordered multitude of rebellious Black bodies, had become the first site to overthrow a specifically colonial government and abolish slavery, setting a dangerous example for the rest of the world's colonies. López de Cancelada's edition of Dessalines's biography was introduced as a tool that could help contain this changing reality by anticipating it and immunizing New Spanish readers against the effects of rebellion circulated by a worldly event like Haiti's revolution.

López de Cancelada's ideas about censorship differed from those held by most of his contemporaries: he sought not to suppress information but to control how it circulated and was received. As a result, he devoted his editorial efforts to experimenting with ways to adequately frame the content published under his supervision. López de Cancelada's editorial decisions as head of the *Gazeta de México* reflect emerging ideas about the press as a technology of control that could be used to shape, manage, and guide readers' sensibilities, slowly "engraving" in them emotions that supported the colonial order.[19] His racist evocation of monstrosity aimed to foster in New Spanish readers the sense that racial conflicts were the most undesirable outcome of political struggle. He thus pushed back against the perceived inevitability of the historical repetition of uprisings like those in Haiti, Jamaica, and other colonial sites of the Caribbean, offering his book as a preventative that could support in containing the global expansion of these "monstrous" rebellions. The book served as what I call an affective racial pedagogy, one that aimed to guide readers' bodies and minds in absorbing Haiti's revolution as untranslatable and distant. With this framing, López de Cancelada thought it safe to expose New Spain's audience to carefully curated scenes from the island's revolution. Presented as foreign and untranslatable, these glimpses would help New Spain's audience engender a racialized distancing sensibility that would, in turn, protect the colony.[20]

Consider an article that was printed in the *Gazeta de México* the same year that López de Cancelada's book was published. The article, likely penned by López de Cancelada himself, offers details about how Dessalines's biography was supposed to be received. The text provides information about the book's cost and where it and its images could be acquired, as well as a brief summary of its storyline; its author also explains that one of the primary reasons for its publication was to prepare "the tender and sensible hearts of the sons of New Spain for a text that is most *foreign* to their gentle customs."[21]

The author alludes to the bodily and sensory dimensions of reading ("the tender and sensible heart"), illustrating how texts were thought to be capable of impressing and shaping readers' sensations and emotions.

In doing so, he introduces *Vida de J. J. Dessalines* as a mediator between the public and the private, as a tool that could help readers internalize the parameters of the colony's racialized order via their contact with the text, preemptively disciplining their sensory responses and priming them to reject not only Haiti's revolution but race war itself as a desirable political paradigm.

At first glance, the passage seems not to address the question of race, but its reference to the "gentle customs" of New Spain's sons establishes a tacit racialized difference between these customs and those of Haiti's rebels, which, readers should infer, were, instead, coarse. Similarly, López de Cancelada's opening of the book contrasts New Spanish readers' alleged tenderness and softness with the "ferocious cruelty" of Haiti's revolutionaries. He thus ties race to a differential capacity to feel, to experience a given emotional response in the face of a political event such as the Haitian Revolution.[22]

Crucially, López de Cancelada depicts his local audience as emotionally discerning. As he praises New Spain for its "calm" and "tranquility," and for remaining impermeable to the ideas that "had disturbed the peace of other regions," he positions his readers as both open to their milieu and at the same time capable of disciplining their sensory susceptibility.[23] *Vida de J. J. Dessalines* was meant to be an important device in cultivating its audience's ability to receive and reflectively respond to the world's stimuli. It is in this sense that the New Spanish edition of Dessalines's biography partakes in eighteenth-century trans-imperial discourses about refinement and adequate or cultured behavior as tied to one's alleged capacity to be and remain impressed or affected by an external force. These ideas would later provide the building blocks for notions of impressibility that, as Kyla Schuller studies, involved theories about "the capacity of matter to be alive to movements made on it, to retain and incorporate changes rendered in its material over time."[24]

Another passage, this time from a translated portion of Louis Dubroca's text, brings to the forefront the idea that only certain bodies had the moral readiness required to be trusted with freedom. The passage presents freedom as a privilege that needed to be unevenly disseminated, made accessible only to hearts (and bodies) exposed to previous experiences that had allegedly prepared them to handle it responsibly: "Man poorly enjoys the first and most significant of merits if the principles of all virtues are not carved into his heart; principles that are only received by means of a well-arranged and directed education. Thus, it is not strange that freedom has manifested itself in Saint-Domingue in the appearance of a fury, running this way and that with an axe in one hand, a dagger in the other, and death always ahead of it."[25] According to Dubroca, freedom was yielded adequately and with beneficial results in Europe, while it could only be deployed destructively in the colony. This was the case because the *hearts* of people from the colonies had not been primed for the experience of freedom with the appropriate pedagogical content ("a well-arranged and directed education").

The logics of impressibility support the racist discourses advanced by both Dubroca and López de Cancelada in the original and translated versions of the book. In both texts, Blackness is configured as a spectrum of low capacities to adequately receive and assimilate external stimuli. All of Haiti's rebels are ascribed a minimal capacity to absorb, retain, and manage sensible impressions, but Dessalines, the lead role in the text, is assigned the lowest marker on the scale. Although it is known that the revolutionary was born into slavery in Saint-Domingue, the book describes him as a "ferocious African" who had undergone the middle passage fairly recently and whose body only retained impressions made by the "barbarity and ferociousness of the climate into which he'd been born."[26] According to the author, Dessalines's habits were unaffected by the moral influence of Western culture, customs, and civilization, and the only lasting impression in his soul "was that of the desire for vengeance."[27]

Unlike Dessalines, who is marked by this alleged incapacity to self-regulate ("wildness and ambition"),[28] the Toussaint Louverture of the text is presented as having a slightly higher degree of impressibility. In reference to Louverture's education, the book describes how the revolutionary leader had learned how to read and write under his master's tutelage and thus assigns him a certain capacity to retain and manage impressions. Louverture's Blackness, unlike that of Dessalines, is not a marker of an absolute incapacity to be and remain affected. Instead, it is associated with "hypocrisy," a word that in the context of the text acquires the meaning of a racialized propensity to reversibility.[29] Louverture's steps toward "civilization" are easily undone, giving way to his so-called natural ferociousness, which only intensifies as he becomes more and more involved in the uprising.[30] His Blackness thus occupies a different place in the racial spectrum construed by the text. It is tied not to a supposed inability to be impressed but rather to not being capable of *retaining* impressions. Underlying the different racist characterizations of both revolutionary leaders (Dessalines and Toussaint) are ideas that associate Blackness with absolute and relative notions of "barbarism." While

Dessalines is a figure of complete exteriority to "civilization," Louverture is figured as having an uncertain capacity to progress. These ideas are metonymically used in the book to position the revolution itself not as a political event inscribed in the progressive movement of history but rather as a return to "savagery."

In the nineteenth century, ideas about how barbarism lurked beneath the sensible structures of all mankind would become increasingly prominent. In these discourses, racial difference was a matter of ascribing varying levels of temporal depth to the "civilizational" layers impressed onto different bodies; the racialization of the actors of *Vida de J. J. Dessalines* anticipates the peak of these theories' circulation. Racial difference emerges in the book not as an immutable or fixed characteristic but rather as a dynamic palimpsestic relation. Race appears as a temporalized difference, where bodies are perceived to have varying degrees of past, present, and future capacities to experience and retain stimuli.[31] The distinction between the "civilized" and the "barbaric" is not a dichotomy but a complex and uneven distribution of capabilities along a fluid yet hierarchized spectrum, where bodies and their political claims to life are differentially organized, managed, and regulated.[32]

INDELIBLE MESSAGES: RACIALIZED DEPICTIONS OF HAITI FOR NEW SPANISH READERS

Although the historical characters of the book are described as nearly unimpressible, López de Cancelada's prologue locates his New Spanish audience on the opposite side of the spectrum of affectability. His use of the theatrical metaphor of the "spectacle" was important in helping to create the affective racialized distance between New Spanish readers and Haiti's rebels. This metaphor gave his audience in Mexico City an image of themselves as a homogeneous block of spectators who watched from afar as Haiti's revolution unraveled. The text presents readers as viewers, thus separating them from the immediacy of the "terrible catastrophe" disturbing France's Antillean territories; this distance was meant to allow the audience some space to absorb, reflect, and "adequately" respond to the revolutionary theater.[33]

Specialists in colonial Mexico's print culture have remarked on how the physical operations of the printing press—its use of stamped type blocks to literally impress text into paper—served as a metaphor for how the ideas in printed texts operated on the public's minds and hearts. Indeed, discussions of how printed texts "engraved" indelible messages in the "souls" of New Spanish subjects are not only present in the book but also common in contemporary articles published in the *Gazeta de México*.[34] At the time, images were thought to be particularly effective in imprinting emotions, for they were presumed to have a greater capacity to "penetrate the hearts" of viewers than even printed text itself.[35] It is unsurprising, then, that López de Cancelada's unique edition of Dubroca's text includes several images, although they made its publication quite expensive.[36] These ten illustrative engravings were commissioned by López de Cancelada from two well-regarded colonial artists, José Simón de la Rea and Manuel López López.[37] In the context of New Spain's iconography, these images emphasized the spectacularization of Haiti's revolution and López de Cancelada's attempt to immunize his readers' hearts against it.[38]

Although his descriptions speak of a homogenous New Spanish, and even of an American, audience, one can't help but wonder whether López de Cancelada assumed his text would be read differentially across caste lines. Given the distribution of alphabetic literacy in Mexico City at the time, his readership would have been small and mostly limited to wealthy Spaniards and some criollos.[39] However, the images had the potential to make the work accessible to a broader illiterate audience in general. The set of ten images was sold separately (though not cheaply) to those interested.[40]

Amid growing concerns about the alleged danger of racial undifferentiation in colonial governmentality discussed in the previous chapters, the images in López de Cancelada's *Vida de J. J. Dessalines* affirmed and reproduced the hierarchies of the colonial caste system. The vignettes, which purport to illustrate scenes from Haiti's revolution, are in fact embedded in contemporary visual imaginaries of *casta* in New Spain. As Jesús Paniagua Pérez remarks, the etchings' lack of detail, as well as their incipient realist aesthetic, betray the artists' ignorance of the actual Haitian landscape.[41] Also, the images do not focus only on portrayals of important battles and other historically significant incidents to the Haitian Revolution. Instead, many of them illustrate seemingly arbitrary and minor passages from the text, a result of López de Cancelada's primary project in publishing the book: not necessarily historical and factual accuracy but rather a narrative designed to work within the viceroyalty's social context to create an affective racialized distance between his New Spanish readers and Haiti.[42] But the images' misrepresentations of Haiti's landscapes and history make them no less interesting. This is especially the case if one looks at them not for what they capture about the island and its revolution but for what they can express about New Spanish elites' preoccupations with race and the race war paradigm more broadly. Interestingly, too, in some ways the images can be seen as working against the grain of López de Cancelada's message about the distance between Saint-Domingue and New Spain, for they actually imply a certain degree of translatability between these two colonial sites.[43]

A VIEW TO THE SHARED STRUCTURES OF WHITENESS

One of López López's etchings is an exemplar of the illustrations' attempts to racially train the reader's sight and sensibility. The image shows the dismembered and decapitated body of a white mother with her baby lying dead beside her, his face still fixed to her bare breast. The caption presents the image as illustrating a factual event, offering specific narrative details that were not included in Dubroca's original: the mother had been murdered when she resisted rape by Dessalines's soldiers, and the hungry baby had starved to death trying in vain to extract milk from her dead breast.[44] The two bodies, mother and child, are depicted against a bucolic background of trees, grass, and rolling hills, a scene that is interrupted in the distance by the figure of a Black revolutionary, dressed in military uniform and holding what the viewer is meant to conclude is the dagger he used to take the woman's life. Read beyond a realist aesthetic, the figure of the white woman's dismembered body can be seen as an allegory of elite peninsular and criollo anxiety about the prospect of an internal fracture between these two groups. Such a fracture could lead to the disruption of the colony's order. López de Cancelada himself warned as much in his introduction, stressing that the most significant lesson in the book was "the importance of the unity of all those whites who inhabit a colony where there are blacks and other castes."[45] Although, as I will show in chapter 4, the racialized economic and social structures of New Spain and Saint-Domingue were very different from one another at the end of the eighteenth century, a point of translation between both contexts emerged through the fear the Haitian Revolution triggered in Saint-Domingue's plantation owners, which circled beyond the island's confines. A vast body of scholarship has touched upon how this fear spread to elites in many other Atlantic colonies. Few, however, have asked what the condition of possibility of that shared perception was. In other words, how did elites in colonies that otherwise were quite distinct from each other come to see themselves as analogous and, therefore, equally endangered by alleged race wars? (See fig. 3.1.)

The Haitian Revolution was certainly not the first time Spanish elites had expressed concern over the potential irruption of racial conflict linked to Black conspiracy. With the transatlantic slave trade increasing the presence of African and Afro-descendent groups in New Spain, fantasies and anxieties about such conflicts were regularly expressed by both colonial authorities and peninsular and criollo elites.[46] But after Haiti, the texture of these anxieties changed, as local histories of race were overlaid with the experience of an increasing globality.

Reactionary responses to the revolution in Haiti illuminate the development of a transatlantic structure of "whiteness" that was coming together while ideas about race war being the most dangerous type of political conflict facing colonial societies were also taking shape and circulating widely throughout the region. These ideas moved from one colonial context to another in translations like the one prepared by López de Cancelada. Repeating content about the dangers that racialized majorities posed to white colonists in Saint-Domingue, he abstracted the singular conditions of the Caribbean island and asserted that "the unity of whites" was essential not only for New Spain but also for any other colony inhabited mostly by nonwhite groups. Indeed, his text underscores that in this period a transatlantic structure of whiteness was beginning to crystallize and to be named explicitly as such.

Although the geographical, economic, social, and demographic contexts of Atlantic colonies differed widely, elites' affirmations about a shared fear and anxiety over other racialized majorities in colonial societies seems to have been an important aspect in the consolidation of what Charles W. Mills has called a global white supremacy: a polycentric racial structure of privilege built and sustained by international jurisprudence and a shared colonial history of pacts and treaties.[47] Mills writes, "Though there is no centralized planetary seat of formal white governing power, though whites the world over are divided by national membership, citizens of countries and empires sometimes in conflict with each other, and internally divided by class and gender, there are nonetheless binding transoceanic and trans-societal links."[48]

This shared vision of whiteness, partly forged against the radical force of the Haitian Revolution, is apparent in excerpts from the diplomatic correspondence between Charles Maurice de Talleyrand and the US secretary of state on the topic of the island's revolution. The letters were reprinted under López de Cancelada's supervision in the *Gazeta*

FIGURE 3.1. *Manuel López López,* Fue muerta y destrozada en el campo esta infeliz p[o]r haver resitido a los deseos brutales de los Negros y el niño perezio de hambre a su lado buscando el pecho yerto de su Madre. *Courtesy of the John Carter Brown Library.*

de México, and they showcase how international law was an important piece in building the transatlantic edifice of whiteness.[49] Seeking to end the commerce in weapons and other goods between US merchants and Haitian rebels, Talleyrand invokes the United States' duty to support the "civilized powers" of the world and demands that its government uphold the pact to not incite rebellion in each other's subjects.[50] Talleyrand's appeal to international law underscores the fact that, in his views, the United States and France held parallel positions. As "civilized powers" they both were called upon to fight and resist the uprising of other racialized majorities of the world, in this particular situation of those in Haiti. To assume this duty was thus to accept the presumed connection between these two nations as forgers of "civilization," placing them together within a shared structure of whiteness. The fact that these letters were reprinted in New Spain's most important newspaper is indicative not only of their widespread circulation but, most important, of the role that the publication of international diplomatic correspondence played in forging a transatlantic public sphere. Notably this sphere was a site where localized ideas of whiteness were translated and retranslated into different contexts, becoming interwoven to produce an encompassing web that allowed elites in different colonial sites to increasingly identify with each other. Through this web, elites in different locations started to view themselves as being similarly white.

López de Cancelada's introduction to *Vida de J. J. Dessalines* illustrates the point. The editor emphasizes the problem of discord among whites even more than he did the "monstrosity" of Black rebels. In fact, this was the editor's dominant strategy in reframing Dubroca's narrative about Haiti's revolution for the New Spanish context. At the time of the biography's publication, any potential translatability between New Spain and Saint-Domingue resided not so much in a parallel between the racialized majorities of each colony but rather in the analogy of the positions occupied by their white elites.

Of course, whiteness is produced by what it excludes, and at the same time that López de Cancelada sought to show that Haiti was incommensurable with New Spain, he was also laying the groundwork for a tacit analogy to emerge between the racialized majorities in both places. When he emphasizes the importance of white unity in places inhabited by "negros y otras castas" (Blacks and other castes), he creates an implicit parallel between these two racial categories. While contemporary censuses documented the negligible size of New Spain's Black population, the "casta" population was significant. Indeed, López de Cancelada's text implicitly hints at the possibility that in New Spain the threat of an uncontrollably growing population of *castas* could be read in parallel to the threat of Black insurgency in Saint-Domingue.[51] This is visible in the syntax of the sentence used by López de Cancelada in which the conjunction "y" equates "negros" with "otros castas," presenting as equal the threat posed by each group. Thus, López de Cancelada's deliberate attempt to emphasize white unity in New Spain—while also insisting on the distance that separated it from Haiti's Blackness—returned to haunt him through the back door.

While the documents on the 1767 Bajío riots studied in the previous chapters showcase the consolidation of *white* as an explicit racial category in New Spain, *Vida de J. J. Dessalines* signals how the category started operating at a transatlantic level. It points toward the emergence of whiteness as a category that connected elites in different nations and colonies of the region, making clear the analogous positions held by privileged groups within these racialized societies. López de Cancelada's edition of Dubroca's text inserted New Spain into this network.

Insofar as the visual representation of the body was a common strategy to allude to the body politic, the depiction of the woman's dismembered body offered a violent visual rendition of "white disunity" that was meant to impress readers with ideas about a preemptive counterinsurgent solidarity with white elites both within and beyond the confines of the colony.[52] The woman's severed body—her hand over here, her head over there, her foot some distance away—thus allegorizes the fear of a potential rupture between white elites in New Spain. As tensions between *peninsulares* and criollos increased under Bourbon rule, preoccupations with a fracture between them grew in proportion. The engraving's depiction of the dead mother and child—both symbols of life and reproduction—documents a new stage in the consolidation of the race war paradigm. At this moment in New Spain and in connection to events occurring in other Atlantic colonies, race wars were starting to be presented as the most significant threat to the reproduction and continuation of colonial systems writ large.

RACE WAR AND GENDERED VIOLENCE

During the colonial period in Mexico, images constituted a kind of grammar that allowed residents, mostly those living in urban spaces, to visualize their place in the racialized structure of the Spanish Empire. If we view López López's image as part of the visual vocabulary of its time, it seems hardly coincidental that a white woman's body was portrayed at its center.

The representation of bodies was a strategy often used to illustrate the intersection between the individual and the social.[53] Kelly Donahue-Wallace has studied how gender was constructed in New Spanish iconography, paying particular attention to the portrayal of women's bodies. In addition to shaping normative ideas about womanhood, says Donahue-Wallace, the representation of the female body was central to visually depicting the colonial order at large.[54] Women's physical bodies were indeed central to New Spain's reproduction. As María Elena Martínez puts it, "As symbols of power for men and vehicles of their reproduction, women's bodies—their wombs, really—were at the center of the racialized order and, in particular, of the struggle between blackness and whiteness."[55]

López López's etching concretely maps the place assigned to white female bodies in New Spain and illustrates how the racializing logics of the colonial order were projected and disputed upon them. While certain forms of gendered violence were condoned, even fostered, at this time in New Spain, others were more carefully policed, particularly when they were perceived to be transgressions that jeopardized order in the colony, such as cross-racial or cross-caste violence.

By portraying a white woman with a lifted skirt, López López visually referred to sexual violence, presumably attempted by the Black man in the background who had committed the murder. The image reactivated certain threads in the historical construction of Blackness in colonial Mexico, calling upon a repertoire of racializing discourses that ascribed to Black male bodies a propensity toward licentiousness and the transgression of sexual boundaries.[56] These discourses had come into being in the early stages of the transatlantic slave trade, as New Spain's African and Afro-descendent populations grew.[57]

Given that in New Spain caste lines were determined along both paternal and maternal lines, Spaniards' preoccupation with having nearly exclusive "access" to white women's bodies was deemed essential to reproducing a social order with them at the top of the hierarchy and Black populations at the bottom.[58] The union between a Black man and a Spanish woman, particularly a violent one as portrayed in the illustration, was perceived as endangering Spanish male lineage, risking the stability of the colonial order.[59] It was during this period that bans prohibiting the marriage of Spaniards with Africans and mixed-blood people

FIGURE 3.2. *Manuel López López, Dessalines. Courtesy of the John Carter Brown Library.*

were reinstated.[60] In addition, while a few *casta* paintings illustrate the union of a Black man and a Spanish woman, this combination is the least common of the unions depicted in this type of art.[61] López López's suggestive illustration of the white woman's abused body added fodder to these historical anxieties. By repurposing New Spain's long-standing myth of Black sexual licentiousness, the engraving mediated and shaped readers' (and thus the colony's) relation to Haiti.[62]

One of the portraits of Dessalines included in the book uses the same visual rhetoric: it depicts the Haitian revolutionary holding the severed head of a white woman, her body and clothes discarded in the background, once again visually suggesting her rape.[63] Beyond emphasizing the text's written representation of Dessalines as incapable of self-regulation in all realms, including the sexual, the image extends this trait and ultimately presents violent licentiousness as an intrinsic marker of Blackness. The duplicated image of a white woman's dismembered and violated body, first by the hand of an anonymous Black soldier and then by Dessalines's, accomplishes this extension. It therefore both offers a cautionary image of the horrors of white disunity and at the same time builds on the racialization of Black masculinity (see fig. 3.2).

Notably, both Dubroca's textual representation of Dessalines and the illustrations in López de Cancelada's edition converged in depicting Black men as brutalizing white women. This repetition across both versions illuminates the gendered and racial dynamics that supported the transatlantic edifice of whiteness; it showcases how diverging histories of race in France and Spain could come together as Dubroca and López de Cancelada placed "maternal" female white bodies at the center of imperial reproduction.

CONCLUSION

The last engraving printed in the book seems to ignore López de Cancelada's hitherto-central racist focus on monstrosity. There is no violence depicted in it at all. Instead, the image shows Dessalines as new emperor of Haiti, sitting on his throne in white royal garments and a crown, surrounded by a court full of Black women and men who are also dressed in sumptuous attire. Some suggest that the artist still registered something about the violence at the time associated with Haiti's revolution in the visual vocabulary that underpins the image. According to Donahue-Wallace, for instance, the book's illustrations of Haiti's Black revolutionaries used the visual codes reserved for portraits of aristocrats. In these individual depictions, Dessalines, Biassou, Louverture, and Christophe wear opulent military attire and are often in the foreground of the frame, gazing steadily toward the viewer. Donahue-Wallace suggests that these codes were likely deployed to illustrate how the uprising had flipped the colonial order on its head. Even the images that did not explicitly depict violent acts were thus used as visual reminders of Haiti's monstrosity, its unnaturalness. In other words, through the use of conventional visual codes, the images intended to show the undesirable and unexpected results of a rebellion that had turned Saint-Domingue's colonial world upside down (see fig. 3.3).[64]

The emancipating force that haunts the engravings far exceeds the editor's and artists' intentions. The portrait of Dessalines's coronation is thus an image that a few years prior would have been unimaginable. The vignette visually registers the way that Haiti's revolution opened a discrepancy, an abyss, between itself and the epoch's representational codes. The tension that belies the use of the conventions of portraiture, which Donahue-Wallace describes as an editorial decision, is in fact the result of the *real* pressure exerted by Haiti over colonial orders and their racialized symbolic and material apparatuses. As Michel-Rolph Trouillot famously (and controversially) observed, "the Haitian Revolution . . . entered history with the peculiar characteristic of being unthinkable even as it happened."[65] Haiti broke out into a modern history that had "no adequate instruments to conceptualize [it]."[66]

If we follow Trouillot's assessment, we might say that in the image of Dessalines's coronation, Haiti's "unthinkability" is registered twice: first in the fact of the historical event the image depicts and second in how it is in excess of the epoch's visual codes. The image presented New Spanish spectators with an unprecedented scene of the triumph of Black power. This illustration, meant to impress a racializing fear in the hearts of readers, at the same time offered them a tangible image of the subversive power of freedom that was unraveling slavery and the colonial order on an island located just a few leagues away.

López de Cancelada's edition of *Vida de J. J. Dessalines* registered the encounter with an expanding globality that, among other things, begged for new ways of navigating the relation between the distant and the proximate. Faced with this new scenario, the editor seemed aware that events happening far away might not be as distant as he'd hoped. Read through the lens of this encounter, the book becomes not merely a tool used for the production of a racializing fear that aimed to contain

FIGURE 3.3. *Manuel López López*, Coronación de Juan Santiago Dessalines—Primer Emperador de Hayti. *Courtesy of the John Carter Brown Library.*

Haiti's power and affirm New Spain's colonial order, but also a record of the emerging crisis accompanied by a new encounter with the "totality of history."[67] The book's pages are filled with the glimmers of a new global moment, one that would be marked by rising racialized multitudes across the hemisphere and a correlated counterinsurgent concern with expansive "race wars." Indeed, the book anticipated and responded to the growing and immanent presence of the "political monster."

{ FOUR }

Staging Fear and Freedom
HAITI'S SHIFTING PROXIMITIES
AT THE TIME OF MEXICAN INDEPENDENCE

In September 1810, a sweeping popular rebellion once again took over the Bajío region.[1] Just a few days later, the renowned bishop Manuel Abad y Queipo published a response to this rebellion, likening the events in Dolores, Guanajuato, and environs to the historic slave uprising in Haiti (1791–1804). It is telling that the bishop chose as his analogy neither the revolution in the United States (1776) nor that in France (1789). Instead, he compared the Bajío's rebellion to the "horrendous anarchy" that in 1791 struck Saint-Domingue:[2]

> But we can find the most analogous example of our situation in the French part of the island of Santo Domingo, the owners of which were the richest, happiest, and most comfortable men to be found on this earth. The population was composed *almost* like ours, consisting of European French, criollo French, Indians native to the country, blacks, mulattos, and other castes resulting from such classes. . . . But the anarchy in Saint-Domingue cut the throats of all white French and criollos, not sparing a single one; and it killed four-fifths of all other inhabitants, leaving the final remaining fifth of blacks and mulattos in eternal hatred and moral war, in which they must eternally destroy themselves. It devastated the entire country, burning and destroying all possessions, all cities, villas, and pleasant sites once boasted by the best-populated and -cultivated country in all the Americas; it is now a desert harboring tigers and lions. Such is the horrendous but faithful portrait of how anarchy has ravaged Saint-Domingue.[3]

As discussed in chapter 3, a few years earlier in 1806, peninsular elites such as Juan López de Cancelada had described New Spain's society as being far removed from and impermeable to Haiti and its revolution. Yet by 1810, Abad y Queipo was expressing deep concern over the collapse of that distance. For him, the boundaries, both imagined and material, that had once separated Haiti from New Spain were now dangerously crumbling.

New Spanish responses to Haiti, even those emerging from those occupying posts in colonial state institutions, were not monolithic. In fact, they were traversed by cracks and contradictions stemming from the fragmented information that circulated on and shaped narratives about revolution in the Caribbean island.[4] Nevertheless, between 1806 and 1810, a significant change in colonial authorities' engagement with Haiti and its relevance for the New Spanish context is noticeable. In the early 1800s, López de Cancelada wrote about the distance that separated former Saint-Domingue and New Spain as a gulf, a gap between two foreign milieus that was nearly unbridgeable. By 1810, this distance had seemingly vanished, allowing Abad y Queipo to suggest that the problems plaguing New Spain were the same problems that had once plagued Saint-Domingue. While López de Cancelada's 1806 take on Haiti's revolution showcased ideas about white unity and supposed racial harmony in the colony, Abad y Queipo's intervention illustrates instead that at the dawn of struggles that would lead to independence, Haiti's case was increasingly used to frame and interpret internal fractures within Mexico's racialized colonial society.

There has been extensive study of contemporary responses to Haiti's revolution, particularly in areas that were geographically close to the island and where fears of copycat revolutions appeared to be more immediate. Many have pointed out that the international impact of Haiti's revolution must be considered in its full complexity, accounting for both rebels' demands for radical emancipation and for the contradictory reactive narratives that marked the revolution's reception abroad.[5] Haiti offered a powerful example of radical abolitionism that resonated across the world, and the world responded with an array of discursive and material efforts to both support and curtail the dissemination of the Haitian message.[6] Rarely, however, has Mexico been considered a part of this scenario.[7] Perhaps Haiti's struggle had a slighter impact on New Spain than on other colonial regions that were geographically closer or whose racialized socioeconomic structures more closely resembled Haiti's, such as Cuba, Santo Domingo, or even Venezuela. But, as I will argue in the pages that follow, the events in Haiti were still a significant filter through which peninsular and criollo elites and authorities reconceptualized race in early nineteenth-century Mexico. In this chapter I explore what may lay behind the shifting perception of Haiti's proximity to New Spain. I argue that political crises in the Spanish Empire underpinned a reframing of domestic affairs in the viceroyalty that registered the intensification of colonial authorities' fear that events like the Haitian Revolution—which they understood to be the clearest example of contemporary race war—could, in fact, also happen there.

While news about Haiti's revolution was available in New Spain through both the press and popular oral transmission, local newspapers covered the events unevenly, with marked periods of almost complete silence.[8] For this reason, to trace Haiti's shifting discursive proximity to Mexico, I look at a decentralized corpus that includes a range of variegated sources from colonial newspapers, to inquisitorial censorship documents on plays staged in Mexico City's coliseum addressing the topic of slavery, to texts written in response to and as part of the 1810 Bajío uprisings. I also make use of different analytic methodologies, from speculative thinking to reading against the grain, in order to interpret these sources and piece together the story they might tell us about the shifting reception of Haiti's revolution in New Spain. I call this a decentralized corpus because the traces left by Haiti appear, as Sibylle Fischer has aptly argued, only in fragments in the archives.[9] While some of the sources studied here address the Haitian Revolution explicitly, others that help me trace and speculatively interpret authorities' shifting engagement with the events that unraveled in the Caribbean island as the 1810 Bajío rebellions broke out must be read between the lines and against the grain.

In the documents examined throughout the chapter, the portrayal of Haiti's distance from New Spain is contradictory and fragmentary. While, as shown in the previous chapter, the revolution was in 1806 portrayed as a "monstrous" yet distant event, things had changed by 1810, when Abad y Queipo responded to the Bajío revolt. In four short years, Haiti went from being portrayed as remote and unrepeatable to being invoked as the internalized mirror that reflected the "monstrosity" and dangerous impurity of New Spain's racialized social body. In this mirror, colonial figures such as Abad y Queipo saw the now-uncontainable image of a rebellious, racialized "plebe" that was determined to take over. In the following pages I attempt to grapple with how this shift took place.

SAINT-DOMINGUE AND NEW SPAIN: TWO DIFFERENT COLONIES

Before the eruption of the Haitian Revolution, the two colonies, Saint-Domingue and New Spain, were quite different. The French-held Saint-Domingue was the model of the sugar plantation slave system, and it had nearly cornered the market in sugar production. New Spain, the Spanish Empire's most profitable colony, depended instead on silver mining.[10] Although both colonies were economically central to their respective imperial grids, the social and racial conditions of the two colonies' workforces were also quite distinct. Haiti's sugar plantations were worked almost entirely by Black slaves; New Spain's silver was mined by a diverse workforce that mostly comprised free mulattos and "indios vagos." Although these workers were subjected to precarious labor conditions, they were not enslaved.[11] Indeed, slavery, which was only increasing in Saint-Domingue, had been declining in New Spain since the late seventeenth century. Although it still existed in urban areas in the form of domestic servitude and in regions with sugar plantations and textile manufacturing, slavery was not the dominant mode of production in New Spain by the early nineteenth century.[12]

Saint-Domingue's and New Spain's populations also had very different racial makeups, a note worth making given that emerging narratives about how Haiti could be repeated in other colonies relied heavily on census data about the racial makeup of colonial populations.[13] In 1789, the population of the French-controlled western half of Hispaniola was 88 percent Black slaves (more than 465,000 of them); only 5.9 percent of the population was white (31,000 people), and 5.3 percent (28,000) were "freedmen."[14] New Spain's racial makeup was quite different. According to censuses taken around the time of the 1810 Bajío uprising, only 10 percent of the New Spanish population was of African descent, and of this 10 percent, only a minuscule percentage remained enslaved.[15] As Alexander von Humboldt puts it in his well-known *Political Essay on the Kingdom of New Spain*, "The kingdom of New Spain is, of all the European colonies under the torrid zone, that in which there are the fewest Negroes. We may almost say that there are no slaves."[16]

Humboldt's commentary on the reduced size of New Spain's slave population is relevant because it exemplifies a growing trend to associate this factor with a lesser risk of race war. Although at different moments of *Political Essay* Humboldt discusses the dangers that European families faced while living in the racialized societies of American colonies, he implies that there was an important difference in how this threat gained expression in societies where slaves constituted the racialized majority. As he compares New Spain to the United States, Humboldt insists on the one advantage the former held over the latter: "The kingdom of New Spain has one decided advantage over the United States. The number of slaves there, either Africans or of mixed race, is almost nothing; an advantage which the European colonists have only begun rightly to appreciate since the tragical events of the revolution of St. Domingo."[17] While Humboldt insists that New Spain was the most unequal society in all the Americas (and he associates this inequality with racialization), he still suggests that European colonists living there had a better chance of reducing the gap between themselves and the largely impoverished nonwhite populations of the colony than those living in the United States did. In places like New Spain, where such racialized groups were mostly filled by Indian and unenslaved people, Humboldt hints, the eruption of a revolution like Haiti's appeared to be less likely.

In fact, in writing about the 1780 Tupac Amaru rebellion, Humboldt warns "European families" invested in protecting their interests and tranquility "that they should interest themselves in the Indians, and rescue them from their present barbarous, abject, and miserable condition."[18] Conversely, when writing about the United States, he emphasizes the tardiness with which the young nation had moved to obstruct the slave trade and the entry of slaves into the country. His remark about the belated response of the latter is tainted by a sense of irreversibility that is absent in his injunctions about the Peruvian context. Although never explicitly, Humboldt's essay not only touches on what he perceived to be the exceptional marginalization of Black slaves across imperial lines but also suggests that this marginalization was an important difference that separated colonial sites such as Mexico from the United States and also from former Saint-Domingue and, therefore, from the likelihood of a race war erupting there.[19]

Under the light of narratives that affirmed the distance between differently racialized colonies such as New Spain and Saint-Domingue, the analogy that Abad y Queipo established between them at the dawn of the 1810 Bajío rebellion is, to say the least, intriguing. Indeed, one wonders what allowed the Michoacán bishop to ignore the differences that separated the two colonies (New Spain and Saint-Domingue) when asserting that they had "almost" the same racialized social composition.

In *En el espejo haitiano*, Luis Fernando Granados argues that the Haitian Revolution is similar to the Bajío rebellion in that both were popular irruptions sparked by the most marginalized workers of each empire: *indios vagos* in New Spain and Black slaves in Saint-Domingue. In both cases, groups on the margins of these colonial societies rose up to crush the racialized colonial structures that oppressed them, in Saint-Domingue destroying the plantations and abolishing slavery, and in the Bajío dismantling the tributary system.[20] This similarity did not escape New Spanish colonial authorities or clergymen such as Abad y Queipo. But the conditions allowing the perception of the similarity between the two colonies had not always been present; they were a product of contingent events that shook the Spanish Empire and eroded ideas about the alleged racial harmony in New Spain.

In the wake of the age of Atlantic revolutions, the repeated outbursts in the Bajío pointed to the irruption of racialized populations onto New Spain's political stage. Shifting ideas about Haiti's proximity to the colony mediated this transition, both explicitly and implicitly. In other words, unstable and crystallizing figurations about Haiti's revolution provided a backdrop against which New Spain's colonial authorities negotiated and revised ideas about the heterogeneous society under their command. Following the circuits of political instability, it becomes clear that it was in the aftermath of the imperial and local turmoil initiated after Napoleon's Spanish invasion of 1808 that colonial authorities began to see New Spain's racialized groups as explicitly analogous to Saint-Domingue's. In the context of these crises, Haiti's "Blackness" and New Spain's "Indianness" no longer seemed incommensurate with one another but parallel, overlapping, even identical.

SHIFTING GROUNDS: A SCENE OF ABOLITION

Colonial authorities' shifting perception of Haiti's distance/proximity to New Spain did not occur overnight. While Abad y Queipo's counterinsurgent speeches established an explicit analogy between the "anarchy" of Saint-Domingue and the rebellions in New Spain, a more stealthy ungrounding underlay the conditions of possibility for the bishop's enunciations. I here suggest that one way of tracing this less explicit ungrounding is to look at changing ideas at the level of colonial governmentality regarding the circulation of political ideas among the New Spanish public, more concretely the dissemination of critiques of slavery. I specifically turn to theater as a privileged medium from which to explore the fictions of power at the heart of late colonial governmentality as it attempted to manage and shape New Spain's racialized public sphere.

Theater was an important medium through which empires forged and managed colonial relations.[21] It was also a medium through which local social relations were negotiated.[22] As both a representational and embodied practice, theater articulated a transatlantic circuit of symbolic exchanges between the metropolis and its colonies. It also opened spaces for local public gatherings that organized bodies according to colonial social hierarchies of class and race. "Any particular staging of the colonial relation," Elizabeth Maddock Dillon writes, "is also a staging of relations among the members of the audience gathered to respond to the play they are watching."[23] Under the light of these assumptions, theatrical censorship practices offer valuable insight into how colonial authorities had changing perceptions about local social and racial dynamics. After 1808, growing concerns in New Spain's censoring apparatus about the dangers of exposing the colony's inhabitants to certain political content go beyond the capricious practices of cultural censorship. They index a deeper shift at the level of the epoch's political horizons.

Two late eighteenth-century plays, *El negro y la blanca* and *El negro sensible*, were staged in the early 1800s in Mexico City's coliseum. Although initially censors agreed to include both plays in the coliseum's billboard, a few years after their first staging, both plays were banned by the Inquisition for their allegedly revolutionary nature. While censorship practices of the time were inconsistent and often volatile and arbitrary, colonial authorities' wavering decisions on these two plays' censorship still allow us to explore the shaky ground of race in New Spain's late colonial period. Although the plays make no explicit reference to Haiti and its revolution, inquisitorial bans seem to be haunted by the island's events, more importantly by the idea that something similar might happen in New Spain. Indeed, it is surprising that both plays' mildly critical engagement with the topic of slavery would have suddenly been perceived to be so threatening in a colony where, as was discussed previously, slavery was not a dominant institution.

In July 1797, the audience at the Madrid Príncipe theater watched a staging of *El negro y la blanca*.[24] This two-act exoticist melodrama by Vicente Rodríguez de Arellano is set in Africa, in the kingdom of Benin, and includes in its scenes a dramatic take on the abolition of slavery. The theater censors in the city reviewed the work and accepted it for staging. It proved popular with peninsular audiences, returning to the stage of the Príncipe theater in 1801 and 1802, and shortly thereafter playing at the colonial coliseums across the Atlantic.[25]

The piece was inspired by classic French Enlightenment works like Voltaire's *Zaïre*, Favart's *Soliman II*, and the anonymous novel *Histoire de Louis Anniaba: Rois D'Essenie en Afrique sur la Côte de Guinée* (1740), which has a similar plot.[26] The story circles around the romantic relationship between Clarisa, a white Christian woman, and Góndar, an aristocratic Black man. Traveling on a Dutch ship with her betrothed, Gerardo, Clarisa is taken captive when the ship in which she travels falls into the hands of African pirates. She remains hostage in Benin under Góndar's watch. Góndar had been raised in Europe by a Portuguese friend of his father's, and upon returning to Africa he had helped pacify the social unrest that unsettled the region and shortly thereafter was proclaimed king of Benin.

A brief scene in the second act touches on the potential abolition of slavery. A Portuguese ship arrives at Benin's coast, and at the shore Góndar meets Don Tello, a Portuguese merchant, who declares his intention to involve himself in the African slave trade, in which Benin had played a crucial role. Góndar refuses to satisfy the merchant's expectations (and perhaps that of some members of the audience), firmly informing the visitor that, during his reign, slavery and human trafficking are forbidden for "breaking the just and natural order."[27]

By setting the play in Benin, Rodríguez de Arellano represented slavery as ending at its starting point; he thus circled around the trade's other destinations (mostly plantations that cut across colonial spaces), leaving them intact. Imagining abolition in Africa as a starting point, rather than in the Americas as a destination, had specific political implications: while the play evoked contemporary efforts to restrict the Atlantic slave trade, it did not address the economic and social dynamics of slavery in the colonies.[28]

El negro y la blanca hit the stage during the age of Atlantic revolutions. By the 1797 premiere of Rodríguez de Arellano's work, the "Black Jacobins" of Haiti, as C. L. R. James would call them, had already pushed France to abolish slavery in all its colonies despite the initial resistance of France's Revolutionary Assembly to carry the proclamation of universal equality to its ultimate logical end.[29] This hesitation revealed the gendered and racial constraints of equality as articulated in the 1789 *Declaration of the Rights of Man and of the Citizen*. However, in the face of turmoil in the island, the assembly decreed abolition in 1793. The pressure exerted by the uprisings prompted Léger-Félicité

Sonthonax and Étienne Polvérel to decree the emancipation of northern slaves in Saint-Domingue and freedom from slavery reigned in the French portion of the island.[30]

Although news about the events in Saint-Domingue were printed in the Spanish press, it is unlikely that Rodríguez de Arellano was thinking about the island when he wrote his play.[31] At this time, a cohesive narrative around the Haitian Revolution and the singular path it took toward the abolition of slavery had not coalesced. Furthermore, scattered notes covering the conflict in the Spanish press consisted mostly of fragmented reports arriving in ships from Jamaica, London, and Paris that framed the news as part of inter-imperial rivalry and metropolitan affairs.[32] At this point the events in Haiti were not a touchstone (positive or negative) on matters of slavery and abolition, at least not in Spain. In this sense, *El negro y la blanca* was in sync with its time and place. The play touched on the controversial issue of abolition and framed it in the same terms the press regularly used to discuss it: as a concern bound by disputes around the slave trade. Several articles debating international efforts to ban this trade were published throughout the 1790s in the *Gaceta de Madrid*. From the perspective of a Madrid-based audience, particularly for those familiar with the news, Rodríguez de Arellano's play must have been received as a dramatic take on the issue.

Yet for a colonial audience such as the one that in July 1806 gathered in Mexico City's coliseum to witness the staging of *El negro y la blanca*, the play may have evoked other histories.[33] We know not only that peninsular and New Spanish audiences differed significantly, but also that nearly a decade had passed since the play's initial staging in Madrid and many things had changed on the question of slavery and abolition in the world. By 1806, the terrain of these discussions had shifted as Haiti emerged as "an independent nation in which slavery was forever abolished and citizenship was predicated on blackness."[34] Perhaps New Spanish spectators acquainted with the former Dominguan context saw the scene of abolition included in Rodríguez de Arellano's play through the filter of these recent events. Perhaps for some the scene even redirected the shockwaves radiating from the island, theatrically altering the circumstances that led Haiti down its revolutionary path toward abolition. In contrast to what happened on the island, *El negro y la blanca* played out the abolition of the slave trade via a royal decree that circumvented the path of revolutionary violence. The play thus embodied contemporary contractualist tendencies that, as Moira Fradinger suggests, shifted modernity's relation to violence.[35]

The racial and political dynamics in *El negro y la blanca* must be discussed according to the differing contexts (and historical moments) in which the play was staged.[36] Of course, we cannot know definitively what audiences of the day thought of the play, but we can speculate that the piece was received differently in the different locations (and moments) where it was performed. Being open to the changing reception of the play carves a path for considering how the meaning and content of Góndar's Blackness might have shifted as the play traveled across the theaters of Spain's imperial geography.

Frieda Koeninger suggests that in light of Spain's historical legacies, Madrid spectators are likely to have focused on *El negro y la blanca*'s story line of Catholicism triumphing over pagan religions. One can therefore imagine that the union between Góndar and Clarisa, as performed on the stage of the Príncipe theater, would have evoked Spain's racial frameworks in which Blackness was often construed in religious terms. Consider, for instance, a scene that precedes the one about abolition in which Góndar prevents his people from carrying out a pagan ritual sacrifice to celebrate the five-year anniversary of his coronation. As he interrupts the "barbaric" festivities, the king declares the universality of Catholicism, aligning himself with dominant ideas about religion and "civility" in Spain. It is only through this gesture that he can later proceed to abolish slavery and human trafficking of all types and present himself—and, by extension, his African subjects—as a full participant of an Enlightenment morality that worked well with Spain's religious bent.

Góndar's ban on paganism and his declaration of the universality of the Catholic faith are thus whitening mechanisms through which Góndar is ultimately assimilated into Spain's hegemonic social structures. Clarisa herself, in an instance of evident wordplay, announces Góndar's racial transition to the viewers: "Come into my arms, virtuous negro, for of all my loving cravings you shall now be the *target/blanco*."[37] The play's conclusion with the couple's happy marriage was easily adapted to the metropole's racialized political and religious horizons.

But it is possible that Góndar and Clarisa's love story evoked other racial histories in the minds of spectators gathered in the Mexico City coliseum. Rather than appearing as a story of religious whitening, Góndar's union with Clarisa might have conjured complicated emotions around interracial relations in the colony. Unlike the etching by Manuel López López discussed in the previous chapter, which depicted the union of a Black man with a white woman as the product of rape, the relationship between Góndar and Clarisa is the product of two individuals. The play could thus have easily opened another channel for peninsular and criollo Spaniards' racial fantasies and anxieties about Blackness and sexuality. In it, the Black man appears threatening not because of his violence but because of his moral superiority and the fact that a white woman chooses him over a white man. In both fantasies, however, the reproduction of Spaniards' status and the connection this had to continuing the colonial order were at stake.

It might seem extreme to presume that the marriage between a Black man and a white woman was enough for colonial authorities to consider the play's staging dangerous. Nevertheless, in 1809, three years after its premiere in Mexico City's coliseum, an inquisitorial edict prohibited further stagings of *El negro y la blanca* as well as the circulation of its printed scripts. The play was censored on the grounds that it was "revolutionary, and for plotting in its depths great ruin in civil, political, and moral terms."[38]

Another onstage exploration of slavery was offered to peninsular audiences in a piece by the popular Spanish playwright Luciano Francisco Comella. The play combines moral criticism of slavery as an institution with scenes that expressed elites' distress over the potential violence of Black slaves in the colonies. Performed for the first time in Madrid in 1798, it was highly popular with European audiences. As Rodríguez de Arellano's play had done, Comella's *El negro sensible* traveled across the Atlantic to be staged in colonial theaters in the early nineteenth century.[39] Unlike *El negro y la blanca*, which takes place in Africa, however, Comella's piece is set in a sugar mill located, according to stage directions, "somewhere in the Americas."[40]

The play begins by considering how slavery sowed the seeds of resentment in the enslaved, opening the door to new forms of violence against their masters. Its central character is Catul, a slave at the sugar mill whose wife has been unexpectedly sold to another master, making him solely responsible for their infant son. Through the soliloquy that opens the play, Catul explains his situation, presenting to the audience a dramatic interrogation of slavery's (il)legitimacy and the unequal distribution of humanity across imperial geographies. On stage, Catul lays out the unsustainable conditions of his life: not only has he lost his wife, but Jacobo, the foreman and overseer in charge of the mill, threatens and bullies him into abandoning his son during the day so that he can fulfill his quota of daily work, preventing him from adequately caring for his child. Catul, who would have been played by a white man in blackface, thinks aloud to the audience about the options and implications of seeking revenge—that is, of perpetrating on his masters the same violence he has been subject to.[41]

At the beginning, the play is structured as an Aristotelian tragedy, establishing a growing tension between two parallel and divided stories: that of Catul and his desire for vengeance, and that of Doña Martina, a European white woman who appears onstage after the protagonist's initial monologue. Not until the end of the play does the audience discover that Martina, who embodies the melodrama's moral critique of the slave system, was traveling from the metropole to the colonial sugar mill to buy slaves (including Bunga, Catul's wife) in order to free them. In the play, Martina returns to the sugar mill to search for the rest of Bunga's family and comes across Bunga and Catul's baby, who is hungry and alone. Unaware that he is the son of the woman she had already freed, Martina takes the child into her arms to comfort and "save him," offering him the sacrament of baptism and promising to take him back with her to Europe.

The turn of events, or the reversal of the dramatic action, occurs when the two stories intersect. When Catul returns home and finds that his son is missing, he immediately thinks that Jacobo has sold the child. He decides to stop holding back his hurt and anger. Theatergoers would have seen his character pacing the stage, searching for someone on whom he could unleash his fury. Catul discovers Martina sleeping under a tree with a child in her arms. He approaches her, showing the audience his intention to murder the child in order to punish her, forcing her to feel the same anguish that he himself felt at the loss of his son. The tension of the audience, who knew that the little boy in Martina's arms was Catul's son, would have dissipated only when, terrified by Catul's threats, Martina unswaddled the baby to reveal his Black face, proving to Catul that the child was his.

At this point, Comella's play departs from its tragic structure and becomes a melodrama. Catul relents when he sees the child's face and learns that Martina has bought his wife to free her—and that she now plans to do the same with him and his son. The menace of his violence is transformed into gratitude so profound that he recognizes that he has erred in having judged (white) Europeans to be capable only of cruelty, and as a result of this change of heart, he begs Martina to let him and his family serve her for the rest of their lives. Martina refuses to accept Catul and his family as slaves, insisting that the institution of slavery does not exist in Europe, and agrees instead to take them with her as servants. The final scene marks the start of their return journey to the metropolis with a collective celebration proclaiming the triumph of Catholic virtues and the "end of the affliction" of the "sensitive negro."

Catul's last words onstage seal the performance as he reinstates the colonial relation he had initially questioned: "I was averse to the European; I gazed with horror at his holy cult, because I did not know its greatness, its generosity, its noble features; but now that you have made me fully aware of my fatal deceit, I venerate the European, I bless him, and I seek to follow his sacred rites."[42] *El negro sensible* reconstructed and reaffirmed the colonial relation: it framed slavery as an institution restricted to the colonies, distancing the so-called corruption of colonial societies from the supposedly pristine morality of the metropolis.

The work is also based on the racialization of Black male subjectivity according to the widely common trope of the "submissive" or "good slave."[43] While Comella's work opens with an interrogation of the (il)legitimacy of slavery, its conclusion forecloses any potentially subversive response to slavery, giving form to a fantasy about the perennial submission of Black subjectivity. Even after slavery, Catul and his family's freedom is staged as a new servitude conceived here as a voluntary act of submission. Comella's work plays out the reconfiguration (but not the end) of the material and symbolic racialization of Black subjectivity, which would continue to exist within the framework of "universal equality" after slavery was abolished. The play thus imagines the legacies of slavery after abolition in terms of the emerging configuration of what Saidiya Hartman has called (with respect to the US context) a "burdened individuality of freedom."[44] The play performs the liberal disjunction between morality and politics; in its plot, the "effective" struggle against the abuses of slavery depend on an individualized ethical position, in this case a gendered one that is embodied by the female European character of Martina.

Given this potential reading of the play's dynamics, a similar question emerges about why colonial authorities perceived it to be threatening after approving it for an initial staging. In 1805, before López de Cancelada's edition of the biography of Dessalines was even circulating, the censors affiliated with Mexico City's coliseum accepted *El negro sensible* for staging. Yet once again in 1809, just four years later, the conditions for the production of this work (and others with similar subject matter, such as *El negro y la blanca*) seemed to have changed. The Inquisition banned *El negro sensible* for "cunningly promoting the insurrection of slaves against their legitimate owners."[45]

VALENCES OF THE ONTIC: A FIRST TAKE ON CENSORSHIP

The question of how to interpret the shift in these two plays' horizons of legibility is a vexing one. There is not enough documentation to fully ascertain whether these changes are merely a reflection of volatile censorship practices or, as I suggest, there was a deeper political ungrounding underlying the Inquisition's decision to interrupt the staging of both *El negro y la blanca* and *El negro sensible* in the same year. In any case, engaging with the questions does open up several possible speculative interpretations that are worth exploring.

A first reading centers on tracking changes in how colonial proximity (or distance) from the metropolis was viewed. In this reading, edicts banning the staging of the plays might indicate a change of focus in the censoring apparatus: a shift from an emphasis on the mimetic dimension of representation—for example, regulating the content and support structure of dramatic fiction—to an emphasis on the ontic or embodied dimension: the consequences that might ripple out from concrete interactions between the audience and the plays in the stages of colonial coliseums.[46] This interpretation is supported if we consider that, since the late eighteenth century, regulations to reframe and control the interactions between the audience and the stage had been implemented in New Spain.

The first document compiling regulations for the Mexico City coliseum was published at the request of viceroy Bernardo de Gálvez (José de Gálvez's nephew) in 1786. The *Reglamento u Ordenanzas de Teatros* was in effect until 1830.[47] Widely disseminated in pamphlets that were distributed among the public and pasted on the walls of the theater, the *Reglamento* included several clauses designed to manage and curtail interactions between the audience and the actors, but also among spectators themselves. It also established specific sanctions ranging from fees to time in jail for infractions. One of the clauses, for instance, determined that *mosqueteros* (those standing in what today we would call "general admission") could chant to demand a song be repeated only once per performance.[48] Another clause banned spectators from expressing their appreciation or dislike for the play by throwing objects onto the stage.[49] Yet another demanded that spectators remain silent during the performance.[50] At the time, theater nights were about social engagement and discussion with others.[51] Regulations from 1786 onward gave theater overseers the power to rein in the effervescent interactions that regularly took place inside the theater, sanctioning spectators for overstepping the newly imposed boundaries. The increased policing that took over the theater in the late colonial period already points toward the concern that colonial authorities expressed about what could happen inside the venue.

The 1809 edicts that banned the plays could therefore be read alongside increasing regulations and anxieties about the embodied responses elicited by staged performances among spectators in the coliseum. Implied in this shift was also a growing awareness about the differential effect of the plays *as they were staged* across different locations. In other words, the act of censorship itself could be read as indexing the fears about how racialized colonial audiences might respond to and interact with the plays. Theatrical authorities who had at first been oblivious to these questions seem to have suddenly begun to consider how the plays, which had previously circulated indiscriminately from one side of the Atlantic to the other, might open up different horizons of legibility for different local audiences. The placards of early nineteenth-century theaters in Madrid show that plays that were banned in New Spain, including *El negro sensible*, continued to be performed on stages of the metropolis uncensored.[52]

In 1797, spectators in peninsular theaters might have understood Góndar's Blackness through the lens of historical tensions between Catholicism and Islam, but by 1809 in colonial spaces, authorities expressed their concern about the political, civil, and moral ruin plotted by a play whose main story line circled around the relation between a Black man and a white woman. These anxieties seemed to be latent in or unimportant to the censors prior to 1806, but just three years later, as political instability knocked on the doors of the Spanish Empire, they loomed so large that the play was seen as so "revolutionary" as to be unstageable.

Similarly, while it is likely that *El negro sensible* appeared to European audiences as a play that affirmed and protected the distance and structure of the relation between the metropolis and the colonies, in the New Spanish context the play seemed to suddenly awaken censors' anxieties about the possibility of it promoting racial violence. If a race war in fact happened there, the region's status as colony could be jeopardized. Coliseums, at least the one in Mexico City, were points of convergence for people of all social strata and caste ascription.[53] The censorship edicts reflect concerns about how a racialized audience would receive the play, indicating that the alleged racial harmony of New Spain—as once predicated by López de Cancelada in the face of Haiti—was no longer a sturdy framework on which colonial authorities could (even wishfully) rely on. Not only was the plays' dissemination of certain ideas and affective dynamics seen as potentially undermining the colony's order, but they also seemed to invite questions about the internal harmony between "castas" in New Spain itself. In the midst of political turmoil in the empire, theatrical and religious censors seem to have suddenly grasped upon this reality and begun to consider the potential danger of exposing racialized audiences to plays that touched on certain difficult topics, such as slavery.

VALENCES OF PERIPETEIA:
A SECOND TAKE ON CENSORSHIP

The second possible reading of the 1809 censorship of these plays is that it registered the destabilizing of the colony's racialized political, affective, and aesthetic boundaries by the irruption of history. As I have discussed, in 1806, López de Cancelada published a text explicitly addressing the Haitian Revolution, reproducing as an appendix both Dessalines's full speech to his followers on his proclamation as emperor and a translation of the 1805 Haitian constitution, which called for universal abolition of slavery. The publication of this text in 1806 indicates colonial authorities' certainty that New Spain was comfortably distant and different from Haiti. In 1806, New Spain was not threatened by any sense of proximity—geographical, affective, or racial—to Haiti. But by 1809, theatrical stagings of racial tension were now seen as potentially opening the door to racial violence.[54]

In 1808, Napoleon invaded Spain. As scholars have suggested, the vacuum in sovereignty caused by the invasion unleashed a chain reaction of deep political instability that spread like fire across the Spanish Empire. The crisis of 1808 was the spark that brought the ripening conditions for a massive uprising to its final combustion. In a matter of years, independence was proclaimed in different sites of Spanish America.[55] The events of 1808 that shook the political structures of the empire also indexed the impossibility of safeguarding the racialized distance that had once seemed to separate New Spain from Saint-Domingue.

More importantly, they altered the racialization of New Spain's popular sectors; after 1808, Haiti's *Blackness* began to seem analogous to New Spain's *Indianness*. The censorship edicts thus expose internal changes in colonial authorities' perceptions, even if these were not monolithic or homogenous. New Spanish censors had once been confident that spectators' interpretations of both *El negro y la blanca* and *El negro sensible* would remain within the limits of the colonial order. Even if for some this reception diverged slightly, the political conditions in the colony were stable. But by 1809, they seemed to no longer be so sure about this. It was as though recent historical events brought the plays' potentially plural reception and "hidden transcripts" to the fore.[56]

In the case of *El negro sensible*, the interpretation of the play's conclusion hinged on the transformation of Catul's rage into gratitude. After 1809, the other side of the peripeteia—Catul's unknowing threat to kill his own son to take revenge on the whites—haunted the play, exposing the complex workings of this dialectic. According to Fredric Jameson, the basic dynamic of the peripatetic is a dialectic of successes and failures in which both poles are attuned and "profoundly identified with one another."[57] According to Jameson, the moment of "recognition" or "reversal" is actually one of profound ambivalence, the resolution of which may unfold in either direction. Resolution cannot be understood as simple, but through a complex premise in which every success is at the same time a failure and every failure is simultaneously a success.[58]

The 1809 ban of *El negro sensible* might suggest that the story line that played out onstage did not fully erase the haunting presence of the other story line, the path not taken. It is as if the two potential outcomes of the play's peripeteia, its oscillation between tragedy and melodrama, remained equally open despite what the audience witnessed on stage. It's as if in 1809 censors were in tune with the basic ambivalence of the dialectic turning point that framed the irruption of history as *undecidable*. At this moment of intense political uncertainty, any resolution or path seemed possible: the stability of racial boundaries that had organized life in New Spain seems to have, in the views of colonial authorities involved in theatrical censorship, entered into a kind of ungrounding. In 1805, the ending of *El negro sensible* declared the containment of racial violence while at the same refusing the audience the pathos of Catul's suffering and fury. Colonial censors perhaps even thought that the play would guide the public toward a happy ending in which the empire's hierarchical and racial order remained intact, even affirmed. By 1809, the inquisitorial ban's characterization of the play as inciting the rebellion of slaves against their masters suggests that for censors the play's ending seemed not only ineffective but also unsustainable. It showed itself to be out of sync (or too in sync?) with present conditions, and its shadow potential of race war as allegorized by Catul's announced revenge, which went unexecuted onstage, became more visible as a possibility. This shifting horizon indexed colonial authorities' growing perception that New Spain's society was perhaps too much like the one that ignited the revolutionary spark in former Saint-Domingue.

CONCLUSION

After 1809, when the plays were banned, the empire's crisis of sovereignty continued to deepen, seeping into New Spain's colonial structure and further weakening it. In September 1810, popular revolts lit up the Bajío region. Faced with the spreading wave of uprisings, other departments of colonial governmentality appear to have also felt the threat of race war on the heels of the colony. That same year, Felipe Zúñiga y Ontiveros's press reprinted a 1789 royal decree promoted by Charles IV on the topic of master-slave relations in Spanish American colonies.[59] The decree was initially formulated as part of the king's efforts to expand slavery in the empire: with more slaves arriving into the colonies, the state found it crucial to establish clear regulations that outlined the rights and duties of both slaves and masters.[60]

The decree reiterated certain already established provisions on slavemaster relations such as the prohibition of work on Sundays, the importance of promoting marriage among enslaved populations, the masters' obligations to provide food and clothing for the enslaved, and cumulative fines for masters who failed to follow these regulations.[61] While it determined that slaves had an obligation to obey and respect the master as a father, the decree also introduced new regulations that limited the punishment that could be applied to them. It strictly forbade placing slaves upside down when receiving punishment and warned against whippings that caused bleeding or exceeded twenty-five lashes. Finally, the decree also gave local syndics and clergymen the power to report abuses perpetrated by masters and overseers, and protected the anonymity of the denouncers.[62] Printed and distributed widely, the decree elicited a controversial response among slaveholders. They were concerned that the regulations would be misinterpreted by the slaves, causing turmoil in their plantations. In Santo Domingo, Louisiana, Caracas, and Havana, planters objected to the new instruction and demanded its repeal.[63] Indeed, enslaved people throughout the American colonies found ways to use the decree to their advantage and took their masters to court for abuses based on its stipulations.[64] Prompted by the controversy, the Crown rescinded the decree in 1794, weakly requesting that slaveholders uphold its spirit.[65]

New Spanish editors' decision to reprint the 1789 decree in 1810 deserves some attention.[66] While the practice of reprinting old codes and decrees was common, doing so was usually a response to local events. In this light, one could suggest that growing tensions in the colony pushed elites to recall the Crown's recent efforts to soften the punitive practices of slavery. With the colony on the verge of widespread rebellion, perhaps the decree would remind enslaved people about the peaceful avenues available to voice their grievances. Perhaps too, it would remind slaveholders about the utmost importance of attenuating social tensions by not abusing their power. This reading of the decree runs against planters' initial responses to it in slaving colonies such as Caracas or Cuba, where they rejected it on the basis that it might incite turmoil. However, given the closeness of the Zúñiga y Ontiveros press to the colonial state, seeing the decision to reprint the decree as an effort to assuage racial tensions in the colony makes sense, particularly in the midst of the crisis. What would seem more surprising is the editors' overestimation of the role of plantation slavery in New Spain, as if New Spain were indeed a mostly slaving colony and as if recalling the decree could forestall the waves of upheaval. Nevertheless, the reprinted decree points, once again, to authorities' and elites' growing concern about race war in the colony.

Similarly, Manuel Abad y Queipo would continue to give voice to counterinsurgent ideas, expanding in subsequent speeches and publications the analogy between New Spain and Saint-Domingue that he had made in his first speech. In his "Instructive Edict," addressed to his diocesans on September 30, 1810, the bishop of Michoacán once again equated the conditions leading to the Haitian uprising with contemporary circumstances in the Bajío, based in the alleged sudden translatability between the two colonial spaces. In apocalyptic terms, he claimed that, like in Haiti, the devastating destruction of the colonial economy would be inevitable if the Hidalgo-led insurrection were to continue. In his first speech, he had stated that Mexico and Haiti had "almost" the same racialized composition; in this second intervention Abad y Queipo closed the gap even further, attributing the "same cause" to both insurrections:

> And here the explosion of the mine is slowly approaching. Such shall be the onset of your ruin and the devastation of the entire Kingdom. All that follows shall be horrifying and tremendous: all divine and human laws shall cease, and only the fury of ire and vengeance shall reign, destroying all things by fire and by iron, and soon our cities, villas, and places, our flowering agriculture, deserted and uncultivated, shall become woods and brambles, as befell the French part of the island of Saint Domingue as a result of *the same cause*. No one can foresee the extent of the atrocities and misfortunes of this anarchy.[67]

The censorship of the two plays symptomatically anticipated what Abad y Queipo's response to the 1810 popular insurrections made explicit: that in the aftermath of the 1808 political crisis, the fractures within New Spain's racialized social body would be increasingly read through the filter of Haiti. The full-fledged analogy between both sites would hold for years to come. Indeed, once independence became the clear horizon of the political crisis, both peninsular and criollo leaders, royalists and insurgents, continued to ambivalently invoke the "tragic history" of Saint-Domingue, the former French portion of the Caribbean island, to gain fodder in favor of their own political projects.

{ CODA TWO }

Haiti in Mexico's Early Republican Context

Far away from Mexico City, in Cádiz, Juan López de Cancelada published his second work on the Haitian Revolution. Titled *Código formado por los negros de la isla de Santo Domingo*, this 1810 book displayed a different approximation to the Caribbean island's uprising than what had been captured by its author in his 1806 piece, *La vida de J. J. Dessalines*. The new book was mostly dedicated to analyzing Haiti's 1807 constitution, which recognized Henri Christophe as president and *generalísimo* of the northern nation. Caught in the midst of the war between France and Spain, López de Cancelada turned his gaze to the Americas and saw Christophe's political project as a successful blueprint for preserving a form of centralized power after the turmoil unleashed by revolution. According to the author, Spain could use this model to imagine its own future in the aftermath of the political crisis caused by Napoleon's expansionist projects and the abdication of Ferdinand VII.

Although *Código formado por los negros* showcased the Haitian Revolution as a source of possibility from which new political horizons could be explored, López de Cancelada's vision of Haiti as a potential political model for Spain was still undercut by his anti-Black racism. At the moment when the courts in Cádiz were coming into being, he insisted that if Haitians, whom he refers to as "black imbeciles," had been able to form a constitution for themselves, then Spaniards should be able do the same, and better: "A group of black imbeciles, with no principles other than those inspired by the humiliating education of slavery. These negroes, I say, have triumphed over death itself and granted themselves some laws (whose translation I present here) full of energy and simplification, which certain nations that declare themselves to be cultured may find they lack. And why cannot we not only imitate them but also improve on them?"[1] It is tempting to speculate about how the lapse of time and geographic relocation allowed López de Cancelada to shift his position and view Haiti's revolution through a different lens. After picturing the island's events as the source of a negative affective racial pedagogy in New Spain, he now viewed it as a potential model that Spain could emulate and even improve on. It is certainly plausible to consider that this shift was tied to colonial difference: as discussed in chapters 3 and 4, imagining the translatability of the Haitian Revolution for an American audience versus a peninsular one was not seen as a parallel endeavor, nor was this task thought to entail equally potentially risky outcomes. Yet even if López de Cancelada's relocation opened a new possibility for framing Haiti's revolution, his second take continued to depict Dessalines as a figure of unassimilable "monstrosity."

López de Cancelada was not an exception in his changing take on the Haitian Revolution. Other political thinkers also showcased more complex and shifting engagements with the events of the Caribbean island as they unfurled. As Sibylle Fischer has examined, Simón Bolívar offers one of the most interesting examples in the context of the Spanish American struggles for independence.[2] Looking at the relationship between the "Libertador" and the postrevolutionary Haiti of Alexandre Pétion, Fischer offers a counterweight to her own previous work that studied how Haiti appeared in contemporary discourses predominantly through figures of trauma and disavowal.[3] In her more recent work she suggests instead that for criollo insurgents in Spanish America, Haiti must not have simply been a paradigm of fear and failure but likely also showed important glimmers of possibility: "When compared with the war-torn Spanish American states in the first decades after independence, Haiti looks rather like a success story. One wonders whether the refugees from the insurgent Spanish colonies, traumatized by brutal colonial warfare and grateful for having found a safe haven, might not have seen it that way."[4] The question is compelling. Insofar as both Haiti's experience and images of it were not monolithic, criollo insurgents, particularly those who, like Bolívar, had spent time on the island and were familiar with its history and political context, were likely to be aware of the empirical and theoretical richness that Haiti's example presented before them, prompting them to selectively navigate through the aspects that could prove to be sites of political inspiration versus those they continued to see as examples of race war and anarchy to be avoided at all costs.[5]

The issue, as Fischer aptly illustrates, is that in the documents of the epoch these nuanced engagements with Haiti are traversed with opacities that present methodological challenges for those attempting to read them today. Including reading against the grain of expected patterns of legibility and, most important, balancing the potential openings of speculation and contextual specificities, scholars have their work cut out for them.[6] One might wonder, for instance, how the efforts of political authorities in the Haitian Republic to protect its precarious position in the Atlantic and present the young nation as avoiding interference with international and transimperial affairs might be written in between the lines of communiqués and governmental decisions to support or not insurgent political projects in Spanish America.[7] One might also wonder about the nature of changing and contradicting figures that Haiti's revolution acquires when reading closely the discourses and practices of criollo insurgents.

In this coda I explore the vacilitating images that the Haitian Revolution and the notions of Blackness that were constructed around it acquired during Mexico's transition from colony of the Spanish Empire to independent republic. I argue that when in touch with the different ways in which Haiti might have appeared in criollo insurgents' political imaginations, one can also appreciate with more complexity and precision how they mobilized the race war paradigm in connection to the Caribbean island's history. The fear of racial conflict that is expressed in contemporary pamphlets and epistolary diplomatic exchanges becomes more legible as a rhetorical tool that mediated conflicting political horizons at the time of independence, and not just as a nightmarish affective experience.

THE VACILITATING IMAGES OF RACE WAR AND HAITI

Looking at the case of Colombia, Marixa Lasso argues that early republicanism was bounded by the horizons of racial democracy on one side and race war on the other, both carved by the interventions of elites and popular groups alike. Whereas it might seem counterintuitive that these two modes of political expectation would coexist, Lasso makes a compelling case for their connection. In her view, emerging discourses of racial equality were crucial to envisioning the overcoming of colonial legacies and to forging a new type of social body and political organization. This was the case even when the meaning and materiality of what actual racial equality looked like and entailed varied greatly among social sectors.[8]

In a republic that, like Colombia, proclaimed the legal abolition of racial distinctions shortly after independence, grievances about the continuation of these distinctions were strong, and discursive practices targeting the alleged dangers of race war constituted an effective new way of policing and managing the political pressure from these grievances. Insofar as racism had supposedly been legislated into extinction, denunciations of ongoing racial discrimination were seen as critiques of the new order and its constitution and, therefore, as seditious and unpatriotic acts that incited internal conflict and debilitated the strength of the emerging political community. As such, grievances related to ongoing racist practices in the republican context were deemed to be punishable. If elites saw the horizon of racial equality as having been fully accomplished just by its legal proclamation, *pardos*' claims to the contrary were framed as outright unpatriotic attitudes that could (and should) be punished.[9]

As they did in Colombia, in early republican Mexico discourses on racial equality operated alongside elites' notions about the dangers of race war (for more see chapters 5 and 6). Interestingly, however, in the midst of political upheaval with Spain and even shortly thereafter, insurgent criollos mobilized colonial administrators' fear of race war to their political advantage. Some invoked Haiti's specter to gain greater political representation for the Americas during the discussions in the courts of Cádiz, while others, in the first years after independence, used it to ward off foreign intervention and to protect the nation's recently won political autonomy. At this point, discourses about the dangers of race war had not yet begun to demarcate the future republic's political boundaries. Instead, they were mostly invoked to mediate, reshape, and ultimately break the colonial relation between New Spain and Spain.

The work of insurgent Fray Servando Teresa de Mier offers a good starting point to trace this. In his outline of the Cádiz debates about representation for the Americas, Mier discusses how New Spanish representatives used Haiti's past in their case for a generalized legal understanding of Spanish citizenship that included those "that by some line have African ancestry".[10] "Our representatives, not all substitute deputies, advocated the orders they had from their respective provinces in New Spain, so as to procure the extinction of all distinctions with respect to color, as illusory as they are unjust and detrimental. And they otherwise threatened with the revenge injured peoples might seek, which could repeat elsewhere the tragedy of Saint-Domingue, inflicting it on whites."[11] While it is unclear whether New Spanish representatives in Cádiz were actually worried that those excluded from citizenship in the colonies would take "revenge" and riot, Mier's passage implies that they intentionally mobilized race war arguments to sway Spaniards' votes, pushing them to include free men of African ancestry in the constitutional definition of Spanish citizenship. Mier ridicules this rhetorical tactic, insisting that it would have been more effective to disprove Spaniards' misconceptions about the racial composition of the colonies than to stoke racial fears in them. Although Mier believed American territories were more populated than Spain and therefore deserved to have more representative weight in constitutional debates, he also insists that including men of African ancestry in Spanish citizenship would have a negligible impact on representation, adding only four or five representatives to the Spanish American table.[12]

Rather than focusing on local racial tensions, Mier demographically whitens the New Spanish population, arguing that there were far fewer mulatto, *pardo*, and Black inhabitants in the Americas than was commonly thought. This not only rendered unlikely the irruption of a Haiti-type "race war" in New Spain but also diminished the political importance of including Afro-descendent groups into Spanish citizenship, even if Mier supported the motion. To underscore his point, Mier also repurposes Black-legend Atlantic discourses that racialized Spain through notions about the "impure blood" of its people, arguing that Spain itself had an Afro-descendent population much larger than that of any of its colonies.[13]

Like López de Cancelada, Mier argued that the Haitian Revolution was unlikely to be repeated in New Spain. However, Mier's argument hinged not on constructing a racialized affective and moral distance between the two sites (Saint-Domingue and New Spain), but on statistics about the "reduced" presence and contained mobility of Black bodies in Spanish American colonies, New Spain specifically. Mier presented his readers with an imagined racialized colonial geography where Black bodies were exclusively restricted to the islands and coastal zones, the points where African slaves had initially entered. He supported this vision of quasi segregation by referring to colonial policies that had allegedly helped to shape it: namely, prohibitions on racial mixing between "black men" and "Indian women" that set the punishment for men who disobeyed as corporeal mutilation.[14]

Mier's text illustrates how perceptions of Haiti filtered the disputes related to the role and support of Black and other racialized groups in political debates about Spanish American independence within the region's crumbling viceroyalties. In an unpublished appendix to his "Idea de la constitución," he asserts that Simón Bolívar's abolition of slavery in Caracas, which—according to his narrative—had been enacted "suddenly" or "immediately" (*de un golpe*), had been a concession to the threat of a *pardo* uprising.[15] However, Mier does not underscore rebellion as a motivation for concession; instead (and as López de Cancelada had previously done) he highlights white disunity, ultimately showcasing that this type of discourse also permeated emerging republican criollo imaginations. Mier critiques how Spaniards, both in Popayán and in Caracas, had poisoned *pardos* and mulattos against criollos:

> The Europeans in Popayán, seeing that they could counteract the criollos, led the negroes to believe that their dispute with the criollos, their masters, was because the Courts had granted them their freedom and their masters had resisted. They convinced them to rise up and sow chaos. But how shall they subject them again? When they grow disillusioned, they will turn wrathfully against the Europeans who tricked them into killing their masters, compatriots, and defenders. They began to practice the same cruel maneuver in Caracas, driving Bolívar to the tremendous measure of suddenly decreeing the freedom of all slaves.[16]

Mier's take on the events of Popayán drew upon the historical stereotype of Black subjectivity as immature and easily affectable. Blackness, as Mier constructs it in this passage, was linked to being susceptible to others' power. The actual political dispute was for him located in the intersection between white criollos and Spaniards, who used Black slaves' alleged affectability as a weapon. This implied that political crises could be averted by "white unity" and the refusal of whites (criollos and Spaniards) to use Black support in their disputes against each other. Constrained as it was by the colonial legacies of race, Mier's intervention nevertheless contains a kernel of truth: it reveals the power that popular and nonwhite groups held in the struggles, showing that negotiations for their support would be crucial to the outcome of independence.[17]

Despite Mier's dismissal of his colleagues' strategy to stoke racial fear in colonial authorities, there is documentation suggesting that imperial administrators were in fact quite concerned by the possible outburst of race wars in Spanish colonies, and that the strategy might have been more effective than Mier avowed. Writing to Felix Calleja in 1816, Luis Onis, the plenipotentiary minister of Spain in the United States, warns the viceroy of a number of insurgent expeditions that planned to meet and depart from Port-au-Prince with military and financial support from the Haitian Republic to different points of Spanish America looking to expand the potency of ongoing rebellions. Francisco Xavier Mina was leading the expedition destined for New Spanish shores, and Mier was one of its members. In his missives, Onis notifies Calleja of running rumors about a plan to "revolutionize blacks in all Spanish colonies" and states that just like Bolívar's prior expedition, Mina's was likely to grow in strength and number during its stationing in Haiti with the support of "colored men" and arms provided by Pétion himself.[18]

Demanding that Haiti be admonished for its unneutral behavior, in one of his missives, Onis seems to refer to the known agreement between Pétion and Bolívar in which the president of Haiti's republic agreed to give financial and military support to the Libertador's revolutionary project with the guarantee that slavery would be abolished in liberated territories, thus expanding through the Americas Haiti's commitment to radical antislavery.[19] But Onis's letters also suggest that he might have been aware of, or at the very least concerned with, other plans to "revolutionize blacks in all Spanish colonies" beyond Bolívar's pact with Pétion. Whether these plans existed and were officially agreed upon or they were a figment of Onis's expansive imagination is uncertain.[20] What becomes clear through the minister's insistence on the topic, however, is that the potential politicization of racialized groups (particularly that of free Blacks and slaves) in favor of insurgent efforts was deeply concerning to colonial authorities and thus easily weaponized by insurgent criollos and Spaniards. This might also explain why, when reporting on the failure of Mina's 1817 expedition, Calleja reassures Onis by happily sharing with him the detail that after disembarking in Soto la Marina, very few people of the *"infima plebe"* had decided to join the rebels.[21]

Haiti's support to early Spanish American insurgent projects has been somewhat discussed in the relevant scholarship, but its persistence as an anchor for republican imaginations after independence is less explored.[22] An instance of coalition with Haiti that also combined the strategic use of rhetoric associating the island's revolution with race war appears in 1829 during the presidency of Vicente Guerrero. In the context of Ferdinand VII's efforts to invade and reconquer Mexico and push back against republican projects in Spanish America more broadly, Guerrero enlisted the support of Haiti's new president, Jean-Pierre Boyer, in order to safeguard the newly won autonomy of the nation he commanded. The plan of the coalition was to use Haiti's neighboring location with Cuba to destabilize the most important stronghold of what was left of the Spanish Empire in the Americas, also operating as the base from which reconquering expeditions such as the one led by Isidro Barradas to Tamaulipas were launched. To this effect, Guerrero sent a secret commissioner who, from Haiti, was supposed to diplomatically organize the alliance of both nations and guarantee the safety of Mexico's independence.[23]

Considering that in the midst of political instability during the early decades after achieving independence, Haiti might have provided a blueprint of success for Mexico and other young nations in the region, Guerrero's call upon Boyer's support might be read beyond the mere interest of strategically using the island's closeness to Cuba.[24] It might be seen, instead, as an effort to build a hemispheric coalition on the basis of a shared political vision. Vicente Rocafuerte's enthusiasm for Guerrero's plan in Haiti conveys the point:

> The best way to prepare to defend our territory, in case of invasion, is to combine our forces with the cooperation of Colombia and Santo Domingo. Prudence advises us to convene with these governments and keep them pleased so that we can take advantage of them when potentially needed in future circumstances. Santo Domingo is the terror of the Island of Cuba: let's use the alliance that can be formed with Boyer to take a threatening stance and make the Spaniards of Havana understand that, if they invade us, they will be invaded too; that if they come to Mexico to end the anarchy, as they say, we will go to Cuba to end the enslavement of blacks.[25]

To be sure, the passage showcases Rocafuerte's strategic thinking and his recommendation to use Haiti and Colombia's support to Mexico's advantage.[26] But it also presents these two nations as republican anchors on which Mexico could rely to protect its tenuous independence. Haiti, recently unified under Boyer, likely continued to appear in 1829 as a source of political inspiration and a solid base of support for emerging and unstable Spanish American nations. Nevertheless, at the heart of Rocafuerte's positive take on Guerrero's secret mission is once again the recourse to Haiti's historical valence as a racial nightmare, more concretely as "the terror of Cuba." While recourse to the abolition of slavery is certainly figured here as a threatening political scheme to incite fear of racial uprising in Spaniards living in Havana, the passage also betrays—perhaps even against its author's intentions—how Haiti's revolutionary antislavery resonated well beyond the nation's borders and came to underpin and outline the boundaries of anticolonial disputes in the early 1800s. At the same time, Rocafuerte's passage also underscores how the politicization of racialized groups, in this case Cuba's Black slaves, was mobilized and placed at the center of the battle between early republican and royalist projects. In other words, Rocafuerte's comments on the Mexico-Haiti mission already elucidated the ways in which certain aspects of antislavery rhetoric would be absorbed and tamed by an emerging common sense at the point where positions against slavery would become sutured to criollo republicanism. Situating themselves against what was increasingly viewed as the "barbaric" institution of slavery, this ultimately allowed Latin American countries to, for a period of time, inhabit the position of what James E. Sanders calls the "vanguard of the Atlantic."[27]

But the use of Haiti's example as a race war in efforts to negotiate and protect Mexico's independence was far from uncontroversial. Critiques of the strategy shed light on concerns about how the emerging nation should balance its position in the international arena, carefully selecting its allies. As he denounced being kept in the dark regarding the secret mission in Haiti, Lorenzo de Zavala (the head of Mexico's treasury at the time of Guerrero's plan) warned his colleagues about the complications this strategy could bring to the country's international affairs. In his eyes, trying to incite rebellion in the "degraded class of Haiti's neighboring island" was an affront to jus gentium and could provoke complaints from "civilized nations," further endangering Mexico's already precarious standing in the international arena.[28] The racializing shadow of "barbarity" that early on was cast upon Haiti and its revolution continued to pierce through Zavala's appraisal of Guerrero's plan as he counseled him to reevaluate his alliances in favor of inserting Mexico in another geopolitical circuit more closely tied to the structures of whiteness and in line with what he called the "civilized nations."

The image of Haiti that criollo discourses in Mexico constructed and mobilized at different stages of the early nineteenth century thus vacillated between two modalities. On one hand, Haiti could sometimes be used as a figure of race war that, while deeply concerning to colonial authorities, was mostly the source of inspiration for those searching for new political horizons as well as for visions of potential future stability under a republican framework. On the other hand, Haiti could also be invoked as the name of a racial excess that while mobilized against colonial power would nevertheless return to haunt the visions of criollo statecraft. Navigating international affairs through the race war paradigm was thus not an isolated issue, disconnected from internal matters. As I stated before, the rhetoric and its practical implications would slowly become internalized as a mechanism to patrol and police the nation's boundaries once the colonial relation was finally severed. This underscores how efforts deployed to manage foreign relations resonated with, and even mirrored, measures taken to regulate internal affairs, and vice versa. As Haiti's amphibological image was absorbed by emerging criollo imaginations under the sign of the nation, the contradictions and tensions between the two poles of its figure played out. A concluding reading of José Joaquín Fernández de Lizardi's rewrite of Luciano Comella's play *El negro sensible* (discussed in the previous chapter) will help us parse out how.

EL NEGRO SENSIBLE AFTER INDEPENDENCE

In 1825, José Joaquín Fernández de Lizardi wrote a second part to Comella's *El negro sensible*. The new piece was scheduled to be staged as part of a celebration commemorating the new presidency of Guadalupe Victoria, who had proclaimed a conciliatory order that "conceded freedom to those slaves who could redeem themselves with funds raised for this purpose, and those voluntarily freed by their owners."[29]

Although the play reached the rehearsal phase, the performance was canceled at the last minute by the authorities of the coliseum due to a dispute over the earnings.[30] Lizardi's *El negro sensible* would not appear on a Mexican stage until 1827, after the death of its author.[31] It is worth noting that this play, meant to celebrate this important moment in the new nation's political life and independence, was an adaptation of a popular late colonial piece on the topic of slavery. Even more strikingly, in writing about the play and the cancellation of the performance, el Pensador Mexicano (as Lizardi is known) described his adaptation of *El negro sensible* as a piece that was "utterly American and original."[32] This description may have revealed more than its author intended, for it speaks to the continuities between the colonial and postcolonial periods in matters of race.

While Lizardi's *El negro sensible* preserves the central plot of Comella's original version, he uses different dramatic strategies in the second part. These changes in technique underscore the contradictions that traversed racializing discourses and practices after the end of the colonial period. In addition to adding new characters—including Bunga, Catul's wife, who was only mentioned in Comella's original work—Lizardi's piece stages a different affective dynamic, one marked by the tensions that accompanied the rise of liberalism and its paradoxical combination of universal liberties (for some) with racialized constraints (for others). On the one hand, the piece discursively applauds the position of Doña Martina, the "sensitive" European woman who had freed Catul and his family, who advocated for the abstract equality and liberty of all men, and who would inspire the "common sense" of liberalism in the viewers. It also demonizes the cruelty of the slave-owning characters, who are depicted as obsolete and out of step with modernity. However, some passages contradict the supposedly emancipatory discourse offered up by Martina and, ultimately, by the play itself, allowing the inconsistencies and contradictions of the emerging national political imagination to pierce through.

For example, Lizardi made use of asides, a classic theatrical technique in which a character (Martina, in this case) says something to another character onstage and then changes her tone to say something different "offstage," directed at the audience and supposedly inaudible to other characters. These asides often contradict characters' previous onstage lines to other figures in the play, producing dramatic irony. The device stages before the public at least two dimensions of theatrical discourse that are at odds with each other, thus making explicit the hidden thoughts and motivations of the speaking character. The technique encourages viewers to look deeper and beyond the play's explicit message, which in the case of Lizardi's rewriting of *El negro sensible* touched upon notions of freedom and universal equality.

The play clearly undercuts its own ostensible message in an added scene: after Martina has already bought Catul, Jacobo (Catul's previous master) and Martina (the "benevolent" European) lie to Catul about his slave status. After she has bought Catul in order to grant him his freedom, Martina and Jacobo pretend that the transaction hasn't occurred; they tell him that Martina has bought his son but not Catul himself, and that they will be separated. They seek to drive him to desperation, thereby forcing him to reveal his "true feelings" about whites—particularly about Martina. A despairing Catul rails against the "inhumane whites," readying his knife to kill himself and his child. Martina finally intervenes, informing him that it had all been a joke and that she had in fact also purchased him in order to free him. In this perverse game of first denying and then recognizing Catul's liberty, the play betrays that, at bottom, criollo elites' perception of freedom as a contingent privilege to be granted (and taken away) by the "white master" or "savior" depended on the "good" behavior of other racialized citizens. The play thus anticipated and echoed the introduction of similar caveats about "good behavior" into the constitution and other legislation to racially segment citizenship in different states of the Mexican Republic, even after the legal abolition of the caste system. It also gestured toward the persistence of paranoid ideas about racialized subjects' "hatred of whites." Jacobo and Martina's desire to uncover Catul's "true feelings" toward them ultimately indexes the play's anxiety about postindependence racial tensions and potential racial violence in Mexico.

The play, like the vacilating images of Haiti, moves between recognizing, including, and disavowing the political existence of racialized subjectivities; this is the same ambivalence that would shape Mexico's political landscape throughout the nineteenth century. Indeed, the rewritten play added another dimension to the paranoid fear of racial violence that had once been projected onto Haiti and framed as external and distant from New Spain's society or used as a political tool in breaking the colonial relation. However, the fear of "race war" did not disappear; in fact, as I show in chapters 5 and 6, an internal race war was perceived as being ever more immanent after the nation had consolidated itself as an independent polity, ever more so when this nation was supposed to be governed by the principles of "freedom" and "equality."

{ PART III }

Yucatán

{ FIVE }

On Criminality, Race, and Labor
INDENTURE AND THE CASTE WAR

Two miles from the shores of Sisal, Yucatán, the first material remainders of a network that in the mid-nineteenth century placed thousands of Maya men, women, and children into indenture were recently discovered.[1] Buried underneath the sand of the Caribbean Sea, the hull of the ship *Unión*, which in September 1861 perished in the flames of an engine fire, was unearthed by a team of subaquatic archaeologists.[2] The vessel, part of the fleet of the Spanish merchant house Zangroniz Hermanos y Compañía, operated between the ports of Tampico, Veracruz, Campeche, Sisal, and Havana, transporting goods, correspondence, and travelers across these locations.[3] The ship was also among the vehicles upon which thousands of indigenous people from the Yucatán Peninsula, alleged "rebels" of the Caste War, were transported to the neighboring island of Cuba and coerced into indenture.

As reported in the media, the recent findings confront Mexico with its disavowed "slaving past."[4] The occurrence of this clandestine trade has been widely ignored in official narratives of Mexican history, and few scholarly studies on the topic exist.[5] In fact, even as it occurred, the trade's controversial nature led to multiple attempts from those involved in it to erase its evidence. As Terry Rugeley acknowledges, "The murky history of this business constitutes one of the most frustrating of all dimensions of the Caste War, mainly for the paucity of information. Most of the trade occurred without benefit of paperwork, and the few records that do exist are mainly diplomatic correspondence, or else bogus contracts used to legitimize the trade."[6] Certainly, it is hard to accurately estimate the breadth of the network. There is little information, either quantitative or qualitative, about those who were sent to Cuba against their will.[7] However, the "paucity of information" should not be discouraging but perhaps seen as providing an opening to interrogate a new iteration of the race war paradigm. The fragmentary nature of the documentation of the trade is not incidental; rather, it results from a series of silences and distortions produced in the archive by authorities and landowners involved in the trade, stakeholders who sought to legitimize and whitewash their business or even to erase any record of its occurrence. The piecemeal documentation of the trade correlates with how efforts to stealthily sell indigenous people into indenture created a zone of legal anomaly that allowed this "exceptional" punitive practice to thrive for over two decades.

Despite efforts to conceal it, the trade generated quite the controversy. Not only were numerous op-ed articles and novels published on it in Mexico's most important and well-distributed newspapers, but the situation also led to an intense diplomatic conversation about the boundaries of liberal freedom that resonated beyond the confines of the nation. The discussions had important implications for Mexico's foreign and national affairs. Diplomats from Mexico, Spain, Cuba, and Britain all exchanged letters that touched on the "uncomfortable" evidence that a new form of forced labor was emerging: Was it slavery? Were the people being sent to Cuba workers or prisoners? Was the labor they performed on the plantations "free"? Was this "freedom" safeguarded by the fact that the "workers" had signed contracts and had passports?[8]

Bureaucracy certainly helped to mask the coercive nature of the migration of indigenous men and women to Cuba. Upon embarking on the ships destined for the island, authorities issued passports to the people on board. They also pressed them to sign contracts written in Spanish, which were likely illegible to many and stipulated a full decade of service with no rescinding clauses.[9] As they entered into Cuba, Maya migrants were dispersed throughout the island and expected to undertake any form of labor assigned to them. This could involve agricultural activities in tobacco or sugar plantations, working on roads and in factories, or domestic labor. Like Asian (mostly Chinese) "coolie" laborers, Maya migrants were considered free, and their lives and labor were to be allegedly protected from slavery under decrees specifically outlined for this type of population. However, far from establishing regulations to safeguard these groups' rights, the decrees served as a bureaucratic prosthesis that facilitated racialized coerced work.[10]

In contemporary discussions, participants and detractors of the trade often aimed to situate it in relation to slavery, whether to defend it or to defame it. Echoes of these discussions continue to shape historiographical accounts about it. This chapter, instead, follows a less explored thread that, nevertheless, was also an important part of the debates, one that associated the trade of indigenous indentured labor with the need to implement "exceptional" penal practices to regulate the peninsula's indigenous rebels. After all, the trade came into being as a means of managing and repressing the massive indigenous uprising that in 1847 shook the Yucatán Peninsula and expanded its shockwaves into other regions of the country. Supporters of the trade defended it by criminalizing the indigenous people who were forced to migrate. In doing so, they appealed to international law, war regulations, and ideas about the reformative potential of penal labor. As far as these defenders were concerned, those forced to board ships destined for Cuba were "savage rebels" who were incapable of understanding the legal procedures of "civilization" and who, therefore, deserved whatever penalty came their way.

Following the rhetoric of exceptionality that surrounded it, in this chapter I situate the Yucatán-Cuba trade as a piece in a larger puzzle of global forced migration. The relation between indenture and slavery has received substantial attention, but only recently have scholars begun to explore nineteenth-century global networks of indenture in relation to histories of incarceration and confinement. Here I build on this new approach, reading the Yucatán-Cuba trade as a form of penal practice.[11]

The Yucatán-Cuba trade marked the pulse of public debates shaping the contours of what constituted publicly accepted measures to contain "caste wars." To follow the controversy that accompanied the trade from its initial to its final stages is, thus, to follow the changes in the widespread "common sense" among elites and governing groups about the dangers of indigenous uprisings and the racializing strategies employed to manage and contain them. As the trade began its operations, the transactions between the peninsula and the island became quickly attached to disputed ideas about what it meant to uphold "civilized" and "humane" behavior toward indigenous groups, specifically toward those taken to be rebels. Notably, both detractors and supporters of the trade presented themselves as upholding the highest standards of "humane" behavior toward indigenous rebels, who, they often argued, did not even deserve such consideration. That these two opposing groups battled each other in the same rhetorical space illustrates that by the mid-nineteenth century notions of "humanitarianism" had become an index to measure ideas about both individual and collective civilizational status.[12] At stake in these debates, however, was more than a mere discussion about the nation's morality and degree of civilization: underpinning these different understandings of humane treatment of caste war rebels were diverging understandings of *Indianness*, or more concretely, diverging ideas of what Indian labor meant in the new nation and what role it was to play within (or outside of) it.

The trade was polemic from the outset both within Mexico and abroad. It entailed a collaboration between the government, the army, and transatlantic private businesses, and it strengthened the transatlantic ties that had historically connected the peninsula to Cuba.[13] Internally, politicians' positions on the indentured labor trade sometimes demarcated their party affiliations (conservative or liberal). Most who defamed it using arguments about how the practice stood against humanitarian and civilized behavior strongly identified with the liberal party. But the lines dividing Mexico's two political parties did not split neatly; the scenario was much more complex than that. The trade was backed by members of both parties, and regional differences affected opinions on the practice, with different receptions in places such as Yucatán, Veracruz, and Mexico City.[14] In fact, regional differences on the trade reignited recently mitigated tensions between the state of Yucatán and the Mexican federal government, and brought into the spotlight the tenuous process by which Yucatán had finally been incorporated as a state of the Mexican Republic in 1848 after several episodes of secession.

Those who supported the trade tended to see domestic Mexican reliance on indigenous labor as undesirable. They argued that it would create a dangerous populational imbalance tilted in favor of the Indians.[15] Although the widespread labor scarcity placed intense pressure on hacendados and homeowners in the aftermath of the first wave of insurgency in Yucatán, trade supporters were not invested in how the peninsula's shattered economy would be reconstructed through internal agricultural ventures; instead, they pictured entering into and profiting from the contemporary global networks of forced migration.[16] Headed by Yucatec hacendados, Cuban plantation owners, and Spanish contractors, the enterprise was designed to export nearly 6 percent of the region's Maya population at a rate of approximately 120 to 160 pesos per worker, with the price varying according to gender, age, and physical health.[17] The trade thus had the prospect of yielding millionaire fortunes, reactivating the state's paralyzed economy. This source of revenue would have exceeded the peninsula's contemporary loan capital by more than double.[18]

Alternatively, those who opposed the trade connected their stance against it not only to ideas about how it violated the most basic principles of humanitarianism but also to their own concerns with the nation's depletion of indigenous populations. Detractors of the trade perceived indigenous bodies and labor as invaluable to filling the ranks of the army and for employment in the development of the country's agriculture.

One of the longest and largest indigenous rebellions in Latin America's history, Yucatán's Caste War is the most significant case around which a new iteration of the race war paradigm coalesced in the mid-nineteenth century. This multifaceted conflict is traditionally said to have begun in 1847, when a group of rebels led by the Maya *bataab* Cecilio Chi took over the town of Tepich.[19] The proximate cause of this initial revolt was the execution of Manuel Antonio Ay (*bataab* of Chichimilá), who had been accused of plotting (with Cecilio Chi) against criollo officials and institutions.[20] But Ay's execution was only a match to a pyre that had long been under construction, for the uprising was rooted in a long history of colonial violence. As the hacienda system and the sugar industry in Yucatán expanded to meet global demands, tracts of communal land were being continually expropriated while the laboring conditions of their racialized workforce grew more dire.[21] The insurgents sought to overturn this situation: broadly speaking, they aimed to renegotiate the terms of their involvement in the peninsula's economic and political affairs.[22] The uprising was not unified, but there was communication among leaders of different groups, who wrote letters that were read aloud in rebel communities and used to strategize among themselves. Rebels also used letters to negotiate with both Yucatec government officials and British merchants based in the neighboring region of Belize, from whom they acquired, among other things, gunpowder and weapons. As in the cases studied in previous chapters, the racialized exaction of taxes and tributes, which in Yucatán continued to operate after independence, was a key issue against which rebels organized their struggle for equality, freedom, and "husticia" (justice).[23]

The uprising shook the region to its core. Moving from the southeastern side of the peninsula toward the capital city of Mérida, the insurgency destroyed villages, ranches, churches, and sugar plantations in its path. Hundreds of thousands were killed or displaced in the clashes, and Yucatec criollos' vision of the peninsula as a future sugar empire "lay in cinders."[24] Intellectuals, politicians, hacendados, and authorities within and beyond Yucatán despaired of their efforts to contain the havoc. Two years into the rebellion, the first ships carrying indigenous men and women from the peninsula were on their way to Cuba.[25]

ZONES OF ANOMALY: INDENTURE AND THE PALIMPSESTIC COLONIAL ROUTES OF CONVICT LABOR

On March 12, 1849, Buenaventura Vivó, the Mexican consul in Havana, received an unexpected visitor in his office. The man introduced himself as José Antonio Migangos from the town of Halachó, Yucatán, and expressed that he was at the consul's office to voice the concerns of his fellow countrymen and women. He spoke on behalf of 135 indigenous people from the Yucatán Peninsula who had complained to him of being abducted from their hometowns and transported to Cuba aboard the Spanish steamboat *Cetro*. They were now facing the prospect of forced labor in the island's sugar and tobacco plantations. All of these men and women, Migangos stated, had expressed their desire to write the consul themselves, but because they couldn't they had asked him to do so on their behalf.[26]

According to Migangos, the men and women had been imprisoned by Yucatec authorities for their alleged involvement in the Caste War. Shortly thereafter, with their ankles and wrists shackled, they were sent to the seaport of Sisal and put aboard the Spanish ship without knowing what awaited them. It was only as they reached the Cuban shore that they learned their whereabouts. Stating that they had been sent to the island against their will, the people demanded to be freed and refused to follow Cuban landowners' plans to coerce them into agricultural labor. Through Migangos, they requested that the consul intervene on their behalf so that Cuban authorities would grant them permission to relocate within the island or even back in Yucatán according to their will.[27]

Upon receiving Migangos's testimony, Vivó sought to contact both the governor in Yucatán and the captain general in Cuba. In the letters he wrote, Vivó made clear his concern with protecting the "dignity of Mexico's good name" as a civilized and enlightened nation. Dispatching from the island, where slavery was still lawfully permitted, the consul was aware of the diplomatic intricacies that could arise from the complaints of the recently arrived migrants.[28]

Vivó's distress about the trade was mostly diplomatic: he empathized with Yucatec authorities' plight to expel Maya rebels from the region, given the "atrocious war they waged against the white race," but requested that this be done through the appropriate bureaucratic channels and in compliance with the "principles of politics, convenience, and humanity."[29]

Nevertheless, when writing to the captain general of Cuba, Vivó introduced himself as a "protector of foreigners" and demanded permission to visit the incoming people aboard the *Cetro*, accompanied by a Maya translator and a Cuban official, to further inquire about the conditions of their arrival to the island.[30] The captain general responded promptly, denying Vivó's request and reminding him that his diplomatic functions were strictly limited to mercantile issues.[31] He thus closed the door on the eager consul's investigation. Vivó's failed efforts to curtail the dubious introduction of indigenous people from Yucatán into Cuba illuminate the blind spots in international diplomacy that allowed the trade to persist and thrive as an opaque practice for years, puzzling contemporary beholders for whom categorizing it as either slavery or "true free" labor was a vexing endeavor.

The practice of selling Maya men, women, and children into indenture in Cuba generated a de facto ambiguous legal space. Notably, this ambiguity is not fully explained by contemporary efforts to disguise or justify it. Instead, its use as a mechanism to pacify indigenous rebels acquires more density when placed in the context of Mexico's broader histories of convict labor.

A precursor to the enterprise can be found in the historical infrastructure of convict labor sustained by Spanish imperialism. It is only recently that scholars have begun to explore in more depth the role of convict labor in building the Spanish Empire. Starting in the early sixteenth century and lasting into the late nineteenth, tens of thousands of convict laborers were transported from node to node in Spain's polycentric dominium.[32] The networks of convict transportation not only connected the different corners of the empire but also intertwined multiple punitive regimes operating within it.[33] Convicts of the highest and lowest orders could find themselves traveling alongside each other and alongside non-convicted migrants who shared the convicts' destinations: the Philippines, California, North Africa, Havana, Veracruz, San Juan, and many others.[34]

New Spain was an important node in the geographies of Spanish convict labor. Thousands of prisoners crossed its lands on their way to a range of destinations. Some were sent from Acapulco to Manila; others coming from Spain arrived to Veracruz and traveled north toward the California garrisons; others moved from the Gulf of Mexico to different parts of the Caribbean, including Cuba, Puerto Rico, and Florida.[35]

In his *Political Essay on the Kingdom of New Spain* (1811), Alexander von Humboldt described how convict labor complemented the strategies deployed by colonial authorities to "pacify" the indigenous tribes of northern territories. As part of his critique of Spanish colonialism, Humboldt asserted that so-called *barbaric* Indians made captive during the violent encounters with missionaries and Spanish militias were often imprisoned in the infamous Mexico City jail La Acordada, to then be shipped to Veracruz and Havana as convict laborers, where, confronted with the different conditions of life on the island, the prisoners usually found their deathbed.[36] While Humboldt's anecdotes about convict labor in New Spain may not be as accurate as he'd hoped, still they shed light on a colonial imaginary that employed penal labor to pacify indigenous rebels. The legacies of this imaginary seem to have come to new life in the Yucatán Peninsula during the Caste War years.

As nineteenth-century Yucatec government officials, soldiers, hacendados, and contractors plotted the trade of indigenous men and women with Cuba, they created a route of convict labor that, like a palimpsest, was layered over the routes that had been circuited by Spanish ships since the early years of colonial rule. Moving through Sisal, Veracruz, Tampico, New Orleans, and Havana, the ships that transported indentured prisoners from the peninsula to Cuba followed the patterns of transportation that had created the Great Caribbean geography through which commodities and people (including convict laborers) traveled.

After the wave of Spanish American independences broke apart the empire, emerging Latin American nations, including Mexico, continued to use convict labor. While some see these continuities as anachronistic residues of a dying colonialism, I see them as adaptations or repurposings ("refunctionalizations," to use Christian G. De Vito's terminology) of colonial punitive practices.[37] At stake in the repurposing of these previously established routes of commerce and convict labor was something more than convenience: the production of zones of legal exception.

In her comparative study on colonial systems of convict labor, Lauren Benton argues that these networks peaked in the eighteenth century, cresting a wave of increasing interimperial tensions and global militarization. Western empires increasingly used islands under their jurisdiction as sites of both military fortresses and convict labor. During this epoch, "the reliance on forced labor to expand and consolidate empires in a period of intense, global inter-imperial rivalry" increased, complicating the question of sovereignty in these spaces:[38] while empires vied to construct imperial structures that were ever more tightly woven and integrated, the sites of convict labor created new legal anomalous zones within their grids.[39]

The *presidiarios* (criminals sentenced to penal labor in presidios, or Spanish military fortresses) faced not only degrading conditions but also a peculiar legal status, an exception within Spain's legal bureaucracy that put them in a kind of legal limbo in which they had almost no path to appeal punitive decisions or to request clemency. This limbo, Benton tells us, emerged from two factors: the nature of exile as a penal sentence and the frequency with which officials ordered it without due legal process or trial. When convicts entered the presidios, they entered into a military world that lacked the bureaucratic infrastructure to channel their petitions to the king. Although access to the monarch was not directly foreclosed, the garrisons that housed transported convicts had no court, leaving the prisoners stranded with no avenue for their claims. Although, as Benton states, this circumstance paralleled that of galley slaves, it was an unusual situation in Spain's imperial structure, where petitioning the king was a common and long-standing prerogative of Spanish subjects, irrespective of their social and caste status.[40]

The deportation of indigenous "Caste War convicts" to Cuba opened a zone of legal anomaly that resonated with the one described above. Like those moving through the routes of eighteenth-century Spanish convict labor, indigenous rebels found themselves in legal limbo, sentenced to exile without due process. This anomalous status was cast on them both before leaving Mexico and upon arrival to Cuba. In May 1849, for instance, Governor Miguel Barbachano was involved in an intense epistolary exchange with federal officials in Mexico City about his decision to sanction the network of indentured labor with Cuba. Barbachano defended his decision to support the trade of Maya men, women, and children by insisting that the rebels had not even been classified as prisoners. He asserted that while those sent to Cuba had in fact been detained under the state's jurisdiction for a short amount of time, they had not been sentenced nor processed, and therefore took ship as "free" men, not prisoners: "But what law or decree forbids the government of Yucatán from granting passports to one or many men who wish to work in a foreign country without losing their freedom, nor doing so by the immediate action of a court, given that while these men have been imprisoned they have not yet been tried nor processed?"[41] Barbachano's apologia for the trade, and his insistence that those traveling to Cuba had not been processed by the state, indicates that these transactions deliberately skirted the margins of the law: the trade itself was purposefully not encoded as a penal practice, although it very much operated as such. Indeed, the trade generated much of its force from remaining in this informal or anomalous legal space.

Conversely, the anomaly of indentured workers' status upon arrival to Cuba was tied to how international legal frameworks used by nations to negotiate the status of their citizens in foreign countries was barely emerging in this period. In addition, Cuba's apparatus for managing indentured "colonist" populations was relatively new and perhaps intentionally opaque, and Mexico itself had basically foreclosed the indentured workers' connections home with its extralegal process of deportation. Although the contracts of indenture had no rescinding clauses and the avenues for appeal were slim, the first arrivals to the island strove to make their voices heard through local acquaintances who addressed the Mexican consul in Havana on their behalf. As they found themselves unjustly and unwillingly transported to Cuba, indigenous men and women from the Yucatán resorted to the historic practice of petitions and claimed their freedom, demanding just treatment.

IN FAVOR OF THE TRADE: CRIMINALITY, INTERNATIONAL LAW, AND THE USES OF HUMANITARIANISM TO PROTECT RACIALIZED SOVEREIGNTY

In the late 1850s and early 1860s, during a rising second wave of the Yucatán-Cuba indentured labor trade, the federal government increased its investment in shutting down the network. In fact, the constitution of 1857 introduced a ban on all forms of involuntary labor.[42] The federal government's crackdown on the trade led its supporters to actively search for narratives to sustain their business without entering into direct contradiction with either federal law or public opinion. To support their investment in selling indigenous people into indenture in Cuba, they entered the disputed rhetorical arena of "humanitarianism" and intertwined it with two discursive threads in contemporary public discussion: the country's penal practices and international law. Relying on these two frameworks, supporters of the trade figured Maya deportees as rebel criminals whose behavior justified stripping them of all constitutional protections, placing them beyond the pale of national legislature and even rendering them candidates for (by then abolished) capital punishment.

In February 1858, the Mérida-based official newspaper of Yucatán, *Las Garantías Sociales*, published on its front page a series of municipal letters written from Hecelchakán, Tizimín, and Valladolid to Governor Martín Francisco Peraza requesting that he officially sanction the trade of indigenous people with Cuba. The requests had a strong local precedent. A decade prior, Governor Miguel Barbachano had given his official support to the first forced deportations of indigenous people to the island.[43]

The letters to Peraza were written in the context of a renewed wave of tensions with Maya insurgents. A recent attack on the village of Tekax, in September 1857, had sparked concerns about the reignition of the Caste War. The letter writers' preoccupations were not unfounded: only two weeks after the letters were printed, rebel groups recaptured Bacalar and attacked the city of Valladolid.[44] A passage in one of these letters frames deportation and forced labor as the most "humanitarian" possible response to the insurgents. Cloaking a racist desire to remove Maya inhabitants from the peninsula in the epoch's growing concern with "humane" punitive techniques, the writer presents the trade as a conservative measure, one that halted the state from rightfully "waging total war" against the "uncivilized Indians" and showing no mercy to its political captives:

> Faced with the need to take the most adequate measures to achieve the desired end, it is entirely essential to adopt the most humanitarian [action] of all with respect to the enemy as a new campaign begins[.] This is so because what is most important is to maintain public morals and not provide people with examples of cruelty; but in considering that they belong to an uncivilized race that does not understand the laws of war, or the acts of clemency implemented in their favor, they have done nothing more than further stimulate their barbarism, which should be a motive to wage total war against them without mercy; however, it is necessary to instead adopt the measure of expelling them from the State, in accordance with the principles of civilization and humanity.[45]

The signatories' claim in favor of the humanitarianism of expelling indigenous rebels from the country and sending them to Cuba repurposed a long-standing practice inherited from both Roman and early modern European law whereby a (presumably) justified death sentence could be *humanely* replaced by exile or banishment.[46] Letter writers argued that the death penalty would be a legitimate response to the enemy's "barbarism," which then allowed them to frame their push to send indigenous inhabitants to Cuba as a benevolent willingness to compromise.

When trade supporters reiterated the justifiability of a death sentence for captured "rebels," they were also rehashing recent public conversations that had led to the initial abolition of the death penalty in the federal constitution of 1857.[47] Drawing on the general consensus reached by the country's congressmen, who saw the abolition of the death penalty as an expression of the nation's humane, forgiving, and by extension "civilized" nature, Yucatec inhabitants and politicians who backed the trade cast their alleged benevolence toward Maya rebels as being in line with those who had opposed the death penalty, leading to its abolition. As such, letter writers who asked the governor to reinstate the trade between Yucatán and Cuba revealed their investment in preserving the pristine "public morals" of their state. In other words, their main intervention occurred at the level of shaping public opinion. Supporters of the trade connected debates around it to an important national polemic on criminality and exposed how humanism's contradictory legacies allowed them to press for the official approval to sell captured "rebels" into indenture.

The petitions presented in these letters worked within the logic of sovereign power to kill and let live.[48] Even the claim of having "shown mercy"—in this case formulated under the premise that traders were allowing the "rebels" to live by banishing them from the country—affirmed the operation of sovereign power.[49] What is most striking in the letters, however, is the repeated request for the state to sanction a trade that was already in place. These petitions, which sought legitimization from the state, open a path by which to explore the racializing operations of sovereign power in the context of Mexico's mid-nineteenth-century republican horizon.

Political theorists have stated that popular sovereignty, integrated as a key tenet of modern nation-states (in Mexico under the 1857 liberal constitution), relocated and displaced but did not eliminate sovereign power. The power to kill or let live that had formerly been concentrated in the figure of the monarch was now, within the new parameters of democracy, redistributed and disseminated among the individuals who constituted the collective body of the "people." In this new order, any man could be invested with enacting this sovereign power on the bodies of others.[50] While discussions on the dissemination of sovereignty among the "people" situate this distribution as a general attribute of all modern nation-states, what often escapes this analysis is how this shift had its own, singular, historical expression in racialized polities. Indeed, Lisa Guenther's critique of Jacques Derrida's seminars on the death penalty suggests as much. Guenther, who complements Derrida's ideas with the critical interventions of radical abolitionism, writes, "This is the logic of sovereignty in the so-called democracy of the United Sates; the power to kill or let live is not centralized in the body of the king, or even in 'the king's two bodies,' but rather dispersed throughout the white body politic, such that any white man, no matter how poor or otherwise disempowered, is positioned as sovereign in relation to the black man whose 'rights' he is enjoined by law to disregard."[51]

Although the production of race in Mexico (specifically in Yucatán) was very different from that of the US context that Guenther analyzes, her insight is still useful in examining what the case of Mexican indenture reveals about the singular racializing operations of sovereign violence in Mexico. I am interested in how trade supporters presented themselves as the bearers of a disseminated sovereignty, searching to be invested with the power to decide upon the lives and deaths of Caste War indigenous "rebels." Insofar as the trade's operation required the involvement of private citizens, hacendados, and local businessmen, letter writers' requests for the state's official sanction of the trade can be read as a request placed by the constituents of Hecelchakán, Tizimín, and Valladolid to be deputized by the state with the power to participate in the violent and coercive displacement of indigenous people from their homes, families, and villages, and to be able to profit from this endeavor.

Despite the efforts that trade supporters made to frame their interests in the allegedly race-blind rhetoric of humanitarianism, the racializing implications of their position are evident. They are palpable not only in the requests that Yucatec inhabitants made to the governor to reinstate the trade but, perhaps more tellingly, in state authorities' own supportive discourses of it.

Governor Miguel Barbachano, who in 1849 wrote an extensive apologia for his position on the trade, seemed appalled by federal government officials' expectation that he should have respected the lives and freedoms of those he perceived to be "barbarians" as much as he respected the lives and freedoms of Yucatán's white constituents. Barbachano believed the exact inverse: in his view, the state and its links to whiteness should be preserved at all costs: "Is it by chance that those barbaric killers who are at odds with all principles of civilization and Christianity are more worthy of consideration than the white race of the state against which they wage a crude war?"[52] For Barbachano, anything short of supporting the deportation of indigenous rebels meant favoring the lives of "those barbaric killers" over the lives of Yucatán's white constituents. His assumptions thus made explicit his administration's commitment to protecting the historical edifice of whiteness. Barbachano's apologia evinced that the alleged general defense of the state from the rebellion was in fact an investment in preserving and even expanding the interests, privileges, and property of Yucatán's criollo elites to the detriment of the state's indigenous inhabitants.

Certainly, discussions of the (il)legitimacy of using the trade to contain the Caste War further illustrate how the premise that the "white race of the state" should be protected at all costs implied that whiteness was associated with notions of access and property.[53] An anonymous article printed in 1860 in Mérida and signed by "Los amantes de la felicidad yucateca" illustrates this. The article was a retort to an anti-trade pamphlet written by Joaquín Villalobos in Veracruz who had visited Yucatán under President Juárez's command and acquired sensitive information about the involvement of the then governor of Yucatán, Agustín Acereto, in the trade of indigenous people with Cuba.[54] "Los amantes de la felicidad yucateca" aimed to defend the governor from defamation. The group also laid out the legal epistemologies that trade supporters would use to advocate for their interests. The article showcases one of the most poignant examples of how in the context of the Caste War whiteness was imagined as a quality that allowed unobstructed access to and ownership of certain tangible and intangible "goods":

> What remedy should one seek in such a painful conflict? The right to self-preservation, sacred and necessary, justifies all means to secure it. It is this same right that allows a State or the representative of a Nation to use the necessary force to move the enemy toward the end of guaranteeing its future security and repairing its grievance or demanding a just compensation. This war is legitimate, as is the one we have sustained in defense of religion, humanity and civilization for fourteen years to date, even if in obtaining these precious goods it is necessary to kill anyone who opposes.[55]

Like Barbachano's apologia, the passage makes the defense of Yucatán's racial state coextensive with the defense of religion, humanity, and civilization writ large. The most salient aspect of this racializing metonymic gesture is that its authors defined these values as "precious goods" and thus framed them as intangible possessions. Whereas in some ways the authors wanted to present "religion," "humanity," and "civilization" as abstract universal principles, the text also betrays its underlying racialized presumptions where such "precious goods" are thought to be accessible to only those threatened by the insurgency—in other words, and according to the logic of the article, to whites. In fact, the authors evinced how the value of these "goods" were shored up precisely through the dynamics of war when they stated that it would be legitimate to take the lives of others in order to defend them.

It was precisely this relation between whiteness, property, and sovereignty—sometimes implied, sometimes explicit, always pervasive—that enabled supporters of the trade to request that it be resanctioned, allowing for their open participation in deciding the fate of indigenous rebels. Both texts' rapid framing of the insurgency as a threat to both the state and whiteness was the basis upon which any strategy for suppressing the uprising could be presented as legitimate. These responses, the trade included, reaffirmed the long-standing patterns and practices that had made political power and whiteness deeply intertwined.

Supporters also linked their take on the trade as a humane form of punishment to the legacies of international law. The article signed by "Los amantes de la felicidad yucateca" is also helpful in analyzing how trade supporters used this common legal knowledge to discursively construct Maya rebels as existing outside the boundaries of national law and citizenship. Much of this framework depended upon Emmerich de Vattel's influential work *Le droit des gens, ou Principes de la loi naturelle, appliqués à la conduite et aux affaires des nations et des souverains* (1758). The article's authors argued, based on the Swiss philosopher's well-known theories, that indigenous rebels had taken their uprising so far that they had created a battlefield, on which two sovereignties were now at odds. This situation, wrote the authors, called for the application of the code of war between two nations: the rebels were no longer to be viewed or treated as brothers, as citizens under the same jurisdiction, but as external enemies and prisoners of war: "'There are two bodies,' says Vattel, 'that seek to be absolutely independent and have no common judge. They resolve their quarrel through arms, as two different nations would do. The obligation to observe, in their mutual dealings, the common laws of war is thus absolute, indispensable for both parties, and the same natural law is imposed on all nations from State to State.' This, regrettably, is our situation with respect to the uprising of the barbaric Indians."[56] In what would become typical trade supporter rhetoric, the article praised Acereto's government for the "philanthropic gesture" of not enforcing his authority as severely as he might have, instead "simply requesting" that indigenous prisoners leave the country for a decade. By framing the insurgency in terms of international law, its supporters sidestepped concerns about the unconstitutionality of the trade. Under the code of war between two nations, divesting "rebels" of their rights as citizens, treating them instead as "prisoners," smoothed out the potential legal contradictions of their actions. As trade supporters saw it, "barbaric Indians" were in absolute excess of the nation and the state's body politic. Even their labor could not be directly absorbed by the state. Instead, it had to be expelled and sold to Cuba.

DEMARCATING GUILT AND INNOCENCE: PACIFIED VERSUS REBEL INDIANS

The appeal to international law developed by "Los amantes de la felicidad yucateca" was implicitly premised on a crucial distinction: the dichotomy between "civilized" and "barbaric," "rebel" and "pacified" indigenous groups, which pervaded contemporary journalism and official documentation on the Caste War in the peninsula. As has already been shown, trade supporters' rhetoric did not assert that the entire indigenous population of the peninsula was eligible for deportation, only those they categorized as "rebels," "barbarians," or "savages."

During the early years of the struggle, the army categorized Maya groups as either "pacified" or "rebel" Indians. The opposition stemmed from multiple efforts to separate indigenous groups who had surrendered or never joined the insurgency from those who were actively involved in the uprising. The army's indigenous captives were grouped in more specific categories: *prisioneros* (those who had been captured with arms), *presentados* (those who had surrendered their arms), and *recogidos* (those who had been rescued from enemy lines).[57]

This distinction between "rebel" and "pacified" groups aimed to sow divisions among the region's villages and towns, to create internal factions to weaken the insurgency and make it easier to control. Indeed, many government and army-backed policies implemented in the early years of the uprising sought to spatially fix and police this distinction: according to the operating narrative, rebel groups were relegated to the southeastern portion of the peninsula, while its west side was relatively conflict free.[58]

Legal decrees controlling the mobility, circulation, and contact between populations of the region were instated as soon as the uprising began. For example, the constitutional right to travel freely from one part of the state to another was immediately suspended; local government and military groups demanded that people use passports to circulate through the peninsula. These stipulations, which were introduced at various points during the years of struggle, reproduced and safeguarded racial distinctions. They mainly targeted the mobility of Indian bodies, for men and women classified as indigenous were required to carry their documents with them at all times.[59] The papers supplied by the authorities contained information on the ethnicity and home locality of each individual, as well as their occupation. As illustrated in the 1853 iteration of the decree, the use of passports also had a military objective: keeping the army's ranks full. As a precondition for receiving the document that would allow people to move across the peninsula, they had to provide confirmation of having completed service in the army or of having been conscripted to the National Guard.[60]

Of course, the boundaries these measures intended to police were porous and volatile. The movement across towns and villages of the peninsula and the connections among people from different areas remained fluid and alive. Indeed, the constant reiteration of various decrees intended to control people's mobility indicates how difficult it was for authorities to patrol these boundaries, and to instate a legible and static distinction between the "peaceful" and the "rebellious."

The network of alliances the insurgents built was vast and mobile. Their communities were supported by many "spies" who were willing to infiltrate regions controlled by the government and army, carrying back with them relevant information. Likewise, when villages were plundered—a strategy that insurgents used to amass resources they then sold or bartered to Belizean settlers in order to fund the rebellion—it was not uncommon for inhabitants of the plundered villages to become allies and spontaneously join the revolt.[61]

But although the murkiness of the two categories of "pacified" and "rebel" in some ways favored the insurgents, in others the distinction supported Caste War–era governmentality. The proliferating discourses that were used during the Caste War to distinguish between the civilized and the barbaric, the pacified and the rebel, can be understood as repurposing categorizations of the "faithful/unfaithful Indian" dichotomy that had been, at different conjunctures, crucial to colonial governmentality. María Josefina Saldaña-Portillo argues that the raison d'être of Spanish colonialism was precisely to sustain the ambivalence and undecidability of this duple.[62] She explains that in the colonial version of the faithful/unfaithful Indian dichotomy, the value lay not so much in deciding effectively which *Indians* belonged to which side but rather in always sustaining the potentiality of both types. In other words, it was crucial for the colonial project to maintain the ambivalence between the two sides of the distinction, sustaining the simultaneous and persistent potential of Indians being both faithful and unfaithful, pacified and rebellious: "Rather than any Indians being either docile converts or rebellious infidels, it was most important that they always be potentially both. Thus they were never discretely designated points in the landscape, but rather they are constantly shifting along the dual axis of fidelity and infidelity. For the duration of Spanish colonialism, as long as Indians are so ambivalently positioned—not either/or but both/and—the raison d'être of the Spanish colonial project continued to exist."[63] In a similar way, the volatility of Caste War–era distinctions between pacified and rebellious groups always held open the possibility of the potential rebelliousness— and thus the potential *criminality*—of the region's indigenous populations. This potential criminality underpinned and made possible the Yucatán-Cuba trade. Yucatec government officials, soldiers, landowners, and entrepreneurs made a conveniently liberal use of the term "rebel," criminalizing and extending it to many who were not actually involved in the uprising and deporting them to Cuba. I do not intend here to reinstate a clear line of innocence and guilt between the "pacified" and the "rebel." Instead, I aim to capture how this spurious dichotomy was overlaid as part of an expanding carceral order, which was (and still is) racialized, one that increasingly depended upon the disposability of those who were socially and legally categorized as "criminals."[64]

"Los amantes de la felicidad yucateca" engaged precisely in this kind of binary thinking. According to the authors, the punishments meted out to the rebels (e.g., the trade in forced indenture, the death penalty, or any other penalty, including incarceration, corporeal punishment, or mutilation) were no violations of civil or constitutional rights, for the rights of "humanity" and "civil freedom" were suspended in the case of people who had put themselves outside of that order by their own criminal actions. These liberal "rights" belonged only to those citizens capable of retaining these "gifts" (*don*); "criminals" (in this case indigenous rebels) were divested of them by their own actions. In fact, the authors of the article emphasized that the fundamental operation of liberal constitutions was to establish and safeguard the distinction between those who were "virtuous" and those who were "evil" individuals.[65] Of course, this position obliterated any potential structural analysis of the causes of the rebellion. Furthermore, the distinction encoded the deployment of racialized punitive practices in the moral language of liberal individualism.

THE IMAGINED REFORMATIVE POTENTIAL OF PENAL LABOR

To avoid associations with the mostly abolished Atlantic slave trade while disguising the profit motive that drove them, supporters of Maya indenture also fused the languages of criminality and labor, joining the growing global chorus about the promise of penal colonies and the reforming potential of labor in "criminal" settings.

In making this argument, I follow Clare Anderson, who studies indentured Indian labor in relation to the emergence of new ideas and practices of migration and criminality. Anderson's intuition that indentured migration should be analyzed in the context of disciplinary innovations in incarceration and confinement connects the trade with modes of biopolitical governmentality that placed life itself as the object of power. "Los amantes de la felicidad yucateca" cite Benjamin Constant's *Principes de politiques applicables à tous les gouvernments representatifs* (1815), linking the liberal thinker's take on the conditions of prisoners sent to Botany Bay with the reformative potential of penal colonies: "Benjamin Constant, from whose fountain our illustrious Mexican general had surely also drunk, had written for his politics course: . . . 'Experience has confirmed what we have just said, as we have seen that the men deported to Botany Bay for criminal acts have begun their social life anew; no longer believing themselves to be at war with society, they have become peaceable and even commendable members of it.'"[66] The parallels between the Botany Bay penal colony and the Yucatán-Cuba trade of Maya prisoners seemed so transparent and obvious to the authors that they did not dwell much on making the analogy more explicit. The passage does illustrate, however, that by placing their business in the purview of contemporary global experiments with penal labor, trade supporters legitimized their interests. They borrowed discourses about the reformative potential of penal labor and blended them with philanthropic humanist rhetoric: uprooting "criminals" from their social context meant giving them the "gift" of a blank slate, the possibility to "forget" and "reform" in order to become "peaceable" and "commendable" members of society. These discourses whitewashed the clandestine trade connecting Yucatán and Cuba as it entered the global practices of penal forced migration.

Uprooting "rebels" from their lands not only served to disperse and fragment the insurgent communities but also commandeered newly vacant land for the growing henequen economy and other agricultural enterprises in the area. It also promised to produce useful "worker-citizens" who, disciplined by the harsh working conditions of indenture, could return to Mexico and join a racialized workforce on their now-usurped lands.[67]

These fantasies about the reformative potential of coerced labor appeared in literary fiction of the period.[68] The Caste War accompanied a print boom in the peninsula, and numerous newspapers and serial novels were published in hopes of shaping ideas about the conflict.[69] One of these ideological novels was *Los misterios de Chan Santa Cruz*, penned in 1864 by the conservative journalist, political leader, and twice-governor of Yucatán Pantaleón Barrera.

The novel was published serially, presenting itself as the Yucatec iteration of the cosmopolitan literary trend that had reached its apex with Eugène Sué's *Les mystères de Paris* (1842–1843), which had been rapidly translated into several languages and had circulated profusely across the Atlantic.[70] While most iterations of this subgenre sought to depict in literary language the impact of industrialization on urban spaces, Barrera refigured the trend to address the social and economic transformations in the peninsula during the Caste War by juxtaposing Chan Santa Cruz (the capital of the rebel territories within the peninsula) with Paris, London, and Berlin.

Los misterios de Chan Santa Cruz offers perhaps the most acute literary passage condensing the connection between the Yucatán-Cuba trade and contemporary fantasies of penal labor's reformative power. Barrera had supported the trade, and through his novel he sought not only to present an apology for his position but also to engage in a literary pedagogy that could shape readers' responses to and views on the trade.

The novel attempts to describe the everyday life of the rebel community that was founded in 1850 on the eastern side of the peninsula and dubbed Chan Santa Cruz (today Felipe Carrillo Puerto). Its plot is mostly dedicated to the complicated life of Pastora Naré, a fictitious anagram for Pastora Rean, a young white woman who had been captured by rebels from the town of Tunkás and who married the Cruzo'ob leader Cresencio Poot in 1874.[71] The novel, which depicts everything from political conspiracies to intricate love affairs, documents the epistolary circuit that shaped many of the negotiations between the rebels and the Mexican and Yucatec governments, offering a critique of the alliances between British merchants in Belize and the insurgent communities.

Mentions of the clandestine trade of indentured labor are woven into the plot through an internal narrative involving a fictionalized letter sent to Chan Santa Cruz by Fernando Ek, a minor character in the novel. In the story, Ek is a former indigenous rebel turned small property owner who shipped his personal correspondence from Cuba to Mexico via an English merchant who occasionally visited the community of Chan Santa Cruz. The merchant circulates the correspondence through his acquaintance, Leandro Santos, a leader of the rebel groups, a good friend of Ek, and a central character in the novel. Santos narrates, "[The merchant] brought me the first news of my friend Fernando in 1861, and he has done so successively over the past three years, as he has a correspondent in Havana due to that business.... But last September he conveyed the letter to me that you shall now see and which will serve us better today than ever before."[72]

The letter's recipient, the reader soon discovers, is Casiana, a close acquaintance of Pastora Naré's. Unlike her white captive friend, Casiana is of indigenous descent, and Fernando Ek, the writer of the letter, is none other than Casiana's father. He had participated in the uprising and, according to the novel, had been captured by the army in 1855. He was sent to Cuba, where he remained for the rest of his life. After her mother's death, Casiana had been left in the care of Ek's closest friend, Leandro Santos; along with her grandfather, he had been entrusted with Casiana's education. Growing up in Chan Santa Cruz, Casiana became Pastora Naré's confidant and companion. In the novel, her father's letter reaches her at a crucial moment, right after the community leaders have discovered Casiana's and her husband's participation in a conspiracy to overthrow them. Casiana's husband is murdered while transporting conspiracy-related correspondence from Chan Santa Cruz to Bacalar. The letter, sent by her father, opens up the possibility that Casiana might escape from Chan Santa Cruz to Cuba, where she could find safe haven and reunite with her father. After the letter reaches Santos, the characters in the scene read Fernando's letter aloud, ensuring that the readers also hear the letter in its entirety, including the "happy ending" of Ek, who is redeemed by his forced labor.

The letter was probably included in the novel as an apology for indenture and Barrera's own involvement in it. By including this missive, Barrera appropriated the voice of an indigenous man who had been sold to Cuba. This fictitious testimony, told in first-person narration, aims to effectively convince readers that despite its hardships, the trade had positive outcomes. Here, Ek, the fictitious survivor of indenture, offers arguments in favor of his experience. The letter's key aspect—its erasure of indigeneity and its replacement with white-coded Spanish identity—is articulated in the letter's opening paragraph, where Fernando announces to the reader that he has changed his surname: it is no longer the Mayan Ek, but now the Spanish Estrella (star).

> My dear Leandro: in Havana, on my return from Sagua la Grande, I met Mr. **, who gave me news of you all. He said that my darling Casianita is radiant as a star, and this is why I have decided to give her this surname. You must know, laugh as you may, that I am no longer called Fernando Ek but rather Fernando Estrella. The owner of a small cigar factory in the town of Bejucal cannot be called Ek but rather Estrella.[73]

Ek's transition from a Maya to a Spanish surname is a literary gesture that condenses the political and economic implications of the indenture trade: the erasure of the Maya language in Fernando Estrella's name resonates with material efforts to eliminate indigenous presence in the peninsula. In the novel, Barrera cites parallels between Ek's surname shift and the name change of Juan Sotillo, the main character in the Spanish playwright Juan Martínez Villergas's dramatic trilogy *Sotillo, Soto, Soto Mayor* (1845). Sotillo changes his name as he climbs the social ladder. By comparing the two, Barrera subsumes Ek's experience in Cuba into the workings of the ideology of liberalism, for it is as Ek transitions through the island's different economic institutions—the sugar plantation, the tobacco plantation, and the small factory—that he changes his subjective position from indigenous rebel to small property owner who now distances himself from his indigeneity:

> When I was a worker at one of the sugar factories owned by the Bemba party on this island, I could continue being Ek; when I wandered these fields, learning how to farm tobacco, I was still called Ek; but now that I represent five thousand pesos in capital and own a cigar factory in direct contact with the esteemed "respectable class," and as I have a beautiful daughter worthy of a better fate, how can I resign myself to being Ek in the Mayan tongue when I can be Ek in Spanish?[74]

This passage places these two subject positions—small property owner and indigenous person—as incommensurable, as mutually exclusive. Both the novel and supporters of the trade seem to see the displacement and elimination of the latter as the precondition to becoming the former. *Ek* had to become *Estrella*, had to crave becoming Estrella, before he could become the honest owner of a small cigar factory. Through Ek, Barrera thus gives voice to the normative desire of the liberal subject: to be a "free," self-made person entering into the world of private property. His novel presents indenture as a central step to producing assimilated, *whitened*, subjects out of indigenous rebels. While Barrera's fantasy of indenture was linked to the desire to deracialize criminalized indigenous groups, the very core of the trade depended on reinscribing and reproducing racial difference; the novel operated on the basis of an experience of indenture that targeted only "Maya rebels" and that was narrativized to give those thrown into it an accelerated path toward becoming "civilized."

CONCLUSION: AGAINST THE TRADE, NATION-BOUND SYSTEMS OF INDENTURED LABOR

Around the peak of the trade in indigenous people with Cuba, between 1858 and 1860, debates about it intensified. Politicians who opposed the trade portrayed it as an absolute departure from the moral principles upheld by a "civilized" country, as a form of slavery. This position bore upon Mexico's standing on the international stage: at a time when slavery still existed in the United States, Latin American countries that challenged it were situating themselves at the vanguard of modernity and emphasizing their commitment to humanitarianism and democracy.[75] Many of those who opposed the trade surrounded Benito Juárez and would become part of his presidential administration after his 1858 election, including Francisco Zarco, Melchor Ocampo, and General Juan Suárez y Navarro. These men, and others who opposed the trade, sought to counter any association between Mexico and slavery, now viewed as a barbaric institution. These men were invested in maintaining Mexico's position on the international stage as a modern, civilized country. They argued against using the trade of indentured labor as a means of pacification, insisting that the country would not support the selling of its own "brothers" and citizens; instead, they called for internal trials and judicial punishment for rebels.

For example, the renowned liberal politician Melchor Ocampo characterized the trade as an inhuman endeavor in an 1859 letter addressed to the governor of Yucatán. Ocampo suggested that Mexico should request that the British navy patrol Mexican waters and enforce the "respect that humanity deserves."[76] Ocampo thus set the terms of the debate as being about philanthropy and humanitarianism while at the same time framing the trade as an issue of international import.

But detractors' concerns with the trade were indeed not only about "humanitarianism." Certainly economic, not only ethical, considerations were behind their condemnation of the trade. In the aftermath of the decline of the sugar plantation economy, which was largely prompted by the Caste War, the region was restarting after the depredations of the conflict, developing a rising henequen industry; vacant lands required more labor to make them productive. It is no coincidence that the federal ban on the indentured labor trade was proclaimed during this period.[77]

An anti-trade article published in *El Constitucional* in 1860 exposes the economic and nationalistic motivations behind the curtailment of the Yucatán-Cuba indentured labor trade: "This trade alone is more harmful and destructive to our society than the Caste War itself and all our civil disputes. . . . It leaves not only agriculture and industry without workers, but also our homeland without soldiers."[78] The trade was not simply "inhumane" in itself; it also depleted the nation of its "workers" and "soldiers." It is important to acknowledge, then, that the anti-trade stance was not necessarily just a principled position against slavery and other forms of unfreedom; it was also a justification for new ways to exert control over racialized labor within the boundaries of the nation.

The dispute that pitted supporters and detractors of the trade against each other was thus rooted in a deeper issue: whether racialization techniques should be covert or overt, state-sanctioned or extralegal. Ultimately, this was a dispute over whether the racializing mechanisms that configured the nation's body politic should be public and explicit or whether they should be internally (and stealthily) managed and administered.

Supporters of the trade saw their endeavors as legitimate, framing indigenous "rebels" as *exterior* to the nation and therefore as not having the same rights as other, law-abiding citizens. In contrast, detractors coded the response to the rebellion, and to the racialized system of coercive labor that crystallized around it, as *internal* to the nation, placing rebels within the nation's juridical framework.

After 1861, the Yucatán-Cuba trade of indentured labor began to wane, replaced by a boom in racialized forced labor within Mexico itself. An oft-dismissed episode in history, the indentured labor trade between Yucatán and Cuba was nonetheless a hotly debated issue of its time. At its center were not only the contradictory responses of governing elites but also the resistant voices of the indentured. In demanding their freedom, they made a statement about their place within the polity, questioning its boundaries and the social categories that constituted it. The murky and unstable terminology that accompanied the diplomatic discussions around the Yucatán-Cuba trade may seem to impede access to historical information about it, but we might instead read this instability as marking the deep contradictions that traversed the rise of liberalism in Mexico during the second half of the nineteenth century. By placing this case of human trafficking within the broader context of indentured migration taking place internationally before, during, and after the ban on the Atlantic slave trade, we can see it not as a marginal event in the histories of the Atlantic world but rather as a crystallization of major adjustments and shifts taking place within political modernity.[79]

{ SIX }

The Shapes of a Desert
THE RACIAL CARTOGRAPHIES
OF THE CASTE WAR

In 1856, Antonio García Cubas, a renowned geographer, writer, and member of the Mexican Society for Geography and Statistics (Sociedad Mexicana de Geografía y Estadística; SMGE), published what would become the most widely circulated map of the Mexican republic.[1] Created amid intense political uncertainty from all sides—the US invasion (1846–1848), the loss of vast tracts of land in the north, and the wave of popular rebellions surging up from Yucatán all the way to the Sierra Gorda—García Cubas's map had unprecedented political significance. It depicted the latest changes in the country's territorial limits and was perceived as an important piece in achieving a much-desired national cohesion.[2] Indeed, governing elites from both the conservative and liberal parties agreed that symbolically demarcating the boundaries of the nation would play a crucial role in fostering the political stability the country lacked on the ground (see fig. 6.1).[3]

García Cubas published two versions of his *Carta General*. The first version, printed in 1856, was the most broadly consulted and distributed map of the country for at least two decades; the second, released in 1858, added more detail to the first and was printed in the form of an atlas that included pages for each of the individual states that had been incorporated into the Mexican Republic. The surface of the nation traced by the acclaimed geographer in 1858 already included the state of Yucatán. The peninsula had seceded several times but in 1848 was definitively annexed to the federal republic after criollo leaders tried (and failed) to incorporate Yucatán under US jurisdiction as the Caste War broke out. Governing Yucatec elites, who were desperate for military support to suppress the indigenous rebellion, reluctantly accepted the reintegration of Yucatán into the Mexican republic. Upon examining the traces that chart the

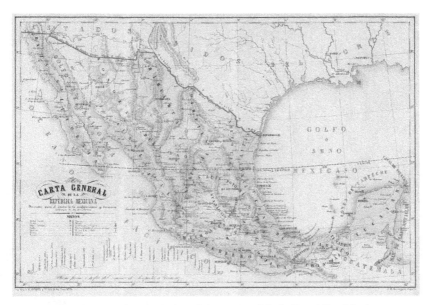

FIGURE 6.1. *Antonio García Cubas,* Carta general de la República Mexicana (1858). *David Rumsey Map Collection, www.davidrumsey.com.*

Yucatán Peninsula on García Cubas's map, the viewer might appreciate how the region is gradually divided into two uneven zones, apparently differentiated on the basis of how densely populated and developed they were. The towns and villages of the western side are carefully outlined, charted, and named. The eastern portion, instead, is figured as a nearly empty zone of barren lands. It is a blank space that stands in contrast to the chartings of surrounding towns and rivers. Such tracings are remarkable especially when considering that toward the east, rebel communities held a semiautonomous territory that dynamically intersected with the lands occupied by English settlers in Belize and with other local geographies, including sites disputed and controlled by the state forces of Yucatán. Yet the map draws the peninsula's eastern region not as a site of friction, exchanges, and conflicts among numerous interests, but simply as an empty tract of land (see fig. 6.2). García Cubas's depiction of Yucatán's eastern region thus deploys a cartographic knowledge that desocializes the territories it charts.[4] The map effectively erases the fluidity and dynamism of the interactions that took place among rebels, settlers, soldiers, foreign travelers, and government officials, many of them documented in the Caste War archives.

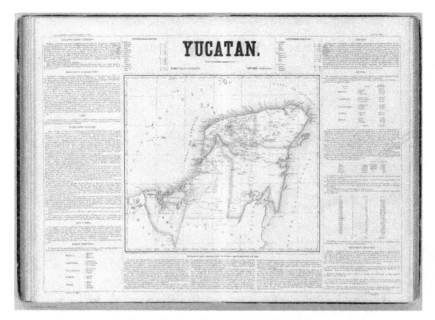

FIGURE 6.2. *Antonio García Cubas,* Yucatán *(1857). David Rumsey Map Collection, www.davidrumsey.com.*

One might see in García Cubas's representation of this region as barren echoes of what has been a persistent strategy in processes of land appropriation and dispossession: the "invention" of certain spaces as terra nullius, so essential to the paradigmatic enclosure of communal lands in England and to fueling colonization in imperial regimes across the globe.[5] Indeed, it is well known that figuring spaces as vacant has allowed settlers to legitimate their territorial interventions with arguments about how the occupation of said lands will lead to their betterment and "improve their usage."[6] Nevertheless, to understand the actual effectiveness of this strategy, a case-by-case approach that works in tandem with the transhistorical awareness of its recurrence seems imperative. One must look not only at the persistent reiteration of the terra nullius trope throughout history but also to the particular ways in which concrete territories have been constructed as barren. Certainly, not all configurations of land as "void" are equivalent, and attempts to grasp the historical traction of this trope must therefore explore its variations, its contextual specificities, and the diversity of its material expressions.[7]

In this chapter I examine how at the core of the *Guerra social Maya*, or the Caste War, lay disputes over different modes of producing and relating to space. I show that cartography played an important role in the local and national government's efforts to regain state control over the area. I study how both textual and visual mappings of the region engendered particular racial geographies that aimed to demarcate and regulate access to and use of land.[8] I ultimately argue that the restructuring of land and labor that accompanied and followed the Caste War occurred not only via direct disputes over *the ground* itself but also through contrasting and overlapping strategies for producing, envisioning, and representing space.[9]

CARTOGRAPHIES OF THE VOID

A first interpretation of the void that shapes García Cubas's mapping of the eastern side of the Yucatán Peninsula might focus on how this particular depiction of the area was connected to the geographer's larger project of producing the national space as ready for capitalist modernization. According to Raymond B. Craib, García Cubas's minor adjustments to the second version of his map are indicators of a sprouting national sensibility. This is conveyed by how the geographer tied his production of the national space (geography) to a narrative about its temporality (history): the second version of the *Carta General* included reflections on past events that García Cubas framed as part of the single shared history of the cohesive political space called the "Mexican Republic." He illustrated these historical events with colorful vignettes that sat in the margins of his maps, creating a visual grammar for the emerging nation (see fig. 6.3).[10]

But García Cubas's cartographies were also determined by contemporary economic projections. The maps he created were part of a broader effort to shape Mexico's geography—both within and beyond the country—as one of abundant natural resources, ready to be exploited in the name of progress and development, calling for the intervention of foreign investors.[11] That a national sensibility coalesced alongside the production of the country's landscapes as raw material for economic development is telling of how the nation-state would become the main political technology managing foreign investment and spearheading capitalist accumulation throughout the nineteenth century.

According to García Cubas, Mexico's deficit in the exploitation of and access to its natural resources was heavily determined by the coun-

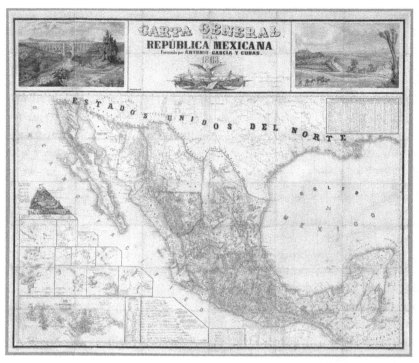

FIGURE 6.3. *Antonio García Cubas*, Carta general de la República Mexicana (1863). *David Rumsey Map Collection, www.davidrumsey.com.*

try's weak cartographic tradition. In his view, to map the space of the nation was to open its territories to economic expansion and development: as he says in the first lines of his *Atlas geográfico estadístico e histórico de la República Mexicana* (1858), "The primary objective of this atlas is that its readers may learn about this beautiful country, so rich in natural productions. The lack of maps and geographical information has posed an obstacle to the execution of great projects."[12]

Under this light, the void in García Cubas's map might be seen as having a certain anticipatory quality to it, projecting multiple efforts to incorporate the Yucatán's eastern region into the national economy. But there is another possible reading of this void, one rooted in the context of the Caste War and the concrete disputes and crises over land and labor that accompanied it.[13] The uprising engendered massive waves of migration across the spectrums of race and class. Refugees from all backgrounds fled to Tabasco, Campeche, Cuba, the United States, the Guatemalan Petén, and emerging refugee towns in Belize.[14] The Caste War displaced hundreds of thousands of people, and the towns and villages they had once inhabited were left abandoned. The southeastern side of the peninsula, once a zone of fertile and active sugar plantations, remained uncultivated for years.[15] The conflict effectively interrupted the area's prosperous future in the sugar industry.

Alongside those who fled the violence, fugitivity was a practice of resistance during the years of the rebellion. It was used in tandem with more acknowledged insurgent tactics such as raids, sweeps, and even a few direct confrontations and armed battles.[16] In the early years of the struggle, hundreds of workers, from domestic servants to *luneros*, abandoned their posts. Local hacendados' difficulty trying to retain laborers affected the entire peninsula: the closer a hacienda was to the eastern line that demarcated rebel territories, the more likely it was that peons would drop their tools and flee into the neighboring insurgent communities.[17]

Fugitivity also impacted the army. The issue of desertion plagued the minds and communiqués of highly ranked military commanders. Starvation conditions, inclement weather, uncontrollable epidemics, low wages, and continuous attacks by enemy groups all made being a soldier at this time in the peninsula quite undesirable, and many of the army's combatants fled on a regular basis.[18] Even in 1865, after the most intense episodes of the conflict had passed, chief commanders advocated for better incentives and general improvements to working conditions, hoping to retain the few soldiers who were willing to serve from the frontier lines of the peninsula, where they now fought for the imperial army of Maximilian of Habsburg.[19]

The blank space on García Cubas's map can therefore also be read as a concrete visualization of the fact that during the Caste War fugitivity presented an active and deep challenge to capital accumulation. This can be further appreciated in another map, published in 1885, drafted by the renowned Mexican geographer. This map, which was created to collect and visually organize information about Mexico's internal and external commercial routes, once again rendered the peninsula's eastern portion as a vacant and static space, a zone that did not partake in the nation's routes of commerce and economic productivity. None of the commercial routes traced on the map's surface pass through the eastern region. The blank space that shapes this zone documents not only the fugitivity of the population in the region but the fugitivity of the area itself, its effective withdrawal from the circuits of trade and accumulation propelled by the nation.

The region contrasts with others drafted in the map in that there

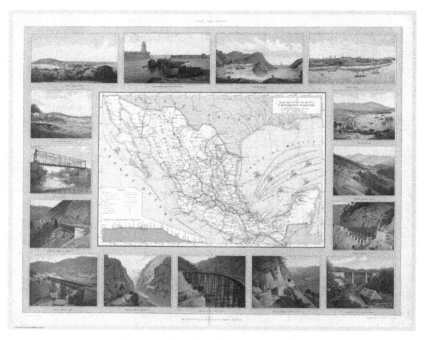

FIGURE 6.4. *Antonio García Cubas,* Vías de comunicación y movimiento marítimo *(1885). David Rumsey Map Collection, www.davidrumsey.com.*

are no traces of the commercial exchanges that connected this area of the peninsula to the world.[20] And there were connections; communities in the eastern region were not isolated. Although many rebel groups had strategically withdrawn from the national economy, they still had arrangements with their English neighbors and held some control over how the lands and forests they inhabited were inserted into global networks of exportation. Some communities tried to negotiate an incorporation to the British Crown; others maintained commercial liaisons with English settlers in British Honduras. Although these trade relations were not without tension, they yielded gunpowder, weapons, and other goods that were exchanged for logging access to specific areas of the jungle-forests that housed globally demanded woods such as mahogany and blackwood (see fig. 6.4).[21]

García Cubas's cartographic work was not based on empirical research and exploration, but on historical documents. The geographer drew up most of his maps from the comfort of his office in Mexico City.[22] Though he insisted that the maps he charted were based on the most current information available at the time, García Cubas's map of the Yucatán Peninsula seems to have omitted contemporary territorial changes. Instead, it charted the region by repeating a number of historical patterns that can be appreciated by looking at the peninsula's cartographic archives.[23]

Political instability was often accompanied by cartographic anxiety. In the late 1840s, as the first stages of the Caste War unraveled, the state of Yucatán joined forces with the SMGE to create a map of the state. Supported by local engineers and landowners, members of the geographical society collected the necessary data to produce the first official postcolonial map of the peninsula.[24] The map was created at the request of private interests and was drafted by the engineer Santiago Nigra. It was first published in New Orleans, then reprinted in scale for distribution in Mexico (see fig. 6.5). Nigra's map served as the primary source behind national mappings of Yucatán in the nineteenth century, for it was easily accessible: an article in *El Fénix* from November 15, 1848, announced that colored copies of the map were available for sale to the public at a price of eight *reales*.[25] The map was so well disseminated that it was probably the main source behind Antonio García Cubas's chart-

FIGURE 6.5. Plano de Yucatán (1848). *Bibliothèque nationale de France.*

ing of the peninsula in the 1858 *Atlas geográfico estadístico* and beyond.[26] Both cartographies rendered nearly identical depictions of Yucatán; both also charted the eastern region of the state as completely barren.

But the history of this void stretches further back in time. Documents from the colonial period often also figured the eastern side of Yucatán as an "unpeopled" area.[27] While less densely populated than in the times of Nigra and García Cubas, during the colonial period the east was not completely uninhabited: its lands were home to Maya communities that sought to remain as distant as possible from the encroaching colonial order. The emptiness in García Cubas's map thus apprehended multiple historical temporalities of fugitivity in the region, not just the most recent one related to the Caste War. His map captured something about the political landscapes of its time while also reproducing the colonial legacies that charted the eastern region as empty. García Cubas's figuration of Yucatán echoed past traces of the region, but it was also proleptic, promoting a vision of futurity in which these *unpopulated* lands that were already cartographically drafted within the boundaries of the nation would also be incorporated into the expanding economy of the criollo nation-state project.

THE RUIN AND THE DESERT:
ON THE ARRESTED TEMPORALITIES OF REBELLION

In 1865, Severo del Castillo arrived in the Yucatán Peninsula as general commander superior of the first territorial division, part of Maximilian's imperial forces. As he learned more about the actual impacts of the Caste War in the area, del Castillo changed the initial plan he had been sent there to implement—to lead an offensive attack against rebel groups. Once on the ground, the commander saw that reinforcing frontier lines and increasing the capacity of militias stationed in Tekax, Peto, and Valladolid to contain raids from rebel groups was both a higher priority and more cost effective.[28]

As del Castillo saw it, his army was charged with the task of reactivating Yucatán's arrested economy and agriculture, and he therefore commanded his military forces to create the necessary conditions for abandoned towns to be repopulated. His military forces expected the collaboration of political authorities and local hacendados, who were asked to supply laborers for *fagina* (the local term for uncompensated municipal work, here racialized by specifically recruiting Maya peasants).[29] These

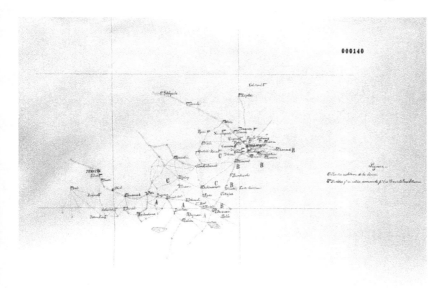

FIGURE 6.6. Mapa militar de pueblos en la Zona Rebelde Península de Yucatán (1865). Archivo Histórico de la Secretaría de la Defensa Nacional, Military Operations, file XI/481.4/9987.

uncompensated *fagina* workers were assigned major public projects such as reconstructing destroyed buildings and rehabilitating roads.[30]

To put del Castillo's plan into effect, he needed to chart and organize the peninsula's territory, for the Caste War had left behind it an uneven and confusing space punctuated by dead or dying towns, ranchos, and haciendas. Del Castillo created a grid that organized the state's villages and towns according to their current productivity and livelihood. The commander compiled a list of all the "depopulated" towns and estates within the disconnected municipalities of Tekax, Peto, and Valladolid. The list of abandoned towns, which were marked with a "D" for *despoblado*, was several pages long. Although *despoblados* were scattered throughout the state, the villages in the southeast, closest to rebel lands, were the most affected. Between Peto and Tihosuco, del Castillo insisted, lay only a desert. Town after town, everything had been abandoned, leaving only a chain of ruined villages covered with thick growing vegetation to evidence more fortunate times (see figs. 6.6 and 6.7).[31]

Del Castillo's road rehabilitation project was in line with the rising hegemony of liberal capitalism, which was conceived as depending upon the unrestricted flow of goods. Indeed, his military vision was only an ex-

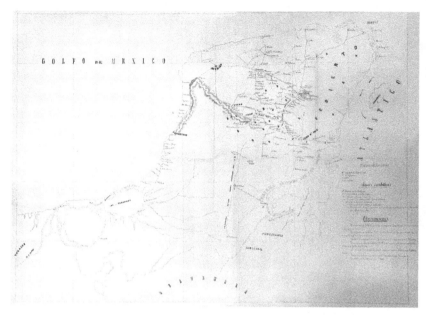

FIGURE 6.7. Mapa militar de la Península de Yucatán *(approx. 1865)*. Archivo Histórico de la Secretaría de la Defensa Nacional, Military Operations, file XI/481.4/9987.

pression of a broader historical conjuncture where the main function of the modern state was to establish a *regime of movement*.[32] As del Castillo saw it, the uprising had stopped time in the Yucatán, and his army's job was to bring the region back into modernity. Peeling away the overgrown jungle covering the ranches and haciendas that had once been the most opulent and productive of the state, the *fagina* workers, overseen by the army, worked to knit together the fragmented social geography of the peninsula, creating the conditions that would allow it to rejoin the flows of modern capitalism, readying it for development and industry.[33]

Del Castillo's interest in the geography of the eastern Yucatán persisted even after his military service had ended. When he was imprisoned in San Juan de Ulúa as a traitor to Benito Juárez's liberal government, the commander translated his military experience into literary discourse. Published in 1869, his novel *Cecilio Chi* is an interesting textual companion to García Cubas's cartographic voids. In this text, informed by del Castillo's firsthand experience as leader of the military campaigns in the peninsula, *ruin* and the *desert* are the two main spatial categories that shape the eastern region of Yucatán.[34]

In broad strokes, the novel narrates in parallel the development of the armed conflict and a love story. In the latter, the daughter of the rebel leader, who is descended from Maya nobility, renounces her indigenous lineage to marry a Yucatec soldier, a hero of the counterinsurgent campaign. On the one hand, the novel can be read within the parameters of what Doris Sommer has called a "foundational fiction": the story of the nation and the indigenous insurgencies that interrupt its consolidation is resolved in the allegorical romance between the Maya princess and the heroic criollo soldier. However, and as was common in the historical fiction of the epoch, the novel's fictionality is periodically interrupted by footnotes that assert the facticity of the episodes it narrates.

For the purposes of this chapter, I am interested in analyzing these moments in which "history" enters the scene, for I argue that these moments show the author's effort to grapple literarily with the effects of fugitivity in the peninsula's economy. In its translation of military policy to the novelistic register, *Cecilio Chi* fictionally represents the arrested temporality at the heart of Yucatán's racial state, thrust there by practices of fugitivity. While del Castillo's military correspondence recounts the region's concrete or material obstructions to production and circulation, the novel registers the temporal experience of *interruption* caused by the uprising:

> The scene presented to the heroic saviors of Yucatán was both sad and moving when they occupied, after a year, the towns that had been under the control of the savages; debris everywhere, ruins blackened by the devastating torches of the barbarians and still covered in bodies, with which they had obstructed even the wells of potable water, thus rendering the villages inhabitable; this was what remained of those beautiful populations where, mere months before, a calm and industrious neighborhood bustled as it advanced the commerce, agriculture, and civilization of the Yucatán.[35]

With its descriptions of stagnant water, piled up bodies, and burned buildings, the passage is more than a simple documentary record of Caste War devastation. It is a literary image that attempts to grapple with how fugitivity had interrupted processes of accumulation and economies of progress, and their consequences for the state.

In a sense, this passage (like del Castillo's military campaign) seeks to regain control over the peninsula's arrested sites, but it does so not by mapping a grid to track the effects of fugitivity but by creating a literary cartography that temporalizes the peninsula's devastated geography. In this literary cartography, abandoned towns and haciendas are the sites of disputation—attempts to recognize and record the outer limits of history. Whatever lay beyond these borders was nothing more than a primitive, uncivilized desert. By recovering the devastated towns from the vestiges of the desert, the counterrevolution sought to reinstate time, to reinsert the lost villages into the moving regime of progress and modernity.[36]

The novel thus emerges from the pulsating desire to reterritorialize (and thus reconquer) these fugitive spaces. It also documents a racial fear about the encroaching desert, for the passage is also an account of governing criollo elites' encounter with the fragility of their own ideas about "progress." The passage illustrates that "development"—here marked with terms such as "commerce," "civilization," and "agriculture"—was fragile and could be unexpectedly derailed or interrupted, as it had been by the Caste War. In the novel, "civilization," like "progress" and "development," did not equate with a steady, reliable arrival point. Civilization, which was linked to whiteness, appeared instead as a state of intense paranoid vulnerability, besieged by the constant threat of possibly collapsing into its undifferentiated opposite. The aesthetics of the *desert* and the *ruin* were tools to deal with this potential collapse. They presented an opposition to the void that fugitivity had created, ways of reterritorializing that absence. The ruin, the void, and the desert thus establish some order in the undifferentiated and confused spaces where time and progress were allegedly suspended.

Cecilio Chi discursively frames the government as victorious in two ways. It shows the Yucatec army regaining control over many of the once prosperous, now devastated towns and villages in the peninsula. The novel cements this victory by bracketing the areas that could not be immediately recovered and inserted into the state's economy; it converts the lands of rebel settlement into a vast desert in the eastern region, marking that land as not yet unrecovered and vacant. But neither the *desert* nor the *void* was a space of absolute exteriority from the state of Yucatán or the nation. Instead, these spatial figurations were both interior and exterior at the same time; they sustained and used the undecidability and potentiality of both configurations.

As I described in the previous chapter, María Josefina Saldaña-Portillo has argued that the engine of Spanish colonialism lay in maintaining the undecidable duality of Indian faithfulness/unfaithfulness. The spatial politics of Caste War cartographies invites us to consider a secularized nineteenth-century version of this raison d'être. In this version, the Crown's interest in "spiritual accumulation" is replaced with the nation-state's "civilizing" accumulation, both motives that are underpinned by a logic of economic expansion.[37]

This disputed area of the peninsula was thus mapped as a space of uncivilization that could yet be incorporated into the nation's economy. It was traced as both exterior (not yet territorialized) and yet interior (potential territory) to the state. The blanks in García Cubas's maps were concrete apprehensions of Caste War–era fugitivity and as such illustrated the social practices of resistance that effectively thwarted the region's economy. These rebellious practices were the target of state-led pacifying efforts for nearly fifty years. The area's very emptiness indexed projects for its future enclosure as well as the desire to erase the existence of rebel settlements (such as Chan Santa Cruz, the main rebel settlement in the eastern side, established around 1852). In the very gesture of erasure, which is only made possible by representation, the maps incorporated the area, performing a kind of cartographic territorialization that included the "empty" spaces within the boundaries of the nation.

TO PLUNGE INTO THE JUNGLE: ESCAPING THE SYSTEMS OF RACIALIZED EXPLOITATIVE LABOR

In both his military and literary writings, Severo del Castillo insisted on the barrenness of nonrecovered eastern territories—lands that he described as empty deserts. But at moments, possibly despite himself, he acknowledged that in fact, this desert was home to communities fighting to protect their autonomy:

> The forces of that line established their general barracks at Peto, but its troops did not remain inactive; one division, marching through the villages of Saban and Sacalaca, and another, advancing along the royal road on December 12, attacked and occupied Tihosuco and were met with no resistance, the Indians scattering in all directions and plunging into the dense eastern jungles, where they would come to found their new homeland and where the fortitude of those untamed hearts would secure their independence.

In acknowledging that these lands were, in fact, populated, del Castillo's account begins to align with archives produced beyond the constraints of the national perspective. In contrast to a geography that was bounded by ruin, desert, and the void, documents by foreigners, many of them travelers, map a different spatial configuration of the rebel areas of the peninsula.

These travelers were often men of science, for nineteenth-century Yucatán was a site prized by antiquarians and amateur archaeologists who were eager to "discover" the "secrets" of the region's lost Maya cities. Travelers and explorers such as John Lloyd Stephens, Frederick Catherwood, Karl Heller, Karl Hermann Berendt, Desiré Charnay, and the Le Plongeons recorded their impressions of the Yucatán in textual accounts, illustrations, and photographs. This archive is another indispensable element in examining the intersecting geographies of the Caste War.

Two of these foreign visitors were Augustus and Alice Dixon Le Plongeon, who traveled from New York to Yucatán in 1873 to search for the "Maya past." Ignoring their Yucatec colleagues' attempts to dissuade them from their explorations, they insisted on photographing and excavating at length (they stayed in the Yucatán until 1880) areas that straddled the dividing lines between "peaceful" and "rebel" zones.[38] The then governor Liberio Irigoyen sent with them an escort of soldiers, tasked with protecting them in case "barbaric Indians" decided to attack their camp. The Le Plongeons' photographic archive (which is now held at the Getty Research Institute in Los Angeles) is to my knowledge the largest collection of nineteenth-century traveler images from the Yucatán Peninsula.

During their trip, Augustus Le Plongeon was especially invested in studying the region's "ruins," seeking vestiges of the Mayan past. Alice D. Le Plongeon, on the other hand, found ways to study the contemporary reality around her. Most of her writings, particularly those addressing the Caste War, were published in the late nineteenth century in American newspapers such as the *New York Evening Post, The Woman's Tribune,* the *Commercial Advertiser,* and the *Los Angeles Times,* among others. Although a fearful tone permeates the personal diaries she kept during her expeditions, her published writings register (albeit with some incredulity and surprise) the complex network of exchange between Yucatán's southern and eastern communities and their trade with settlements in British Honduras: "But those people do not live like savages: they have good houses, utensils, clothes and other necessaries and commodities. Among them there are clever mechanics and musicians provided with instruments from British Honduras from which place they also procure many small luxuries, such as potted meats, wines and perfumes, which they delight in."[39]

Alice Dixon Le Plongeon's articles do not escape the racializing dichotomization prevalent in many contemporary narratives about the race war between Indians and whites. However, her descriptions do capture a different angle to García Cubas's void: the multiracial space of fugitivity that was formed in the eastern lands of the peninsula, in Chan Santa Cruz and on Mexico's border with British Honduras:

> The population [of Chan Santa Cruz] is not more than three or four thousand, but several thousand people are believed to live in surrounding ranches and villages. In the city there are now all sorts of people— mestizos, escaped negro convicts, and a lot of Chinese who were brought as servants to British Honduras, and [who] deserted *en masse*. The people of Chan Santa Cruz received them well, saying that they are their brothers, and, indeed, after a while they became quite similar to them in appearance and manners.[40]

Although the passage romanticizes the scene it narrates, eastern rebel communities did open their space to those fleeing systems of racialized exploitative labor in neighboring regions. Fugitives of peonage and indentured labor created modes of collective life in the *rancherías* that were scattered throughout the eastern lands. For example, in 1866, a group of Chinese laborers who had been brought to British Honduras by force through Cuba from Xiamen, fled to the rebel zones. They had been commissioned to labor in sugar plantations located in northern British Honduras. In complicated negotiations with Santa Cruz rebels, British landowners and local government officials demanded the return of the escaped laborers. They were refused; the fugitive Chinese indentured workers who had plunged into the depths of the jungle never went back.[41] Shortly thereafter, Edwin Adolphus, magistrate of Corozal, received a communiqué from the trader and mediator José Andrade. This message contains contradictory information about the rebels' refusal to expel the Chinese escapees. The letter suggests that the workers regretted their decision but could not return, for they were now held captive as servants to rebel Maya leaders. But the letter also states that Santa Cruz rebels refused to comply with their British neighbors' request because the fugitives of indentured labor were "Indians like themselves" and were "to be well treated and taught to work."[42] The reliability of the letter remains an open question; to my knowledge there is no surviving firsthand documentation of how the eastern rebel settlements' motley inhabitants lived with one another. Fugitivity thus remains beyond both romanticism and condemnation, despite these accounts' efforts to fix and historicize it.

MAPPING, SURVEILLANCE, AND REPRESSION

Maps that were drawn during military expeditions to rebel zones tend to also offer a different depiction of the eastern region of the peninsula, for they aimed to capture the actual physical and social geography of insurgent areas.

General Rómulo Díaz de la Vega, who led the Yucatec military branches during the most algid years of the Caste War, believed that the government's success in repressing the rebellion depended upon producing accurate knowledge about rebel territories.[43] In 1852, he commanded Colonel Manuel Hernández and German engineer Juan Hübbe to travel across the frontier into rebel lands in order to chart and measure them. The expedition produced a "sketch of the theater of war currently being waged in the State of Yucatán against rebel Indians." According to Michel Antochiw, this sketch is "the only map that indicated the names and locations of many towns, ranches, and *haciendas* inhabited by the insurgent Maya, sometimes destroyed and abandoned during the painful conflict."[44] The map, for instance, included Chan Santa Cruz, the rebel capital that was frequently omitted from other cartographic tracings of the peninsula (see fig. 6.8)

Years after it was created, Colonel Hernández based a more detailed map titled *Carta de Yucatán* on the sketch he had previously charted while on the road. Curiously, the map was never published or publicly circulated, though it seems to have been lithographed in Mexico City and was cited by the acclaimed geographer Manuel Orozco y Berra (García Cubas's mentor). For this reason, the configuration of rebel space offered in the map had a tardy and nuanced influence over other national and state maps being produced for circulation, purchase, and education.[45] In fact, the first map to use the information collected by Hernández and Hübbe was printed in Paris in 1878. It was the work of Andrés Aznar y Pérez and Hübbe himself, who had accompanied Colonel Hernández in the exploration that led to the creation of the sketch. This map was retouched and enlarged by the German traveler Karl Hermann Berendt shortly before his death.[46] The 1878 cartography was so exceptional in its detail that the State of Yucatán later planned to use it in schools as educational material.[47] Additionally, the map was received enthusiastically

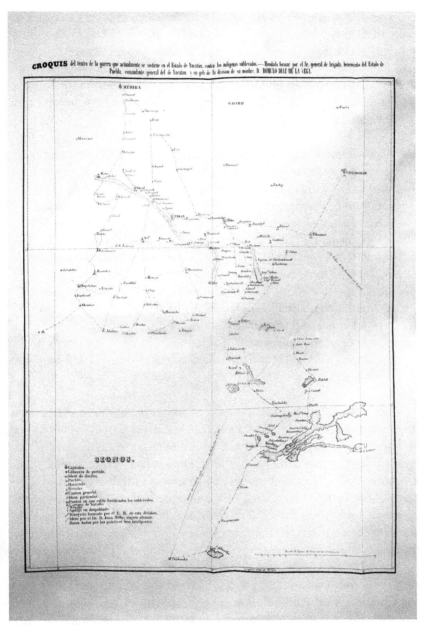

FIGURE 6.8. Croquis del teatro de la guerra que actualmente se sostiene en el Estado de Yucatán. *Archivo Histórico de la Secretaría de la Defensa Nacional, Military Operations,* file XI/481.3/3257.

overseas, and it is noteworthy for how it effectively captures the various competing geographies of Yucatán's east (see fig. 6.9). The explorer and antiquarian Philipp Valentini wrote about the production of the map, giving us insight into how it registered the overlap of numerous and not always complementary interests (those of the rebel communities, state government, hacendados and landowners, antiquarian travelers, and members of scientific expeditions):

> We understand that the map is the work of experts, and persons born and living on the soil of Yucatan itself. Its composition has grown out of a large amount of data, given by engineers who made surveys either for the Government or for owners of vast estates; by military officers, who in their expeditions against the Indians laid down the lines of their marches; and by foreign travelers and scientists, who in the interest of their special pursuits revised former data, and rectified them by means of more correct methods of observation. A special commission performed the labor of examining and selecting the material used in the formation of the map, which was reduced to a common scale, adapted to such astronomical positions of the main cities as were known, and especially to that frame of the coast line which is laid down and published in the mss. sheets of the Hydrographical Bureau at Washington.[48]

Aznar and Hübbe's map yields yet another depiction of the eastern side of the peninsula. Neither a void (as in García Cubas's version) nor a mere inscription of names of insurgent towns (as in del Castillo's strategic military version), the 1878 map acknowledges communities' semi-autonomous practices and modes of living by registering the words "Indians of the east" on its tracing of the region's surface. This inscription, which first appeared in some of the maps of Yucatán previously elaborated by foreign travelers and engineers, conveys the spatial and representational dilemma posed by Yucatán during the Caste War. As we have seen, mapping absence did ideological and political work: tracing the region as a void or a desert desocialized the area by depicting it as unpopulated. This configuration represented the eastern side as barren and therefore in need of intervention and economic exploitation. Yet, and perhaps somewhat paradoxically, depictions of the void in the east also underscored the state's lack of control over the area; this was further emphasized with the inscription "Indians of the east," which acknowledged both the continuous roiling of the uprising and the existence of

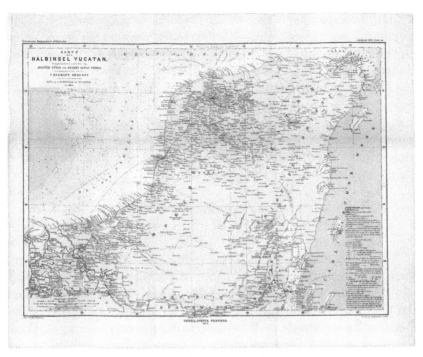

FIGURE 6.9. *Juan Hübbe and Andrés Aznar y Pérez,* Karte der Halbinsel Yucatan (1879). *Bibliothèque nationale de France.*

fugitive communities that resisted assimilation to a criollo state. To complicate things further, the increasing cartographic accuracy displayed in maps such as the one charted in 1878 by Aznar and Hübbe adds another layer of complexity to the mix insofar as its growing body of cartographic knowledge constituted a direct threat to the fugitivity that had allowed Maya rebels to live autonomously in uncharted lands for several years.

AGAINST REPRESENTATION: OBSTRUCTED REBEL CARTOGRAPHIES OF THE CASTE WAR

In 1888, the English topographer William Miller visited Chan Santa Cruz. The objective of his trip was to corroborate and correct extant "geographic information" about the peninsula. Miller was particularly interested in remapping the southern and eastern areas of the region and used Aznar and Hübbe's map as the basis for his empirical cartographic contrast. In a report addressed to the Royal Geographic Society, Miller narrates his experience as allegedly the third white man to visit the rebel capital in nearly fifty years of conflict. The report points out a series of discrepancies or errors in the 1878 map.[49]

Although the annotations might seem minute, Miller arrived at these corrections by comparing the information on Aznar and Hübbe's map with the spatial knowledge and practices of local inhabitants. This is crucial. One of the ways that rebel communities challenged their assimilation to Yucatán's racial state was through resisting the government's attempts to surveil, measure, and ultimately map eastern lands; rebels had their own ways of living in, charting, seeing, and relating to space. What is unique about Miller's corrections is his attempt to reconcile these two competing regimes of spatial knowledge, and his privileging of local practices when the two regimes were in conflict.

On the one hand, Miller's travels through the peninsula's eastern corridor were constrained by a "regime of visibility" that prevented him from seeing his surroundings as anything more than ruined buildings and overgrown vegetation that complicated his access to the area.[50] On the other hand, though, certain passages in his report interrupt this experience, revealing his encounter with other regimes of visibility and spatial production. Miller discusses, for instance, how Indians measured the roads by marking them with crosses and how they used churches as intermittent housing spaces; he also mentions rebel forces' use of local terrain in their guerrilla strategies.[51]

There is one especially relevant moment of Miller's report that registers rebels' sense that the survival of the autonomy they had carved out during the struggles for their communities was tied not only to sustaining material control of the lands they inhabited but also to obstructing symbolic representations of them. Miller mentions in the report that he has failed to achieve a more accurate charting of the eastern region than the one already provided by Aznar and Hübbe's cartography. He excuses himself by stating that he has been incapable of corroborating the distances inscribed in older maps due to limited access to his measuring instruments: "I had no instruments, and so had to accept the Indians' version of the number of leagues travelled. It would not be safe to use any surveying or astronomical instruments there, as the people are constantly in dread of and watching for spies."[52]

Although some might read this as yet another version of the "Indians mistrust technology" trope, one of a long chain of stereotypes employed to racialize indigenous people as resistant to (or incapable of) historical change, there is a different possible reading of Miller's comment. In it, Indians do not fear the instruments themselves, but the uses that "spies" might put them to. This indicates that the rebels did not obstruct the collection of geographic information because they were "backward" or "uncivilized." Rather, they were both aware of and concerned with the implications and intersections of different forms of symbolic, political, and economic power over their lands.[53] In other words, local communities seem to have been well aware that in order to protect the material autonomy of the territories they inhabited, they also had to protect their graphic autonomy. In fact, innumerable travelers made their way through this region, capturing and shaping the "splendor of the Maya ruins" with their pencils or cameras during the long years of the Caste War, yet, to my knowledge, there are no remaining visual images or photographs of Chan Santa Cruz and other rebel communities during this period, even within the Le Plongeons' vast photo archive.

Other accounts underscore how rebels' refusal to allow their terrains to be mapped or scouted was both strategic and political. In a letter dated September 9, 1851, José María Tzuc, the then leader of the southern town of Chichanhá, wrote to the general commander of the Yucatec army, Juan María Novelo, to explain why his community was refusing to allow the state's forces to enter the *monte*. The letter suggests that the refusal was above all a defensive strategy, a response to Yucatec authorities' constant violation of agreements established with indigenous communities: "About what your lordship says, that you and your men must come and see where we are if you are to know us, that will not be possible as it once was, because we have experience now; the first time you took our weapons and harmed us; is that what you will do again? Why can you not leave us in peace once and for all and your lordship see what to do somewhere else?"[54]

The letter conveys the persistence of national and local military forces' attempts to gain terrain (actual ground held or even information about terrain) over rebel areas. At this point, territorial control and spatial surveillance were becoming increasingly entwined with visions of a consolidating national sovereignty. The letter expressed exasperation at the government's continual requests to enter the communal lands of Chichanhá, demanding freedom from state surveillance: "Why can you not leave us in peace once and for all?"

Toward the end of the century, spatial surveillance appeared ever more central to "national" attempts to fully repress the uprising, and authorities joined forces with other international powers to map and even-

FIGURE 6.10. Tropas del general Ignacio Bravo en Chan Santa Cruz Qroo. *Fototeca Pedro Guerra de la Facultad de Ciencias Antropológicas, Universidad Autónoma de Yucatán, 2A08265.*

tually reterritorialize rebel spaces. When Porfirio Díaz resumed diplomatic relations with the British Crown (relations that had been broken by Benito Juárez, who rejected ties with nations who recognized the empire of Maximilian of Habsburg), the new treaty allowed British military ships along the Caribbean coasts and into Mexican waters. The surveilling presence of ships such as the *Independencia* and the *Zaragoza* was meant to help record information on insurgent communities' spatial practices. From the shores where they anchored, army sailors attempted to track and monitor rebels' movements, gaining knowledge about the routes they used, who they allowed into the forests, and what kind of trade relations they had, both among local communities and with inhabitants of British Honduras.[55]

This naval strategy marked the beginning of an invasive campaign to besiege the region and dismantle the autonomy that rebel communities had constructed and safeguarded for nearly fifty years. Although it was aimed at gaining direct material control over rebel grounds, this strategy also functioned symbolically, for the spectacle of national ships on the Caribbean coastlines was a public display of Mexico's increased military capacities under the Díaz regime.

In 1901, as Chan Santa Cruz fell to the hands of the Mexican army led by General Ignacio Bravo, the first image of the rebel capital was produced and circulated, marking the official end of the "Caste War." The picture establishes a connection between representational and military conquest; it stages the tightening strings stretching between the expansion of state sovereignty, capital accumulation, and the material and symbolic surveillance of space. The image shows Bravo's troops lined up in Chan Santa Cruz, the heart of the rebellion, the village that had long operated as the major political center for allied rebels' strategic planning (see fig. 6.10). This first photograph of Chan Santa Cruz marked the beginning of the end of fugitivity, the collapse of rebel autonomy.[56] It also marked the acceleration of state-led efforts to develop the area.

As Díaz pushed to increase henequen production in Yucatán, new railroads that connected the previously disjointed villages of Peto, Tekax, Valladolid, and others were built and put in motion. The booming global economy of the region was erected on a growing base of racialized peonage. To gain greater control over the eastern side of the peninsula, the emerging territory of Quintana Roo was separated from Yucatán and placed under the military command of Ignacio Bravo. The vision behind this was to stabilize the once disputed area and later incorporate it into the nation's economy.

CONCLUSION: OTHER TRACES, OTHER SPACES

An 1849 entry in the baptism registry of the Espita parish reads, "Book 15 of Indian baptisms in the parish of Espita, which was stripped of its pages when seized by the rebel Indians who captured the archive of this parish last year in 1848."[57] Church books such as the one referred to in this passage were used to register towns' inhabitants according to racial categories. This was the basis upon which church officials demanded differential payments from parishioners receiving and participating in sacraments. The destruction of the records from the Espita parish is thus noteworthy for the act of tearing out the pages of the baptism records, as it suggests more than a simple act of vandalism on the rebels' part. The act could be read as an attempt to dismantle the legacy of a colonial racialized revenue system and its continuing role in the production of race in Mexico after independence.

But rebels went beyond efforts to demolish the basis of race-making; they also imagined alternative social arrangements to it. Many of the letters penned by rebel leaders during the Caste War contain fascinating political speculations about how to undo, unfix, and rechart social and spatial relations in the region, even in the world at large. Like the cosmopolitan projections of Yucatec hacendados, journalists, historians, and politicians that were printed in novels and newspapers, Maya rebels, too, projected their visions of the world beyond the local through a rich epistolary network radiating from rebel zones throughout the peninsula. Rebels used letters to communicate with each other, share political messages with their communities, and negotiate with federal, local, and foreign actors. Often written in Maya and then translated into Spanish, these letters provide a window into the spatial and political imagination of insurgent communities. I offer readings of some of these letters, paying particular attention to the connections they established between dismantling mechanisms of racialization and reconfiguring spatiality from which alternative arrangements of life could emerge.

First, I turn to an anonymous manifesto containing a series of rebel demands. The 1848 document offers a genealogy of struggles—conflicts preceding the Caste War—that emerged and died down throughout the early postindependence years in Yucatán. This text, like many others, references the constant pledges made by different Yucatec governors, all of whom promised to stop levying tribute on indigenous communities and all of whom failed to deliver. The text connects this history of broken promises to the practices of dispossession and displacement that were central to the expansion of the Yucatec state: "Fourth: the whites must not set foot on indigenous land. They [the whites] set the price until men are left with nothing. Is it not the case that without [legal] dispute some whites get their way, sending the indigenous people into the hills of the haciendas? Who supports the indigenous requests?"[58]

The passage is quite poignant. On one hand, it stages the complex relation between fugitivity and displacement, showing that "whites" relate to land only as property, setting a price on it, and ultimately generating an economy of displacement that pushes indigenous groups into the *monte*. The passage, also, clearly refers to the extra-legal operations of racialized primitive accumulation in the region, remarking that "some whites" can appropriate land almost automatically and forcefully, without regard for legal procedures.

Although the text uses the stark racial rhetoric that permeated most Caste War narratives, it actually is underpinned by a more nuanced and complex perspective about the social (and racial) relations in the region. It is only *some* whites who get their way. In the same vein, the letter insists that *men* (perhaps not only indigenous men) are left with nothing in this process. These two specificities unfix any reference to a rigid racial framework, prompting instead a series of questions: Is the text pointing to an intersection between class and race, where only certain "whites" are leading the process of land appropriation and displacement that the letter narrates? Analogously, does the text also recognize that indigenous groups are not the only ones affected by this violent process, in stating that "men" are "left with nothing"?

The text ends with an open-ended series of questions that interpellate readers as it attempts to move them beyond racial fixity. By repeating questions that begin with the word "who," the text frames the problem of dispossession as relevant and painful not only to indigenous groups but to everyone who witnesses these displacements. The text poses an almost direct challenge to the dehumanization of indigenous rebels that the state promotes in both practice and discourse, asking, "Who will not feel pain at what is being done to the indigenous?"[59] The violence inflicted upon indigenous communities is therefore a matter that concerns and affects not only said communities but anyone who is aware of it, whether they are indigenous or not.

Notably, many of these letters juxtapose their challenges to racialization with ideas about alternative configurations of space and land usage. A letter from 1850 signed by Juan de la Cruz—a fictive signature that rebels from different communities perhaps used, as David Kazanjian suggests, to project the configuration of a stable, solidified rebel leadership—envisions an end to the segmented geography mostly instituted by the state.[60] As explained in chapter 5, Yucatec forces aimed to set apart the "east" of Yucatán in an attempt to quarantine the rebellion. The letter at hand proposes instead breaking down the established division and constructing a new, unregulated spatiality in lieu of it: "The boundaries that the whites have placed in the east, and anywhere else they have placed them, shall be broken down."[61] In imagining the undoing of the fragmented geography, the letter seems to also imagine the collapse of the pillars of racialization in the region. To break down geographical divisions is also to put an end to measures aimed at policing the mobility of indigenous people, disappropriating land and making it accessible and open to the fluid movement of all.

Another letter, dated April 7, 1850, expands the vision of a new spatiality stemming from the erosion of state-sponsored racial divisions. The letter, which was addressed to the priest José Canuto Vela and signed by the Maya leaders José María Barrera, Francisco Cob, José Isaac Pat, Calixto Yam, Pantaleón Uh, Juan Justo Yam, and Apolinar Sel, also condemned the government's failure to honor the agreements signed with rebel communities on the outskirts of Tekax. The missive accomplished the objective of allowing Maya leaders to state the reasons for continuing their struggle after said negotiations had been violated:

> You were fully aware of the agreement that had been made with us. That is why we fight. We demand that no contribution be paid, whether by the white man, the black man, or the indigenous man: ten pesos per baptism for whites, blacks, and indigenous; ten pesos per marriage for whites, blacks, and indigenous. As for the old debts, they will no longer be paid by whites, blacks, or indigenous; and the *monte* shall not be bought. Wherever whites, blacks, or indigenous may plant their "milpa," no one will impede it.[62]

The letter complicates the "race war paradigm" that Yucatec newspapers used to structure their narratives of the conflict, which they figured as a race war perpetrated by "barbaric Indians" who sought the total extermination of "whites." Instead, it constitutes an effort to grapple with an imagined form of equality traversed by difference. The passage undoes the *abstract* universal equality of liberal citizenship by instead demanding that "the white man, the black man, and the indigenous man" *all* be subject to the same payments and stipulations for baptism and marriage. In its list of particularities, the passage experiments with other ways of creating a ground for a universal equality that does not naively negate the actual material operations and existence of racial difference. Following Kazanjian, we might say that the letter articulates a mode of "plural universality."[63]

Most important, however, the letter's conceptualization of this mode of equality depends on the deregulation of spatial practices. It outlines the possibility of a *non-appropriative* relation with the *monte*, requesting that land be neither sold nor bought. The text imagines a political geography marked by the "free" and indiscriminate access to cultivating these lands, allowing that "whites," "Indians," and "blacks" all start their plots, or *milpas*, wherever they choose.[64] The spatio-political imagination constructed by the text challenges Yucatán's status quo and its dependence on land appropriation and a racialized peasant workforce. This is the case even when, in practice, rebels did not offer unrestricted access to their communities. As we have seen, in the face of land appropriation and military incursions during the conflict, insurgents were highly protective of their communities and carefully regulated outsiders' access to them. Still, the letters that constitute the Caste War's rebel archive offer potent speculations of an open spatiality, one that would be free of the physical and legislative barriers erected by the state to regulate differential access to resources.

Rebels' efforts to envision alternate spatial and social arrangements while obstructing the charting of eastern lands may still be resonating in contemporary plights over the region's geography. One of the largest development projects of the current government of President Andrés Manuel López Obrador, the so-called Tren Maya, for instance, was launched precisely on the basis of repeating tropes about how the peninsula is a fragmented and isolated territory that needs to be further interlinked and incorporated into the nation's economy. The train, a major infrastructural project, promises to connect the entire Maya region with railways running through the states of Tabasco, Chiapas, Campeche, Yucatán, and Quintana Roo, serving for the transport of both cargo and passengers. The recurrent motif that López Obrador cites when defending the controversial project is that the train will not only create numerous jobs by expanding the region's tourism industry but also provide a new system of transportation for local residents. Ultimately, the argument goes, the train will foster the coming together of communities in the peninsula and the entire Maya region of Mexico's southeast. Although the government has promoted the Tren Maya as a hyper-modern development project of inclusive tourism and environmental care, one that would promote the distribution of wealth among local communities, tapping into the rich archaeological legacies of the area while also protecting its many natural reservations, activists from indigenous communities have allied to resist the construction of the railroad. According to the group Múuch' Xíinbal, self-described as an itinerant assembly of Maya men and women seeking to defend the territory, the Tren Maya is truly a project to reterritorialize the peninsula and dispossess indigenous communities from the lands they inhabit. Pedro Uc, one of the leading members of the assembly, has highlighted how the Tren Maya, in tandem with the government's second railroad project (the Trans-Isthmus railroad), is effectively designed to operate, in favor of US interests, as a brickless border containing migrants coming into the country from Central America.[65] In their challenge to the railroad project, Múuch' Xíinbal insists on continuing to foster a nonappropriative relation to land. "Land can neither be sold nor rented," states the group in its main manifesto against the railroad. In doing so they echo the histories of resistance of the region, including the struggle of Caste War rebels described in this chapter. Indeed, as in 1848, their commitment to obstruct the reterritorialization of the peninsula by the railroad project is not only a defense of land but, as the itinerant assembly states, a "defense of life itself."[66]

{ CODA THREE }

"Barbarous Mexico"
RACIALIZED COERCIVE LABOR FROM SONORA TO YUCATÁN

By the first decade of the twentieth century, things had shifted greatly in Yucatán. The state's once stalled economy had become among the most profitable in the country. Supported by an extensive railroad system and a broad network of racialized coerced labor, local haciendas kept up with the high demand for henequen fiber: Yucatán's so-called green gold, which by the turn of the century was a cherished raw material in the international market.[1]

In his renowned muckraking piece *Barbarous Mexico* (1908), the American journalist and political activist John Kenneth Turner presented his readers with an image of Yucatán that differed enormously from the narrative of the region's labor scarcity described in previous chapters. His best-selling book instead showed the consolidation of large plantation economies in both Yucatán and the Valle Nacional, where local haciendas employed thousands of workers in conditions that, according to the author, amounted to chattel slavery. This situation, he argued, explained how Yucatán, an otherwise small state within the Mexican Republic, had come to be more densely populated than the United States itself.[2]

Turner did not name the sources behind these demographics, and it is certainly possible that they were inflated to match his hyperbolic tone. Historians have reported that labor scarcity troubled Yucatec hacendados even at the height of the state's economy.[3] Numbers aside, Turner's depiction of Yucatec haciendas is nevertheless valuable, for it opens a window into how discourses that relied on tropes of labor scarcity in the peninsula (i.e., its "lack of arms" [*falta de brazos*]) were mobilized to instate a widespread system of racialized coerced labor in the aftermath of the Caste War. In this coda I study the discursive practices of race that supported the emergence of this system. I specifically analyze the overlap between projects of colonization and convict labor that racialized workers who were transported from other countries and states of the Mexican Republic to labor in the region's plantations. These projects resonated with the network of indentured labor that was established years prior between Yucatán and Cuba (see chapter 5) at the height of the Caste War and that, ultimately, constituted the discursive backbone to the growth of the henequen industry and the dire labor conditions that Turner described in his famous book.[4]

Turner traveled through Mexico guided by his friend and comrade Lázaro Gutiérrez de Lara.[5] They were respectively disguised as an American investor interested in purchasing a plantation in the Mexican tropics and his translator and assistant. Role-playing their way from the northern border down to the southeast, Turner and Gutiérrez de Lara gained access to the darkest secrets of the alliances between American investors and Mexican elites. With many of their comrades imprisoned in the Los Angeles County Jail after attempts to stir up social disturbances in Mexico from the other side of the border, the two men sought to collect evidence and influence international public opinion against both Díaz and American investors.[6] To this end, Turner's rhetoric echoed that of other investigative journalists of the period who denounced the abusive laboring conditions of expanding extractive economies all over the world.[7] His book sought to strike an emotional chord with the American public by showcasing how US capital was involved in sustaining workers' dire living conditions in the neighboring country. This is perhaps the reason behind *Barbarous Mexico*'s central comparison between Mexico's peonage system and US chattel slavery.

Throughout the pages of his articles, Turner returned time and again to the same trope: he argued that his text presented undeniable evidence that slavery indeed plagued the henequen, coffee, and tobacco plantations of southeastern Mexico. He supported this claim by including documentary photographs taken during his travels and by constantly reminding readers that he had been a firsthand witness to all the circumstances described in each of the chapters. For Turner, slavery in Mexico was both pervasive and hidden in plain sight. It was encoded in a widely spread language and practice that normalized indebted labor (i.e., peonage) and that rendered thousands of lives disposable. Although other publications within both Mexico and the United States discussed the precarious working conditions in Mexico's export-oriented industries, Turner's piece highlighted racialization as a crucial factor organizing the distribution of this precarity. As the author filtered, however inaccurately, life in henequen and tobacco plantations in southeastern Mexico through the lens of chattel slavery, *Barbarous Mexico* provided his readers (within the United States and in Mexico) with a language that was intended to pierce through the racial dynamics that punctuated labor relations in Mexico's agricultural sector.

"FALTA DE BRAZOS": PROJECTS OF FOREIGN COLONIZATION AND THE TROPE OF LABOR SCARCITY

The radical shift that separated mid-nineteenth-century visions of the peninsula's landscape as a ruined desert from Turner's early twentieth-century depiction of Yucatán's haciendas as overpopulated sites of dynamic capital accumulation and brutal racialized exploitation was underpinned by a rising interest to experiment with foreign colonization. Nearly thirty years before Turner would travel through Yucatán disguised as an American investor, the Caste War continued to challenge the region's economy. The fugitivity of labor connected to the rebellion had in fact deeply impacted the state's agriculture and left Yucatec hacendados desperately searching for opportunities to reconsolidate their wealth. Many were eager to join the national conversation about how to accelerate the country's economic capacities.

In March 1878, Yucatec governor Manuel Romero Ancona was presented the opportunity to evaluate the state's productivity and to come up with potential measures that could be implemented to fortify it. He commissioned three state representatives to respond to a federal survey collecting information about the economic difficulties facing each of the states in the republic as well as ideas about how federal funds could be employed to address them. The survey was created by the Secretary of Development, Colonization, and Industry and followed Díaz's public statements about Mexico's need to consider the advantages of foreign colonization.[8]

Discussions that touched upon the idea of introducing foreign laborers into Mexico had been on the rise for a few years, but the survey marked the beginning of colonization as a central project of the Díaz administration, amplifying debates on the issue and giving them a nationwide platform.[9] Mostly mediated by the press, these conversations spun around two core ideas: first, that Mexico's unparalleled natural richness remained untapped, and second, that there was a concerning lack of capable laborers in the country who could perform the task of exploiting these riches.[10] In other words, supporters of colonization were not really troubled by a general lack of populational density. They were, instead, concerned with the *low quality* of workers, most of them racialized as *indios*.[11]

The Yucatán report put forth by Pedro de Regil Peón, Manuel Dondé, and José García Morales translated the two pillars of the debate into the local context. The report showcased how the trope about the *falta de brazos* in the region was connected to the ongoing rebellion and to efforts to contain it. While initially the trope might have been conditioned by the actual fugitivity of labor described in chapter 6, elite and governing authorities repeated it well into the twentieth century, when social, economic, and political conditions in Yucatán had significantly changed, well into the prosperous period in which Turner observed the hundred thousand Maya, Yaqui, and Asian slaves. The trope was used continuously to support the steady flow of racialized labor from within the country and abroad for the expansion of the area's monocrop production.

Although in 1878 the henequen boom had not yet reached its peak, Regil Peón, Dondé, and García Morales recognized the growing revenue tied to the burgeoning industry. Their report enticed the federal treasury with visions about the expansive riches that could be extracted from the peninsula, recalling that the region's most fertile terrains remained under the control of rebel communities in the east and south. In their view, the peninsula's economy would not reach its full and destined potential until the state succeeded in putting an end to the Caste War, incorporating those vast and fertile lands into the national economy and increasing the number of capable workers available to render them productive.[12]

The report discussed the difficult conditions facing ranches and settlements near the rebel frontier. As expected, the three commissioners advocated for military intervention and other measures, including the federal government granting localized exemptions to liens and taxes for venturous landowners who attempted to make their living near the rebel line and return the *baldíos* to "productivity."[13] While these guidelines resonated with past strategies to promote settlements in so-called barren lands in the border between rebel and pacified zones, the commissioners' colonizing fantasies acquired new racializing tones that are worth discussing.

Throughout the nineteenth century, the question of national colonization plagued the minds of intellectuals and state officials in Mexico.

Mesmerized by the fast-growing economy of the United States, from the early decades of the century onward politicians fantasized about implementing a range of policies to foster foreign settlements in what was often described as the country's "vast" and "uninhabited" lands. Elites and authorities insisted that colonization would kickstart the nation's agriculture and accelerate the accumulation of riches. Their proposals often explicitly intended to mimic the settler practices used throughout the United States that were seen as the main motor behind the northern neighbor's booming economy. During the first half of the century, fantasies that figured colonization as the panacea for Mexico's social and economic problems mostly centered on attracting European immigration. Supporters of these efforts thought that bringing in "white" immigrants would not only improve the economy but also foster a process of miscegenation that could "dilute" the presence of indigenous and Black populations in the country, ultimately neutralizing the risk of racial conflict.[14] Mexico's efforts to promote European immigration were not an exception. Many other countries in the Americas, including the well-known case of Argentina, buttressed projects with similar objectives.[15]

But things seemed different by the time the three Yucatec commissioners responded to the federal survey. Unlike others before them (including the illustrious José María Luis Mora), Regil Peón, Dondé, and García Morales did not recommend that foreign white settlers be courted; indeed, they stated that projects of white colonization were doomed, recalling the failed attempt to establish a German colony in the Yucatec town of Santa Elena under Maximilian's reign.[16] They attributed this failure to the fragility of whiteness itself, the inability of European settlers (whom they referred to interchangeably as either European or white) to adapt to and labor in tropical climates such as that of Yucatán. In their view, the peninsula, with its harsh climatic and unstable social conditions, was not an attractive nor suitable place for white immigrants, whose "natural ambition" drove them instead to richer, safer places such as the United States.[17] Further, the commissioners argued that white colonization would actually increase, not decrease, local racial tensions; European settlers, they wrote, would inevitably note their superiority in relation to the local population and seek to dominate indigenous groups, which would in turn awaken indigenous inhabitants' supposed rebellious nature, ultimately undermining any chance for political stability.[18]

Despite these critiques, the commissioners did not recommend that projects of colonization be completely abandoned; Regil Peón, Dondé, and García Morales recommended instead that, like Peru, Mexico should bring Asian and African laborers to the peninsula. They were not alone in this suggestion. In fact, debates about how Mexico should open its borders to Chinese laborers leaving Cuba had ensued since the late 1860s, shortly after the island published a decree of expulsion for coolie laborers whose contracts had expired and who refused to renew them.[19] While the commissioners agreed that white colonization was the most desirable, they also insisted that Yucatec authorities come to terms with the fact that this project was unsuitable given the region's conditions. The commissioners were careful to assuage their colleagues' potential concerns about introducing Asian and African laborers and emphasized that strict regulations would be implemented to adequately manage the presence of these *colonos* in the peninsula. Written in the midst of the Caste War, the report attended to criollo anxieties about bringing in populations that could allegedly complicate already existing racial conflicts, and it framed the solution to this problem in terms of controlling the living and laboring conditions of imported workers as well as their numbers. They advised that the population of incoming Asian and African laborers should always be limited and only respond to economic necessity.[20]

The commissioners' dismissal of white colonization was neither uncommon nor uncontroversial. Representatives from different states of the republic held diverging views on the matter. It is noteworthy, however, that the difference that separated those who still expressed enthusiasm for white colonization from those who embraced opening the country to nonwhite populations outlined a racial geography that divided the center and northern regions of the republic from its coastal zones. This division also overlapped with the racialization of different economies and modes of labor: discussions purported that the central region of the country, mostly dedicated to mining and railway industries, would be best served by the introduction of white settlers, whereas tropical areas, devoted to agricultural production for exportation, would thrive by attracting nonwhite workers, who were supposedly better suited to endure the harsh climatic conditions of the coast.[21] The racial geography that accompanied fantasies about colonization during the late nineteenth century highlights how peripheral zones were constructed as spaces where experiments with racialized labor could ensue at a supposedly lower risk of political instability. Even if racial disturbances were ignited in these sites, their marginality in relation to the central portion of the country made the deployment of exceptional measures to contain them easier. Further, their promise to exponentially boost the nation's economy made such experiments worth trying.

Yucatán's 1878 response to the federal survey highlights this point. Peripheral zones were not only sites that more openly embraced experimenting with racialized labor but also areas that deepened the use of coerced labor as a way of regulating the lives of incoming nonwhite settlers. Unlike white colonization, which was supposed to be voluntary (though it was not always so), the commissioners implied that Asian and African workers transported to Yucatán, for instance, would arrive there involuntarily and remain only "partially free" for the time of their employment in Mexico. Their presence would be carefully managed by time-bound contracts that notably, and unlike what was discussed in chapter 5, were presented not as documents that guaranteed an individual's free will but rather as surveilling mechanisms that could be used to constrain and regulate the parameters within which incoming *colonos* could exist in the peninsula.[22]

Of course, the commissioners did not explicitly demarcate the distinction between "free" and "partially free" labor. Instead, they did it through accidental slips: when they described the labor of European migrants as *"enteramente libre"* (entirely free), for example, they tacitly set it in opposition to other types of racialized labor that were, thus, not entirely free.[23] The commissioners were likely careful not to explicitly categorize the labor of Asian and African immigrants as "unfree," for this would have contradicted federal law. Since 1857, the Mexican constitution had explicitly banned all forms of involuntary labor in the country, even those supported by a contract.[24] However, in 1863, Yucatán reestablished decrees from the 1840s allowing the use of forced labor, hoping to repair the economic impact of the Caste War. By the late 1870s, state censuses were openly documenting the number of "servants" laboring in local haciendas. These censuses complicate the narrative of labor shortages that would be reiterated only a few years later: the "servant" population in the area was rapidly increasing, especially in regions devoted to the cultivation of the henequen plant.[25]

The racial geography of colonization also gave rise to a distinction between settlers and workers.[26] Initially, incoming foreigners were all lumped under the same category of *colonos*. But as potential incoming groups were given different statuses based on the desirability and alleged value of their presence in the country, the roles they were envisioned to perform during their stay also increasingly diverged. In other words, the racialized hierarchy that emerged from projects of colonization meant that foreign immigrants had different paths charted out for them depending on where they were coming from and how they were racially marked. These paths diverged in a number of ways, including in how the relation to property and labor of different *colono* groups was imagined to take place.

The Yucatán report, for example, constructed a racial difference between white and nonwhite *colonos* based on the fantasy that white settlers were allegedly adept, self-regulated subjects who didn't need to report to superiors. In fact, white settlers could be potential landowners, given that their racial status was perceived to coincide with that of those who occupied the highest ranks in Yucatán's racial hierarchy. The commissioners openly recognized the racialized structure of their state's society, even as they attempted to attenuate their description of it by stating that its existence was not in any way tied to or produced by legal exclusion: "The indigenous class is almost exclusively dedicated to agriculture; mestizos are dedicated to crafts and, in part, to agriculture as peons or small-property owners; and whites are the almost exclusive owners of commerce and large agricultural properties. However, these lines of separation are not so marked that one wouldn't find individuals from all classes in all these different professions, for there is no legal exclusion."[27] The report did not suggest control via indenture contracts for European settlers, who were perceived to be fully capable of self-management. In contrast, although the report put Asian and African workers in the same category as white settlers, it also consistently framed them as subordinate workers who ought to be managed by employers, or *patronos*.[28] This implied that unlike European migrants, Asian and African settlers were incapable of self-regulation, of laboring autonomously, or of becoming landowners. The report insisted that the freedom of incoming Asian and African laborers was thus to be carefully regulated and even constrained. The commissioners somewhat disingenuously framed these directives not as protecting the rights of the *patronos* but of the workers, insisting that if the workers misunderstood the boundaries of their freedom ("*mal entendida libertad*") this would ultimately infringe upon their rights; however, they did admit that this same *mal entendida libertad* could harm the interests and rights of the employers.[29]

Following a logic that connected whiteness with self-sufficiency, the commissioners also associated whiteness with the right of having one's individual liberties protected. They expressed concern for the safety of white settlers given the state's political instability as they sustained that the political danger of the ongoing Caste War meant that Mexico could not guarantee the individual safety of incoming European settlers. Emphasizing a dichotomic framework of the rebellion, the report does not extend the same concerns to potential Asian or African migrants. Instead, it frames these lives as being less affected by risk and less worthy of concern. Although Asian laborers were, like white settlers, racialized as weak and unfit for the rough labor of the countryside, there were no concerns for Asian laborers' safety, as there had been for that of European migrants, and this fragility was not seen as a mark of superiority or of "natural ambition" to settle in gentler regions. The supposedly fragile incoming Asian *colonos* were best suited for employment in "accessory activities," freeing up local indigenous workers for strictly agricultural labor.[30]

Finally, nonwhite workers were expected to assimilate to the local culture to varying degrees. The Yucatec commissioners reminisced about how German settlers who had arrived there twelve years prior had been expected to fully incorporate into Yucatec life and, through this, to allegedly attenuate the presence of rebellious indigenous groups in the state. Alternatively, they suggested that Asian and African workers who were destined to enter the region with limited-time contracts would also have limited opportunities to mix with the local population. In fact, colonization by Asian workers, who they racialized as reclusive and reluctant to acculturate, was favored because these traits were supposed to preemptively limit their assimilation into the already complicated racial dynamics of the peninsula.[31] Nevertheless, assimilation was a thorny subject in conversations about colonization. While mixing between groups whose presence in the country was deemed to be "undesirable" was framed as something that had to be discouraged, promoting the presence of racialized groups that would remain unassimilated could also reignite the dreaded threat of race war, hence efforts to demarcate a racial geography that would limit the presence of certain groups of coerced laborers to peripheral and coastal zones.

Despite their best efforts, the commissioners' fantasies of promoting Asian and African colonization did not materialize until decades later. Concrete projects to incorporate Asian laborers into the peninsula did not gain traction until after 1891. Nevertheless, their response to the federal survey underscores that in Yucatán the national conversation about colonization grew out of efforts to contain and respond to the Caste War. Projects of foreign colonization not only shaped a persistent narrative about the importance of solving the region's scarcity of labor but linked this to the importance of maintaining a careful balance among racialized sectors so as not to increase the risks of race war. Such discussions laid the groundwork for the slavelike racialized labor that Turner would document in the early twentieth century, including later experiments with intranational racialized coerced labor.

THE YAQUI AS LABORING SUBJECT

At the turn of the century, Mexico's southern and northern frontiers became connected by the networks of coerced labor: somewhere between eight thousand and fifteen thousand men and women, most of them members of the Yaqui tribe, were deemed rebels and deported from the state of Sonora to Yucatán.[32] This deportation accompanied the experiments with foreign racialized labor described above and also echoed the use of coerced labor to expel Maya rebels from the peninsula to Cuba during the Caste War. This time, however, the deportation was intranational rather than international. Since the 1860s, when the international trade in deported subjects had been banned, Mexico's internal use of convict and indebted labor had expanded.[33] The plan to deport specifically Yaqui men and women from Sonora to labor in southeastern henequen plantations was created by Yucatec entrepreneurs such as Olegario Molina and Sonoran military and political authorities such as Luis E. Torres, a partnership that makes clear the direct and explicit connection between strategies of pacification and the use of coerced labor in the country's two frontier zones.[34]

Toward the late 1800s, the impending threat of race war had seemingly relocated, moving out of the southern border in Yucatán and to the northern border in Sonora, home of native tribes such as the Yaqui, Mayo, Pima, and Opata. During the colonial period, many of these tribes had negotiated with colonial state authorities to retain their autonomy, but after independence their relationship with the government was tense; waves of Yaqui uprising recurred throughout the nineteenth century, resisting encroaching national projects and economic expansion in the region. The valley that stretched between the Yaqui and Mayo Rivers, often described as the "best [land] in the state," was coveted for its fertility and abundance of water.[35] The government sought to divide these rich, communally owned lands, targeting the indigenous residents for dispossession.

In 1880, a petition was passed by the Sonoran congress requesting support from the federal army to contain uprisings described as a "caste war, a merciless and fierce one, like all the wars of its type."[36] According to this narrative, the relative autonomy that Yaqui and Mayo tribes had held on to in those rich and fertile lands constituted a "horrible anomaly" that needed to be smoothed out, flattened by the power of the state.[37] To achieve this, a new set of exceptional practices was legitimated by both the local and federal governments. The narratives that insisted on the need to eradicate the dangers of race war transformed the Yaqui Valley into an anomalous region, one characterized not by a negotiated autonomy but by the sanctioned suspension of the rule of law, and with it the violation of the rights of native groups living within it.

The government made numerous attempts to repress the surges of rebellion in the second half of the century, from attempts to promote national and foreign colonization to varying degrees of military intervention by both federal and local forces. In 1900, the first group of Yaqui people were deported from Sonora to Yucatán's henequen plantations, transported in a complicated circuit via trains and boats, with improvised structures at stops along the way to contain and cage the deportees.[38]

Despite authorities' admission of the economic importance of gaining control over the Yaqui valley, they still framed the indigenous uprising in terms of the race war paradigm. Colonel Ángel García Peña, for instance, who was enlisted by the Sonoran government to chart rebel territories and provide information about roads, potential strategic points of access, dangerous zones, river tributaries, and the like, insisted in his report to the secretary of marine and war that the rebellion was not about land but about the hatred the Yaqui held toward the "yori" (white man) and their desire to expel them from the area.[39]

The racial hatred attributed to the Yaqui was intricately gendered; in his renowned piece *Las guerras contra las tribus yaqui y mayo del Estado de Sonora* (1905), Francisco del Paso y Troncoso argued that it was the Yaqui *women*, not the men, who were responsible for the rebellions.[40] This conveniently meant that the Yaqui men could remain, continuing to contribute their labor, often framed as indispensable and central to the state's economy: "The Yaqui man is incrusted in our social way of being: he is the peon in the fields, the cowboy in the ranch, the *peón de raya* in the haciendas, the miner in the mines, the worker repairing the railroads, the worker doing construction in the City, the daring sailor and, in many cases, the trusted man of accommodated families."[41] Any proposed government projects that would exterminate and/or expel Yaqui men from the region were thus initially discounted, not because they were unjust but because they would alter the state's racialized economy.[42] This explains why García Peña's report defended a project of deportation focused on Yaqui women so as to quell the uprising at the level of social reproduction and erode communal and familial ties without compromising labor supply, a tactic that would grant the government time to figure out how to shift the state's dependency on Yaqui men's labor. García Peña argued for the interruption of the transgenerational transference of hatred toward whites and thus positioned Yaqui women and children as the bearers of the initial stages of the banishment project. Indeed, a group of Yaqui women, many of whom were widowed after a confrontation between rebels and the army known as the Mazocoba massacre, were among the first deportees to be transported from Sonora to Yucatán in 1900.[43]

Between 1900 and 1908 the number of deportations grew considerably and was certainly not restricted to Yaqui women. However, because "peaceful" Yaqui men were racialized as the best and strongest indigenous workers in the entire country, and because their labor was highly coveted in local businesses, including farms, mines, and railroad construction, the decision to support deportation was complicated for government authorities. Balancing efforts to contain the uprisings and keeping landowners and entrepreneurs satisfied with the availability of indigenous labor was a difficult task. Tensions ran high when the waves of deportation sanctioned by the local government increased.[44]

Just as they had in Yucatán, authorities in Sonora mobilized a distinction between "pacified" and "rebel" Yaqui people in order to justify their deportation to the peninsula and avoid angering hacendados. Instating this distinction allowed government authorities to implement measures for the control and surveillance of Yaqui workers' movement aiming to limit their contact with rebel groups. In 1902, the Sonoran government sponsored a detailed census of all Yaqui men over age fifteen working locally and granted workers passports or identification cards; these were said to be intended for hiring, but they could be inspected at any given moment.[45]

But on the ground, the boundary separating the "pacified" from the "rebel" was hazy and hard to police, just as it was in Yucatán. The outcomes of this blurriness cut both ways. On the one hand, authorities were constantly frustrated by how easily Yaqui men moved between the lines, presenting themselves as peaceful workers when in fact they were rebel sympathizers who had been using their time at work in local haciendas to amass resources for the uprising. On the other hand, authorities benefited from the hazy distinction, for it allowed them to criminalize and deport anyone who seemed suspicious, regardless of their tribal belonging or whether there was evidence for their involvement in the rebellion.[46] While torture and extortion were commonly used to force prisoners to "confess" their supposed Yaqui identities, diplomatic correspondence shows that by 1908, during the highest waves of deportation, authorities had resorted to long-standing racializing discourses about the untrustworthiness of Indians' confessions, in this case specifically applied to the Yaqui population. They had also begun to explicitly recognize the futility of the "pacified" versus "rebel" distinction. At this point, authorities began articulating clear desires and projects to expel *all Yaquis* from the state of Sonora.[47]

Like the Yucatán-Cuba trade in indentured labor, Yaqui deportation was a highly mediatized issue, nationally and internationally, as both the governments of Sonora and Yucatán and opposition groups used the press to gain support for their positions. As Turner's *Barbarous Mexico* and numerous articles in the newspapers of border states such as Arizona and California showed, this was an international debate that impacted Mexico's status as a "progressive," "civilized" nation.

However, even publications that sharply criticized the ongoing deportation and the Díaz administration for allowing it also often fell into the rhetorical trap of the "pacified" versus "rebel" distinction, reproducing discourses that framed the value of Yaqui men in terms of their laboriousness. Ideas about labor and productivity that developed throughout the century had now come to permeate all levels of social life across the political spectrum. Consider a 1905 article printed in the revolutionary newspaper *Regeneración* titled "El Yaqui rebelde," which states that the tribe's uprising was directly caused by unjust measures taken by the government. To articulate this argument, however, the author insists on proving that Yaqui men were, under "just and dignified conditions," highly productive and laborious subjects: "No one denies the aptitude and vocation of the Yaqui for labor. . . . [The Yaqui man is] an energized worker, gifted with more physical vigor than any individual of another race. Intelligent and sagacious, he has accepted all forms of labor and to all he has brought extraordinary resiliency and exceptional intelligence."[48]

Turner himself did something similar in *Barbarous Mexico*, which centered much of its critique of deportation projects around the fact that it was mostly "pacified" Yaqui men and women who were being wrongly deported to Yucatán's henequen plantations, as if deporting "rebels" was justified. Turner insisted that the vast majority of "pacified" Yaqui men and women had completely lost touch with the isolated "renegade" groups who were the actual source of the rebellion: "Yet the existence of this handful of 'renegades' is the only excuse the Mexican government has for gathering up peaceful Mexican families and deporting them—at the rate of 500 per month! Why should a lot of women and children and old men be made to suffer because some of their fourth cousins are fighting away off there in the hills?"[49] Certainly, though Turner's piece itself succumbed to the "pacified" versus "rebel" distinction, it also successfully highlighted how authorities were exploiting that distinction to criminalize all native inhabitants of the region. Likely, Turner carefully planned this framing of the matter, for he sought to spark the moral outrage of his reading public; for example, he underscored that the Mexican government was deporting vulnerable sectors of the population, such as women, children, and the elderly. Perhaps Turner's critique of the deportation of "pacified" working Yaqui men was similarly intentional, for his readers would have been more likely to show sympathy for the "unjustly deported" than for "rebels," who could be "legitimately" punished for their unruly behavior. Whether Turner shared these preconceptions or not is beside the point. Whatever Turner's motivation, *Barbarous Mexico* and the *Regeneración* article illustrate how drawing lines around innocence and guilt increasingly became a way to determine the boundaries of disposability, and to position the lives of "criminals" and "renegades" as not deserving of defense.

Barbarous Mexico also shows how the charting of these lines of innocence and guilt intersected with processes of racialization. Turner traveled on a ship from Veracruz to Progreso with a group of deportees, and his transcription of the conversation he had with one of them underscores the importance of racialization to deportation. Responding to Turner's question about why he and his companions were being deported given that they were Pima and Opata workers and not active participants in the rebellion nor members of the Yaqui tribe, his interlocutor said, "Ah, we are all Yaquis to General Torres. It makes no difference to him. You are dark. You dress in my clothes and you will be a Yaqui—to him. He makes no investigation, asks no questions,—only takes you."[50] Public and official discourses insisted that race was no longer an issue of the "great Mexican family," but Turner's piece shows otherwise.

The question of race and political–economic banishment was not confined to constructions of Indianness. As deportations ramped up and the scarcity of indigenous labor once again became a concern, discussions about foreign colonization were revisited; in this discussion, a whole new range of discursive practices of racialization were revitalized and repurposed. A 1908 article published in *La Opinión* discusses the "terrible exodus" of the Yaqui to Yucatán, but the author does not critique deportation for its own sake. Instead, he criticizes a new problem supposedly generated by it: the depletion of idealized Yaqui labor, which was now beginning to be replaced with Asian immigrants—a dangerous "invasion" that was taking over commerce in the country's Northern Pacific region. The author ends by lamenting the extermination of the Yaqui race and hoping that those who had been forcibly dispersed throughout the country would spread their greatness by mixing with the "degenerated ethnic elements" that peopled most of the country. The article ultimately points toward growing discourses about indigenous assimilation that would later feed into ideas about *mestizaje* during and after the Mexican Revolution. It also highlights the new direction of racial fear, which would increasingly be aimed at incoming Asian, mostly Chinese, migrant laborers.[51]

Toward the end of the years of turmoil of the Mexican Revolution, the Monterrey-based newspaper *El Porvenir (The Future)* published a futuristic mini-serial novel titled *La guerra de razas en el año de 1977*. The anonymous author of this brief science-fiction piece imagined the coming of a geopolitical order marked by a war of worldly proportions between two racialized coalitions: the Confederation of the Nations of the White Race ("Conferederación de las Naciones de la Raza Blanca") on one side and the United Powers of the Yellow Race ("Potencias Unidas de la Raza Amarilla") on the other, each struggling to devise scientific weapons to destroy their enemy. Although a minor work and generally unknown, the serial novel is telling of postrevolutionary racial discourses in Mexico. Indeed, it is noteworthy that the editors decided to publish and widely publicize this text in a newspaper that, like *El Porvenir*, had the explicit goal of using print media to overcome the social fissures left by the revolution.[52]

Showcasing the eugenicist trends of his time, the author of *La guerra de razas* displaced the rhetoric of race war into a global context, and from the present to the future. In doing so he disavowed social frictions internal to the nation. One could even say that the serial novel's mapping of race war as a global conflict between "white" and "yellow" coalitions was only afforded by the consolidating national ideology of *mestizaje* premised on both the symbolic assimilation of Indianness and the exclusion of indigenous, Black, and Asian people on the ground.[53] Avoiding any references to mestizo ideology per se, *La guerra de razas* illuminates the outer boundaries that underlie it and prompts us to consider how *mestizaje* as a national state discourse would in fact operate by encoding in its alleged project of inclusion the exclusionary historical privileges of whiteness.

Epilogue

On January 1, 1994, Mexico's southeastern region became center stage for one of the most important and internationally influential indigenous uprisings of the twentieth and twenty-first centuries. From the confines of the Lacandon Jungle, the Zapatista Army of National Liberation (Ejército Zapatista de Liberación Nacional; EZLN) issued a declaration of war against the neoliberal reforms promoted by the Institutional Revolutionary Party (Partido Revolucionario Institucional; PRI) and in pursuit of the political, economic, and cultural autonomy of allied Tojolabal, Tzeltal, Zoque, Tzotzil, Chole, and Mame communities. Only five days later, in one of his administration's initial public responses, President Carlos Salinas de Gortari refused to acknowledge the uprising as indigenous. "Este no es un alzamiento indígena" (This is not an indigenous uprising), he stated in a televised message delivered from the presidential chair. Instead, he declared the Zapatista uprising the action of an isolated group, anathema to the interests of Chiapanecan local communities and composed of "professionals in violence."[1] Taking up arms against the state, the "violent group" had, in Salinas's words, struck the heart not only of the Chiapanecan people but also of the entire Mexican nation.[2]

I have shown that throughout the long nineteenth century, elites and government officials frequently relied on the rhetoric of "race war" to depoliticize indigenous and popular struggles and to legitimate, by contrast, racializing measures that would increase state control over rioting populations and facilitate the absorption of their labor into the logics of capitalist development and accumulation. Historical reverberations permeate this story but do not operate in simple chronological order. For some readers, the Mexican Revolution of 1910 might seem to be the logical next step in the temporal arc traced here, but I argue that aspects of the race war paradigm have reemerged and resonate most strongly with the neoliberal economic and political transformations that began in the 1990s.[3]

To a large extent, Salinas's response to the Zapatista movement remained within the bounds of the political framework through which the state dealt with domestic affairs for most of the twentieth century.[4] But when Salinas dubbed the EZLN an "armed group" of "professionals in violence," he used a securitizing rhetoric that echoed the operations of the race war paradigm from a century prior. Similar to how the rhetoric of race war provided a catch-all concept to manage and pacify popular and indigenous uprisings during the nineteenth century, present-day governing groups have resorted to smokescreen categories such as "organized crime" to depoliticize a wide spectrum of complex social dynamics, including indigenous communities' resistance to neoliberal measures. This rhetoric has also been used to justify an increasingly invasive, often military range of interventions in the name of national security.[5] While these measures are presented as objectively logical and necessary to protect public safety, they operate on the ground to recognize as legitimate only those actors and activities that contribute to a "friendly environment for capital alongside neoliberal commitments to deregulation, privatization, and liberalization, which translates to minimal taxation and regulation, low wages, lax labor conditions, and restricted opposition."[6] What is seldom acknowledged is the extent to which such security measures are shaped by ongoing processes of racialization, however concealed or creatively recast these may be.[7]

ERASING INDIGENEITY AS LEGACY OF THE RACE WAR PARADIGM

The genealogy I have traced here of connections between race-making practices and state-led pacification efforts helps to render more legible the contemporary effects and affordances of racial difference. On the one hand, Salinas's message illustrates that contemporary struggles for life and against the encroachment of transnational capital, enclosure, and environmental destruction are no longer framed and contained through the rhetoric of race war. On the other hand, it also illustrates how easily these movements continue to be racially criminalized and politically defanged.

Salinas's insistence that the EZLN "is not an indigenous uprising" bears the marks of racial discourses engendered and hegemonized in the aftermath of the 1910 revolution. As many have pointed out, the consolidation of Mexico's "mestizo state" depended on two simultaneous, if contradictory, factors: the cultural appropriation and celebration of Indian ancestry, and the simultaneous demand that indigenous people de-Indianize themselves in order to be recognized as political subjects and assimilate to the premises of a mestizo citizenship with no room for practices of communal self-governance.[8] In this way, those unable or unwilling to assimilate have been (and continue to be) materially exploited and discursively mobilized as the inferiorized alterity that constitutes the condition of possibility for *mestizaje*.[9] The now ex-president's message was congruent with his decision to reform Article 27 of the constitution, thus breaking with the pact that had marked the relation between the state and peasant organizations since 1917. Although Salinas revitalized *indigenista* cultural policies, his reform to Article 27 foreclosed actual economic and political opportunities for peasants tied to the revolutionary legacies of land redistribution.[10]

Most important, Salinas's message was tailored to an emergent liberal multicultural public sphere for which an explicitly repressive campaign against the indigenous rebellion would have been intolerable. Despite its shrewd framing, his characterization of the EZLN as a non-indigenous organization can be read precisely as a refusal to recognize the political valence of the uprising, its demand for recognition for indigenous communities as collective subjects, and its challenge of racialized precarities exacerbated by the Salinas administration's neoliberal agenda. Rather than invoke the rhetoric of race war, Salinas's pacification strategy relied on a version of the developmentalist discourse that has long rendered indigenous subjects the target of assimilationist projects in the name of progress.[11] In the televised message, the president contrasted the uprising's purported detrimental impact for both the state of Chiapas and Mexico at large with the benefits of programs his administration had implemented in the southeastern state to "aid poverty-stricken communities." He insisted that local indigenous groups were, in fact, against the uprising and in support of the government's intervention to promote "peace" and "well-being" in the region.[12]

The emphasis Salinas placed on indigenous communities' alleged rejection of the Zapatista movement, as well as his refusal to acknowledge it as an indigenous uprising, are haunted by the specters of the race war paradigm chronicled in this book. Although the explicit rhetoric of racial war is absent (even deliberately erased) from the message, the move to de-Indianize the Zapatista movement suggests a special concern with the potential dangers of "racial conflict." But whereas nineteenth-century governing and elite groups explicitly racialized uprisings in order to depoliticize them, Salinas's message is but one example of the Mexican state's shift in the twentieth and twenty-first centuries to the strategic disavowal of Indian difference. Only seemingly opposite, both gestures share a historical preoccupation with the potential and actual power of organized indigenous groups—a concern that persists and constitutes a central target of state-led pacification efforts to this day.

DEVELOPMENT AS RACIALIZED PACIFICATION

In 2012, when Captain Gustavo Cuevas Gutiérrez was asked what he considered the most dangerous threats facing Mexico at the time, the head of security for Enrique Peña Nieto's campaign responded without hesitation: "el tema social," a euphemistic term to refer to social movements and, more specifically, to indigenous resistance.[13] After Peña Nieto was elected, Cuevas was one of three members of the presidential guard Estado Mayor Presidencial to be promoted by the president into major civilian positions, and he was put in charge of security policies in one of Mexico's most important state-owned institutions.[14] As subdirector of physical security for the Federal Commission of Electricity (Comisión Federal de Electricidad; CFE), Cuevas oversaw the security of the country's electric infrastructure, from hydroelectric and thermoelectric plants to lines of transmission, distribution, and substations. When protesters blocked highways and occupied pertinent installations, challenging the dispossession and environmental devastation stemming from the expansion of the country's systems of energy and resource extraction to indigenous communities and communally owned lands, Cuevas did not hesitate to threaten violent repression.[15]

That military men should occupy positions overseeing the security of Mexico's energy infrastructure was nothing new. In fact, the Departments for Physical Security of both the CFE and Pemex (Mexico's state-owned oil company) were created under Salinas's administration and in direct response to the Zapatista uprising.[16] The militarization of Mexico's electric and oil infrastructures underscores the extent to which the specter of indigenous resistance continues to haunt governmental fantasies (and policies) of pacification. What is more, sites of development where energy infrastructures are built or expanded constitute new zones of legal exception where race-making processes tied to state-led pacification are still both advanced and challenged. A recent example from the Peña Nieto administration illustrates the point.

In March 2017, a coalition of indigenous activist groups from the Isthmus of Tehuantepec demanded protection from local courts against Enrique Peña Nieto's recent law creating special economic zones (SEZ) in the country. Leaders from the organized groups recognized in the law not only the threat of expansive land dispossession and entrenchment of the economic marginalization of local communities but also an effort to pacify and fragment indigenous resistance to mega-development projects.[17] Many of these groups had been organizing for years against the devastating environmental and social impacts of large wind farms constructed and controlled by transnational firms in the region. Under Peña Nieto's SEZ law, new and existing wind farms would enjoy greater protection against such resistance.

The SEZ law was part of Peña Nieto's broader effort to frame poverty as an issue of national security and, through this, to legitimate the intertwined deployment of militaristic and entrepreneurial interventions in certain regions. In his 2014–2018 Program for National Security (PNS), Peña Nieto sought to distance his administration from the exclusively militaristic strategy developed by his predecessor, Felipe Calderón, to deal with the problem of so-called drug-related violence. The distancing, however, was purely symbolic. Far from restricting the militarization that began in the early 2000s, Peña Nieto's program strengthened the army's presence across Mexico and expanded the breadth of issues around which its intervention could be justified. The program document discursively reframes the concept of national security as "multidimensional."[18] Among the matters it deemed existential threats to the nation, the PNS named poverty, thus constructing a link between economic dispossession and delinquency. Its authors argued that educational and economic marginalization render people vulnerable, making them more likely to participate in violence and join in criminal organizations, but they made no effort to provide a structural analysis of this relationship.[19] As such, the document fed into long-standing narratives about the alleged social threat posed by the destitute and fostered policies that criminalize already largely impoverished racialized groups.

An expression of both Peña Nieto's Program for National Security and his ambitious energy reform projects, the SEZ law was approved by the Mexican House of Representatives in 2016. It provided the juridical infrastructure to create nodes for socioeconomic development in designated areas of Mexico's ten most impoverished states. Following models from China, India, Bangladesh, and other nations, the SEZ law was meant to alleviate regional economic disparities and address security issues associated with poverty. On the ground, however, the law created a special legislative body for designated geographic areas that would pave the way for unfettered land enclosure under the gun of foreign and national private capital. It resorted to the recurrent historical practice studied in the previous chapters of protecting the interests of groups in power (generally tied to the global structures of whiteness) through tax relief and other economic incentives. In doing so, it essentially created zones of legal anomaly within the nation's grid, areas where the law of capital could explicitly rule unchecked in the name of improving economic and social conditions while outstanding fiscal and other exemptions for investors were not only allowed but encouraged.[20] The generic language of the SEZ law allowed it to justify the penetration of an array of industries into allocated regions: energy, monocrop agroindustry, pharmaceutical laboratories, maquiladoras, and the extraction and transformation of raw materials were all pushed forward by this project.[21] Similarly, because it did not include the names of the specific locations where the special zones were to be created, the law constituted a scalable model that could be extended and applied ad infinitum to new regions.[22]

Beyond incentivizing economic investment, the SEZ law also laid the groundwork to assemble a cheap and disciplined workforce. It stipulated that investors and local authorities were to be responsible for implementing "social programs of development" in each zone. Among other things, said programs would educate and train inhabitants of surrounding areas in pertinent labor skills, depending on each given zone's economic potential. As the introduction of the law stated in unapologetically biopolitical terms, the SEZs were designed to "expand opportunities for healthy and productive lives."[23]

Crucially, the law was also conceived as a policing tool aimed at "strengthening public security."[24] This is evident not only in the law's stated guidelines but also in how it was presented to the public. Consider, for instance, the comments that Silvano Aureoles, then governor of the violence-stricken state of Michoacán, made in support of the installation of an economic zone in the Pacific port of Lázaro Cárdenas. In a June 2017 press conference, the governor declared that the only way to resolve the situation of insecurity in Michoacán was for the authorities to provide their respective populations with adequate opportunities, like those created by the SEZ in Lázaro Cárdenas, for development and employment.[25] By framing the SEZs as enclaves that would foster public security, the law incorporated caveats for emergency situations and opened the way for unquestioned army, police, and private security service interventions, all in order to "guarantee and safeguard the adequate operation" of the special economic zones.[26] This also laid the basis for criminalizing indigenous activist groups that for years had been fighting against the encroachment of transnational capital and environmental destruction in the states that would harbor these special zones.

Without a single explicit mention of its effort to repress indigenous organized resistance, yet fully in keeping with the logic and aims of the race war paradigm, the SEZ law seamlessly granted security forces the power to intervene and, among other things, restrict the movement of people through the designated areas.[27] Likewise, without referencing race directly, the law's racializing impact was also ensured by its implementation within and across preexisting racial geographies. It played, for instance, into the historical division of the "productive north" versus the "unproductive south" described in coda 3. Furthermore, and not coincidentally, the southeastern states where these special economic zones were to be first created included Guerrero, Michoacán, Chiapas, Oaxaca, Veracruz, and Yucatán, where most of Mexico's indigenous populations live and where struggles over communal lands and natural resources are ongoing.[28] It is in this way, by targeting largely indigenous regions, that the law constituted a pacifying mechanism to contain and control Mexico's *tema social*.

The SEZ law didn't stipulate concrete guidelines for the social programs that were to be implemented. It did, however, include vague language that enlisted municipal and other pertinent authorities, as well as investors, to make sure that local inhabitants were "adequately incorporated" into the development plans designed for each zone. In her study of Oportunidades (now Prospera), a program that promotes "co-responsibility" by granting funds to women heads of low-income households with certain caveats, such as mandating gynecological exams and children's school attendance, Mariana Mora argues that when behavioral changes are set as preconditions for receiving economic aid, such social programs actually devalue the lives of the target population—more often than not, impoverished indigenous people.[29] Combined with securitizing measures, the programs render permissible the deaths of the marginalized. Peña Nieto's plan to develop "special zones" expands similar racializing mechanisms. To be sure, the primary goal of the SEZ program was profit and the incursion of private capital for development, but its underlying social and political agenda and implications should not be overlooked. The premise that the model would open new opportunities to "improve" the lives of those who participated in it not only presumes a racialized target population that is there to be molded at the whim of state authorities and entrepreneurs. It also implicitly reactivates the pervasive legacies of racial discourses that, since colonial times, have constructed Indian subjectivity as both plastic and in need of improvement.

Social programs that promise that improvement reinforce two simultaneous, if contradictory, racializing premises: first, they presume that the desired betterment of the target population can only take place through the influence of external forces; second, they place the burden for the success or failure of these programs to alleviate poverty on the target population itself.[30] In addition, insofar as the plan to create special economic zones was meant to address issues of insecurity, it also laid the groundwork for the criminalization of racialized poverty. Although presented as placing the interests of marginalized (mostly indigenous) communities at the center, the SEZ law ultimately resonates with and refashions historical discourses of race in ways that reinforce the idea that the lives of those it was destined to help are, in fact, expendable.

Although the creation of special economic zones went into effect in 2016, it promises to be short-lived. Early into his presidency, Andrés Manuel López Obrador announced his plan to cancel the program following his decision to favor, instead, major infrastructural interventions such as the rail projects in the Isthmus of Tehuantepec and the Yucatán Peninsula. Yet once again, while using different methods, this plan targets the same populations and regions, and reactivates similar tropes about underdevelopment and lack of economic productivity. Whether these projects will continue the legacies of the race war paradigm is yet to be seen. What is certain is that, on the ground, a number of indigenous social movements have already expressed their concerns around how such infrastructural projects might deepen and exacerbate existing racialized precarities and facilitate the containment and surveillance of migrant flows.

The turn toward securitization has not been made by Mexico alone; it is occurring at a nearly global scale. By placing it in a broader genealogy of legal exceptionality and tracing its links to processes of racialization, however, I have sought here to show how securitization expands and reactivates the legacies of the race war paradigm. Under the current regime, more and more aspects of life are subsumed and treated as threats to "national security," thereby expanding the opportunities to criminalize and racialize people while militarizing territories in favor of logics of extraction and accumulation. Yet, at the same time, the securitizing turn is far from advancing without resistance; indeed, as the "turn" evolves, it doesn't just provoke resistance but must also respond and adapt to it, forcing all "sides" to continually adjust their strategies. Multiple environmental and indigenous social movements are fighting against the ongoing state and corporate operations of pacification for which the previous race war paradigm has been both disavowed and repurposed. Subcomandante Marcos has called this the fourth world war: a total war against humanity.[31] Its outward appearance may change, but the struggle continues.

Notes

INTRODUCTION

1. All translations are mine unless noted otherwise. See Domingo F. Sarmiento, *Conflicto y armonía de las razas en América* (Buenos Aires: D. Tuñez, 1883), viii–ix.

2. Sarmiento, *Conflicto y armonía*, xxi–xxii.

3. Sarmiento, *Conflicto y armonía*, xii.

4. Patrick Wolfe defines settler colonialism as a project of replacement, one that destroys in order to replace. See "Settler Colonialism and the Elimination of the Native," *Journal of Genocide Research* 8, no. 4 (2006): 388, https://doi.org/10.1080/14623520601056240. See also Wolfe, *Traces of History: Elementary Structures of Race* (London: Verso, 2016), chap. 1. For discussions on the nonapplicability of the term "settler colonialism" to the Latin American context, see Lorenzo Veracini, *Settler Colonialism* (London: Palgrave Macmillan, 2010); Gustavo Verdesio, "Colonialismo acá y allá: Reflexiones sobre la teoría y la práctica de los estudios coloniales a través de fronteras culturales," *Cuadernos del CILHA* 13, no. 17 (2012); and Verdesio, "Endless Dispossession: The Charrua Re-emergence in Uruguay in the Light of Settler Colonialism," *Journal of Settler Colonial Studies* (2020), published online October 6, 2020, https://doi.org/10.1080/2201473X.2020.1823752. For a discussion on the applicability of the term to Latin America, see Richard Gott, "Latin America as a White Settler Society," *Bulletin of Latin American Research* 26, no. 2 (2007), and a recent dossier with several articles on the topic published in *American Quarterly* 69, no. 4 (December 2017).

5. María Josefina Saldaña-Portillo, "'How Many Mexicans [Is] a Horse Worth?': The League of United Latin American Citizens, Desegregation Cases, and Chicano Historiography," *South Atlantic Quarterly* 107, no. 4 (2008): 812.

6. With "racial state," I refer to the conglomeration of governing institutions whose policies and practices call into being the racial hierarchies that govern Mexico's body politic. As Michael Omi and Howard Winant point out, the state does not

have clear boundaries. In their words, "although based in formally constituted institutions and grounded in a contentious historical process, the state extends beyond administrative, legislative, or judicial forms of activity." Omi and Winant, *Racial Formation in the United States* (London: Routledge, 2014), 138. On the term "racial state," see also David Theo Goldberg, *The Racial State* (Malden, MA: Blackwell, 2002). On the racial state in Mexico specifically, see Jason Oliver Chang, *Chino: Anti-Chinese Racism in Mexico, 1880–1940* (Urbana: University of Illinois Press, 2017), 23.

7. The idea that racial differentiation eroded in the face of class and *mestizaje* becoming more prominent is usually highlighted in two moments of Mexican history: at the end of the Porfiriato and the Mexican Revolution, and in the late colonial period. For examples on the former, see Alan Knight, "Racism, Revolution, and Indigenismo: Mexico, 1910–1940," in *The Idea of Race in Latin America, 1870–1940*, ed. Richard Graham (Austin: University of Texas Press, 1990), 71–113; Ben Vinson III, *Before Mestizaje: The Frontiers of Race and Caste in Colonial Mexico* (Cambridge: Cambridge University Press, 2017). For examples on the latter, see Douglas R. Cope, *The Limits of Racial Domination: Plebeian Society in Colonial Mexico City, 1660–1720* (Madison: University of Wisconsin Press, 1994); and Felipe Castro Gutiérrez, *Nueva ley y nuevo rey: Reformas borbónicas y rebelión popular en Nueva España* (Zamora, Mexico: Colegio de Michoacán, 1996).

8. For studies on colonial legacies in Latin America that develop an argument akin to the one presented here, see Jeremy Adelman, ed., *Colonial Legacies: The Problem of Persistence in Latin America* (London: Routledge, 1999); María Josefina Saldaña-Portillo, *Indian Given: Racial Geographies across Mexico and the United States* (Durham, NC: Duke University Press, 2016); David Viñas, *Indios, ejército y frontera* (Buenos Aires: Siglo XXI Editores, 1982). My take on this issue is also informed by discussions about postcolonialism in Latin America. These approaches tend to highlight the epistemological continuities of colonialism, and here I'm interested in tracing more concrete repurposings of race-making colonial practices. See Aníbal Quijano, "Coloniality of Power, Eurocentrism, and Latin America," *Nepantla: Views from the South* 1, no. 3 (2000): 533–580; and Mabel Moraña, Enrique Dussel, and Carlos A. Jáuregui, eds., *Coloniality at Large: Latin America and the Postcolonial Debate* (Durham, NC: Duke University Press, 2008). My thinking about the residues of colonialism beyond the Latin American context is also indebted to the work of Ann Laura Stoler; see *Duress: Imperial Durabilities in Our Times* (Durham, NC: Duke University Press, 2016), and "Imperial Debris: Reflections on Ruins and Ruination," *Cultural Anthropology* 23, no. 2 (2008), https://doi.org/10.1111/j.1548-1360.2008.00007.x.

9. At the time, Garay and Gálvez occupied the position of president and secretary of the Direction of Colonization and Industry, respectively. The Direction was founded in 1846.

10. See Dirección de Colonización e Industria, *Memoria de la dirección de colonización e industria* (Mexico City: Imprenta de Vicente G. Torres, 1850), 5.

11. See Juan Almonte, *Memoria del Ministro de Guerra y Marina, presentada a las Cámaras del Congreso General Mexicano, en Enero de 1840* (Mexico City: Oficina del Águila, 1840).

12. Charles A. Hale credits these texts to Lucas Alamán. See Charles Hale, "Jose María Luis Mora and the Structure of Mexican Liberalism," *Hispanic American Historical Review* 45 (1965): 216n68.

13. See "Guerra de Castas," *El Universal*, December 8, 1848, 1. Accessed through the hndm.unam.mx portal.

14. The Caste War was accompanied by a journalistic boom in Yucatán's press; see David Kazanjian, *Brink of Freedom: Improvising Life in the Nineteenth-Century Atlantic World* (Durham, NC: Duke University Press, 2016), 164–167.

15. Benedict Anderson, *Imagined Communities: Reflections on the Origin and Spread of Nationalism*, rev. ed. (London: Verso, 2016). Anderson's influential thesis has been widely critiqued. For an example of this critique, see John Charles Chasteen and Sara Castro-Klarén, *Beyond Imagined Communities: Reading and Writing the Nation in Nineteenth-Century Latin America* (Washington, DC: Woodrow Wilson Center Press, 2003).

16. I'm here borrowing from David Kazanjian's engagement with Laura Gotkowitz's and Thomas Holt's work on race: "If we ask with Laura Gotkowitz and Thomas Holt, not 'what race means' but rather about 'the consequences of race and the work that races does.'" See Kazanjian, *Brink of Freedom*, 163. See also Laura Gotkowitz, "Introduction: Racisms of the Present and the Past in Latin America," in *Histories of Race and Racism: The Andes and Mesoamerica from Colonial Times to the Present*, ed. Gotkowitz (Durham, NC: Duke University Press, 2011); Thomas Holt, "Marking: Race, Race-Making, and the Writing of History," in *American Historians Interpret the Past*, ed. Anthony Molho and Gordon S. Wood (Princeton, NJ: Princeton University Press, 1998).

17. See Enrique Florescano, *Etnia, estado y nación* (Mexico City: Aguilar, 1997), 405–431.

18. On the term "rebel archive," see Kelly Lytle Hernández, "Introduction," in her *City of Inmates: Conquest, Rebellion, and the Rise of Human Caging in Los Angeles 1771–1965* (Chapel Hill: University of North Carolina Press, 2017).

19. Kazanjian, *Brink of Freedom*, 216.

20. Kazanjian, *Brink of Freedom*, part 2.

21. Spanish version of the letter compiled in Fidelio Quintal Martín, *Correspondencia de la Guerra de Castas: Epistolario documental, 1843–1866* (Mérida, Mexico: Ediciones de la Universidad Autónoma de Yucatán, 1992), 78. For a detailed discussion of this letter, see chapter 6.

22. Wolfe, *Traces of History*, 6. Also see Omi and Winant, *Racial Formation*, and Daniel Nemser, *Infrastructures of Race: Concentration and Biopolitics in Colonial Mexico* (Austin: University of Texas Press, 2017).

23. Wolfe, *Traces of History*, 18.

24. Wolfe, *Traces of History*, 10, 18.

25. Wolfe, *Traces of History*, 10, 18.

26. Perhaps the most paradigmatic of these cases is the Haitian Revolution, which is further discussed in chapters 3 and 4. References to racial fear in the context of the Haitian Revolution are almost ubiquitous, and the bibliography on this historic episode has grown in recent years. For select studies that touch upon Haiti and the question of racial fear, see Michel-Rolph Trouillot, *Silencing the Past: Power and the Production of History* (Boston: Beacon, 1995); Sybille Fischer, *Modernity Disavowed: Haiti and the Cultures of Slaves in the Age of Revolution* (Durham, NC: Duke University Press, 2004); Susan Buck-Morss, *Hegel, Haiti, and Universal History* (Pittsburgh, PA: University of Pittsburgh Press, 2009); James Alexander Dun, *Dangerous Neighbors: Making the Haitian Revolution in Early America* (Philadelphia, PA: University of Pennsylvania Press, 2016); David Geggus, ed., *The Impact of the Haitian Revolution in the Atlantic World* (Columbia: University of South Carolina Press, 2001). In studies about Mexico's history, discussions of the fear of racial conflict have mostly been tied to the Yucatán Caste War. For more on this, see chapters 5 and 6.

27. For more on pacification as both destructive and constructive, see Mark Neocleous and George Rigakos, "On Pacification: Introduction to the Special Issue," *Socialist Studies/Études Socialistes* 9, no. 2 (2013).

28. For more on the term "flashpoint," see David Kazanjian, "Introduction," in his *The Colonizing Trick: National Culture and Imperial Citizenship in Early America* (Minneapolis: University of Minnesota Press, 2003).

29. For a study on the concept of friction, see Anna Tsing, *Friction: An Ethnography of Global Connection* (Princeton, NJ: Princeton University Press, 2011).

30. See Giorgio Agamben, "Che cos'è un paradigma?," in his *Signatura rerum: Sul metodo* (Turin, Italy: Bollati Boringhieri, 2008).

31. For more on discourses on racial harmony in Latin America, see Paulina L. Alberto and Jesse Hoffnung-Garskof, "'Racial Democracy' and Racial Inclusion," in *Afro-Latin American Studies: An Introduction*, ed. Alejandro de la Fuente and George Reid Andrews (Cambridge: Cambridge University Press, 2018). See also Marixa Lasso, *Myths of Harmony: Race and Republicanism during the Age of Revolution in Colombia* (Pittsburgh, PA: University of Pittsburgh Press, 2007), and James E. Sanders, *The Vanguard of the Atlantic World: Creating Modernity, Nation, and Democracy in Nineteenth-Century Latin America* (Durham, NC: Duke University Press, 2014).

32. For a study of the Black Legend that addresses it in the context of imperial conflict within Europe and beyond, see Margaret R. Greer, Walter Mignolo, and Maureen Quilligan, eds., *Re-Reading the Black Legend: The Discourses of Religious and Racial Difference in the Renaissance Empires* (Chicago: University of Chicago Press, 2007).

33. For a historical study on the shapes of partial sovereignty in isolated spaces

such as hills and islands, see Lauren Benton, *A Search for Sovereignty: Law and Geography in European Empires, 1400–1900* (Cambridge: Cambridge University Press, 2014), chapters 4 and 5.

34. The term "anomalous zones" comes from Lauren Benton's work. See the preface of *Search for Sovereignty*.

35. Here, I'm following Achille Mbembe's argument about how colonialism creates zones of exception. See Mbembe, "Necropolitics," *Public Culture* 15, no. 1 (Winter 2003): 11–40.

36. Giorgio Agamben, *The State of Exception*, trans. Kevin Attell (Chicago: University of Chicago Press, 2005), 10–23.

37. Agamben, *State of Exception*, 23.

38. This is particularly the case for postindependence conflicts, as inscribing explicit legal distinctions based on racial difference would have, by that time, been illegal.

39. Brian Loveman, *The Constitution of Tyranny: Regimes of Exception in Spanish America* (Pittsburgh, PA: University of Pittsburgh Press, 1993), 67–91.

40. Loveman, *Constitution of Tyranny*, 71.

41. Loveman, *Constitution of Tyranny*, 86.

42. For more on congressional discussions around the topic of martial law, see "Congreso General, Cámara de diputados. Sesión del día 14 de mayo," *El Sol*, June 28, 1828; *Diario del Gobierno de la República Mexicana*, January 28, 1847; *El Universal: Periódico Independiente*, July 19, 1850. Available through hndm.unam.mx. See also Basilio José Arrillaga, *Recopilación de leyes, decretos, bandos, circulares, y providencias de los supremos poderes y otras autoridades de la República Mexicana del 25 al 31 de diciembre de 1860* (Mexico City: Imprenta de Vicente G. Torres, 1861), 217–219. Loveman situates the first attempts to incorporate the state of siege into Mexican legislature in the 1843 *Bases de organización política de la República Mexicana*. See Loveman, *Constitution of Tyranny*, 80–81.

43. The decree was reprinted and can be accessed in Arrillaga, *Recopilación de leyes*, 217–219.

44. The decree was discussed in relation to France's legislation on the state of siege. For more on the 1857 constitution as inaugurating Mexico's liberal regime of exception, see Gareth Williams, *The Mexican Exception: Sovereignty, Police, and Democracy* (New York: Palgrave Macmillan, 2011), 26. See also Loveman, *Constitution of Tyranny*, 67–91.

45. The most important of these mutinies was planned and funded from Cuba by Antonio López de Santa Anna. See Pantaleón Tovar, *Historia Parlamentaria del cuarto congreso constitucional*, vol. 1 (Mexico City: Imprenta de I. Cumplido, 1872), 86–90.

46. On the paradoxical nature of martial law, see Nasser Hussain, *The Jurisprudence of Emergency: Colonialism and the Rule of Law* (Ann Arbor: University of Michigan Press, 2003), 106, and Benton, *Search for Sovereignty*, chap. 4.

47. To follow these discussions, see Tovar, *Historia Parlamentaria*, vol. 1, 86–

90, 105–106, 116–124, 127–132, 136–147. For discussions on repealing article 29 of the constitution, see *Diario de los debates del Congreso de la Unión correspondiente al periodo de sesiones extraordinarias y al segundo de las ordinarias del año de 1870 a 1871*, vol. 4 (Mexico City: Imprenta del Gobierno en Palacio a cargo de José María Sandoval, 1871), 288–292, 477–485, 498–539, 595–598, 612–623, 682–688. See also Claudio Lomnitz, *Deep Mexico, Silent Mexico: An Anthropology of Nationalism* (Minneapolis: University of Minnesota Press, 2001), 67, 293.

48. One exception to this is the diplomatic discussion that surrounded the indenture of indigenous men and women from the Peninsula in Cuba. For more on this discussion, see chapter 5.

49. See Tovar, *Historia Parlamentaria*, vol. 1, 140. Notably, anxieties about regimes of exception appeared even when discussing the proposal to suspend bandits' and *plagiarios*' (kidnappers') civil liberties to contain the threat they posed to Mexico's economic and political structure. For more on this, see *Diario de los debates del Congreso de la Unión*, vol. 4, 294, 515–539. For a cultural and historical study about banditry in Latin America, see Juan Pablo Dabove, *Nightmares of the Lettered City: Banditry and Literature in Latin America, 1816–1929* (Pittsburgh, PA: University of Pittsburgh Press, 2007).

50. See Michel Foucault, "*Society Must Be Defended:*" *Lectures at the Collège de France, 1975–76*, ed. Mauro Bertani and Alessandro Fontana, trans. David Macey (New York: Picador, 2003), 254–255.

51. See Joshua Lund, "They Were Not a Barbarous Tribe," *Journal of Latin American Cultural Studies* 12, no. 2 (2003), 182.

52. For more on coloniality and zones of exception, see Mbembe, "Necropolitics."

53. This is the rebellion that Rosario Castellanos famously represented in fiction in *Oficio de tinieblas* (1962).

54. Ver, "Proclama al mundo civilizado," quoted in Leticia Reina, *Las rebeliones campesinas en México, 1819–1906* (Mexico City: Siglo XXI Editores, 1980), 53.

55. "Otro de los medios que pudiera ensayarse es el de juzgarlos conforme a la ley, pero esto es impracticable porque no es posible encarcelar a pueblos enteros ni hay recursos para mantener las fuerzas con qué custodiarlos entre tanto se concluyen los procesos, en cuya instrucción hay que tropezar con la malicia y rebeldía de los indios que impiden una averiguación perfecta. El único partido adoptable en las actuales circunstancias es sacarlos de sus madrigueras y trasladarlos a distintas localidades del estado, para formar con ellos otras tantas poblaciones que puedan ser útiles a la República" (quoted in Reina, *Rebeliones Campesinas*, 56).

56. See Reina, *Rebeliones Campesinas*, 55–56.

57. See Reina, *Rebeliones Campesinas*, 56.

58. The term "burdened individuals" is a nod to Saidiya Hartman's concept of the burdened individuality of freedom. Although Hartman specifically addresses the burdens in the context of the United States after what she calls the non-event of emancipation, I am here thinking about how another form of burdened individual-

ity emerged for indigenous people in Mexico's postindependence context. See Saidiya Hartman, *Scenes of Subjection: Terror, Slavery, and Self-Making in Nineteenth-Century America* (New York: Oxford University Press, 1997), chap. 4.

59. See Reina, *Rebeliones Campesinas*, 56.

60. See Christon I. Archer, *The Army in Bourbon Mexico, 1760–1810* (Albuquerque: University of New Mexico Press, 1977), 12–13. See also María del Carmen Velázquez, *El Estado de guerra en Nueva España, 1760–1808* (Mexico City: Colegio de México, Centro de Estudios Históricos, 1997).

61. See Ben Vinson III, "Articulating Space: The Free-Colored Military Establishment in Colonial Mexico for the Conquest to Independence," *Callaloo* 27, no. 1 (Winter 2004).

62. The military solution would engender a new dilemma: the strategy of immunization—that is, establishing an army—would be accompanied by the constant fear (and the efforts to manage it) that the militias would turn against the very order that had produced them and that they were supposed to protect. See Archer, *Army in Bourbon Mexico*, 12–13. On the Bourbon army in Mexico, see also Velázquez, *Estado de guerra*; Vinson, *Bearing Arms for His Majesty: The Free-Colored Militia in Colonial Mexico* (Stanford, CA: Stanford University Press, 2001), and "Articulating Space"; Juan Ortíz Escamilla, "Las fuerzas militares y el Proyecto de Estado en México, 1767–1835," in *Cincuenta años de historia en México*, ed. Alicia Hernández Chávez and Manuel Miño Grijalva, vol. 2 (Mexico City: El Colegio de México, 1991).

63. See "Guerra de Castas."

64. For more on the imbrication of the army in Mexico's political structure, see Loveman, *Constitution of Tyranny*, 67–91. See also Ortíz Escamilla, "Las fuerzas militares," and Guy P. C. Thompson, "Bulwarks of Patriotic Liberalism: The National Guard, Philharmonic Corps and Patriotic Juntas in Mexico 1847–88," *Journal of Latin American Studies* 22, no. 1 (March 1990): 31–68.

65. Nemser, *Infrastructures of Race*, chap. 3. See also Carlos de Sigüenza y Góngora, *Alboroto y motín de México del 8 de junio de 1692*, ed. Andrés de Pez and Irving A. Leonard (Mexico City: Talleres gráficos del Museo Nacional de Arqueología, Historia y Etnografía, 1932). For more on the topic of the riots, see Cope, *Limits of Racial Domination*, chap. 6; Natalia Silva Prada, *La política de una rebelión: Los indígenas frente al tumulto de 1692 en la Ciudad de México* (Mexico City: El Colegio de México, 2007).

66. Nemser, *Infrastructures of Race*, chap. 3.

67. Nemser, *Infrastructures of Race*, chap. 3.

68. Nemser, *Infrastructures of Race*, chap. 3.

69. See Nemser, *Infrastructures of Race*, 104.

70. In the words of Antonio Negri, who sees this internalization as a tendency of capitalist expansion, "If the peasant's existence was (in part) outside the accumulation of capital, that of the workers, as generic labor power, was inside it. This 'being inside' was what determined the frightened acknowledgement, the hatred, and

the repression: the more resistance and opposition are internal, the more frightening they are." See Antonio Negri, "The Political Monster: Naked Life and Power," in *In Praise of the Common: A Conversation on Philosophy and Politics*, ed. Cesare Casarino and Antonio Negri (Minneapolis: University of Minnesota Press, 2008), 202. To a certain extent, Negri's narrative is the negative blueprint of what Foucault articulated as the transition from sovereignty to biopolitical modes of governmentality. See Michel Foucault, *The Birth of Biopolitics: Lectures at the Collège de France 1978–1979*, ed. Arnold Davidson, trans. Graham Burchell (London: Palgrave Macmillan, 2008), and *"Society Must Be Defended."*

71. The concept of metonymic displacements of race builds on the work of Lea Geler in the Argentine context. Geler studies what she calls negritud popular, that is, a mode of being of popular classes that, independent of skin color or other visual markers of race, are associated with Blackness. See Geler, *Andares negros, caminos blancos: Afroporteños, Estado y Nación: Argentina a fines del siglo XIX* (Rosario: Prohistoria Ediciones; TEIAA (Universidad de Barcelona), 2010), and "Categorías raciales en Buenos Aires: Negritud, blanquitud, afrodescendencia y mestizaje en la blanca ciudad capital," *RUNA, Archivo para las ciencias del hombre* 37, no. 1 (July 2016).

72. Indeed, the participation of indigenous men in militias was not exclusively burdensome. Scholars have studied how joining the corps of the National Guard, for instance, constituted an important space for subaltern sectors to negotiate their participation in building the nation. See Florencia E. Mallon, *Peasant and Nation: The Making of Postcolonial Mexico and Peru* (Berkeley: University of California Press, 1995), and Thompson, *Bulwarks of Patriotic Liberalism*. Similarly, Caste War leaders in Yucatán used their previous military training surrounding previous events such as the 1839–1840 Santiago Imán revolt in the uprising. See Terry Rugeley, *Yucatán's Maya Peasantry and the Origins of the Caste War* (Austin: University of Texas Press, 1996).

73. This will be further developed in chapters 5 and 6. See Karen D. Caplan, *Indigenous Citizens: Local Liberalism in Early National Oaxaca and Yucatán* (Stanford, CA: Stanford University Press, 2010), 182. A similar issue emerged in the federal legislature; see the conservative and liberal constitutions of 1836 and 1857, respectively. See also Sanders, *Vanguard of the Atlantic World*, 104; Graciela Velázquez Delgado, "La ciudadanía en las constituciones mexicanas del siglo XIX: Inclusión y exclusión político-social en la democracia mexicana," *Acta Universitaria* 18, no. 1 (September 2008): 41–49, https://doi.org/10.15174/au.2008.131; Antonio Annino and Marcela Ternavasio, coords., *El laboratorio constitucional iberoamericano: 1807/1808–1830* (Madrid: Iberoamericana y Estudios AHILA, 2012); Fernando Escalante Gonzalbo, *Ciudadanos imaginarios: Memorial de los afanes y desventuras de la virtud y apología del vicio triunfante en la República Mexicana: Tratado de moral pública* (Mexico City: Centro de Estudios Sociológicos, El Colegio de México, 1992).

74. See Moisés González Navarro, *Raza y tierra: La guerra de castas y el henequén* (México: Colegio de México, 1979), 102; Charles A. Hale, *Liberalismo mexi-*

cano en la época de Mora (Mexico City: Siglo XXI Editores, 1999), 246; Luis Chávez Orozco, *La gestión diplomática del doctor Mora* (Mexico City: Editorial Porrúa, 1970), 155.

75. Chávez Orozco, *La gestión diplomática*, 81.

76. See Letter from José María Luis Mora to Secretaría de Relaciones de México in Chávez Orozco, *La gestión diplomática*, 151.

77. As reproduced in Chávez Orozco, *La gestión diplomática*, 151.

78. Many of these studies extend toward the postrevolutionary period as well. See, for example, Beatriz Urías Horcasitas, *Historias secretas del racismo en México (1920–1950)* (Mexico City: Tusquets, 2007); Knight, "Racism, Revolution, and Indigenismo"; Karin Alejandra Rosemblatt, *The Science and Politics of Race in Mexico and the United States, 1910–1950* (Chapel Hill: University of North Carolina Press, 2018); Claudio Lomnitz, *El antisemitismo y la ideología de la Revolución Mexicana*, trans. Mario Zamudio (Mexico City: Fondo de Cultura Económica, 2012); Leopoldo Zea, *El positivismo en México* (Mexico City: El Colegio de México, 1943). For studies that connect race to land spatial interventions in nineteenth-century Mexico, see Joshua Lund, *The Mestizo State: Reading Race in Modern Mexico* (Minneapolis: University of Minnesota Press, 2012), and Chang, *Chino*, chap. 1.

79. See, for example, Vinson, *Before Mestizaje*.

80. See Christina A. Sue, *Land of the Cosmic Race: Race Mixture, Racism, and Blackness in Mexico* (New York: Oxford University Press, 2013), 14. Sue notes that the pillars of *mestizaje* have depended on (1) presenting *racial mixing* as a positive process leading to the overcoming of racial distinctions; (2) *nonracism*, that is, contending that racism is nonexistent in the country; and (3) the negation of African and Asian, mostly Filipino and Chinese, heritages in Mexico. For a study of anti-Chinese racism, see Chang, *Chino*. For more on the disavowal of racism in Mexico and Latin America, see Tanya Katerí Hernández, *Racial Subordination in Latin America: The Role of the State, Customary Law, and the New Civil Rights Response* (Cambridge: Cambridge University Press, 2012); Claudio Lomnitz, "Mexico's Race Problem and the Real Story behind Fox's Faux Pas," *Boston Review*, November–December 2005; Fernando Navarrete Linares, *México racista: Una denuncia* (Barcelona: Grijalbo, 2016).

81. Dirección de Colonización e Industria, *Memoria de la dirección*, 5.

82. See Nemser, *Infrastructures of Race*, 106–107; Anna More, *Baroque Sovereignty: Carlos de Sigüenza y Góngora and the Creole Archive of Colonial Mexico* (Philadelphia: University of Pennsylvania Press, 2013), 164–169.

83. For an influential study on the relation between whiteness and property in the context of the United States, see Cheryl L. Harris, "Whiteness as Property," *Harvard Law Review* 106, no. 8 (June 1993): 1707–1791. This is further developed in chap. 5.

84. See Gastón Gordillo, "The Savage Outside of White Argentina," in *Rethinking Race in Modern Argentina*, ed. Paulina Alberto and Eduardo Elena (Cambridge: Cambridge University Press, 2016), 263.

85. Friedrich Katz, ed., *Riot, Rebellion, Revolution: Rural Social Conflict in Mexico* (Princeton, NJ: Princeton University Press, 1988), 16.

86. The bibliography is vast. For some of the most important studies, see Romana Falcón, *Las rasgaduras de la descolonización: Españoles y mexicanos a mediados del siglo XIX* (Mexico City: El Colegio de Mexico, 1996), and *México descalzo* (Mexico City: Plaza y Janés, 2002); Reina, *Rebeliones campesinas*; Katz, *Riot, Rebellion, Revolution*; Mallon, *Peasant and Nation*; Gilbert M. Joseph and Daniel Nugent, eds., *Everyday Forms of State Formation: Revolution and the Negotiation of Rule in Modern Mexico* (Durham, NC: Duke University Press, 1994); Allen Wells and Gilbert M. Joseph, *Summer of Discontent, Seasons of Upheaval: Elite Politics and Rural Insurgency in Yucatán, 1876–1915* (Stanford, CA: Stanford University Press, 1996); Gilbert M. Joseph and Jürgen Buchenau, *Mexico's Once and Future Revolution: Social Upheaval and the Challenge of Rule since the Late Nineteenth Century* (Durham, NC: Duke University Press, 2013); John Tutino, *From Insurrection to Revolution in Mexico: Social Bases of Agrarian Violence, 1750–1940* (Princeton, NJ: Princeton University Press, 1986); Elisa Servin, Leticia Reina, and John Tutino, eds., *Cycles of Conflict, Centuries of Change: Crisis, Reform, and Revolution in Mexico* (Durham, NC: Duke University Press, 2007); Eric Van Young, *La crisis del orden colonial: Estructura agraria y rebeliones populares en la Nueva España, 1750–1821* (Mexico City: Alianza Editorial, 1992), and *The Other Rebellion: Popular Violence, Ideology, and the Struggle for Mexican Independence, 1810–1821* (Stanford, CA: Stanford University Press, 2001); William B. Taylor, *Drinking, Homicide, and Rebellion in Colonial Mexican Villages* (Stanford, CA: Stanford University Press, 1979); Antonio Escobar Ohmstede and Leticia Reina, eds., *Indio, nación y comunidad en el México del siglo XIX* (Mexico City: Centro de Investigaciones y Estudios Superiores en Antropología Social, 1993).

87. Katz, *Riot, Rebellion, Revolution*, introduction.

88. Ann Laura Stoler, "The Pulse of the Archive," in her *Along the Archival Grain: Epistemic Anxieties and Colonial Common Sense* (Princeton, NJ: Princeton University Press, 2009).

CHAPTER ONE: VANISHING INDIANNESS

1. See John Tutino, *Making a New World: Founding Capitalism in the Bajío and Spanish North America* (Durham, NC: Duke University Press, 2011), chap. 4. See also Felipe Castro Gutiérrez, *Nueva ley y nuevo rey: Reformas borbónicas y rebelión popular en Nueva España* (Zamora: Colegio de Michoacán, 1996).

2. "Indios vagos" is the term used to describe Indians who were not attached to Indian republics. See Tutino, *Making a New World*, 234.

3. See Tutino, *Making a New World*, chap. 4.

4. See Tutino, *Making a New World*, chap. 4. On garrisons and militarization see Lauren Benton, *A Search for Sovereignty: Law and Geography in European Em-

pires, 1400–1900 (Cambridge: Cambridge University Press, 2014), chap. 4. See also Gabriel Haslip-Viera, *Crime and Punishment in Late Colonial Mexico City* (Albuquerque: University of New Mexico Press, 1999), chap. 5; and Kelly Lytle Hernández, *City of Inmates: Conquest, Rebellion, and the Rise of Human Caging in Los Angeles 1771–1965* (Chapel Hill: University of North Carolina Press, 2017), chap. 1. On New Spain's army, see Christon I. Archer, *The Army in Bourbon Mexico, 1760–1810* (Albuquerque: University of New Mexico Press, 1977). See also Ben Vinson III, "Articulating Space": The Free-Colored Military Establishment in Colonial Mexico for the Conquest to Independence," *Callaloo* 27, no. 1 (Winter 2004): 150–171.

5. See Tutino, *Making a New World*, chap. 4; see also Cynthia E. Milton and Ben Vinson III, "Counting Heads: Race and Non-native Tribute Policy in Colonial Spanish America," *Journal of Colonialism & Colonial History* 3, no. 3 (2002), https://doi.org/10.1353/cch.2002.0056.

6. See Tutino, *Making a New World*, chap. 4.

7. See letter from Croix to Arriaga, August 26, 1767, transcribed as appendix 9 in Isaura Elvira Gallart y Nocetti, "Las rebeliones populares de 1767 en Nueva España" (undergraduate thesis, Universidad Nacional Autónoma de México, 1981), 209.

8. According to John Tutino, this military expedition was "the largest non-militia force ever assembled in New Spain." Gálvez was backed by six hundred regular troops. See Tutino, *Making a New World*, 248.

9. The Spanish word for inspector is *visitador*. As discussed by Felipe Castro Gutiérrez, *Nueva ley*, 102–103, the inspectors in the Spanish governmental system were officials with total license to assess and modify the operations of an administrative sector and offer in-depth solutions to situations of inefficiency, corruption, or conflict. José de Gálvez was also behind the implementation of *intendencias* as part of the administrative system, a key feature of the Bourbon Reforms. For more on Gálvez and his relation to the Bourbon Reforms, see David Brading, *Miners and Merchants in Bourbon Mexico 1763–1810* (Cambridge: Cambridge University Press, 1971), and *The First America: The Spanish Monarchy, Creole Patriots and the Liberal State, 1492–1866* (Cambridge: Cambridge University Press, 1993), particularly "The New State"; Herbert Ingram Priestly, *José de Gálvez, Visitor General of New Spain (1765–1771)* (Berkeley: University of California Press, 1912); David J. Weber, *Bárbaros: Spaniards and Their Savages in the Age of Enlightenment* (New Haven, CT: Yale University Press, 2005), specifically chap. 4. For some studies on the topic, see Horst Pietschmann, *Las reformas borbónicas y el sistema de intendencias en Nueva España: Un estudio político administrative* (Mexico City: Fondo de Cultura Económica, 1996); Barbara H. Stein and Stanley J. Stein, *Apogee of Empire: Spain and New Spain in the Age of Charles III* (Baltimore, MD: Johns Hopkins University Press, 2003); Allan J. Kuethe, *The Spanish Atlantic World in the Eighteenth Century: War and the Bourbon Reforms, 1713–1796* (Cambridge: Cambridge University Press, 2014); Susan Deans-Smith, *Bureaucrats, Planters, and Workers: The Making of the Tobacco Monopoly in Bourbon Mexico* (Austin: University of Texas Press, 1992); Car-

los Marichal, *Bankruptcy of Empire: Mexican Silver and the Wars between Spain, Britain, and France, 1760–1810* (Cambridge: Cambridge University Press, 2007).

10. For a document on the faculties granted to Gálvez for the repression of the rebellions, see "Poder recibido por el visitador José de Gálvez del virrey Marqués de Croix, México 7 de julio de 1767," published as the first appendix in José de Gálvez, *Informe sobre las rebeliones populares de 1767 y otros documentos inéditos*, ed. Felipe Castro Gutiérrez (Mexico City: Universidad Nacional Autónoma de México, Instituto de Investigaciones Históricas, 1990), 83–84.

11. Gálvez, *Informe sobre las rebeliones*.

12. I am here building on Joshua Clover's reading on surplus populations and race in *Riot Strike Riot: The New Era of Uprisings* (London: Verso, 2016), chap. 8. Clover writes, "Thus we might finally argue that the term 'race riot' has an inverted sense: not that of race as cause of riot, but of riot as part of the ongoing process of racialization. It is not that race makes riots but that riots make race" (168).

13. Onur Ulas Ince, "Primitive Accumulation, New Enclosures, and Global Land Grabs: A Theoretical Intervention," *Rural Sociology* 79, no. 1 (2014): 112, https://doi.org/10.1111/ruso.12025.

14. For information on demographics in the Bajío region during Bourbon Reform, see Eric van Young, *La crisis del orden colonial: Estructura agraria y rebeliones populares en la Nueva España, 1750–1821* (Mexico City: Alianza Editorial, 1992).

15. Castro Gutiérrez, *Nueva ley*, 214.

16. Castro Gutiérrez, *Nueva ley*, 214. This narrative is quite common. For a similar argument about class relations becoming more determinant than race, see R. Douglas Cope, *The Limits of Racial Domination: Plebeian Society in Colonial Mexico City, 1660–1720* (Madison: University of Wisconsin Press, 1994).

17. See Manuel Escobar, *Verdad reflexa, platica doctrinal sobre los varios sucesos que intervinieron en la ciudad de San Luis Potosí desde el día 10 de mayo hasta el día 6 de octubre del mismo año, en que se ejecutaron los últimos suplicios de los tumultuarios* [. . .] (Mexico City: Imprenta Real del Superior Gobierno por el Br. D. Joseph Antonio de Hogal, 1768). See also Carlos Herrejón Peredo, *Del sermón al discurso cívico: México, 1760–1834* (Zamora, Mexico: Colegio de Michoacán, 2003), 70–76.

18. See William B. Taylor, *Drinking, Homicide, and Rebellion in Colonial Mexican Villages* (Stanford, CA: Stanford University Press, 1979), 120.

19. Felipe Castro Gutiérrez, "Introducción," in Gálvez, *Informe sobre las rebeliones*, 11. As indicated by Castro Gutiérrez, a repression of this scale was unusual for the Spanish government. See also Taylor, *Drinking, Homicide, and Rebellion*, 120.

20. Escobar, *Verdad reflexa*, 57.

21. Escobar, *Verdad reflexa*, 10.

22. Escobar, *Verdad reflexa*, 65.

23. As quoted in Castro Gutiérrez, *Nueva ley*, 233.

24. The trope of the vanishing Indian has been central for settler colonial stud-

ies in the US context. It would be interesting to note the differences, yet chronological simultaneity, in how this trope played out in the eighteenth century in New Spain and the United States. For more on the trope of the vanishing Indian in the US context, see Brian W. Dippie, *The Vanishing American: White Attitudes and U.S. Indian Policy* (Middletown, CT: Wesleyan University Press, 1982); Eric N. Olund, "From Savage Space to Governable Space: The Extension of United States Judicial Sovereignty over Indian Country in the Nineteenth Century," *Cultural Geographies* 9, no. 2 (April 2002): 129–257; Stuart Banner, *How the Indians Lost Their Land: Law and Power on the Frontier* (Cambridge, MA: Harvard University Press, 2007); Renée L. Bergland, *The National Uncanny: Indian Ghosts and American Subjects* (Hanover, NH: University Press of New England, 2000); Ned Blackhawk, *Violence over the Land: Indians and Empires in the Early American West* (Cambridge, MA: Harvard University Press, 2008); Robert A. Williams, *The American Indian in Western Legal Thought: The Discourses of Conquest* (Oxford: Oxford University Press, 1992); Patrick Wolfe, "Settler Colonialism and the Elimination of the Native," *Journal of Genocide Research* 8, no. 4 (2006): 387–409, https://doi.org/10.1080/14623520601056240; "Yucatán: Una guerra escrita," in part 2 of David Kazanjian, *The Brink of Freedom: Improvising Life in the Nineteenth-Century Atlantic World* (Durham, NC: Duke University Press, 2016); María Josefina Saldaña-Portillo, *Indian Given: Racial Geographies across Mexico and the United States* (Durham, NC: Duke University Press, 2016), 54, 64. For more on the trope about forms of racial vanishment in Mexico's colonial period, see Joanne Rappaport, *The Disappearing Mestizo: Configuring Difference in the Colonial New Kingdom of Granada* (Durham, NC: Duke University Press, 2014). I here build on Nemser's discussion of Rappaport's work in *Infrastructures of Race*, chaps. 2 and 3.

25. See Nemser, *Infrastructures of Race* and "Primitive Spiritual Accumulation and the Colonial Extraction Economy," *Política Común* 5 (2014), http://dx.doi.org/10.3998/pc.12322227.0005.003. For more on the role that tribute played in constructing Indiannness, see Tutino, *Making a New World*; Luis Fernando Granados, *En el espejo haitiano: Los indios del Bajío y el colapso del orden colonial en América Latina* (Mexico City: Ediciones Era, 2016); Michael T. Ducey, "Viven sin ley ni rey: Rebeliones coloniales en Papantla, 1760–1790," in *Procesos rurales e historia regional*, ed. Victoria Chenaut (Mexico City: CIESAS, 1996), 15–49; Nancy Farriss, *Maya Society under Colonial Rule* (Princeton, NJ: Princeton University Press, 1984), 39–47; Charles Gibson, *Aztecs under Spanish Rule* (Stanford, CA: Stanford University Press, 1964), chap. 8; James Lockhart, *The Nahuas after the Conquest* (Stanford, CA: Stanford University Press, 1992). Few studies have specifically explored the institution of tribute during Bourbon Reform; see Daniela Marino, "El afán de recaudar y la dificultad en reformar: El tributo indígena en la Nueva España," in *De colonia a nación: Impuestos y política en México, 1750–1860*, ed. Carlos Marichal and Daniela Marino (Mexico City: El Colegio de Mexico, 2001), 61–84.

26. See José de Gálvez, *Informe general que en virtud de real orden instruyó*

y entregó el Excmo. Sr. Marqués de Sonora al Virrey D. Antonio Bucarely y Ursúa con fecha de 31 de diciembre de 1771 (Mexico City: Imprenta de Santiago White, 1867), 87 (hereafter *Informe a Bucareli*). It is striking that Gálvez turned to the trope of the disappearance of the "Indians," given that the indigenous population actually tripled over the course of the eighteenth century. See Marino, "El afán de recaudar," 62.

27. See Gálvez, *Informe a Bucareli*, 87.
28. See Gálvez, *Informe a Bucareli*, 86.
29. See Gálvez, *Informe a Bucareli*, 86.
30. See Gálvez, *Informe a Bucareli*, 98.
31. For more on how efforts to increase tribute often resulted in community exodus, see Gibson, *Aztecs under Spanish Rule*, 210.
32. See Gibson, *Aztecs under Spanish Rule*, 210. For studies on how people navigated caste ascriptions, see Cope, *Limits of Racial Domination*; Rappaport, *Disappearing Mestizo*; María Elena Martínez, *Genealogical Fictions: Limpieza de Sangre, Religion, and Gender in Colonial Mexico* (Stanford, CA: Stanford University Press, 2008). Beyond the New Spanish context, see Ann Twinam, *Purchasing Whiteness: Pardos, Mulattos, and the Quest for Social Mobility in the Spanish Indies* (Stanford, CA: Stanford University Press, 2015); Rachel Sarah O'Toole, *Bound Lives: Africans, Indians, and the Making of Race in Colonial Peru* (Pittsburgh, PA: University of Pittsburgh Press, 2012); Matthew D. O'Hara and Andrew B. Fisher, eds. *Imperial Subjects: Race and Identity in Colonial Latin America* (Durham, NC: Duke University Press, 2009).
33. On mercantilism's efforts to maximize profit and productivity, strengthening the state as an agent for the accumulation of capital, see Michel Foucault, *The Birth of Biopolitics: Lectures at the Collège de France 1978–1979*, ed. Arnold Davidson, trans. Graham Burchell (London: Palgrave Macmillan UK, 2008), Lectures 1–3.
34. Gálvez, *Informe a Bucareli*, 95.
35. Gálvez, *Informe a Bucareli*, 95.
36. As Gibson notes, efforts to homogenize tribute traversed colonial governmentality from the early sixteenth century onward. For more on historical changes in the institution of tribute, see Gibson, *Aztecs under Spanish Rule*, chap. 8.
37. Gálvez, *Informe a Bucareli*, 93.
38. Gálvez, *Informe sobre las rebeliones*, 53. "But the truth is that I have found them all to be malicious and intent on harming us."
39. Gálvez, *Informe a Bucareli*, 86.
40. Milton and Vinson, "Counting Heads." See also Marichal, *Bankruptcy of Empire*, 49. Marichal shows how throughout the eighteenth century New Spain was the colony that paid the most taxes, not only within the Spanish Empire but also as compared to the colonies of the French and British Empires.
41. Milton and Vinson, "Counting Heads." See also Tutino, *Making a New*

World; Granados, *En el espejo haitiano*; Ducey, "Viven sin ley ni rey"; Farriss, *Maya Society under Colonial Rule*; Gibson, *Aztecs under Spanish Rule*, chap. 8; Lockhart, *Nahuas after the Conquest*.

42. I'm here building from Benton's use of this term. "Anomalous zones" are spaces where legal variation was in use. See Benton, *Search for Sovereignty*, chap. 1.

43. See Gálvez, *Informe sobre las rebeliones*, 54–55.

44. See Castro Gutiérrez, *Nueva ley*, 200–201, and "La represión."

45. See Benton, *Search for Sovereignty*, chap. 1.

46. See Tutino, *Making a New World*, 248.

47. See Gálvez, *Informe sobre las rebeliones*, 31–32.

48. "In this plan, I set forth two primary ends that were, in my judgment, essential: first, impede the flight of delinquents, the fearful desertion of the workers, and the abandonment of the mines, ensuring at the same time that individuals of commerce and honorable neighbors would not leave their homes and seek refuge elsewhere." See Gálvez, *Informe sobre las rebeliones*, 31–32.

49. See Archer, *Army in Bourbon Mexico*; Vinson, "Articulating Space" and *Bearing Arms for His Majesty: The Free-Colored Militia in Colonial Mexico* (Stanford, CA: Stanford University Press, 2003); María del Carmen Velázquez, *El estado de guerra en Nueva España, 1760–1808* (Mexico City: Colegio de México, Centro de Estudios Históricos, 1997).

50. Gálvez, *Informe sobre las rebeliones*, 31–32.

51. See Joshua Lund, *The Mestizo State: Reading Race in Modern Mexico* (Minneapolis: University of Minnesota Press, 2012); and Nemser, *Infrastructures of Race*. For other takes on the relation between race and space, see Saldaña-Portillo, *Indian Given*; and Paige R. Andersson, "The Only Way: Congregación and the Construction of Race and Land in Mexico, 1521–2017" (PhD diss., University of Michigan, 2018).

52. Nemser, *Infrastructures of Race*, 4.

53. Gálvez, *Informe a Bucareli*, 94.

54. Gálvez, *Informe sobre las rebeliones*, 65–66.

55. Gálvez, *Informe sobre las rebeliones*, 66. See also Tutino, *Making a New World*, 253.

56. Gálvez, *Informe sobre las rebeliones*, 66.

57. Gálvez, *Informe sobre las rebeliones*, 66.

58. See Tutino, *Making a New World*, 253.

59. See *Recopilación de leyes de los Reynos de las Indias, mandadas imprimir y publicar por la Magestad Católica Del Rey Don Cárlos II. Nuestro Señor [. . .]*, 4th ed., vol. 2 (Madrid: La viuda de D. Joaquín Ibarra, 1791), book 4, title 3, laws 18 and 19.

60. See *Recopilación de leyes*, vol. 2, book 7, title 4, laws 1–5, and book 7, title 5, law 4. For a study about vagabondage, racialization, and primitive accumulation in New Spain, see Nemser, *Infrastructures of Race*, chap. 2. See also Richard Warren, *Vagrants and Citizens: Politics and the Masses in Mexico City from Colony to*

Republic (Wilmington, DE: SR Books, 2001), and Rosa María Pérez Estévez, *El problema de los vagos en la España del siglo XVII* (Madrid: Confederación Española de Cajas de Ahorros, 1976).

61. Gálvez, *Informe sobre las rebeliones*, 51.
62. Castro Gutiérrez, *Nueva ley*, 74, 199–201.
63. Castro Gutiérrez, *Nueva ley*, 74.
64. Castro Gutiérrez, *Nueva ley*, 74–76.
65. Castro Gutiérrez, *Nueva ley*, 231.
66. Gálvez, *Informe sobre las rebeliones*, 51–52.
67. For more on this subject, see Castro Gutiérrez, *Nueva ley*, 74–75, and Gálvez, *Informe sobre las rebeliones*, 51–52. A transcription of Gálvez's decree can be found in Manuel Muro, *Historia de San Luis Potosí*, vol. 1 (Mexico City: Sociedad Potosina de Estudios Históricos, 1973). See also Tutino, *Making a New World*, 251.
68. Gálvez, *Informe sobre las rebeliones*, 53.
69. Gálvez, *Informe sobre las rebeliones*, 56.
70. Gálvez, *Informe sobre las rebeliones*, 56.
71. The relationship between power and vision has been amply studied. I'm here thinking specifically of James C. Scott's approach to the topic in *Seeing Like a State: How Certain Schemes to Improve the Human Condition Have Failed* (New Haven, CT: Yale University Press, 1998).
72. See note 46 in Gálvez, *Informe sobre las rebeliones*. A previous instantiation of these laws dates from 1646. See *Recopilación de leyes*, vol. 2, book 6, title 1, laws 21–24.
73. Gálvez, *Informe sobre las rebeliones*, 57.
74. This decision was made with the clear intent to erode, at least practically if not legally, the colonial institution of *repúblicas de indios*. See Castro Gutiérrez, *Nueva ley*, 274. See also note 65 in Gálvez, *Informe sobre las rebeliones*, 74, and Tutino, *Making a New World*, 255.
75. The documents on the 1767 riots often use the term "whites." See, for instance, Escobar, *Verdad reflexa*, 4, where he writes that rebels sought to kill or banish all who "pintasen de blanco" (painted white). For more on this issue see Castro Gutiérrez, "Introducción," in Gálvez, *Informe sobre las rebeliones*, 260–261. Castro Gutiérrez makes an interesting observation in stressing that the authorities tended to present the antagonism of the rebelling "plebs" as directed at whites in general. Nonetheless, a careful study of the documents written and circulated by the rebels speaks to an attack focused more on peninsular privileges and the search to establish certain alliances with select criollos. However, as John Tutino also discusses, these criollo entrepreneurs often sided with colonial authorities and their repressive efforts. See Tutino, *Making a New World*, 237–248.
76. See More, *Baroque Sovereignty*, 164–169; and Nemser, *Infrastructures of Race*, 106–107.
77. Anna More describes this as an "elite identified by its Spanish descent." See More, *Baroque Sovereignty*, 163.

78. See Gallart y Nocetti, "Las rebeliones populares," appendix 9, "Carta de Croix a Arriaga, 26 de agosto de 1767," 209. Emphasis mine.

79. In Gallart y Nocetti, "Las rebeliones populares," 271. See also the reconfiguration of this sentence in Gálvez, *Informe sobre las rebeliones*, 56.

80. The bans on Indians bearing arms had been decreed since 1501. See *Recopilación de leyes*, vol. 2, book 6, title 1, law 31. On bans on other "castes" bearing arms, see *Recopilación de leyes*, vol. 2, book 7, title 5, laws 15 and 16. The bans on horses began to be instated in New Spain as early as 1528. See "Provisiones a la Audiencia de México 1528, 1530, 1534 y 1568 sobre prohibición de utilizar armas y caballos; Real Cédula, Audiencia de México, 28 de septiembre de 1534," in Richard Konetzke, ed. *Colección de documentos para la formación social de Hispanoamérica 1493–1810*, vol. 1, 1493–1592 (Madrid: Consejo Superior de Investigaciones Científicas, 1953. See also *Recopilación de leyes*, vol. 2, book 6, title 1, law 33. As both Delfina López Sarrelangue and Raquel E. Güereca Durán have shown, these bans were irregularly practiced and often regionally pardoned by colonial authorities when convenient. An example to these exemptions were the Tlaxcaltecans. See Delfina López Sarrelangue, *La nobleza indígena de Pátzcuaro en la época virreinal* (Morelia: Morevallado, 1999), 176; and Raquel Güereca Durán, *Milicias indígenas en la Nueva España: Reflexiones del derecho indiano sobre los derechos de guerra* (Mexico City: Universidad Nacional Autónoma de México, Instituto de Investigaciones Jurídicas, 2016), 45–46. Notably, these bans carried over from racialized legal decrees applied to Moorish populations in Spain. See Norma Angélica Castillo Palma, *Cholula sociedad mestiza en ciudad india* (Mexico City: Universidad Autónoma Metropolitana, 2001), 29.

81. Gálvez, *Informe sobre las rebeliones*, 56. See also the sentences transcribed as appendices in Gallart y Nocetti, "Las rebeliones populares," especially 253, 270, and 289.

82. Gálvez, *Informe sobre las rebeliones*, 56.

83. Gálvez, *Informe sobre las rebeliones*, 56. The reinstated law dates from 1576. See *Recopilación de leyes*, vol. 2, book 6, title 1, law 33.

84. Concerns about how hairstyles allowed Indians to be confused with other castes were also present in the 1692 riots in Mexico City. See, for instance, José de la Barrera to Conde Galve, July 1, 1692, AGN *Historia* 413, fol. 14v as cited in Nemser, *Infrastructures of Race*, 110. In his *Vocabulario de Mexicanismos*, Joaquín García Icazbalceta includes the term "balcarrota." In his overview of the term, he discusses how P. Cabo (possibly the Jesuit historian Andrés Cavo) wrote about colonial authorities' concerns with Indian hairstyle around the 1692 riots. See Icazbalceta, *Vocabulario de mexicanismos* (Mexico City: Tipografía y Litografía "La Europea" de J. Aguilar Vera, 1899), 42.

85. See Gallart y Nocetti, "Las rebeliones populares," 271.

86. See, for example, David M. Goldberg, *The Curse of Ham: Race and Slavery in Early Judaism, Christianity and Islam* (Princeton, NJ: Princeton University Press, 2005), and *Black and Slave: The Origins and History of the Curse of Ham*

(Philadelphia: University of Pennsylvania Press, 2017); Benjamin Braude, "The Sons of Noah and the Construction of Ethnic and Geographical Identities in the Medieval and Early Modern Periods," *William and Mary Quarterly* 54, no. 1 (1997): 103–142.

87. Martínez, *Genealogical Fictions*, 267. See also Colin A. Palmer, *Slaves of the White God: Blacks in Mexico, 1570–1650* (Cambridge, MA: Harvard University Press, 1976), 39.

88. Martínez, *Genealogical Fictions*, 267.

89. Martínez, *Genealogical Fictions*, 268.

90. Escobar, *Verdad reflexa*, 39.

91. See Milton and Vinson, "Counting Heads."

92. Milton and Vinson mention a 1633 letter by Lucas Oro Tineo in Quito, in which the author complains about the undefined and confusing use of traditional clothing by "mujeres de la mala vida" (bad-life women). See Milton and Vinson, "Counting Heads."

93. Escobar, *Verdad reflexa*, 40.

94. See Milton and Vinson, "Counting Heads." See also *Recopilación de leyes*, vol. 2, book 6, title 5, law 8.

95. See Milton and Vinson, "Counting Heads."

96. Gálvez, *Informe sobre las rebeliones*, 63.

97. For more on how punishment was incorporated into restoring buildings and specifically erecting new Casas Reales as part of materializing a new colonial bureaucracy, see José Armando Hernández Souberville, *Un rostro de Piedra para el poder: Las nuevas casas reales de San Luis Potosí, 1767–1827* (Mexico City: El Colegio de San Luis y el Colegio de Michoacán, 2013), 55–93.

98. See Gálvez, *Informe sobre las rebeliones*. See also the sentences transcribed as appendices in Gallart y Nocetti, "Las rebeliones populares," especially 237, 253, 270.

99. Gálvez, *Informe sobre las rebeliones*, 78.

100. Castro Gutiérrez, *Nueva ley*, 214.

CHAPTER TWO: "SO THAT THEY MAY BE FREE OF ALL THOSE THINGS"

1. See Felipe Castro Gutiérrez, *Nueva ley y nuevo rey: Reformas borbónicas y rebelión popular en Nueva España* (Zamora: Colegio de Michoacán, 1996), 120. See also Juan José Benavidez Martínez, "Revuelta general y represión ejemplar: Los motines de 1767 en San Luis Potosí," *Revista de El Colegio de San Luis* 6, no. 12 (2016), 48.

2. See Castro Gutiérrez, *Nueva ley*, 120.

3. See Castro Gutiérrez, *Nueva ley*, 120; and Benavidez Martínez, "Revuelta general," 48.

4. See Castro Gutiérrez, *Nueva ley*, 120; and Benavidez Martínez, "Revuelta general," 48.

5. See Castro Gutiérrez, *Nueva ley*, 120; and John Tutino, *Making a New World: Founding Capitalism in the Bajío and Spanish North America* (Durham, NC: Duke University Press, 2011), 238. See also José de Gálvez, *Informe sobre las rebeliones rebeliones populares de 1767 y otros documentos inéditos*, ed. Felipe Castro Gutiérrez (Mexico City: Universidad Nacional Autónoma de México, Instituto de Investigaciones Históricas, 1990), 35.

6. See Castro Gutiérrez, *Nueva ley*, 124. The names of the two San Pedro leaders are mentioned in the document on José de Gálvez's sentence to the San Pedro–area rebels dictated on August 19, 1767. A transcription of this sentence can be found in Isaura Elvira Gallart y Nocetti, "Las rebeliones populares de 1767 en Nueva España" (undergraduate thesis, Universidad Nacional Autónoma de México, 1981), appendix 6.

7. See Castro Gutiérrez, *Nueva ley*, 12; and Tutino, *Making a New World*, 238.

8. As had been the case in other regions, many of the villagers were hanged and their bodies mutilated for public exhibition. Entire families were exiled from the province. Those remaining in the area faced heavy taxation fees and intense public labor sentences to make up for the riots' damages. See Gallart y Nocetti, "Las rebeliones populares," appendix 6.

9. I'm here drawing from Benjaminian approaches to history. For more on this, see Walter Benjamin, "On the Concept of History," in *Selected Writings*, vol. 4, *1938–1940*, ed. Marcus Paul Bullock, Michael William Jennings, Howard Eiland, and Gary Smith, trans. Edmund Jephcott (Cambridge, MA: Belknap, 2006); and "Surrealism," in *Selected Writings*, vol. 2, part 1, *1927–1930*, ed. Jennings, Eiland, and Smith, trans. Eiland, Jennings, Jephcott, Rodney Livingstone, Jerolf Wikoff, and Harry Zohn (Cambridge, MA: Belknap, 2005). See also Peter Osborne, *The Politics of Time: Modernity and Avant-Garde* (London: Verso, 1995).

10. This mode of reading is inspired by the work of several scholars who have opened up the possibility of reading archives beyond the empirical. See Arlette Farge, *The Allure of the Archive*, trans. Thomas Scott-Railton (New Haven, CT: Yale University Press, 2015); Saidiya Hartman, "Venus in Two Acts," *Small Axe* 12, no. 2 (2008): 1–14; Saidiya Hartman, *Wayward Lives, Beautiful Experiments: Intimate Histories of Riotous Black Girls, Troublesome Women, and Queer Radicals* (New York: Norton, 2019); David Kazanjian, *The Brink of Freedom: Improvising Life in the Nineteenth-Century Atlantic World* (Durham, NC: Duke University Press, 2016); Lisa Lowe, "History Hesitant," *Social Text* 33, no. 4 (December 2015): 85–107, https://doi.org/10.1215/01642472-3315790; Susana Draper, *1968 Mexico: Constellations of Freedom and Democracy* (Durham, NC: Duke University Press, 2018).

11. Farge, *Allure of the Archives*, 123.

12. See Rafael Montejano y Aguiñaga, *El Valle de Santa Isabel del Armadillo, San Luis Potosí* (San Luis Potosí, Mexico: Imprenta Evolución, 1964), 32.

13. See Montejano y Aguiñaga, *El Valle de Santa Isabel*, 42.

14. See Montejano y Aguiñaga, *El Valle de Santa Isabel*, 50.

15. See Montejano y Aguiñaga, *El Valle de Santa Isabel*, 39–41.

16. See Gallart y Nocetti, "Las rebeliones populares," appendix 7, "Carta del Gobernador Atanasio de la Cruz, gobernador del pueblo de San Nicolás, a Patricio y Juan Antonio Orocio, cabecillas del Cerro de San Pedro, San Nicolás, 2 de julio de 1767, con explicación que hace Prudencio Ochoa Badiola por mandato de José de Gálvez en la Ciudad de San Luis Potosí el 21 de agosto de 1767."

17. Tutino, *Making a New World*, 240.

18. Tutino, *Making a New World*, chap. 4.

19. See "Carta del Gobernador Atanasio de la Cruz," in Gallart y Nocetti, "Las rebeliones populares," 201.

20. Many theorists and historians of social struggle have remarked on the dominant tendency to dismiss or rationalize the viscerality that is expressed in riots and rebellions. I am here building on Jackie Wang, *Carceral Capitalism*, Intervention 21 (South Pasadena, CA: Semiotext(e), 2018; distributed by MIT Press), 2018), 277. See also Ranajit Guha, "The Prose of Counter-Insurgency," in *Selected Subaltern Studies*, ed. Ranajit Guha and Gayatri Chakravorty Spivak (Oxford: Oxford University Press, 1988); Joshua Clover, *Riot, Strike, Riot: The New Era of Uprisings* (London: Verso, 2016), chap. 8.

21. See "Carta de Croix a Arriaga, 26 de agosto de 1767," in Gallart y Nocetti, "Las rebeliones populares," 209.

22. Michael Omi and Howard Winant, *Racial Formation in the United States* (London: Routledge, 2014), 125.

23. William B. Taylor, *Drinking, Homicide, and Rebellion in Colonial Mexican Villages* (Stanford, CA: Stanford University Press, 1979), 115–121.

24. Taylor, *Drinking, Homicide, and Rebellion*, 115–121.

25. See Castro Gutiérrez, *Nueva ley*, 118–119.

26. See Tutino, *Making a New World*, 246.

27. As cited in Castro Gutiérrez, *Nueva ley*, 119.

28. I'm here building on Ruth Gilmore's influential definition of racism as "the state-sanctioned or extralegal production and exploitation of group-differentiated vulnerability to *premature death*." See Gilmore, *Golden Gulag: Prisons, Surplus, Crisis and Opposition in Globalizing California* (Berkeley: University of California Press, 2007), 28.

29. See Castro Gutiérrez, *Nueva ley*, 12; and Tutino, *Making a New World*, 238. The text is transcribed in Manuel Muro, *Historia de San Luis Potosí*, vol. 1 (Mexico City: Sociedad Potosina de Estudios Históricos, 1973), 179–181.

30. See Kazanjian, *Brink of Freedom*, 31–32.

31. I'm here drawing from Kazanjian's engagement with Fred Moten's idea on the improvisational. See Kazanjian, *Brink of Freedom*, 31–32.

32. Muro, *Historia de San Luis Potosí*, 179–181.

33. See Castro, *Nueva Ley*, 92, 125. See also Gálvez, *Informe sobre las rebeliones*, 51.

34. Tutino, *Making a New World*, chap. 4.

35. My use of the term "racial geography" comes from María Josefina Saldaña-Portillo, who defines it as "not simply a term for describing a given effect in space in racial terms. Racial geography is a technology of power, and when used as an analytic and theory of spatial production, it indexes the series of techniques used to produce space in racial terms." Saldaña-Portillo, *Indian Given: Racial Geographies across Mexico and the United States* (Durham, NC: Duke University Press, 2016), 17.

36. Muro, *Historia de San Luis Potosí*, 179–180.

37. Muro, *Historia de San Luis Potosí*, 180: "el Real con sus contornos" (the real and its surroundings).

38. Muro, *Historia de San Luis Potosí*, 179–181.

39. Muro, *Historia de San Luis Potosí*, 181.

40. Muro, *Historia de San Luis Potosí*, 181.

41. Muro, *Historia de San Luis Potosí*, 179.

42. For more on this tension, see Nancy Fraser, "Behind Marx's Hidden Abode," *New Left Review* 86 (March–April, 2014): 55–72.

43. Muro, *Historia de San Luis Potosí*, 181.

44. Muro, *Historia de San Luis Potosí*, 181.

45. Castro Gutiérrez, *Nueva ley*, 142–144.

46. *Chueca* was an early type of field hockey. See Castro Gutiérrez, *Nueva ley*, 141.

47. Castro Gutiérrez, *Nueva ley*, 141–142.

48. Castro Gutiérrez, *Nueva ley*, 141–142.

49. Castro Gutiérrez, *Nueva ley*, 145.

50. Castro Gutiérrez, *Nueva ley*, 142–145. Rioters also demanded to replace the current lieutenant mayor with the criollo Don Santiago Ortega and to crown as local king Juan de Altamirano Velasco y Flores, count of Santiago de Calimaya (who, it was said, belonged to one of the oldest lines of Mexican nobility). See "Carta del teniente de alcalde mayor, diputados de minería y comercio y procurador del común y propios del real de San Pedro de Guadalcázar al alcalde mayor de San Luis Potosí, Andrés de Urbina. Guadalcázar, 8 de julio de 1767," transcribed as appendix 9 in Gálvez, *Informe sobre las rebeliones*, 100.

51. Taylor, *Drinking, Homicide, and Rebellion*, 119. For more on the meaning of attacks on jails during the riots, see Castro Gutiérrez, *Nueva ley*, 254.

52. "Carta del teniente de alcalde mayor," in Gálvez, *Informe sobre las rebeliones*, 99–102.

53. Gálvez, *Informe sobre las rebeliones*, 100.

54. Kazanjian, *Brink of Freedom*, 202.

55. In the case of the Caste War on the Yucatán Peninsula (described in part 3), David Kazanjian explores how, through reconceptualizing tribute collection, the rebel groups in the Yucatán were both theorizing and speculating about freedom. Kazanjian, *Brink of Freedom*, 207–210. Luis Fernando Granados also explores the political dimensions of the opposition to tribute with respect to the struggle for in-

dependence in *En el espejo haitiano: Los indios del Bajío y el colapso del orden colonial en América Latina* (Mexico City: Ediciones Era, 2016). Similar arguments have been presented in studies of the French Revolution and other imperial networks. See, for example, Michael Kwass, *Privilege and the Politics of Taxation in Eighteenth Century France: Liberté, Egalité, Fiscalité* (Cambridge: Cambridge University Press, 2006).

56. Gálvez, *Informe sobre las rebeliones*, 55.

57. For a study on the emergence of "simplification" and "legibility" as fundamental state practices, see James C. Scott, *Seeing Like a State: How Certain Schemes to Improve the Human Condition Have Failed* (New Haven, CT: Yale University Press, 1998).

58. There is a large body of scholarship on the impact of pactism in New Spain and its relation to Thomist theories of sovereignty. Many of these interventions explore the 1808 crisis of sovereignty that came with Napoleon's invasion of Spain and will be further discussed in chapters 3 and 4. See Mónica Quijada, "From Spain to New Spain: Revisiting the Potestas Populi in Hispanic Political Thought," *Mexican Studies/Estudios Mexicanos* 24, no. 2 (Summer 2008): 185–219. See also the relevant discussion in Rafael Sánchez, *Dancing Jacobins: A Venezuelan Genealogy of Latin American Populism* (New York: Fordham University Press, 2016). In chapter 1, Sánchez maintains that despite the colonial authorities' efforts to promote an absolutist framework through the empire, pactism continued to maintain an undeniable presence in the communities of the empire's most important viceroyalties.

59. See Carlos Herrejón Peredo, *Del sermón al discurso cívico: México, 1760–1834* (Zamora: Colegio de Michoacán, 2003), 77–82.

60. José Manuel Rodríguez, *Cómo deben haberse los vasallos con sus reyes: Plática doctrinal predicada por Joseph Manuel Rodriguez a los terceros de la misma orden* (Mexico City: Imprenta Real Superior del Gobierno de Joseph Antonio de Hogal, 1768), 15.

61. Rodríguez, *Cómo deben haberse*, 16.

62. Rodríguez, *Cómo deben haberse*, 21.

CODA ONE: FROM THE COUNTRY TO THE CITY

1. Hipólito Villarroel, *Enfermedades políticas que padece la capital de esta Nueva España* (Mexico City: Porrúa, 1999). Published as an incomplete version by Carlos María Bustamante, without mentioning its author at all, *Enfermedades políticas* would reach an audience for the first time in 1831. The full manuscript was probably ready in 1787 and comprises six parts addressing different aspects of the viceroyalty's social predicaments. Written in an epistolary format, the recipient is undisclosed and speculations about who it might have been abound. Villarroel's text was relatively unknown at the time of its publication and, while often referenced in recent colonial historiography, the piece has seldom been the object of

monographic or detailed studies. For one of the most recent and thorough engagements with the piece, see Patricia Escandón, "Hipólito Villarroel: Pensamiento ilustrado y autobiografía en las *Enfermedades políticas*," *Revista de Historia de América* 157 (July–December 2019): 107–128. See also Woodrow Borah, "Hipólito Villarroel: Some Unanswered Questions," in *Des Indes occidentales à l'Amérique Latine*, vol. 2, ed. Thomas Calvo and Alain Musset, 505–514 (Mexico City: Centro de Estudios Mexicanos y Centroamericanos, 2006), accessed July 18, 2018, https://books.openedition.org/cemca/2118?lang=en; Mary Austin Collins, "Hipólito Villarroel and the Reforms of Charles the Third" (master's thesis, University of California, 1922); Virginia Gil Amate, "Hipólito Villarroel: Una mirada ilustrada sobre la ciudad de México," *Tema y variaciones de literatura* 32 (January–June, 2009): 255–287; Yolopattli Hernández Torres, "*Enfermedades políticas* de Hipólito Villarroel: Migración, higiene y orden social en la Nueva España ilustrada (Ensayo crítico)," *Chasqui, revista de literatura latinoamericana* (Lima) 44, no. 1 (2015): 77–90.

2. The establishment of *intendencias* has been widely studied by David Brading as a revolutionary transformation in government. See Brading, *Miners and Merchants in Bourbon Mexico 1763–1810* (Cambridge: Cambridge University Press, 1971). *Intendencias* were first adopted in 1718 by Philip V and inspired by the model of French intendencies. See Collins, *Hipólito Villarroel and the Reforms*, 176.

3. Villarroel, *Enfermedades políticas*, 67.

4. Villarroel, *Enfermedades políticas*, 67.

5. Villarroel participated in a case handled by the Audiencia de Guadalajara and also served as a member of the Tribunal de la Acordada. He was the mayor of Tlapa, Oaxaca, for a few years after leaving his post in Cuautla and was accused and charged, although minimally, for mistreating the Indians and for willfully overcharging tributary quotas and bond fees. See Escandón, "Hipólito Villarroel."

6. Escandón, "Hipólito Villarroel."

7. Villarroel, *Enfermedades políticas*, 66–67. For more on Villarroel's personal relationship with Gálvez and the disagreements he had with his projects, see Escandón, "Hipólito Villarroel."

8. Villarroel, *Enfermedades políticas*, 175.

9. Villarroel, *Enfermedades políticas*, 175.

10. Villarroel, *Enfermedades políticas*, 175.

11. See the entry for "policía" in Esteban de Terreros y Pando, *Diccionario castellano con las voces de ciencias y artes y sus correspondientes en las tres lenguas francesa, latina é italiana*, vol. 3 (Madrid: Viuda de Ibarra, Hijos y Compañía, 1788), 169.

12. Villarroel, *Enfermedades políticas*, 195. In discussing "infested castes," the author makes specific reference to the racial categories of *lobos*, *coyotes*, and *salto-atrás*.

13. Villarroel, *Enfermedades políticas*, 195.

14. Villarroel, *Enfermedades políticas*, 195.

15. Villarroel, *Enfermedades políticas*, 61–62.

16. Villarroel, *Enfermedades políticas*, 61–62.

17. Karl Marx, *Capital: A Critique of Political Economy*, vol. 1 (New York: Penguin, 1990).
18. Villarroel, *Enfermedades políticas*, 175–176.
19. For a discussion of race, spatial management, and segregation in an earlier context surrounding the 1692 riot in Mexico City, see Daniel Nemser, *Infrastructures of Race: Concentration and Biopolitics in Colonial Mexico* (Austin: University of Texas Press, 2017), chap. 3.
20. Nemser, *Infrastructures of Race*, 116–118.
21. Villarroel, *Enfermedades políticas*, 176–177.
22. Villarroel, *Enfermedades políticas*, 176–177.
23. "[I deduce] that they begin to work in service not for the salary and rations, but rather for what they might steal to support those they left in the street, their masters living in a state of distrust and with more eyes than Argos, so that they might be thieved less." Villarroel, *Enfermedades políticas*, 176.
24. Villarroel, *Enfermedades políticas*, 177.
25. Villarroel, *Enfermedades políticas*, 179–180.
26. Villarroel, *Enfermedades políticas*, 180.
27. Villarroel, *Enfermedades políticas*, 181.
28. Villarroel, *Enfermedades políticas*, 180.
29. Villarroel, *Enfermedades políticas*, 180–182.
30. See *Reglamento e instrucción para los presidios que se han de formas en la línea de frontera de la Nueva España resuelto por el rey nuestro señor en cédula de 10 de setiembre de 1772* (Mexico City: Oficina de la Águila dirigida por José Ximeno, 1834).
31. Villarroel, *Enfermedades políticas*, 180–182.
32. Villarroel, *Enfermedades políticas*, 180–182.
33. Villarroel, *Enfermedades políticas*, 180–182.
34. Villarroel, *Enfermedades políticas*, 180–182.
35. See Michel Foucault, *Discipline and Punish*, trans. Alan Sheridan (New York: Vintage Books, 1995).

CHAPTER THREE: THE DOMINO AFFECT

1. Juan López de Cancelada, "Nota al lector," in *Vida de J. J. Dessalines, Gefe de los negros de Santo Domingo, con notas muy circunstanciadas sobre el origen, carácter, atrocidades de los principales gefes de aquellos rebeldes desde el principio de la insurrección en 1791 traducida del francés por D.M.G.C año de 1805* (Mexico City: Oficina de Mariano de Zúñiga y Ontíveros, 1806). For the original French version, see Louis Dubroca, *La vie de J. J. Dessalines, chef de noirs révoltées de Saint-Domingue, avec des notes très détaillés sur l'origine, le caractère, la vie et les atrocités des principaux chefs de noirs, depuis l'insurrection de 1791* (Paris: Chez Dubroca et Rondonneau, 1804). For more on the life and work of Dubroca, see Jesús Paniagua

Pérez, *La revolución haitiana en la obra de Juan López de Cancelada* (León, Spain: Universidad de León, 2016), 219–224. As Paniagua Pérez notes, Louis Dubroca remains a mysterious figure despite his prolific output. Prior to his biography of Dessalines, he published, among other pieces, a biography of Toussaint L'Ouverture, which was quickly translated into English. For information on the publication of *Vida de J. J. Dessalines*, both in its original form and in its Spanish translation, see Paniagua Pérez, *La revolución haitiana*, 225–235. See also Kelly Donahue-Wallace, "Ilustrando el terror de rebelión: Los grabados de la vida de J. J. Dessalines," in *Arte y crisis en Iberoamérica: Segundas jornadas de historia del arte*, ed. Fernando Guzmán, Gloria Cortés, and Juan Manuel Martínez (Santiago de Chile: Ril Editores, 2004), 85–87; Johanna von Grafenstein, "Jean Jacques Dessalines: Fundador de la nación haitiana," *Secuencia* 5 (May–August, 1986): 112.

2. López de Cancelada, "Nota al lector," in *Vida de J. J. Dessalines*. See also Paniagua Pérez, *La revolución haitiana*, 259. Emphasis mine.

3. See Paniagua Pérez, *La revolución haitiana*, 226–227.

4. The rhetoric emphasizing Dessalines's monstrosity, animality, and ferocity are present in both the original version and its Spanish translation. The most substantial differences between the original French and the Spanish translation involve questions of international politics; for instance, the translation suppresses scenes that address the Spanish Empire's support of the Haitian rebels during the first years of the conflict. For more on these differences, see Paniagua Pérez, *La revolución haitiana*, 232. See also Ada Ferrer, *Freedom's Mirror: Cuba and Haiti in the Age of Revolution* (New York: Cambridge University Press, 2014), chap. 3. In using the term "racial formations," I echo the work of Michael Omi and Howard Winant in *Racial Formation in the United Sates* (London: Routledge, 2014), 109–113. Omi and Winant define racial formation as follows: "The process of race making, and its reverberations throughout the social order, is what we call racial formation. We define racial formation as the socio-historical process by which racial identities are created, lived out, transformed, and destroyed." *Racial Formation in the United Sates*, 109. I also use the word "formations" in the sense used by Ann Laura Stoler, who discusses imperial formations with respect to the category of empire in considering continual processes of deposition, destruction, displacement, and demands. See "Imperial Debris: Reflections on Ruins and Ruination," *Cultural Anthropology* 23, no. 2 (2008): 191–219, https://doi.org/10.1111/j.1548-1360.2008.00007.x.

5. An expansive transatlantic network boycotted Haiti (both symbolically and materially) after the rebellion. Eventually, this boycott would reconfigure the slave system, which grew beyond Saint-Domingue in Cuba, Brazil, and the United States, among others. As Ada Ferrer has argued, the sugar production boom in Cuba and the restructuring of slavery on the island should be viewed in relation to the abolition of slavery in Haiti. See Ferrer, *Freedom's Mirror*, chap. 1.

6. López de Cancelada's political compass was as volatile as the allegiances and confrontations between the Atlantic empires at the time. In this way, while in *Vida de J. J. Dessalines* López de Cancelada seemed to support the Napoleonic proj-

ect, this was not the case in his earlier and later publications. In his second work on Haiti, for example, he expounded on the well-known parallel between Napoleon and Dessalines, which the Haitian leader himself sought to establish in his gestures and attire. By then, López de Cancelada had altered his reading of the Haitian Revolution (especially during the government of Henri Christophe), beginning to see it as an example for Spain to follow after the crisis of 1808 and Napoleon's invasion. See Juan López de Cancelada, *Código formado por los negros de la Isla de Santo Domingo de la parte francesa hoi estado de Hayti, sancionado por Henrique Cristoval, Presidente y Generalísimo* (Cádiz: Quintana, 1810), 28. For more on political changes in López de Cancelada's work, see also Paniagua Pérez, *La revolución haitiana*, 232–233. For more on the wars with England and the alliance between Spain and France, see Charles Esdaile, *Napoleon's Wars: An International History* (New York: Viking, 2007), chap. 5.

7. See Andrew S. Curran, *The Anatomy of Blackness: Science and Slavery in an Age of Enlightenment* (Baltimore, MD: Johns Hopkins University Press, 2011); Andrew S. Curran and Patrick Graille, "The Faces of Eighteenth-Century Monstrosity," *Eighteenth-Century Life* 21, no. 2 (1997): 1–15. See also Noel Carroll, *The Philosophy of Horror, or, Paradoxes of the Heart* (New York: Routledge, 1990); Theodor W. Adorno and Max Horkheimer, *Dialectic of Enlightenment*, trans. John Cumming (New York: Continuum, 1994).

8. See Curran, "Faces of Eighteenth-Century Monstrosity."

9. See Curran, "Faces of Eighteenth-Century Monstrosity."

10. According to Michel Foucault, the figure of the political monster—which comprised both the tyrannical king and the armed people—first emerged in the late eighteenth century in the context of the French Revolution. The difference between Haiti's "monstrosity" and that of France was colonial difference, which was inscribed along racial lines; Foucault does not consider this in his analysis. See Michel Foucault, *Abnormal: Lectures at the Collège de France, 1974–1975*, ed. Valerio Marchetti and Antonella Salomoni, trans. Graham Burchell (New York: Picador, 2003), chap. 4.

11. See López de Cancelada, *Vida de J. J. Dessalines*, 1.

12. See Immanuel Kant, *The Conflict of Faculties / Der Streit der Fakultäten*, translated and with an introduction by Mary J. Gregor (New York: Abaris Books, 1979), 153–157. The historical indelibility Kant saw in the French Revolution came from the violent and traumatic opening of regicide as an expiable, incomprehensible crime and its "legalized illegality." Yet the same revolution also signaled an affectivity shared by all of "humanity," and thus by the universality of the principles of law. See Rebecca Comay, *Mourning Sickness: Hegel and the French Revolution* (Stanford, CA: Stanford University Press, 2011), chap. 2, Kindle edition. See also Hannah Arendt, *Lectures on Kant's Political Philosophy*, ed. Ronald Beiner (Chicago: University of Chicago Press, 1982).

13. See Comay, *Mourning Sickness*, chap. 2.

14. See Comay, *Mourning Sickness*, 32.

15. "The structure is strictly traumatic: Germany's experience of modernity is registered as a missed experience. The encounter with the French Revolution introduces anachronism—trauma itself—as a henceforth ineluctable feature of historical and political experience. German philosophy around 1800 presents both the theorization and the ideological expression of this traumatic lateness: symptom, legitimation, consolation." Comay, *Mourning Sickness*, 3–4.

16. On Haiti's revolution as a benchmark of modernity, see Sibylle Fischer, *Modernity Disavowed: Haiti and the Cultures of Slaves in the Age of Revolution* (Durham, NC: Duke University Press, 2004).

17. Comay continues, "The 'French' Revolution that provides the measure of 'German' untimeliness is itself untimely. (Marx himself came to see this by the time he moved to Paris and began to contemplate the Revolution at closer quarters.) There is no right time or 'ripe time' for Revolution (or there would be no need of one). The Revolution always arrives too soon (conditions are never ready) and too late (it lags forever behind its own initiative)." Comay, *Mourning Sickness*, 7.

18. Antonio Negri, "The Political Monster: Naked Life and Power," in *In Praise of the Common: A Conversation on Philosophy and Politics*, ed. Cesare Casarino and Antonio Negri (Minneapolis: University of Minnesota Press, 2008), 196.

19. Ronald Briggs, *The Moral Electricity of Print Transatlantic Education and the Lima Women's Circuit, 1876–1910* (Nashville, TN: Vanderbilt University Press, 2017).

20. See López de Cancelada, *Vida de J. J. Dessalines*, 2.

21. *Gazeta de México*, December 24, 1806, 851–852. Emphasis mine.

22. López de Cancelada, *Vida de J. J. Dessalines*, 1.

23. See López de Cancelada, *Vida de J. J. Dessalines*, 1. Of course, these mentions presupposed the risk of possible contagion and therefore tacitly admitted New Spain's vulnerability to a similar racialized popular uprising. They also tacitly admitted the existence of real communication networks through which popular rumors about the situation in Haiti were circulating within the Spanish colony. With respect to the circulation of information about Haiti in New Spain, see Johanna von Grafenstein Gareis, *Nueva España en el Circuncaribe, 1779–1808: Revolución, competencia imperial y vínculos intercoloniales* (Mexico City: Universidad Nacional Autónoma de México, 1997), 269–271; Cynthia García Martínez, "Fugas, ventas y otras noticias sobre la población afrodescendiente en el *Diario de México* y la *Gazeta de México*, 1784–1809" (master's thesis, Instituto de Investigaciones Dr. José María Luis Mora, 2016), chap. 2.3. For more on the general circulation of news about the Haitian Revolution, see Ferrer, *Freedom's Mirror*, chap. 2.

24. "Impressibility," Schuller writes, "denotes the capacity of a substance to receive impressions from external objects that thereby change its characteristics. Impressibility signals the capacity of matter to be alive to movements made on it, to retain and incorporate changes rendered in its material over time." Kyla Schuller, *The Biopolitics of Feeling: Race, Sex, and Science in the Nineteenth Century* (Durham, NC: Duke University Press, 2018), 7.

25. López de Cancelada, *Vida de J. J. Dessalines*, 1.
26. López de Cancelada, *Vida de J. J. Dessalines*, 4.
27. López de Cancelada, *Vida de J. J. Dessalines*, 4. For more on Dubroca and vengeance as a trope in the writing about the Haitian Revolution, see Marlene L. Daut, *Tropics of Haiti: Race and the Literary History of the Haitian Revolution in the Atlantic World, 1789–1865* (Liverpool: Liverpool University Press, 2015), chap. 1.
28. López de Cancelada, *Vida de J. J. Dessalines*, 6.
29. López de Cancelada, *Vida de J. J. Dessalines*, 8.
30. López de Cancelada, *Vida de J. J. Dessalines*, 8.
31. See Schuller, *Biopolitics of Feeling*, introduction.
32. See Schuller, *Biopolitics of Feeling*, introduction.
33. See López de Cancelada, *Vida de J. J. Dessalines*, 2, 10.
34. As Kelly Donahue-Wallace has shown, the process of printing was mobilized as a metaphor by colonial authorities to discuss the affects of the king's subjects; ideas about "impressibility" invoke this same rhetoric. See Donahue-Wallace, "Spinning the King: Prints, Imprinting and the Equestrian Portrait of Charles IV," *Print Quarterly* 29, no. 4 (2012): 411–416.
35. While the Bourbon administration promoted its own visual codes, remnants of how images were viewed and used during the Hapsburg period still carried over. See Alejandro Cañeque, "Imaging the Spanish Empire: The Visual Construction of Imperial Authority in Habsburg New Spain," *Colonial Latin American Review* 19, no. 1 (2010): 31. For more on the power of images, including secular images, see also Kelly Donahue-Wallace, "Abused and Battered: Printed Images and the Female Body in Viceregal New Spain," in *Woman and Art in Early Modern Latin America*, ed. Kellen Kee McIntyre and Richard E. Phillips (Leiden, Netherlands: Brill, 2007), 129–130. See also Magali M. Carrera, *Imagining Identity in New Spain: Race, Lineage, and the Colonial Body in Portraiture and Casta Paintings* (Austin: University of Texas Press, 2003).
36. The versions in other languages contained only a print of Dessalines's portrait. See Paniagua Pérez, *La revolución haitiana*, 225. See also Donahue-Wallace, "Abused and Battered," 138–141.
37. For more on the images included in *Vida de J. J. Dessalines*, see Paniagua Pérez, *La revolución haitiana*, 240–247; Donahue-Wallace, "Ilustrando el terror de rebelión" and "Abused and Battered."
38. For studies on New Spanish iconography, see Serge Gruzinski, *Images at War: Mexico from Columbus to Blade Runner (1492–2019)*, trans. Heather MacLean (Durham, NC: Duke University Press, 2001); Michael Schreffler, *The Art of Allegiance: Visual Culture and Imperial Power in Baroque New Spain* (University Park: Pennsylvania State University Press, 2007); Alejandro Cañeque, *The King's Living Image: The Culture and Politics of Viceregal Power in Colonial Mexico* (New York: Routledge, 2004); David A. Brading, *Mexican Phoenix: Our Lady of Guadalupe—Image and Tradition across Five Centuries* (Cambridge: Cambridge University Press, 2001). Most of these studies are devoted to the political use of images in the pre-

Bourbon period. Here I am building specifically upon the work of Kelly Donahue-Wallace, who expands her analysis into the use of images in the late colonial period. See especially "Abused and Battered."

39. See Hillel Eyal, "Beyond Networks: Transatlantic Immigration and Wealth in Late Colonial Mexico City," *Journal of Latin American Studies* 47, no. 2 (May 2015): 317–348. According to Eyal, 90 percent of *peninsulares* in Mexico City were literate, versus 71 percent of male criollos. "Beyond Networks," 336.

40. See *Gazeta de México*, December 24, 1806, 852. On the circulation of images among illiterate and literate circles in New Spain, see Donahue-Wallace, "Abused and Battered," 128.

41. See Paniagua Pérez, *La revolución haitiana*, 245.

42. See Donahue-Wallace, "Ilustrando el terror de rebelión," 88–89.

43. See Donahue-Wallace, "Ilustrando el terror de rebelión," 88–89.

44. A woman's lifted skirt was among the visual codes associated with rape. See Donahue-Wallace, "Ilustrando el terror de rebelión," 88. See also Donahue-Wallace, "Abused and Battered."

45. See López de Cancelada, *Vida de J. J. Dessalines*, 1.

46. See María Elena Martínez, "The Black Blood of New Spain: Limpieza de Sangre, Racial Violence, and Gendered Power in Early Colonial Mexico," *William and Mary Quarterly* 61, no. 3 (2004): 479–520.

47. Charles W. Mills, "Race and Global Justice," in *Empire, Race and Global Justice*, ed. Duncan Bell, 94–119 (Cambridge: Cambridge University Press, 2019).

48. Mills, "Race and Global Justice," 103.

49. These letters were also published in the form of footnotes in the New Spanish edition of *Vida de J. J. Dessalines*.

50. "Extracto de las cartas de Mr. Talleyrand remitidas al secretario de Estados Unidos," *Gazeta de México*, July 9, 1806, 437. The relation between the United States and Haiti has been the topic of numerous studies. For a recent general overview of this scholarship, see Ronald Angelo Johnson, "Haiti's Connection to Early America: Beyond the Revolution," *History Compass* 16, no. 3 (2018), https://doi.org/10.1111/hic3.12442. See also Elizabeth Maddock Dillon and Michael Drexler, eds., *The Haitian Revolution and the Early United States: Histories, Textualities, Geographies* (Philadelphia: University of Pennsylvania Press, 2016); Donald R. Hickey, "America's Response to the Slave Revolt in Haiti, 1791–1806," *Journal of the Early Republic* 4 (1982): 361–379.

51. See Daniel Nemser, *Infrastructures of Race: Concentration and Biopolitics in Colonial Mexico* (Austin: University of Texas Press, 2017), 128.

52. See López de Cancelada, *Vida de J. J. Dessalines*, i.

53. See Donahue-Wallace, "Abused and Battered," 127. See also Carrera, *Imagining Identity in New Spain*, 7–8 and chap. 3.

54. See Donahue-Wallace, "Abused and Battered."

55. See Martínez, "Black Blood of New Spain," 514. For more on the centrality of the female womb as a resource of colonial accumulation, see also Donahue-

Wallace, "Abused and Battered," 127; Kristine Ibsen, "The Hiding Places of My Power: Sebastiana Josefa de la Santísima Trinidad and the Hagiographic Representation of the Body in Colonial Spanish America," *Colonial Latin American Review* 7, no. 2 (1998): 254.

56. See Donahue-Wallace, "Ilustrando el terror de rebelión," 88. See also Donahue-Wallace, "Abused and Battered," 138.

57. See Daniel Nemser, "Triangulating Blackness: Mexico City, 1612," *Mexican Studies / Estudios Mexicanos* 33, no. 3 (Fall 2017): 365.

58. See Martínez, "Black Blood of New Spain," and *Genealogical Fictions*.

59. See Martínez, "Black Blood of New Spain," 515. See also María Elena Martínez, *Genealogical Fictions: Limpieza de Sangre, Religion, and Gender in Colonial Mexico* (Stanford, CA: Stanford University Press, 2008), chap. 9.

60. See Carrera, *Imagining Identity in New Spain*, 13. See also "Real cédula declarando la forma en que se ha de guardar y cumplir en las indias la Pragmática sanción de 23 de marzo de 1776 sobre contraer matrimonio," in *Colección de documentos para la historia de la formación de Hispanoamérica, 1493–1810*, ed. Richard Konetzke, vol. 3.1, 1691–1779 (Madrid: Consejo Superior de Investigaciones Científicas, 1962), 438.

61. For more on this genre of paintings, see Carrera, *Imagining Identity in New Spain*, and Ilona Katzew, *Casta Painting: Images of Race in Eighteenth-Century Mexico* (New Haven, CT: Yale University Press, 2004).

62. For more on the New Spain's trope of the Black rapist, see Nemser, "Triangulating Blackness."

63. Donahue-Wallace, "Abused and Battered," 138.

64. See Donahue-Wallace, "Ilustrando el terror de rebelión," 89.

65. Michel-Rolph Trouillot, *Silencing the Past: Power and the Production of History* (Boston: Beacon, 1995), 73.

66. Trouillot, *Silencing the Past*, 82.

67. Fredric Jameson, *Valences of the Dialectic* (London: Verso, 2010), 596. Jameson writes,

> If history is a totality, or better still a process of totalization, one which is an ongoing incorporation of ever more extensive parts of the globe, then its experience will necessarily include a new and original relationship of absence to presence, of the far to the near and the external to the internal: it will not only by a "sign" of the historical as Kant thought but a mode of grasping these new and hitherto unsuspected relationships and of bringing them to consciousness.

CHAPTER FOUR: STAGING FEAR AND FREEDOM

1. Much has been written about the 1810 Hidalgo rebellion. For some of the most influential studies on the popular aspect of the events, see Eric Van Young,

The Other Rebellion: Popular Violence, Ideology, and the Struggle for Mexican Independence, 1810–1821 (Stanford, CA: Stanford University Press, 2001); Hugh M. Hamill, *The Hidalgo Revolt: Prelude to Mexican Independence* (Gainesville: University of Florida Press, 1966); John Tutino, *From Insurrection to Revolution in Mexico: Social Bases of Agrarian Violence, 1750–1940* (Princeton, NJ: Princeton University Press, 1986) and *Making a New World: Founding Capitalism in the Bajío and Spanish North America* (Durham, NC: Duke University Press, 2011); Friedrich Katz, ed., *Riot, Rebellion, and Revolution: Rural Social Conflict in Mexico* (Princeton, NJ: Princeton University Press, 1988); Luis Fernando Granados, *En el espejo haitiano: Los indios del Bajío y el colapso del orden colonial en América Latina* (Mexico City: Ediciones Era, 2016); Brian Hamnett, *Roots of Insurgency: Mexican Regions, 1750–1824* (Cambridge: Cambridge University Press, 1986). For studies focused on the impact of the 1808 crisis of sovereignty in New Spain, see Francois-Xavier Guerra, *Modernidad e independencia: Ensayos sobre las revoluciones hispánicas* (Mexico City: Fondo de Cultura Económica, 1992); Jeremy Adelman, *Sovereignty and Revolution in the Iberian Atlantic* (Princeton, NJ: Princeton University Press, 2006); Jaime Rodríguez O., *We Are Now the True Spaniards* (Stanford, CA: Stanford University Press, 2012).

2. Juan E. Hernández y Dávalos, ed., "Primer edicto contra la revolución iniciada en Dolores por el Sr. Hidalgo, fulminado por Don Manuel Abad y Queipo, canónigo penitenciario, electo Obispo de Michoacán," in *Colección de documentos para la historia de la guerra de independencia de Mexico de 1808 a 1821*, vol. 2 (Mexico City: José María Sandoval, 1878), 104.

3. Hernández y Dávalos, "Primer edicto contra la revolución," 104. Emphasis is mine.

4. Here it would be worth mentioning examples such as Spain's support of the rebels during the early years of the uprising as part of its war with France (1793–1796) or the way that Spain's colonies and metropolis (except for Cuba) opened their doors to a group of exiled rebels from the battalion of Haitian rebel leader Jean François. In 1796, the Yucatán saw the formation of San Fernando Aké, a village populated entirely by Haitian ex-soldiers. Imperial strategy wielded a double-edged sword: while it opened its doors to those who had been their allies as part of a negotiation with France, the rebel troops were scattered across various marginal areas of the empire in order to dilute them and avoid the circulation of revolutionary ideas and experience. For more on the establishment of San Fernando Aké, see Jorge Victoria Ojeda and Jorge Canto Alcocer, *San Fernando Aké: Microhistoria de una comunidad afroamericana en Yucatán* (Mérida, Mexico: Universidad Autónoma de Yucatán, 2006); Ada Ferrer, *Freedom's Mirror: Cuba and Haiti in the Age of Revolution* (New York: Cambridge University Press, 2014), 131–145.

5. Hernández y Dávalos, "Primer edicto contra la revolución."

6. The scholarship on the Haitian Revolution is now vast. For a study on how Haiti impacted domestic affairs in the United States, see James Alexander Dun, *Dangerous Neighbors: Making the Haitian Revolution in Early America* (Philadel-

phia: University of Pennsylvania Press, 2016). For other studies on Haiti's impact abroad, see Carla Calargé et al., *Haiti and the Americas* (Jackson: University Press of Mississippi, 2013); Ferrer, *Freedom's Mirror*; David Geggus, ed., *The Impact of the Haitian Revolution in the Altantic World* (Columbia: University of South Carolina Press, 2001) and "The Sounds and Echoes of Freedom," in *Beyond Slavery: The Multilayered Legacy of Africans in Latin America and the Caribbean*, ed. Darien J. Davis (Lanham, MD: Rowman and Littlefield, 2007), 19–36. The bibliography chronicling the "fear" of Haiti is extensive. A few important sources on this topic are Michel-Rolph Trouillot, *Silencing the Past: Power and the Production of History* (Boston: Beacon, 1995); Sybille Fischer, *Modernity Disavowed: Haiti and the Cultures of Slaves in the Age of Revolution* (Durham, NC: Duke University Press, 2004); Susan Buck-Morss, *Hegel, Haiti, and Universal History* (Pittsburgh, PA: University of Pittsburgh Press, 2009). For a very detailed overview on the scholarship on Haiti, see Jesús Paniagua Pérez, *La revolución haitiana en la obra de López de Cancelada* (León, Spain: Universidad de León, 2016), chap. 1.

7. On the relationship between Haiti and Mexico, see Johanna von Grafenstein Gareis, *Nueva España en el Circuncaribe, 1779–1808: Revolución, competencia imperial y vínculos intercoloniales* (Mexico City: Universidad Nacional Autónoma de México, 1997); Cynthia García Martínez, *Fugas, ventas y otras noticias* sobre la población afrodescendiente en el *Diario de México* y la *Gazeta de México, 1784–1809*" (master's thesis, Instituto de Investigaciones Dr. José María Luis Mora, 2016), chap. 2.3; Granados, *En el espejo haitiano*.

8. The first news about the rebellion in Saint-Domingue was published in *Gazeta de México* on August 2, 1794. The paper informed subscribers about the abolition of slavery on the island. Sporadic information was published throughout the following years and until roughly 1795. It was not until 1806, when the *Gazeta* was under Juan López de Cancelada's overview as editor, that a new wave of news about Haiti was printed. For more, see García Martínez, *Fugas, ventas y otras noticias*, chap. 2.3. With respect to the circulation of information about Haiti in New Spain, see also von Grafenstein Gareis, *Nueva España en el Circuncaribe*, 269–271.

9. See Fischer, *Modernity Disavowed*, introduction.

10. For more on this context, see chapters 1 and 2.

11. See chapter 1. See also Tutino, *Making a New World*. See also David Brading, *Miners and Merchants in Bourbon Mexico 1763–1810* (Cambridge: Cambridge University Press, 1971), and Doris M. Ladd, *The Making of a Strike: Mexican Silver Workers' Struggles in Real del Monte 1766–1775* (Lincoln: University of Nebraska Press, 1988).

12. Slavery in the Spanish Empire underwent a fragile yet noteworthy revitalization after the Bourbon Reforms. This brief renaissance was propelled by the Spanish Crown's desire to modernize commerce, including the slave trade, which was expanding and liberalizing. For more on the reopening of the slave trade after the Bourbon Reforms, see Gonzalo Aguirre Beltrán, *La población negra de México 1519–1810* (Mexico City: Ediciones Fuente Cultural, 1946), 77–92, 237; see

also Manuel Lucena Salmoral, *Los códigos negros de la América Española* (Alcalá, Spain: Universidad Alcalá y Ediciones UNESCO, 1996), 15–22; Ben Vinson III, "From Dawn 'til Dusk: Black Labor in Late Colonial Mexico," in *Black Mexico: Race and Society from Colonial to Modern Times*, ed. Ben Vinson and Matthew Restall (Albuquerque: University of New Mexico Press, 2009), 100. For more general studies on slavery and African populations in late eighteenth-century New Spain, see Frank T. Proctor III, *Damned Notions of Liberty: Slavery, Culture, and Power in Colonial México 1640–1769* (Albuquerque: University of New Mexico Press, 2010); Ben Vinson III and Bobby Vaughn, *Afroméxico: Herramientas para la historia* (Mexico City: Fondo de Cultura Económica, 2004); Ben Vinson III, *Bearing Arms for His Majesty: The Free-Colored Militia in Colonial Mexico* (Stanford, CA: Stanford University Press, 2003).

13. For a study on how the Haitian Revolution shaped the emergence of demographic discourses and practices in Cuba, see Ada Ferrer, "Cuba en la sombra de Haití: Noticias, sociedad y esclavitud," in *El rumor de Haití en Cuba: Temor, raza y rebeldía, 1789–1844*, ed. Ma. Dolores González-Ripoll Navarro (Madrid: Consejo Superior de Investigaciones Científicas, 2004), 213. See also Daylet Domínguez, "Imaginarios antillanos: Humboldt, Haití y la Confederación Africana en las Antillas," *Revista Iberoamericana* 84, no. 262 (2018): 45–63.

14. See Laurent Dubois, *Avengers of the New World: The Story of the Haitian Revolution* (Cambridge, MA: Harvard University Press, 2004), 30.

15. According to a comparative table included in Gonzalo Aguirre Beltrán, *La población negra de México 1519–1810* (Mexico City: Ediciones Fuente Cultural, 1946), the population distribution with respect to caste in 1810 was as follows: 15,000 Europeans (0.2 percent); 10,000 Africans (0.1 percent); 3,676,281 indigenous people (60 percent); 1,092,367 Euro-mestizos (17.9 percent); 624,461 Afro-mestizos (10.1 percent); and 704,245 Indo-mestizos (11.5 percent). That said, Aguirre Beltrán maintains that the data obtained from Alexander von Humboldt tends to exaggerate the percentage of the white/European population; he prefers to use the figures provided by the financial officer Noriega. See Aguirre Beltrán, *La población negra de México*, 237. Vinson provides similar numbers for 1793, drawing primarily from the census conducted by viceroy Revillagigedo. Although this census is useful for reconstructing certain aspects of the Afro-descendant populations in the late eighteenth century in the colony, Vinson asserts that the information provided is undoubtedly fragmentary. See Vinson, "From Dawn 'til Dusk," 101.

16. Humboldt does emphasize this difference in his discussion of European whites and criollos in New Spain, pointing out the disproportion between whites and other castes as among the highest in the colonies—higher, even, than in Saint-Domingue. Humboldt's preoccupation with proportional matters, in terms of caste, is certainly striking, for the Prussian traveler presents this in his *Political Essay* as basic knowledge for a government seeking to keep the peace in the colonies. The issue in New Spain, however, does not seem to be either slavery or rising tensions related to racial divisions, but rather being a highly dense population. See Alexander

von Humboldt, *Political Essay on the Kingdom of New Spain*, vol. 1, trans. from the French by John Black (New York: I. Riley, 1811), 177. See also book 2, chap. 8.

17. See Humboldt, *Political Essay*, vol. 1, 12.

18. See Humboldt, *Political Essay*, vol. 1, 152–153. For select recent studies on the Tupac Amaru rebellion, see Sinclair Thomson, *We Alone Will Rule: Native Andean Politics in the Age of Insurgency* (Madison: University of Wisconsin Press, 2002) and "Sovereignty Disavowed: the Tupac Amaru Revolution in the Atlantic World," *Atlantic Studies* 13, no. 3 (2016): 407–431; Sergio Serulnikov, *Revolution in the Andes: the Age of Tupac Amaru* (Durham, NC: Duke University Press, 2013).

19. Scholars have recently studied Humboldt's relation to the Haitian Revolution as a positive one, mostly focusing on his writings about this event in the *Essai politique sur l'île de Cuba* (1826). In his essay on New Spain, Humboldt had already used the example of Saint-Domingue to critique European elites and pressure them to improve the living conditions of racialized majorities in colonial societies. In this more "positive" use of Haiti, he nevertheless seems to still remain within a framework that avoids the revolutionary path toward abolition. Humboldt's work on Cuba was published several years after his essay on New Spain reached the European public for the first time in 1811. The temporal gap between the publication of these two works coincided with the irruption of the struggles for independence in Spanish America. I therefore wonder how this changing political context may have also punctuated Humboldt's public (that is, printed) reflections on Haiti. For studies on Humboldt and Haiti, see Laura Dassow, *The Passage to Cosmos: Alexander von Humboldt and the Shaping of America* (Chicago: University of Chicago Press, 2009), chap. 4; Domínguez, "Imaginarios antillanos"; Michael Zeuske, "Humboldt y la comparación de las esclavitudes en América," *HiN* 6, no. 11 (2005): 65–89.

20. Granados, *En el espejo haitano*, 223–233.

21. See Elizabeth Maddock Dillon, *New World Drama: The Performative Commons in the Atlantic World, 1649–1849* (Durham, NC: Duke University Press, 2014), 32.

22. On the performative dimension of the colonial order in New Spain, see Patricia Seed, *Ceremonies of Possession in Europe's Conquest of the New World, 1492–1640* (Cambridge: Cambridge University Press, 1995); Linda A. Curcio-Nagy, *The Great Festival of Colonial Mexico City: Performing Power and Identity* (Albuquerque: University of New Mexico Press, 2004); Juan Pedro Viqueira Albán, *¿Relajados o reprimidos? Diversiones públicas y vida social en la Ciudad de México durante el Siglo de Las Luces* (Mexico City: Fondo de Cultura Económica, 1987). For considerations on theater and power in other contexts, see Dillon, *New World Drama*; Sergio Bertelli, *The King's Body: Sacred Rituals of Power in Medieval and Early Modern Europe* (University Park: Pennsylvania State University Press, 2001).

23. See Dillon, *New World Drama*, 32.

24. See Enrique de Olavarría y Ferrari, *Reseña histórica del teatro en México*, vol. 1 (Mexico City: La Europea, 1895), 176.

25. For more on the censorship and evaluation of *El negro y la blanca*, see

Frieda Koeninger, "*El negro y la blanca*: La censura de una obra abolicionista en Madrid y México," *Dieciocho: Hispanic Enlightenment* 37, no. 1 (Spring 2014): 123. On the process of censorship in Spanish theater, see Koeninger, "Santos Diez Gonzalez, Civil Censor: Balancing the Theory and Practice of Theater Reform in Madrid, 1788–1804," *Restoration and 18th Century Theatre Research* 29, no. 2 (Winter 2014): 9–26; René Andioc, *Teatro y Sociedad en el Madrid del siglo XVIII* (Madrid: Editorial Castalia, 1987). On censorship in New Spanish theater, see Ricardo Camarena Castellanos, *El control inquisitorial del teatro en la Nueva España durante el siglo XVIII* (Mexico City: Instituto Nacional de Bellas Artes, 1995); Germán Viveros, *Talía novohispana: Espectáculos, temas y textos teatrales dieciochescos* (Mexico City: Universidad Nacional Autónoma de México, 1996), *Teatro dieciochesco de Nueva España* (Mexico City: Universidad Nacional Autónoma de México, 1990), and *Manifestaciones teatrales en Nueva España* (Mexico City: Universidad Nacional Autónoma de México, 2005).

26. See Koeninger, "*El negro y la blanca*," 2; Ivy Lilian McClelland, *Spanish Drama of Pathos 1750–1808*, vol. 2 (Toronto: University of Toronto Press), 392.

27. Vicente Rodríguez de Arellano, *El negro y la blanca: Melodrama en dos actos* (Madrid: J. Sánchez, 1802), 14.

28. Starting in 1776, the British Parliament sought to pass laws restricting the slave trade across the Atlantic, something that would not be legally achieved until 1807 nor actually achieved in practice until much later. See Jenny S. Martínez, *The Slave Trade and the Origins of International Human Rights Law* (New York: Oxford University Press, 2012), 16. For more on the contradictions of British abolitionism and the continuity and rearrangement of slavery after the abolition of trafficking, see Lisa Lowe, *The Intimacies of Four Continents* (Durham, NC: Duke University Press, 2015). On slavery and the slave trade in Spain, see Lisa Surwilio, *Monsters by Trade: Slave Traffickers in Modern Spanish Literature and Culture* (Stanford, CA: Stanford University Press, 2014).

29. In 1802, Napoleon would reinstate slavery in most French colonies, with the exception of Saint-Domingue.

30. See Jeremy D. Popkin, *You Are All Free: The Haitian Revolution and the Abolition of Slavery* (New York: Cambridge University Press, 2010).

31. As Jesús Paniagua Pérez has noted in his preliminary study to *La vida de J. J. Dessalines*, not much has been published about Spain and the Haitian Revolution. He, however, acknowledges that news circulated in the metropolis, particularly in the first years of the conflict. See Paniagua Pérez, *La revolución haitiana*, 36–37. For more on Rodríguez de Arellano, see Cristina Martín Puente, "La Historia de Roma en la obra dramática de Ramón de la Cruz y Vicente Rodríguez de Arellano," in *Cuadernos de Filología Clásica: Estudios Latinos* 32, no. 2 (2013), 347–360, https://doi.org/10.5209/rev_CFCL.2012.v32.n2.41030.

32. For examples see *Gaceta de Madrid*, July 8, 1797, and December 30, 1797.

33. See Olavarría y Ferrari, *Reseña histórica del teatro*, 176.

34. Dun, *Dangerous Neighbors*, 3.

35. Moira Fradinger, *Binding Violence: Literary Visions of Political Origins* (Stanford, CA: Stanford University Press, 2010), 14–15.

36. For more on shifting receptions across the Atlantic, see Dillon, *New World Drama*.

37. "Serás el blanco." See Rodríguez de Arellano, *El negro y la blanca*, 19. Emphasis mine.

38. See Maya Ramos Smith, ed., *Censura y teatro novohispano (1539–1822): Ensayos y antología de documentos* (Mexico City: CONACULTA, 1998), 646–647.

39. According to Olavarría y Ferrari, *El negro sensible* was performed in Mexico on December 2, 1805. See *Reseña histórica del teatro en México*, 174.

40. For more on Comella's theater, see María Angulo Egea, *Luciano Francisco Comella (1751–1812): Otra cara del teatro de la ilustración* (Alicante, Spain: Publicaciones de la Universidad de Alicante, 2006); Ivy Lilian McClelland, "The Comellan Conception of Stage-Realism," *Dieciocho: Hispanic Enlightenment* 1–2, no. 16 (1993): 111–117.

41. Not much has been written about the use of blackface in Spanish-American theater. However, building on studies about Blackness in Golden Age theater, we can assume that blackface and black speech were used in colonial theaters as well. A draft of the theater legislation of 1790 in New Spain reveals that the authorities were discouraging the use of blackface, although it was still being used by actors (hence the need to regulate it): "Quando se haga algún papel de majo, o tuno así en comedias y entremeses como en qualquiera otra pieza, se escusaran los vestidos de andrajos y trapos indecentes que no conducen a demostrar el caracter del papel, ni menos el tiznarse de negro la cara" (When portraying a lowly character in a comedy, interlude, or any other piece, the use of rags and other indecent clothing that do not contribute to accurately presenting the role will be excused [meaning not permitted], as will be the blackening of one's face). See Ramos Smith, *Censura y teatro novohispano*, 523. For a study on blackface in nineteenth-century Cuba, see Jill Lane, *Blackface Cuba, 1840–1895* (Philadelphia: University of Pennsylvania Press, 2005). For a study on Blackness in Spanish Golden Age theater, see Baltasar Fra Molinero, *La imagen de los negros en el siglo de oro* (Madrid: Siglo XXI Editores, 1995). For a recent study on the divergent modalities of Blackness and blackface in the global Indies, see Ashley L. Cohen, "The Global Indies: Reading the Imaginative Geography of British Empire 1763–1871" (PhD diss., University of Pennsylvania, 2013), chap. 2.

42. Luciano Francisco Comella, *El negro sensible: Melodrama en un acto* (Cádiz, Spain: Librería de Murguia), 8.

43. For a study on this topic see, for instance, Fischer, *Modernity Disavowed*, chap. 4.

44. See Saidiya Hartman, *Scenes of Subjection: Terror, Slavery, and Self-Making in Nineteenth-Century America* (New York: Oxford University Press, 1997), chap. 4.

45. See Ramos Smith, *Censura y teatro novohispano*, 646–647. Although I have not been able to confirm this, the plays were also likely staged in theaters in

other colonial regions. It would be interesting to learn about inquisitorial responses to these plays in Cuba. According to José Juan Arrom, the archives that would allow a reconstruction of Cuba's theater scene in the early 1800s are fragmented and dispersed. In his book, however, Arrom does recognize the transatlantic circulation of plays in Cuba and the popularity of Comella's work with Cuban audiences. See José Juan Arrom, *Historia de la literatura dramática cubana* (New Haven, CT: Yale University Press, 1944), 18–21.

46. Here I am building on Dillon's distinction between the ontic and the mimetic. See Dillon, *New World Drama*, 11–17.

47. See Bernardo de Gálvez, *Reglamento u ordenanzas de teatros* (1786) transcribed in Manuel Mañón, *Historia del teatro principal de México* (Mexico City: Instituto Nacional de Bellas Artes, 2013), 22. The original version of the manuscript can be found in Archivo Histórico de la Ciudad de México, vol. 796, exp. 3. See also Viqueira Albán, *¿Relajados o reprimidos?*.

48. Clause 32. See Bernardo de Gálvez, *Reglamento u ordenanzas de teatros*.

49. See Gálvez, *Reglamento u ordenanzas de teatros*.

50. See Gálvez, *Reglamento u ordenanzas de teatros*.

51. Indeed, the viceroy himself acknowledged in his correspondence that because the city lacked coffee shops and other social spaces, Mexico City's coliseum was a crucial space for social interactions. Leonard Irving, "The 1790 Theater Season of the Mexico City Coliseo." *Hispanic Review* 19, no. 2 (1951): 104–120.

52. *El negro sensible* was staged in Madrid in 1809 at the Teatro de la Cruz and in 1811 in the coliseum on Concepción Jerónima Street. María Mercedes Romero Peña, *El teatro de la guerra de independencia* (Madrid: Fundación Universitaria Española, 2007), 426, 428, 899.

53. Viqueira Albán, *¿Relajados o reprimidos?*, 53.

54. It is possible that something about the unrestricted popular reception of theater underpinned the 1809 inquisitorial bans. More news about Haiti was printed on the front page of the *Gazeta de México* in this same year, touching on the events that would lead Spain to recover Santo Domingo. The newspaper included Jean-Louis Ferrand's appeal to Spanish subjects living in the former Spanish area of the island then under French command to join him. It also included a response penned by Puerto Rican inhabitants who challenged and disparaged Ferrand's invitation. The introduction to Ferrand's appeal addressed the "fury of the black army" in Haiti but mostly focused on recent French-Spanish rivalry amid the Napoleonic invasion. It was followed by the response from Puerto Rico and by an article on the "obsequios" presented to Ferdinand VII by the community of Charcas in San Luis Potosí.

55. The bibliography on the crisis of 1808 is vast. For a few of the most important interventions, see Guerra, *Modernidad e independencia*; Adelman, *Sovereignty and Revolution*; Rodríguez, *We Are Now the True Spaniards*.

56. I'm here playing off of James C. Scott's term "hidden transcript." See

Scott, *Domination and the Arts of Resistance: Hidden Transcripts* (New Haven, CT: Yale University Press, 1990).

57. See Fredric Jameson, *Valences of the Dialectic* (London: Verso, 2010), 554.
58. See Jameson, *Valences of the Dialectic*, 554.
59. See Paniagua Pérez, *La revolución haitiana*, 53n137.
60. See "Instrucción para la educación, trato y ocupaciones de los esclavos, Aranjuez, 1789," in Lucena Salmoral, *Los códigos negros*, 95–124. See also Ferrer, *Freedom's Mirror*, chap. 1; Paniagua Pérez, *La revolución haitiana*, 53–55.
61. See Ferrer, *Freedom's Mirror*, chap. 1.
62. See "Instrucción para la educación" and Ferrer, *Freedom's Mirror*, chap. 1.
63. On planters' objections to the edict, see Ferrer, *Freedom's Mirror*; Paniagua Pérez, *La revolución haitiana*, 54; Manuel Lucena Salmoral, *La esclavitud en la América española* (Warsaw: University of Warsaw CESLA, 2002), 286–295.
64. On this use of the edict in Caracas, see Consuelo Naranjo Orovio, "La amenaza haitiana un miedo interesado: Poder y fomento de la población blanca en Cuba," in *El Rumor de Haití En Cuba: Temor, Raza y Rebeldía, 1789–1844*, ed. Ma. Dolores González-Ripoll Navarro (Madrid: Consejo Superior de Investigaciones Científicas, 2004), 89–90; Carlos Edsel, "Los jacobinos negros en la insurgencia de los esclavos de la serranía de Coro," in *José Leonardo Chirino y la insurrección de la Serranía de Coro de 1795: Insurrección de libertad o rebelión de independencia*, edited by Luis Cipriano Rodríguez. Proceedings of the Symposium Held in Mérida, Venezuela, on November 16 and 17, 1995 (Mérida, Venezuela: Universidad de los Andes, Universidad Central de Venezuela, 1996), 161; Ferrer, *Freedom's Mirror*, chap. 1.
65. See Ferrer, *Freedom's Mirror*, chap. 1.
66. This was the same press that printed López de Cancelada's edition of *La vida de J. J. Dessalines*. By this time Zúñiga y Ontiveros had passed away and the press was under the direction of Manuel Antonio Valdés Murguía y Saldaña. See García Martínez, *Fugas, ventas y otras noticias*.
67. Hernández y Dávalos, ed., "Edicto instructivo del obispo electo de Michoacán D. Manuel Abad y Queipo," in *Colección de documentos para la historia*, vol. 3 (1879). Emphasis mine.

CODA TWO: HAITI IN MEXICO'S EARLY REPUBLICAN CONTEXT

1. See Juan López de Cancelada, *Código formado por los negros de la isla de Santo Domingo de la parte francesa hoi estado de Hayti, sancionado por Henrique Cristoval, presidente y generalísimo* (Cádiz, Spain: Quintana, 1810), 28.
2. Sibylle Fischer, "Bolívar in Haiti: Republicanism in the Revolutionary Atlantic," in *Haiti and the Americas*, ed. Carla Calargé et al. (Jackson: University Press of Mississippi, 2013), 28. In the case of New Spain, Francisco Xavier Mina's expe-

dition in 1816 was also linked to Haiti. For more on this and other regencies and minor connections between Haiti and the insurgency in New Spain, see Johanna von Grafenstein Gareis, *Nueva España en el Circuncaribe, 1779–1808: Revolución, competencia imperial y vínculos intercoloniales* (Mexico City: Universidad Nacional Autónoma de México, 1997), chap. 8.

3. Fischer, "Bolívar in Haiti," 28. For her previous study on disavowal, see Sibylle Fischer, *Modernity Disavowed: Haiti and the Cultures of Slaves in the Age of Revolution* (Durham, NC: Duke University Press, 2004).

4. Fischer, "Bolívar in Haiti," 28. In the case of New Spain, Francisco Xavier Mina's expedition in 1816 was also linked to Haiti. See Grafenstein Gareis, *Nueva España en el Circuncaribe*, chap. 8.

5. Fischer, "Bolívar in Haiti," 37.

6. Fischer, "Bolívar in Haiti," 33.

7. Fischer, "Bolívar in Haiti," 33.

8. Marixa Lasso, *Myths of Harmony: Race and Republicanism during the Age of Revolution in Colombia* (Pittsburgh, PA: University of Pittsburgh Press, 2007), chap. 6.

9. Lasso, *Myths of Harmony*, chap. 6.

10. Fray Servando Teresa de Mier, *Escritos inéditos*, ed. Josep María Miquel I. Vergés and Hugo Díaz-Thomé (Mexico City: El Colegio de México, 1944), 290. Mier would sketch out this argument for the first time in his *Historia de la revolución* (1813). See also Christopher Domínguez Michael, *Vida de Fray Servando* (Mexico City: Ediciones Era, 2005).

11. Mier, *Escritos inéditos*, 290.

12. Fray Servando Teresa de Mier, *Idea de la constitución* (México City: Cuadernos Causa/ Centro de documentación política, 1977), 42–43.

13. Mier, *Idea de la constitución*, 42–45.

14. Mier, *Idea de la constitución*, 42–43.

15. Mier, *Escritos inéditos*, 340.

16. Mier, *Escritos inéditos*, 340.

17. In the last few decades, scholars have convincingly shown that members of racialized groups were extremely active participants in these processes. Each sector attempted, through various means, to direct, impact, expand, and curtail the modes of political agency that would be available in the new polis they were forging. See, for instance, Lasso, *Myths of Harmony*; Eric Van Young, *The Other Rebellion: Popular Violence, Ideology, and the Struggle for Mexican Independence, 1810–1821* (Stanford, CA: Stanford University Press, 2001); Luis Fernando Granados, *En el espejo haitiano: Los indios del Bajío y el colapso del orden colonial en América Latina* (Mexico City: Ediciones Era, 2016). On the side of the royalists, see, for example, Ben Vinson III, *Bearing Arms for His Majesty: The Free-Colored Militia in Colonial Mexico* (Stanford, CA: Stanford University Press, 2003).

18. "Carta del 3 de agosto de 1816 de Luis Onis a Felix Calleja," in *Boletín del archivo general de la nación*, 2nd series, vol. 9, nos. 3–4 (1968): 522–523; and "Carta

del 10 de septiembre de 1816 de Luis Onis a Felix Calleja," in *Boletín del archivo general de la nación*, 2nd series, vol. 9, nos. 3–4 (1968): 531–532. See also Grafenstein Gareis, *Nueva España en el Circuncaribe*, 247.

19. Fischer, "Bolívar in Haiti," 39. For more on Haiti and Spanish America, see Paul Verna, *Petión y Bolivar: Cuarenta años (1790–1830) de relaciones haitiano-venezolanas y su aporte a la emancipación de Hispanoamérica* (Caracas: Ministerio de Educación, 1969); Deborah Jenson, *Beyond the Slave Narrative: Politics, Sex, and Manuscripts in the Haitian Revolution* (Liverpool: Liverpool University Press, 2011); and Ada Ferrer, "Haiti, Free Soil, and Antislavery in the Revolutionary Atlantic," *American Historical Review* 117, no. 1 (2012): 40–66.

20. "Carta del 3 de agosto de 1816 de Luis Onis a Felix Calleja."

21. "Carta del 7 de junio de 1817 a Luis Onis a Felix Calleja," in *Boletín del archivo general de la nación*, 2nd series, vol. 9, nos. 3–4 (1968): 541.

22. Fischer explores this looking at Bolívar's 1826 address to the Bolivian Constituent Assembly in "Bolívar in Haiti," 41–49.

23. Luis Chávez Orozco, "Correspondencia de don José Ignacio Basadre, Agente mexicano en Haití," in *Un esfuerzo de México por la independencia de Cuba* (Mexico City: Publicaciones de la Secretaria de Relaciones Exteriores, 1930), 193–204. See also Grafenstein Gareis, *Nueva España en el Circuncaribe*, 250–252.

24. Ideas about the possibility of Mexico invading Cuba and annexing it to its territory had been prevalent since the early days after independence. For more, see Chávez Orozco, "Prólogo," in *Un esfuerzo de México*.

25. As cited in José María Bocanegra, *Memorias para la historia de México independiente 1822–1846*, vol. 2 (Mexico City: Instituto Cultural Helénico/Fondo de Cultura Económica, 1987), 41.

26. Colombia had been the first nation to recognize Mexico's independence, giving rise to an alliance between both governments that, although sometimes wavering, would be an important piece of efforts to build a hemispheric coalition. See Chávez Orozco, *Un esfuerzo de México*, ix.

27. James E. Sanders, *The Vanguard of the Atlantic World: Creating Modernity, Nation, and Democracy in Nineteenth-Century Latin America* (Durham, NC: Duke University Press, 2014).

28. Lorenzo de Zavala, *Ensayo histórico de las revoluciones de México desde 1808 hasta 1830.* (México City: Imprenta a cargo de M. N. de la Vega, 1845), 145–146.

29. As quoted in Jaime Olveda Legaspi, "La Abolicion de La Esclavitud En Mexico, 1810–1917," *Signos Históricos* 15, no. 29 (2013): 26–27.

30. Carol M. Young, "Lizardi's *El negro sensible*," *CLA Journal* 24, no. 3 (March 1981): 369–375; Jefferson Rea Spell, *The Life and Works of José Joaquín Fernández de Lizardi* (Philadelphia: University of Pennsylvania Press, 1931), 65.

31. Felipe Reyes Palacios, "Fernández de Lizardi y la comedia lacrimosa," in *Actas del XIV Congreso de la Asociación Internacional de Hispanistas*, ed. Isaías Lerner et al., vol. 4 (Newark, DE: AIH/Juan de la Cuesta, 2004), 588.

32. Reyes Palacios, "Fernández de Lizardi," 586.

CHAPTER FIVE: ON CRIMINALITY, RACE, AND LABOR

1. Elías Camhaji, "El pasado esclavista que México halló en el fondo del mar," *El País*, September 17, 2020, https://elpais.com/mexico/2020-09-16/el-pasado-esclavista-que-mexico-hallo-en-el-fondo-del-mar.html. See also Instituto Nacional de Antropología e Historia, "Identifica INAH al primer naufragio esclavista de mayas en México," *Boletín* 354 (September 15, 2020), https://www.inah.gob.mx/boletines/9412-identifica-inah-al-primer-naufragio-esclavista-de-mayas-en-mexico.

2. The team is part of a collaboration between the Instituto Nacional de Antropología e Historia and the Subdirección de Arqueología Subacuática. For a note on the "Unión's" shipwreck, see *La Unidad Católica*, no. 128, October 16, 1861, 3. Available through hndm.unam.mx.

3. Camhaji, "El pasado esclavista." See also Instituto Nacional de Antropología e Historia, "Identifica INAH."

4. Camhaji, "El pasado esclavista."

5. Studies on the clandestine trade divide it into two stages: the first lasted only two years, from 1849 and 1850, and the second lasted eight years, from 1853 to 1861. These studies see the emergence of the labor network as a binational response to, on the one hand, the growing internal conflict between Mexican elites and indigenous populations, and, on the other, Cuba's need for alternatives to the decreasing labor force caused by international and particularly British pressures on the African slave trade. Ironically, though, the British Empire—the empire that most strongly pushed to ban the Atlantic slave trade—also built the largest routes of indentured labor, which perpetuated and expanded systems of racialized coerced work. See Moisés González Navarro, *Raza y tierra: La guerra de castas y el henequén* (Mexico City: Colegio de México, 1979); Javier Rodríguez Piña, *Guerra de castas: La venta de indios mayas a Cuba* (Mexico City: Consejo Nacional para la Cultura y las Artes, 1990). For more on the topic, see Izaskun Álvarez, "Indios mayas en Cuba: Algunas reflexiones sobre su comercio," *Estudios Gaditano Cubanos* 3 (2002): 121–141; "De Tihosuco a La Habana: La venta de indios yucatecos a Cuba durante la Guerra de Castas," *Revista Estudios Históricos* 25 (2005): 559–576; and "De españoles, yucatecos e indios: La venta de mayas a Cuba y la construcción imaginada de una nación," *Revista de Pesquisa Histórica de la Universidad Federal de Pernambuco* 30, no. 1 (2012): 1–20. See also Carlos R. Menéndez, *Historia del infame y vergonzoso comercio de indios, vendidos a los esclavistas de Cuba por los políticos yucatecos, desde 1848 hasta 1861: Justificación de la revolución indígena de 1847. Documentos irrefutables que lo comprueban* (Mérida, Mexico: Talleres gráficos de La Revista de Yucatán, 1923); Paul Estrade, "Los esclavos yucatecos como sustitutos de los esclavos negros," in *Cuba, la perla de las Antillas: actas de las I Jornadas sobre "Cuba y su Historia,"* ed. Consuelo Naranjo and Tomás Mallo, 93–108 (Madrid: Doce Calles, 1994); Julio David Rojas Rodríguez, "Trabajo coactivo en Cuba: Inmigración y situación legal de los mayas yucatecos contratados, 1847–1860" (master's thesis, Universidad Iberoamericana, in progress). For more on the emergence of the new forms of coercive work supported by the British Empire after the 1807 ban on the slave

trade, see Lisa Lowe, *The Intimacies of Four Continents* (Durham, NC: Duke University Press, 2015), 46. Building on Lowe's argument about the rise of indentured labor within the British Empire, I argue here that we should question the idea that indenture is a stage in the transition from slavery to free labor. The notion of "transition," as Lowe emphasizes, suggests the idea of improvement, of progress, and implies that older forms of coercion were replaced by modern freedoms. See also Jennifer Martínez, *The Slave Trade and the Origins of International Human Rights Law* (Oxford: Oxford University Press, 2012), 3; Lisa Surwilio, *Monsters by Trade: Slave Traffickers in Modern Spanish Literature and Culture* (Stanford, CA: Stanford University Press, 2014), 4.

6. See Terry Rugeley, *Rebellion Now and Forever: Mayas, Hispanics, and Caste War Violence in Yucatán, 1800–1880* (Stanford, CA: Stanford University Press, 2009), 98.

7. The extant scholarship offers contradictory and diverging information regarding the breadth of the trade. Rodríguez Piña offers a chart showing contrasting estimates of how many indigenous Yucatec people were living in Cuba at different points between 1848 and 1899. He estimates that around two thousand people were sent to Cuba between 1848 and 1861. See Rodríguez Piña, *Guerra de castas*, 178–179. For other perspectives and censuses on Maya migration to Cuba, see Victoria Novelo, *Yucatecos en Cuba: Etnografía de una migración* (Mexico City: CIESAS, 2009). Helena Barba, part of the collaborative research team of subaquatic archaeology for the Yucatán Peninsula, suggests that the ship *Unión* itself was responsible for transporting nearly 3,600 men, women, and children from Yucatán to Cuba over a period of ten years at a rate of thirty people per month. See Camhaji, "El pasado esclavista." In his forthcoming master's thesis, Julio David Rojas Rodríguez works closely with archival information that promises to expand our current knowledge regarding the lives of Maya indentured laborers in Cuba.

8. Although the terminology used to describe this human trafficking is unstable in the sources I study, I will mainly refer to it as a trade in indentured labor. However, sometimes, following the concerns of the primary sources studied here and the terminology used in key previous scholarship by González Navarro and Rodríguez Piña, I will also refer to it as the Yucatán-Cuba slave trade.

9. See González Navarro, *Raza y tierra*, 116.

10. For information on the decree, see Carlos R. Menéndez, ed., *Memorias de Don Buenaventura Vivó y la venta de indios yucatecos a Cuba* (Mérida, Mexico: Biblioteca de Historia del "Diario de Yucatán," 1923), 51–53. See also Rodríguez Piña, *Guerra de castas*, 113. A second, more developed version of the first decree was published in 1854. For diplomatic correspondence on this decree, see *British and State Foreign Papers 1854–55*, vol. 45 (London: William Ridgway, 1865), 1058–1063. For a study of Chinese indentured labor in Cuba focused on laborers' testimonies and resistance, see Lisa Yun, *The Coolie Speaks: Chinese Indentured Laborers and African Slaves of Cuba* (Philadelphia, PA: Temple University Press, 2008).

11. Here I am building on the work of Claire Anderson. See her "Convicts and Coolies: Rethinking Indentured Labour in the Nineteenth Century," *Slavery*

and Abolition 30, no. 1 (2009): 93–109; and Claire Anderson, ed., *A Global History of Convicts and Penal Labor* (London: Bloomsbury Academic, 2018). For a similar approach to Latin America's southern hemisphere, see Christian Giuseppe De Vito, "Convict Labor in the Southern Borderlands of Latin America (ca. 1750s–1910s): Comparative Perspectives," in *On Coerced Labor: Work and Compulsion after Chattel Slavery*, ed. Marcel van der Linden and Magaly Rodríguez García (Leiden, Netherlands: Brill, 2016), 98–126.

12. As I have noted elsewhere, digital searches of nineteenth-century Mexican newspapers show that the concept of humanitarianism arose in the 1840s. The word began to appear in the press at this time and was generally used as a parameter for measuring a given society's degree of civilization. See Ana Sabau, "The Paths of Unfreedom: Indentured Labor from Yucatán to Cuba," *Revista de Estudios Hispánicos* 53, no. 2 (2019): 544.

13. See, for instance, Novelo, *Yucatecos en Cuba*. Novelo, among other things, documents the migration of wealthy Yucatec families into Cuba as product of the Caste War.

14. Politicians across the spectrum, from Antonio López de Santa Anna to José María Luis Mora, offered similar solutions to the threat posed by "caste wars." In their own way, each contributed to implementing these policies, which quite explicitly sought to "neutralize" indigenous populations in the nation, particularly those engaged in rebellions. As I described in the introduction to this book, Mora informally requested British support to contain the rebellions being mounted by the "people of color"; he also suggested more outlandish ways of changing Mexico's demographics, including widespread miscegenation, the promotion of European immigration, and the expulsion of "the elements of color" from the country (qtd. in González Navarro, *Raza y tierra*, 102–103). As for Santa Anna, during his last presidential period, he fully supported and explicitly reinstated the Yucatán-Cuba indentured labor trade, entering into agreements with Cuban and Spanish merchant houses that were eager to import indigenous "workers" to the island. By the time Santa Anna entered the traffic in workers, the initial bubble of the trade had mostly subsided, largely due to the pressure exerted by a network of indigenous men and women across the Atlantic who voiced their opposition through people such as Migangos. See Menéndez, *Historia del infame*, 134; González Navarro, *Raza y tierra*, 120–123; Rodríguez Piña, *Guerra de castas*, 125–140.

15. Governor Miguel Barbachano, for instance, wrote that about three-fifths of Yucatán's population was indigenous. The trade aimed to reduce this population by at least a third. See the reproduction of a letter from Governor Miguel Barbachano to the minister of foreign relations in Mexico City on May 26, 1849, in Menéndez, *Historia del infame*, 123.

16. On the topic of labor scarcity, see Rugeley, *Rebellion Now and Forever*, chap. 3.

17. For an example of an agreement between Yucatán's treasury and the trading house Pou y Compañía, see Menéndez, *Historia del infame*, 228–229.

18. Letter from Governor Miguel Barbachano to the minister of foreign relations in Mexico City, May 26, 1849, in Menéndez, *Historia del infame*, 116–126. See also Rugeley, *Rebellion Now and Forever*, 99.

19. *Bataab* is the Maya word for cacique, the representative of an indigenous town.

20. For some of the most relevant sources on the Caste War and its antecedents, see Ramón Berzunza Pinto, *Guerra social en Yucatán* (Mexico City: Bartomeu Costa-Amic, 1965); Pedro Bracamonte y Sosa, *Amos y servientes* (Mérida, Mexico: Ediciones de la Universidad Autónoma de Yucatán, 1993); Jeffrey T. Brannon and Gilbert M. Joseph, *Land, Labor, and Capital in Modern Yucatán* (Tuscaloosa: University of Alabama Press, 1991); Victoria Reifler Bricker, *The Indian Christ, the Indian King: The Historical Substrate of Maya Myth and Ritual* (Austin: University of Texas Press, 1981); Karen D. Caplan, *Indigenous Citizens: Local Liberalism in Early National Oaxaca and Yucatán* (Stanford, CA: Stanford University Press, 2010); Rocío Leticia Cortés Campos, *Entre héroes y bárbaros: El periodismo yucateco durante la Guerra de Castas* (Mérida, Mexico: Universidad Autónoma de Yucatán, 2013); Don E. Dumond, *El machete y la cruz: La sublevación de campesinos en Yucatán*, trans. Luis F. Verano (Mexico City: Universidad Nacional Autónoma de México, 2005); Romana Falcón, *Las rasgaduras de la descolonización: Españoles y mexicanos a mediados del siglo XIX* (Mexico City: El Colegio de México, 1996); Wolfgang Gabbert, *Becoming Maya: Ethnicity and Social Inequality in Yucatán since 1500* (Tucson: University of Arizona Press, 2004); González Navarro, *Raza y tierra*; Antonio Higuera Bonfil, *Quintana Roo entre tiempos* (Chetumal: Universidad de Quintana Roo, 1997); Gilbert M. Joseph, "From Caste War to Class War: The Historiography of Modern Yucatán (c 1750–1940)," *Hispanic American Historical Review*, no. 65 (1985): 111–134; Gilbert M. Joseph, *Rediscovering the Past at Mexico's Periphery: Essays on the History of Modern Yucatán* (Tuscaloosa: University of Alabama Press, 1986); Gilbert M. Joseph, *Revolution from Without: Yucatán, Mexico, and the United States, 1880–1924* (Durham, NC: Duke University Press, 1988); David Kazanjian, *The Brink of Freedom: Improvising Life in the Nineteenth-Century Atlantic World* (Durham, NC: Duke University Press, 2016); Florencia E. Mallon, *Peasant and Nation: The Making of Postcolonial Mexico and Peru* (Berkeley: University of California Press, 1995); Sergio Quezada, *Los pies de la república* (Mexico City: CIESAS, 1997); Teresa Ramayo Lanz, *Los mayas pacíficos de Campeche* (Campeche, Mexico: Universidad Autónoma de Campeche, 1996); Nelson Reed, *The Caste War of Yucatán*, rev. ed. (Stanford, CA: Stanford University Press, 2001); Leticia Reina, *Rebeliones campesinas en México, 1819–1906* (Mexico City: Siglo XXI Editores, 1980); Matthew Restall, *The Black Middle: Africans, Mayas, and Spaniards in Colonial Yucatán* (Stanford, CA: Stanford University Press, 2009); Matthew Restall, *Maya Conquistador* (Boston: Beacon, 1998); Matthew Restall, *The Maya World* (Stanford, CA: Stanford University Press, 1997); Terry Rugeley, "The Caste War in Guatemala," *Saastun: Revista de Cultura Maya*, no. 3 (December 1997): 94; Terry Rugeley, "The Maya Elites of Nineteenth-Century Yucatán," *Ethnohistory* 42,

no. 3 (Summer 1995): 477–493; Terry Rugeley, *Maya Wars: Ethnographic Accounts from Nineteenth-Century Yucatán* (Norman: University of Oklahoma Press, 2001); Terry Rugeley, *Of Wonders and Wise Men: Religion and Popular Cultures in Southeast Mexico, 1800–1876* (Austin: University of Texas Press, 2001); Terry Rugeley, *Rebellion Now and Forever*; Terry Rugeley, "Rural Popular Violence and the Origins of the Caste War," *The Americas* 53, no. 4 (April 1997): 480; Terry Rugeley, *Yucatán's Maya Peasantry and the Origins of the Caste War* (Austin: University of Texas Press, 1996); Paul Sullivan, *Unfinished Conversations: Mayas and Foreigners between Two Wars* (New York: Knopf, 1989); Paul Sullivan, *¿Para qué lucharon los mayas? Vida y muerte de Bernardino Cen* (Quintana Roo: Universidad de Quintana Roo, 1998); Martha Herminia Villalobos González, *El bosque sitiado: Asaltos armados, concesiones forestales y estrategias de resistencia durante la Guerra de Castas* (Mexico City: Conaculta/CIESAS/INAH/Porrúa, 2006); Alfonso Villa Rojas, *The Maya of East-Central Quintana Roo* (Washington, DC: Carnegie Institution, 1943); Alfonso Villa Rojas, and *Los elegidos de Dios: Etnografía de los mayas de Quintana Roo* (Mexico City: Instituto Nacional Indigenista, 1978); Allen Wells and Gilbert M. Joseph, *Summer of Discontent, Seasons of Upheaval: Elite Politics and Rural Insurgency in Yucatán, 1876–1915* (Stanford, CA: Stanford University Press, 1996).

21. Jennifer P. Mathews and John R. Gust, *Sugarcane and Rum: The Bittersweet History of Labor and Life on the Yucatán Peninsula* (Tucson: University of Arizona Press, 2020), chap. 3.

22. See Kazanjian, *Brink of Freedom*, especially part 2, chap. 4.

23. See Kazanjian, *Brink of Freedom*, especially part 2, chap. 4. The term "justice" appears in the rebels' letters, particularly those dictated by the Cruz Parlante after Chan Santa Cruz was founded in 1850. For a compendium of the letters in Spanish translation, see Fidelio Quintal Martín, *Correspondencia de la Guerra de Castas: Epistolario documental, 1843–1866* (Mérida, Mexico: Ediciones de la Universidad Autónoma de Yucatán, 1992).

24. Rugeley, *Yucatán's Maya Peasantry*, introduction. For more on the production of sugar and coercive labor relations in Yucatán see Mathews and Gust, *Sugarcane and Rum*.

25. See Rodríguez Piña, *Guerra de castas*.

26. See Buenaventura Vivó, *Memorias de Don Buenaventura Vivó, ministro de Méjico en España durante los años 1853, 1854 y 1855* (Madrid, Spain: M. Rivadeneyra, 1856), 302.

27. See Vivó, *Memorias de Don Buenaventura Vivó*, 302–303.

28. See Vivó, *Memorias de Don Buenaventura Vivó*, 303.

29. See Vivó, *Memorias de Don Buenaventura Vivó*, 304.

30. See Vivó, *Memorias de Don Buenaventura Vivó*, 305–306.

31. See Vivó, *Memorias de Don Buenaventura Vivó*, 306.

32. Christian Giuseppe De Vito, "The Spanish Empire: 1500–1898," in *A Global History of Convict and Penal Colonies*, ed. Clare Anderson (London: Bloomsbury Academic, 2018).

33. De Vito, "Spanish Empire," 87.
34. De Vito, "Spanish Empire," 80–85.
35. De Vito, "Spanish Empire," 80–85.
36. Alexander von Humboldt, *Political Essay on the Kingdom of New Spain*, vol. 2, trans. from the French by John Black (New York: I. Riley, 1811), 33–34.
37. De Vito writes, "The persistence of extramural work should not be viewed as the product of the permanence of anachronistic labor relations and punitive projects; rather it reveals a process of re-functionalization of coerced labor relations and preexisting penal practices." See "Convict Labor in the Southern Borderlands," 125.
38. Benton, *Search for Sovereignty*, 165.
39. Benton, *Search for Sovereignty*, 165.
40. Benton, *Search for Sovereignty*, 182–183.
41. Letter from Governor Miguel Barbachano to the minister of foreign relations in Mexico City, May 26, 1849, in Menéndez, *Historia del infame*, 118.
42. See *Constitución Federal de los Estados Unidos Mexicanos sancionada y jurada por el Congreso General Constituyente el 5 de febrero de 1857* (Mexico City: Imprenta de Ignacio Cumplido, 1857), Title I, Article 5. The article states that "no one could be forced to labor without their full consent" nor "sign any agreement leading to their proscription or exile." I cite it here not in a naive attempt to point toward the gap between prescription and practice but to highlight the explicit contradictions that were necessary to sustain the expansion of liberal capitalism. Despite these bans the use of racialized coerced labor, both from within the nation and abroad, prevailed throughout the century. For more see coda 3. The use of these practices was, in many ways, tied to convict labor. After independence, Mexico was quick to embrace the language of penitentiary reform radiating from the United States. The federal penal code of 1871 certainly moved in this direction, enshrining the prison as the bastion of modern punishment and banning the use of garrisons and forced labor. Despite the prevalence that the penitentiary had in Mexican penal discourse, other modes of punishment that were supposedly discarded for being old-fashioned and retrograde, such as banishment and convict labor, continued to be repurposed and used, especially as the country faced the increasing pressures of modernization at the turn of the century, from securing labor for exportation industries, to controlling social unrest and "unruly" populations, to expanding and stabilizing national territorial control. See Ricardo D. Salvatore and Carlos Aguirre, "Colonies of Settlement or Places of Banishment and Torment? Penal Colonies and Convict Labour in Latin America, c. 1800–1940," in *Global Convict Labour*, ed. Christian Giuseppe De Vito and Alex Lichtenstein (Leiden, Netherlands: Brill, 2015), 274–275, 296. See also Diego Esteva Pulido, "La tumba del pacífico: Historia de la colonia penal de las Islas Marías 1905–1939" (master's thesis, Instituto de Investigaciones Dr. José María Luis Mora, 2007), 41.
43. Rugeley, *Rebellion Now and Forever*, 98.
44. Rugeley, *Rebellion Now and Forever*, 176–177.

45. "Parte oficial," *Las Garantías sociales: Periódico Oficial*, February 17, 1858, 1–2.

46. See Lauren Benton, *A Search for Sovereignty: Law and Geography in European Empires, 1400–1900* (Cambridge: Cambridge University Press, 2014), 166–167.

47. By this period, the death penalty was no longer used for "political crimes," being applied only to the following criminals: traitors to the nation in the context of war with a foreign nation, incendiaries, murderers in the first degree, pirates, and those who committed grave military infractions. See *Constitución Federal de los Estados Unidos Mexicanos de 1857*, Article 23.

48. See Michel Foucault, *"Society Must Be Defended": Lectures at the Collège de France, 1975–76*, ed. Mauro Bertani and Alessandro Fontana, trans. David Macey (New York: Picador, 2003), chap. 11.

49. On this discussion see Jacques Derrida, *The Death Penalty*, vol. 1, trans. Peggy Kamuf (Chicago: University of Chicago Press, 2014), sessions 1 and 2.

50. See Foucault, *"Society Must Be Defended."* See also Paul W. Kahn, *Sacred Violence: Torture, Terror and Sovereignty* (Ann Arbor: University of Michigan Press, 2008).

51. Lisa Guenther, "An Abolitionism Worthy of the Name: From the Death Penalty to the Prison Industrial Complex," in *Deconstructing the Death Penalty: Derrida's Seminars and the New Abolitionism*, ed. Kelly Oliver and Stephanie M. Straub (New York: Fordham University Press, 2018), 244.

52. Letter from Governor Miguel Barbachano to the minister of foreign relations in Mexico City, May 26, 1849, in Menéndez, *Historia del infame*, 123.

53. See Menéndez, *Historia del infame*, 123.

54. The article is reproduced in Menéndez, *Historia del infame*, 263–273. See also Rodríguez Piña, *Guerra de castas*, 166.

55. "Los amantes de la felicidad yucateca," as cited in Menéndez, *Historia del infame*, 266.

56. Cited in Menéndez, *Historia del infame*, 270.

57. On the distinction between *prisionero*, *presentado*, and *recogido*, see Rugeley, *Rebellion Now and Forever*, 85–89. Other categories included *hidalgo*, which was assigned to Maya men who joined the army, sometimes in exchange for tax exemptions or other exemptions. See also Caplan, *Indigenous Citizens*, chap. 6.

58. While this distinction did have some empirical grounding, this is an oversimplification of the spatial distribution of pacified and rebel groups. See Rugeley, *Rebellion Now and Forever*, 6.

59. See Martha Herminia Villalobos González, *El bosque sitiado*, 95–96. See also Eligio Ancona, ed., *Colección de leyes, decretos, órdenes y demás disposiciones de tendencia general, expedidas por el poder legislativo del estado de Yucatán: Formada con autorización del gobierno por Eligio Ancona*, vol. 2 (Mérida, Mexico: Imprenta de El Eco del Comercio, 1882), 185. (Decree on September 6, "Exceptúa del pago del impuesto de capitación a los vecinos de las poblaciones fronterizas que expresa," article 2.)

60. See Ancona, *Colección de leyes del estado de Yucatán*, vol. 1, 160. (Order on April 26, "Mandando que ninguno pueda ausentarse de su vecindad sin pasaporte y sin haber acreditado su inscripción a la guardia nacional.")

61. Villalobos González, *El bosque sitiado*, 91–101.

62. Saldaña-Portillo, *Indian Given*, 53.

63. Saldaña-Portillo, *Indian Given*, 53.

64. On the idea of relative innocence, see Ruth Wilson Gilmore, "Geografía abolicionista y el problema de la inocencia." *Tabula Rasa*, no. 28 (2018): 57–77, https://doi.org/10.25058/20112742.n28.3.

65. Cited in Menéndez, *Historia del infame*, 268.

66. See Menéndez, *Historia del infame*, 270.

67. When the trade ended, some "prisoners" returned to Mexico. See González Navarro, *Raza y tierra*; Rodríguez Piña, *Guerra de castas*; Novelo, *Yucatecos en Cuba*.

68. I focus here on Pantaleón Barrera [Napoleón Trebarra, pseud.], *Los misterios de Chan Santa Cruz* (Mérida, Mexico: Imprenta de M. Aldana Rivas, 1864); for a literary work that opposes the trade, see Eligio Ancona's *Uno de tantos: Novela* (Mérida, Mexico: Gobierno del Estado de Yucatán, Secretaría de la Cultura y las Artes, 2015). This novel was specifically written to challenge the trade, and many others mention it in passing.

69. Kazanjian, *Brink of Freedom*, part 2, "Prelude."

70. For information on other texts that followed Sue's tradition, see Kazanjian, *Brink of Freedom*, 274n87.

71. Sullivan, *¿Para qué lucharon los mayas?*, 55.

72. See Barrera, *Los misterios de Chan Santa Cruz*, 67.

73. See Barrera, *Los misterios de Chan Santa Cruz*, 67.

74. See Barrera, *Los misterios de Chan Santa Cruz*, 67.

75. See James E. Sanders, *The Vanguard of the Atlantic World: Creating Modernity, Nation, and Democracy in Nineteenth-Century Latin America* (Durham, NC: Duke University Press, 2014), 71–72.

76. See Menéndez, *Historia del infame*, 244.

77. For detailed studies on the henequen boom, see González Navarro, *Raza y tierra*. See also Joseph, *Revolution from Without*; Mathews and Gust, *Sugarcane and Rum*, chap. 3.

78. See Rodríguez Piña, *Guerra de castas*, 164.

79. This chapter is an extended version of a previously published article. See Sabau, "Paths of Unfreedom."

CHAPTER SIX: THE SHAPES OF A DESERT

1. The Sociedad Mexicana de Geografía y Estadística (SMGE; Mexican Society of Geography and Statistics) was founded in 1833 with support from President

Valentín Gómez Farías; it remained a state-subsidized organization throughout the century. See Raymond Craib, *Cartographic Mexico: A History of State Fixations and Fugitive Landscapes* (Durham, NC: Duke University Press, 2004), 21.

2. Craib, *Cartographic Mexico*, 21.

3. Craib, *Cartographic Mexico*, 21.

4. See J. B. Harley, "Maps, Knowledge, and Power," in *The Iconography of Landscape: Essays on the Symbolic Representation, Design and Use of Past Environments*, ed. Denis Cosgrove and Stephen Daniels (New York: Cambridge University Press, 1988), 303.

5. See Gary Fields, *Enclosure: Palestinian Landscapes in a Historic Mirror* (Berkeley: University of California Press, 2017), introduction. For other studies of this trope as affiliated with the expansion of the Spanish Empire, see Edmundo O'Gorman, *La invención de América: Investigación acerca de la estructura histórica del Nuevo Mundo y del sentido de su devenir*, 4th ed. (Mexico City: Fondo de Cultura Económica, 2006); José Rabasa, *Inventing America: Spanish Historiography and the Formation of Eurocentrism* (Norman: University of Oklahoma Press, 1993).

6. Fields, *Enclosure*, intro.

7. For a similar argument in the Canadian context, see Daniel Clayton, "On the Colonial Genealogy of George Vancouver's Chart of the North-West Coast of North America," *Ecumene* 7, no. 4 (October 2000): 371–401.

8. See Fields, *Enclosure*, 9–11.

9. See María Josefina Saldaña-Portillo, *Indian Given: Racial Geographies across Mexico and the United States* (Durham, NC: Duke University Press, 2016), 23.

10. Craib, *Cartographic Mexico*, 29. See also Héctor Mendoza Vargas, "Las opciones geográficas al inicio del México independiente," in *México a través de los mapas* (Mexico City: Instituto de Geografía, Universidad Nacional Autónoma de México; Plaza y Valdés Editores, 2000), 89–110.

11. See also Mendoza Vargas, "Las opciones geográficas"; Shelley E. Garrigan, *Collecting Mexico: Museums, Monuments, and the Creation of National Identity* (Minneapolis: University of Minnesota Press, 2012), chaps. 2 and 5.

12. Antonio García Cubas, *Atlas geográfico estadístico e histórico de la República Mexicana* (Mexico City: Imprenta de José Mariano Fernández de Lara, 1858), 1.

13. For more on the anticipatory aspect of cartography, see Clayton, "On the Colonial Genealogy," 377.

14. See Terry Rugeley, *Rebellion Now and Forever: Mayas, Hispanics, and Caste War Violence in Yucatán, 1800–1880* (Stanford, CA: Stanford University Press, 2009), chap. 3.

15. Terry Rugeley, *Yucatán's Maya Peasantry and the Origins of the Caste War* (Austin: University of Texas Press, 1996), xii–xiii.

16. For more on how direct combat was not the main aspect of the war, see Rugeley, *Rebellion Now and Forever*, 73.

17. See Rugeley, *Rebellion Now and Forever*, chap 3; Rugeley, *Yucatán's Maya Peasantry*, 127.

18. On the desertion of an entire troop destined for Bacalar in 1849, see the July 4, 1865, letter from General Severo del Castillo to Mexico's minister of war in Archivo Histórico de la Secretaría de la Defensa Nacional (AHSDN), file XI/481.4/9987. Both soldiers and officials fled to Hunucmá; see Rugeley, *Yucatán's Maya Peasantry*, 74.

19. Letter from General Severo del Castillo to the Mexico's minister of war, July 4, 1865, AHSDN, file X1/481.4/9987.

20. In the brief historical vignette accompanying the map of the peninsula that was included in the 1858 atlas, García Cubas did mention the Caste War and its impact on the region's population density. However, his emphasis on how Yucatán might be inserted into the global economy ignored the framework of exchange that already existed there, frameworks in which rebel communities were key participants.

21. As is often the case in massive social conflicts, rebel groups were not always in agreement. The Maya revolt that I now write about as if it were a monolith was not the expression of a homogenous "consciousness" but rather a struggle articulated through shifting local alliances. As Martha Herminia Villalobos González has argued, some of the internal divisions of the rebellion grew out of local communities' diverging management of their alliances with English settlers in Belize and the differing conditions they set for the lease of the "forests" they controlled. See Villalobos González, *El bosque sitiado: Asaltos armados, concesiones forestales y estrategias de resistencia durante la Guerra de Castas* (Mexico City: Conaculta/CIESAS/INAH/Porrúa, 2006), chap. 1. Within the British government, settlers' sale of gunpowder to rebel groups was controversial. The gunpowder trade, however, was not only an economic enterprise but a social one, for well-established British settlers used the trade to maintain an amicable equilibrium between both spaces. On this topic, see Paul Sullivan, "John Carmichael: Life and Design on the Frontier in Central America," *Revista Mexicana del Caribe* 5, no. 10 (2000): 6–88.

22. Craib, *Cartographic Mexico*, 31. See also Héctor Mendoza Vargas, "Historia de la geografía en México siglo XIX" (undergraduate thesis, Universidad Nacional Autónoma de México, 1989); Antonio García Cubas, *El libro de mis recuerdos: Narraciones históricas, anecdóticas y de costumbres mexicanas anteriores al actual estado social* (Mexico City: Imprenta de Arturo García Cubas, Hermanos Sucesores, 1904), 395.

23. Craib, *Cartographic Mexico*, 32.

24. See Michel Antochiw, *Historia cartográfica de la Península de Yucatán* (Mexico City: Centro de Investigación y de Estudios Avanzados del IPN, 1994). For more on the development of cartography/topography in sources contemporary with the Caste War, see Eligio Ancona, *Historia de Yucatán desde la época más remota hasta nuestros días*, vol. 4, 2nd ed. (Mérida, Mexico: Imprenta de J. J. Roviralta, 1889), 402–403; Serapio Baqueiro, *Ensayo histórico sobre las revoluciones de Yucatán desde el Año de 1840 Hasta 1864*, vol. 2 (Mexico City: Imprenta de M. Heredia Argüelles, 1878), 432–433.

25. "Planos de Yucatán," *El Fenix*, November 15, 1848, 4. See also Antochiw, *Historia cartográfica*, 293. The announcement appeared in the same issue of the newspaper that included the fourth chapter of Justo Sierra's novel *La hija del judío* (published under the pseudonym José Turrisa), an essay on the origins of the indigenous uprising, and a section on the "guerras de los bárbaros."

26. See also Antochiw, *Historia cartográfica*, 293.

27. It is worth noting that the maps in question are not specifically devoted to the peninsula but to the entire viceroyalty of New Spain. However, one map of the region, produced in 1798 by Juan José de León, is of particular interest. This map classifies the region in question as "unpeopled." Alexander von Humboldt made use of it in his own cartographic representation of the region (which he never visited himself), and it probably informed other nineteenth-century maps as well. See Antochiw, *Historia cartográfica*, 288.

28. See "Instrucciones para los comandantes militares de Tekax, Peto y Valladolid," AHSDN, file X1/481.4/9987.

29. For more on fagina see Rugeley, *Rebellion Now and Forever*, 128.

30. See "Instrucciones para los comandantes militares."

31. See "Instrucciones para los comandantes militares."

32. See Mehmet Dosemeci, "Social Movement vs. Social Arrest: The Global Occupations of the 21st Century," *Critique and Humanism Journal* 46 (2016): 198–199. See also Paul Virilio, *Speed and Politics: An Essay on Dromology*, Foreign Agents Series (New York: Columbia University Press, 1986), 53.

33. See "Instrucciones para los comandantes militares."

34. The novel has rarely been studied in any depth, although it is often mentioned in the bibliography of the Caste War. For a recent study on the subject, see Kari Soriano, "Geografía militar y humana: La Guerra de Castas en *Cecilio Chi*, de José Severo del Castillo," in *Entre el humo y la niebla: Guerra y Cultura En América Latina*, ed. Javier Uriarte and Felipe Martínez Pinzón, 29–54 (Pittsburg, PA: International Institute of Latin American Literature, University of Pittsburg, 2016).

35. Severo del Castillo, *Cecilio Chi* (Mérida, Mexico: Distribuidora de Libros Yucatectos, [1869] 1978), 275.

36. A similar phenomenon occurred in other Latin American texts of the day; Sarmiento's depiction of the pampas in *Facundo* (1845) may be the most famous.

37. See Saldaña-Portillo, *Indian Given*, 52, 120. On the notion of "spiritual accumulation" in the colonial period, see Daniel Nemser, "Primitive Spiritual Accumulation and the Colonial Extraction Economy," *Política Común* 5 (2014), http://doi.org/10.3998/pc.12322227.0005.003.

38. For more information on the Le Plongeons, see Lawrence Desmond, *Yucatán through Her Eyes: Alice Dixon Le Plongeon, Writer and Expeditionary Photographer* (Albuquerque: University of New Mexico Press, 2009); Lawrence Desmond and Phyllis Mauch Messenger, *Dream of Maya: Augustus and Alice Le Plongeon in Nineteenth-Century Yucatan* (Albuquerque: University of New Mexico Press, 1988).

39. Alice D. Le Plongeon, "The Yucatan Indians: Their Struggle for Indepen-

dence, Their Manner of Living and Method of Warfare," *New York Evening Post,* July 7, 1895. Getty Research Institute, Le Plongeon Papers, box 8*, folder 6.

40. Alice D. Le Plongeon, "Chan Santa Cruz's Fall," *Commercial Advertiser,* June 8, 1901. Getty Research Institute, Le Plongeon Papers, box 8*, folder 6. For a similar argument that draws from the texts of the traveler Karl Hermann Berendt, see David Kazanjian, *The Brink of Freedom: Improvising Life in the Nineteenth-Century Atlantic World* (Durham, NC: Duke University Press, 2016), "Prelude to Part II."

41. See Don E. Dumond, *El machete y la cruz: La sublevación de campesinos en Yucatán,* trans. Luis F. Verano (Mexico City: Universidad Nacional Autónoma de México, 2005), 438–439. See also Sullivan, "John Carmichael," 48–51.

42. See Dumond, *El machete y la cruz,* 438–439.

43. Some years later, Díaz de la Vega would be made governor after overthrowing the administration of Miguel Barbachano with support from the Yucatec conservatives. For more on Rómulo Díaz de la Vega's role in Yucatecan politics, see Rugeley, *Rebellion Now and Forever,* 107–116. For more on General Díaz de la Vega's cartographic interests, see "Fragmento histórico," William L. Clements Library (hereafter CLE), Latin America Collection (1518–1883), box 29, folder 8; Baqueiro, *Ensayo histórico,* 432–433.

44. Antochiw, *Historia cartográfica,* 297–298.

45. Antochiw, *Historia cartográfica,* 298.

46. For more on Berendt and the Caste War, see Kazanjian, *Brink of Freedom,* "Prelude to Part II."

47. See Philipp Valentini, "A New and an Ancient Map of Yucatán," *Magazine of American History* 3 (1879): 295–299.

48. Valentini, "New and an Ancient Map," 296.

49. See William Miller, "A Journey from British Honduras to Santa Cruz, Yucatan," *Proceedings of the Royal Geographical Society and Monthly Record of Geography* 11, no. 1 (January 1, 1889): 23–28.

50. On the idea of "regimes of visibility," see Gustavo Verdesio, "Invisible at a Glance: Indigenous Cultures of the Past, Ruins, Archaeological Sites, and Our Regimes of Visibility," in *Ruins of Modernity,* ed. Julia Hell and Andreas Schönle (Durham, NC: Duke University Press, 2009), 339–354.

51. Miller, "Journey from British Honduras," 26.

52. See Miller, "Journey from British Honduras," 26.

53. See Villalobos González, *El bosque sitiado,* 199, 202, 208–213.

54. Fidelio Quintal Martín, *Correspondencia de la guerra de castas: Epistolario documental, 1843–1866* (Merida, Mexico: Ediciones de la Universidad Autónoma de Yucatán, 1992), 106–107.

55. See Villalobos González, *El bosque sitiado,* 250–260. See also "La guerra contra los mayas," in *El Contemporáneo: Diario Independiente* (San Luis Potosí), September 3, 1899, 1–2.

56. The photograph of Chan Santa Cruz also marked the acceleration of state-

led efforts to develop the area. As Díaz pushed to increase henequen production in Yucatán, new railroads were built connecting the previously atomistic villages in the area (Peto, Tekax, Valladolid, and others). But the region's booming global economy was being erected on a growing base of racialized peonage, and the eastern side of the peninsula remained discontented. To stabilize the once disputed area (so as to later incorporate it into the nation's economy), the emerging state of Quintana Roo was separated from Yucatán altogether and placed under the military command of Ignacio Bravo. For more on the foundation of Quintana Roo, see Carlos Macías Richard, *Nueva frontera mexicana: Milicia, burocracia y ocupación territorial en Quintana Roo, 1902–1927* (Mexico City: Consejo Nacional de Ciencia y Tecnología/Universidad de Quintana Roo, 1997).

57. CLE, Latin America Collection (1518–1883), box 29, folder 8.
58. Quintal Martín, *Correspondencia de la Guerra de Castas*, 131.
59. Quintal Martín, *Correspondencia de la Guerra de Castas*, 131.
60. Kazanjian, *Brink of Freedom*, 206.
61. Quintal Martín, *Correspondencia de la Guerra de Castas*, 87.
62. Quintal Martín, *Correspondencia de la Guerra de Castas*, 78.
63. Kazanjian, *Brink of Freedom*, 216.
64. Kazanjian, *Brink of Freedom*, 218–219. See also Robert Patch, *Maya and Spaniard in Yucatan, 1648–1812* (Stanford, CA: Stanford University Press, 1993).
65. See Dawn Marie Paley, "The Tren Maya and the Remaking of Mexico's South," Toward Freedom, February 1, 2020, https://towardfreedom.org/story/the-tren-maya-and-the-remaking-of-mexicos-south-border/.
66. See Asamblea de Defensores del Territorio Maya Múuch' Xíinbal, "¡No al tren mal llamado maya! Pronunciamiento de la Asamblea de Defensores del Territorio Maya Múuch' Xíinbal," May 21, 2020, https://asambleamaya.wixsite.com/muuchxiinbal/no-al-tren-maya. See also Kazanjian, *Brink of Freedom*, 220–221.

CODA THREE: "BARBAROUS MEXICO"

1. Gilbert M. Joseph, *Revolution from Without: Yucatán, Mexico, and the United States, 1880–1924* (Durham, NC: Duke University Press, 1988).
2. Turner said that Yucatán's haciendas employed "more than one hundred thousand slaves." See John Kenneth Turner, *Barbarous Mexico* (Chicago: Charles H. Kerr, 1910), 12.
3. See, for example, Joseph, *Revolution from Without*; Henry Baerlein, *Mexico: The Land of Unrest; Being Chiefly an Account of What Produced the Outbreak in 1910* (London: Herbert and Daniel, 1913); Claudio Lomnitz, *The Return of Comrade Ricardo Flores Magón* (Brooklyn, NY: Zone Books, 2014), 119.
4. The first chapters of *Barbarous Mexico* were published serially in *The American Magazine* between October and December 1909, and even before the first chapter hit the newsstands, the pro-Díaz newspaper *El Imparcial* was already print-

ing critical responses to it, priming the Mexican audience against it before they could lay their eyes on its pages. In fact, 1,500 copies of *The American Magazine* destined to cross the border from the United States into Mexico were quickly confiscated by Mexican authorities to keep Turner's piece from being disseminated. After the December issue, *The American Magazine* suspended the publication of Turner's piece. In 1910 Turner published nine subsequent chapters in *Appeal to Reason*, *The International Socialist Review*, and *The Pacific Monthly*. See Armando Bartra, "John Kenneth Turner: Un testigo incómodo," *Chiapas* 7 (1999): 209–226. See also Moisés González Navarro, *Raza y tierra: La guerra de castas y el henequén* (Mexico City: Colegio de México, 1979), 223.

5. Gutiérrez de Lara was a Mexican lawyer and journalist who actively organized alongside the Flores Magón brothers and other members of the Partido Liberal Mexicano against the Díaz regime. He was a leader of the 1906 Cananea strike and author of the novel *Los bribones*. For more on Turner and Gutiérrez de Lara, see Lomnitz, *Return of Comrade Ricardo Flores Magón*, chap. 8–10.

6. Lomnitz, *Return of Comrade Ricardo Flores Magón*, 143–146.

7. Indeed, Turner was not the only one to denounce the dire labor conditions in Yucatán and Valle Nacional. See, for instance, Channing Arnold and Frederick J. Tabor Frost, *The American Egypt: A Record of Travel in Yucatán* (London: Hutchinson, 1909). Other similar cases outside of Mexico include the reports made by Roger Casement on the rubber plantations in Putumayo and the Congo. For more on Casement see Carolina Sá Carvalho, "How to See a Scar: Humanitarianism and Colonial Iconography in the Putumayo Rubber Boom," *Journal of Latin American Cultural Studies: Travesía* 27, no. 3 (2018): 371–397.

8. Moisés González Navarro, *El porfiriato: La vida social*, vol. 4 of *Historia Moderna de México*, ed. Daniel Cosío Villegas (Mexico City: Hermes, 1957).

9. Note the meaning of the word "colonization" in this context is not associated with an imperial overseas power structure but rather focused on national development. See Joshua Lund, *The Mestizo State: Reading Race in Modern Mexico* (Minneapolis: University of Minnesota Press, 2012), chap. 1. For more on colonization during the Porfiriato, see Moisés González Navarro, *La colonización en México 1877–1910* (Jalapa, Mexico: Universidad Veracruzana, 1960); González Navarro, *El porfiriato*; Jason Oliver Chang, *Chino: Anti-Chinese Racism in Mexico, 1880–1940* (Urbana: University of Illinois Press, 2017), chap. 1; Carlos Illades, "Poblamiento y colonización: Las políticas públicas, 1854–1910," in *México en el siglo XIX*, vol. 3 of *El poblamiento de México: Una visión histórico demográfica*, ed. Consejo Nacional de Población (Mexico City: Secretaría de Gobernación/Consejo Nacional de Población, 1993), 134–147; Luis Aboites, *Norte precario: Poblamiento y colonización en México, 1760–1940* (Mexico City: COLMEX/CIESAS, 1995).

10. González Navarro, *El porfiriato*, 134–135.

11. González Navarro, *El porfiriato*, 143.

12. Emiliano Busto, *Estadística de la República Mexicana: Estado que guardan la agricultura, indutria, mineria y comercio. Resúmen y análisis de los informes*

rendidos á la secretaría de hacienda por los agricultores, mineros, industriales y comerciantes de la república y los agentes de Mexico en el exterior, en respuesta a las circulares de l de Agosto de 1877, vol. 3 (Mexico City: Imprenta de Ignacio Cumplido, 1880), 265.

13. Busto, *Estadística*, 265.

14. See letters on Yucatán's Caste War compiled in Luis Chávez Orozco, *La gestión diplomática del Doctor Mora*, Archivo Histórico Diplomático Mexicano, vol. 35 (Mexico City: Publicaciones de la Secretaría de Relaciones Exteriores, 1931).

15. On Argentina see, for instance, Juan Bautista Alberdi, *Bases y puntos de partida para la organización política de la República Argentina* (Buenos Aires: F. Cruz, 1914). See also David Viñas, *Indios, ejército y frontera* (Buenos Aires: Siglo XXI Editores, 1982).

16. Busto, *Estadística*, 265–266.

17. Busto, *Estadística*, 265–266.

18. Busto, *Estadística*, 265–266.

19. See "Migración china," *Diario Oficial del Gobierno Supremo de la República*, October 12, 1871. See also González Navarro, *El porfiriato*, chap. 8; José Jorge Gómez Izquierdo, "El movimiento anti-chino en México (1871–1934): Problemas del racismo y del nacionalismo en México durante la Revolución Mexicana" (undergraduate thesis, Universidad Nacional Autónoma de México, 1988), 22–23. For more on the topic of Asian immigration in Mexico, see María Elena Ota Mishima, ed., *Destino México: Un estudio de las migraciones asiáticas a México, siglos XIX y XX* (Mexico City: El Colegio de México, 1997). See also Chang, *Chino*.

20. Busto, *Estadística*, 266–267.

21. González Navarro, *El porfiriato*, 164–165.

22. Busto, *Estadística*, 267.

23. Busto, *Estadística*, 265–266.

24. *Constitución Federal de los Estados Unidos Mexicanos sancionada y jurada por el Congreso General Constituyente el 5 de febrero de 1857* (Mexico City: Imprenta de Ignacio Cumplido, 1857).

25. See González Navarro, *Raza y tierra*, 195–197.

26. González Navarro, *El porfiriato*, 161–165.

27. "La clase indígena se dedica casi exclusivamente a la agricultura; los mestizos a las artes manuales y en parte a la agricultura, como peones o pequeños propietarios, y los blancos son dueños casi exclusivamente del comercio y de la gran propiedad agrícola; sin embargo, las líneas de separación no son tan marcadas que no se encuentren algunos individuos de todas las clases en todas las profesiones, pues no hay exclusión legal." See Busto, *Estadística*, 256.

28. Busto, *Estadística*, 267.

29. Busto, *Estadística*, 267.

30. Busto, *Estadística*, 267.

31. Busto, *Estadística*, 266–267.

32. This is the estimate given by Evelyn Hu de Hart in *Yaqui Resistance and Survival: The Struggle for Land and Autonomy, 1821–1910* (Madison: University of Wisconsin Press, 1984), 188 and 169n37. For more on estimates of how many people were deported and the lack of documentation of these transactions, see also Raquel Padilla Ramos, *Yucatán, fin del sueño yaqui: El tráfico de los yaquis y el otro triunvirato* (Mexico City: Gobierno del Estado de Sonora, Secretaría de Educación y Cultura, Instituto Sonorense de Cultura, 1995), 52, 130.

33. See Ricardo D. Salvatore and Carlos Aguirre, "Colonies of Settlement or Places of Banishment and Torment? Penal Colonies and Convict Labour in Latin America, c. 1800–1940," in *Global Convict Labour*, ed. Christian Giuseppe De Vito and Alex Lichtenstein, 273–309 (Leiden, Netherlands: Brill, 2015). See also Diego Esteva Pulido, "La tumba del Pacífico: Historia de la colonia penal de las Islas Marías 1905–1939" (master's thesis, Instituto de Investigaciones Dr. José María Luis Mora, 2007).

34. Padilla Ramos, *Yucatán, fin del sueño yaqui*, 60.

35. "Los vastos terrenos que contienen los ríos Yaqui y Mayo se han considerado siempre y son en efecto, los mejores del Estado por su feracidad y por tener el elemento preciosismo del agua en abundancia tal, que basta para regarlos todos, sin grandes esfuerzos." Francisco del Paso y Troncoso, *Las guerras con las tribus yaqui y mayo de Sonora* (Mexico City: Tipografía del Departamento del Estado Mayor, 1905), 67.

36. "Una guerra de castas, encarnizada y sin cuartel, como son todas las de esa especie." Del Paso y Troncoso, *Las guerras con las tribus yaqui y mayo*, 70.

37. Del Paso y Troncoso, *Las guerras con las tribus yaqui y mayo*, 71.

38. Padilla Ramos, *Yucatán, fin del sueño yaqui*, 46–48; Hu de Hart, *Yaqui Resistance and Survival*, 147. See also Turner, *Barbarous Mexico*, chap. 2 and 3.

39. García Peña, "Memoria," quoted in Del Paso y Troncoso, *Las guerras con las tribus yaqui y mayo*, 278. See also Padilla Ramos, *Yucatán: Fin del sueño*, 41; and Héctor Aguilar Camín, *La frontera nómada: Sonora y la Revolución Mexicana* (Mexico City: Siglo XXI Editores, 1977), 54–55.

40. Del Paso y Troncoso, *Las guerras con las tribus yaqui y mayo*, 236.

41. "El Yaqui está incrustado en nuestro modo de ser social: es el peón de campo, el vaquero del rancho, el peón de raya de las labores, el barretero de las minas, el trabajador en las reparaciones de los ferrocarriles, el peón de mano de obra de albañilería de la Ciudad, el atrevido marinero y en muchos casos el hombre de confianza de las familias." (García Peña, "Memoria," cited in Del Paso y Troncoso, *Las guerras con las tribus yaqui y mayo*, 265. For another discussion of this passage, see Aguilar Camín, *La frontera nómada*, 54–55.

42. García Peña, "Memoria," cited in del Paso y Troncoso, *Las guerras con las tribus yaqui y mayo*, 265.

43. Ramos Padilla, *Yucatán, fin del sueño Yaqui*, 46.

44. Hu de Hart, *Yaqui Resistance and Survival*, chap. 5; Héctor Aguilar Ca-

mín, *La frontera nómada: Sonora y la Revolución Mexicana* (Mexico City: Siglo XXI Editores, 1977), 63–65; Ramos Padilla, *Yucatán, fin del sueño yaqui*, 60–72.

45. Hu de Hart, *Yaqui Resistance and Survival*, 162n13.

46. Hu de Hart, *Yaqui Resistance and Survival*, 156–172; Ramos Padilla, *Yucatán, fin del sueño yaqui*, 55; Turner, *Barbarous Mexico*, 44–46.

47. Ramos Padilla, *Yucatán, fin del sueño yaqui*, 72; Aguilar Camín, *La frontera nómada*, 65; Hu de Hart, *Yaqui Resistance and Survival*, 186.

48. "Nadie niega las aptitudes y vocación del Yaqui para el trabajo . . . trabajador enérgico, dotado de más vigor físico que cualquier individuo de otras razas, inteligente y sagaz, ha aceptado todas las formas de labor y a todas ha llevado resistencias extraordinarias y excepcionales aptitudes de inteligencia."

49. Turner, *Barbarous Mexico*, 45.

50. Turner, *Barbarous Mexico*, 51.

51. For a study on the heightening of anti-Chinese racism in Mexico during the Mexican Revolution, see Chang, *Chino*.

52. See "Guerra de razas en el año de 1977," *El Porvenir*, March–April, 1919.

53. See Chang, *Chino*, introduction; Christina A. Sue, *Land of the Cosmic Race: Race Mixture, Racism, and Blackness in Mexico* (New York: Oxford University Press, 2013), introduction. For more on the eugenecist trends of the epoch, see Beatriz Urías Horcasitas, *Historias secretas del racismo en México, 1920–1950* (Mexico City: Tusquets, 2007).

EPILOGUE

1. "Salinas de Gortari—6 de enero 1994," YouTube video, posted January 27, 2010, by EstrategiaElectoral. Accessed at "Video: El discurso inicial de Salinas frente al EZLN," Aristegui Noticias, January 6, 1994, https://aristeguinoticias.com/3012/mexico/video-el-discurso-inicial-de-salinas-frente-al-ezln/.

2. See "Salinas de Gortari—6 de enero 1994."

3. One could argue that the institutionalization of the Mexican Revolution created the paradigm of *mestizaje* against the race war paradigm. This is not to say that *mestizaje* overcame the production of racial difference, as it purported to do. Racialization certainly continued to operate, albeit through different mechanisms than those at work in the race war paradigm. For an example of how the 1910 revolution moved away from the race war paradigm, see Manuel Gamio, *Forjando Patria* (Mexico City: Editorial Porrúa, 1960), 10. Gamio criticizes those who feared the potential outbreak of race war amid Mexico's revolution.

4. Oswaldo Zavala, *Los carteles no existen: Narcotráfico y cultura en México* (Barcelona: Malpaso, 2018), chap. 1.

5. Barry Buzan, Ole Wæver, and Jaap de Wilde, *Security: A New Framework for Analysis* (Boulder, CO: Lynne Rienner, 1998). See also Mariana Mora, "La criminalización de la pobreza y los efectos estatales de seguridad neoliberal: Reflexio-

nes desde la Montaña, Guerrero," *Revista de Estudos e Pesquisas sobre as Américas* 7, no. 2 (2013): 174–208, https://doi.org/10.21057/repamv7i2.10027.

6. See Rebecca Berke Galemba, *Contraband Corridor: Making a Living at the Mexico-Guatemala Border* (Stanford, CA: Stanford University Press, 2018), 20.

7. In Mexico the question of racial difference has been displaced from the public to the private sphere, making it very difficult for a shared critical discourse on race to emerge and pinpoint the structural dimensions of how racialization continues to operate. An example of this is the use of the term "morenacos" (joining *moreno* and *naco*) by Victoriano Pagoaga Lamadrid, a CONACYT public servant who described the disappearance of the forty-three students from Ayotzinapa as a *perricidio* (dogicide) characterized by *morenacos* killing each other. For more on this, see R. Aída Hernández and Shannon Speed, "De Ferguson a Ayotzinapa: Racismo y criminalización de la protesta social," *La Jornada*, December 17, 2014. On the question of racism as a private language, see Fernando Navarrete Linares, *Mexico racista: Una denuncia* (Barcelona: Grijalbo, 2016), introduction. On the absence of critical discourses on race that can tackle the structural aspects of racialization in Mexico, see Mariana Mora, "Ayotzinapa and the Criminalization of Racialized Poverty in La Montaña, Guerrero, Mexico," *Political and Legal Anthropology Review* 40, no. 1 (May 2017): 67–85, https://doi.org/10.1111/plar.12208.

8. See María Josefina Saldaña-Portillo, *The Revolutionary Imagination in the Americas and the Age of Development* (Durham, NC: Duke University Press, 2003), chap. 6.

9. See Mora, "Ayotzinapa and the Criminalization," 67–85.

10. Saldaña-Portillo, *Revolutionary Imagination*, 218.

11. Saldaña-Portillo, *Revolutionary Imagination*, 222.

12. "Salinas de Gortari—6 de enero 1994."

13. Todd Miller, *Empire of Borders: The Expansion of the US Border around the World* (New York: Verso, 2019), 187.

14. Jesusa Cervantes and Jorge Carrasco Araizaga, "Premios a quienes custodiaron a Peña-Nieto como candidato," *Revista Proceso*, June 1, 2017, https://www.proceso.com.mx/reportajes/2017/6/1/premios-quienes-custodiaron-pena-como-candidato-185266.html.

15. Arnulfo Mora, "Amagan con desalojar a campesinos de Infiernillo," *Quadtradín*, February 15, 2014, https://www.quadratin.com.mx/sucesos/Amagan-con-desalojar-campesinos-de-Infiernillo/.

16. Cervantes and Carrasco, "Premios a quienes custodiaron."

17. "Pueblos del Istmo (APOYO): La creación de Zonas Económicas Especiales es la validación de política de despojo," Centro de Medios Libres, March 18, 2017, https://www.centrodemedioslibres.org/2017/03/18/pueblos-del-istmo-apoyo-la-creacion-de-las-zonas-economicas-especiales-es-la-validacion-de-politica-de-despojo/.

18. *Programa para la seguridad nacional 2014–2018: Una política multidimensional para México en el siglo XXI* (Mexico City: Consejo de Seguridad Nacional, Presidencia de la República, 2014).

19. Mora, "La Criminalización de La Pobreza."
20. "Ley federal de zonas económicas especiales," *Diario Oficial de la Federación*, June 1, 2016.
21. Alberto Colín Huizar, "El extractivismo de las zonas económicas especiales," *Tercera Vía*, September 4, 2017, https://terceravia.mx/2017/09/extractivismo-las-zonas-economicas-especiales/.
22. Alberto Colín Huizar, "La lucha contra las zonas económicas especiales apenas comienza," *Tercera Vía*, December 13, 2017, https://terceravia.mx/2017/12/la-lucha-contra-las-zonas-economicas-especiales-apenas-comienza/.
23. "Ley federal de zonas económicas especiales."
24. "Ley federal de zonas económicas especiales."
25. Colín Huizar, "El extractivismo de las zonas." See also "Lázaro Cárdenas ya es zona económica especial," *El Independiente*, June 23, 2017, https://www.el-independiente.com.mx/lazaro-cardenas-ya-es-zona-economica-especial/.
26. "Ley federal de zonas económicas especiales." See also Colín Huizar, "La lucha contra las zonas económicas."
27. Colín Huizar, "La lucha contra las zonas económicas."
28. According to a 2020 communiqué from the National Institute of Statistics and Geography (INEGI), nearly 60 percent of the country's indigenous populations live in these states. See "Estadísticas a propósito del día internacional de los pueblos indígenas (9 de agosto)," August 7, 2020, https://www.inegi.org.mx/app/saladeprensa/noticia.html?id=5910.
29. Mora, "La criminalización de la pobreza." The program was first implemented by the Salinas administration under the name Solidaridad. It has since continued to operate under other presidencies as Progresa, then Oportunidades, and now Prospera.
30. Mora, "Ayotzinapa and the Criminalization."
31. *La cuarta guerra mundial (Subcomandante Insurgente Marcos, Noviembre de 1999) / Símbolos (Eduardo Galeano, Octubre del 2001)* (Mexico: CCD Defensores de la República—Frente Zapatista de Liberación Nacional, 2001). Pamphlet accessed through Princeton University's Digital Archive of Latin American and Caribbean Ephemera, https://lae.princeton.edu/catalog/f595d292-6b98-46a6-9d6e-9162457ba288?locale=en#?c=0&m=0&s=0&cv=0&xywh=1345%2C5399%2C3982%2C3599.

Bibliography

ARCHIVES CONSULTED

Archivo Histórico de la Secretaría de la Defensa Nacional (AHSDN)
Archivo Histórico de la Ciudad de México (AHA)
Getty Research Institute
Hemeroteca Nacional de México (HNDM), both on-site and digital
William L. Clements Library (CLE)

PUBLISHED SOURCES

Aboites, Luis. *Norte precario: Poblamiento y colonización en México, 1760–1940*. Mexico City: COLMEX/CIESAS, 1995.
Adelman, Jeremy, ed. *Colonial Legacies: The Problem of Persistence in Latin America*. London: Routledge, 1999.
Adelman, Jeremy. *Sovereignty and Revolution in the Iberian Atlantic*. Princeton, NJ: Princeton University Press, 2006.
Adorno, Theodor W., and Max Horkheimer. *Dialectic of Enlightenment*. Translated by John Cumming. New York: Continuum, 1994.
Agamben, Giorgio. *The State of Exception*. Translated by Kevin Attell. Chicago: University of Chicago Press, 2005.
Agamben, Giorgio. *Signatura rerum: Sul metodo*. Turin, Italy: Bollati Boringhieri, 2008.
Aguilar Camín, Héctor. *La frontera nómada: Sonora y la Revolución Mexicana*. Mexico City: Siglo XXI Editores, 1977.
Aguirre Beltrán, Gonzalo. *La población negra de México 1519–1810*. Mexico City: Ediciones Fuente Cultural, 1946.
Alberdi, Juan Bautista. *Bases y puntos de partida para la organización política de la República Argentina*. Buenos Aires: F. Cruz, 1914.

Alberto, Paulina L., and Jesse Hoffnung-Garskof. "'Racial Democracy' and Racial Inclusion." In *Afro-Latin American Studies: An Introduction*, edited by Alejandro de la Fuente and George Reid Andrews, 264–316. Cambridge: Cambridge University Press, 2018.

Almonte, Juan. *Memoria del Ministro de Guerra y Marina, presentada a las Cámaras del Congreso General Mexicano, en enero de 1840*. Mexico City: Oficina del Águila, 1840.

Álvarez, Izaskun. "De españoles, yucatecos e indios: La venta de mayas a Cuba y la construcción imaginada de una nación." *Revista de Pesquisa Histórica de la Universidad Federal de Pernambuco* 30, no. 1 (2012): 1–20.

Álvarez, Izaskun. "De Tihosuco a La Habana: La venta de indios yucatecos a Cuba durante la Guerra de Castas." *Revista Estudios Históricos* 25 (2005): 559–576.

Álvarez, Izaskun. "Indios mayas en Cuba: Algunas reflexiones sobre su comercio." *Estudios Gaditano Cubanos* 3 (2002): 121–141.

Ancona, Eligio, ed. *Colección de leyes, decretos, órdenes y demás disposiciones de tendencia general, expedidas por el poder legislativo del estado de Yucatán: Formada con autorización del gobierno por Eligio Ancona*. 8 vols. Mérida, Mexico: Imprenta de El Eco del Comercio, 1882–1889.

Ancona, Eligio. *Historia de Yucatán desde la época más remota hasta nuestros días*. 2nd ed. Vol. 4. Mérida, Mexico: Imprenta de J. J. Roviralta, 1889.

Ancona, Eligio. *Uno de tantos: Novela*. Mérida, Mexico: Gobierno del Estado de Yucatán, Secretaría de la Cultura y las Artes, 2015.

Anderson, Benedict. *Imagined Communities: Reflections on the Origin and Spread of Nationalism*. Rev. ed. London: Verso, 2016.

Anderson, Claire. "Convicts and Coolies: Rethinking Indentured Labour in the Nineteenth Century." *Slavery and Abolition* 30, no. 1 (2009): 93–109.

Anderson, Claire, ed. *A Global History of Convicts and Penal Labor*. London: Bloomsbury Academic, 2018.

Andersson, Paige R. "The Only Way: Congregación and the Construction of Race and Land in Mexico, 1521–2017." PhD diss., University of Michigan, 2018.

Andioc, René. *Teatro y sociedad en el Madrid del siglo XVIII*. Madrid: Editorial Castalia, 1987.

Angulo Egea, María. *Luciano Francisco Comella (1751–1812): Otra cara del teatro de la ilustración*. Alicante, Spain: Publicaciones de la Universidad de Alicante, 2006.

Annino, Antonio, and Marcela Ternavasio, coords. *El laboratorio constitucional iberoamericano: 1807/1808–1830*. Madrid: Iberoamericana y Estudios AHILA, 2012.

Antochiw, Michel. *Historia cartográfica de la Península de Yucatán*, Mexico City: Centro de Investigación y de Estudios Avanzados del IPN, 1994.

Archer, Christon I. *The Army in Bourbon Mexico, 1760–1810*. Albuquerque: University of New Mexico Press, 1977.

Arendt, Hannah. *Lectures on Kant's Political Philosophy*. Edited by Ronald Beiner. Chicago: University of Chicago Press, 1982.

Arendt, Hannah. *The Origins of Totalitarianism*. London: Penguin, 2017.

Arnold, Channing, and Frederick J. Tabor Frost. *The American Egypt: A Record of Travel in Yucatán*. London: Hutchinson, 1909.

Arrillaga, Basilio José. *Recopilación de leyes, decretos, bandos, circulares, y providencias de los supremos poderes y otras autoridades de la República Mexicana del 25 al 31 de diciembre de 1860.* Mexico City: Imprenta de Vicente G. Torres, 1861.

Arrom, José Juan. *Historia de la literatura dramática cubana*. New Haven, CT: Yale University Press, 1944.

Asamblea de Defensores del Territorio Maya Múuch' Xíinbal. "¡No al tren mal llamado maya! Pronunciamiento de la Asamblea de Defensores del Territorio Maya Múuch' Xíinbal." May 21, 2020. https://asambleamaya.wixsite.com/muuch xiinbal/no-al-tren-maya.

Baerlein, Henry. *Mexico: The Land of Unrest; Being Chiefly an Account of What Produced the Outbreak in 1910*. London: Herbert and Daniel, 1913.

Banner, Stuart. *How the Indians Lost Their Land: Law and Power on the Frontier*. Cambridge, MA: Harvard University Press, 2007.

Baqueiro, Serapio. *Ensayo histórico sobre las revoluciones de Yucatán desde el año de 1840 hasta 1864*. Vol. 2. Mexico City: Imprenta de M. Heredia Argüelles, 1878.

Barrera, Pantaleón. [Napoleón Trebarra, pseud.]. *Los misterios de Chan Santa Cruz*. Mérida, Mexico: Imprenta de M. Aldana Rivas, 1864.

Bartra, Armando. "John Kenneth Turner: Un testigo incómodo." *Chiapas* 7 (1999): 209–226.

Bartra, Armando. *El México Bárbaro: Plantaciones y monterías del sureste durante el porfiriato*. Mexico City: Universidad Autónoma Metropolitana, 2015.

Benavidez Martínez, Juan José. "Revuelta general y represión ejemplar: Los motines de 1767 en San Luis Potosí." *Revista de El Colegio de San Luis* 6, no. 12 (2016): 40–72.

Benjamin, Walter. *Selected Writings*. Edited by Marcus Paul Bullock, Michael William Jennings, Howard Eiland, and Gary Smith. Translated by Howard Eiland, Michael Jennings, Edmund Jephcott, Rodney Livingstone, Jerolf Wikoff, and Harry Zohn. 4 vols. Cambridge, MA: Belknap, 2004–2006.

Benton, Lauren. *A Search for Sovereignty: Law and Geography in European Empires, 1400–1900*. Cambridge: Cambridge University Press, 2014.

Bergland, Renée L. *The National Uncanny: Indian Ghosts and American Subjects*. Hanover, NH: University Press of New England, 2000.

Bertelli, Sergio. *The King's Body: Sacred Rituals of Power in Medieval and Early Modern Europe*. University Park: Pennsylvania State University Press, 2001.

Berzunza Pinto, Ramón. *Guerra social en Yucatán*. Mexico City: Bartomeu Costa-Amic, 1965.

Blackhawk, Ned. *Violence over the Land: Indians and Empires in the Early American West*. Cambridge, MA: Harvard University Press, 2008.

Bocanegra, José María. *Memorias para la historia de México independiente 1822–1846*. Vol. 2. Mexico City: Instituto Cultural Helénico, Fondo de Cultura Económica, 1987.

Borah, Woodrow. "Hipólito Villarroel: Some Unanswered Questions." In *Des Indes occidentales à l'Amérique Latine*, vol. 2, edited by Thomas Calvo and Alain Musset, 505–514. Mexico City: Centro de Estudios Mexicanos y Centroamericanos, 2006. Accessed July 18, 2018, https://books.openedition.org/cemca/2118?lang=en.

Bracamonte y Sosa, Pedro. *Amos y servientes*. Mérida, Mexico: Ediciones de la Universidad Autónoma de Yucatán, 1993.

Brading, David. *The First America: The Spanish Monarchy, Creole Patriots and the Liberal State, 1492–1866*. Cambridge: Cambridge University Press, 1993.

Brading, David. *Mexican Phoenix: Our Lady of Guadalupe—Image and Tradition across Five Centuries*. Cambridge: Cambridge University Press, 2001.

Brading, David. *Miners and Merchants in Bourbon Mexico 1763–1810*. Cambridge: Cambridge University Press, 1971.

Brannon, Jeffrey T., and Gilbert M. Joseph. *Land, Labor, and Capital in Modern Yucatán*. Tuscaloosa: University of Alabama Press, 1991.

Braude, Benjamin. "The Sons of Noah and the Construction of Ethnic and Geographical Identities in the Medieval and Early Modern Periods." *William and Mary Quarterly* 54, no. 1 (1997): 103–142.

Bricker, Victoria Reifler. *The Indian Christ, the Indian King: The Historical Substrate of Maya Myth and Ritual*. Austin: University of Texas Press, 1981.

Briggs, Ronald. *The Moral Electricity of Print Transatlantic Education and the Lima Women's Circuit, 1876–1910*. Nashville, TN: Vanderbilt University Press, 2017.

British and State Foreign Papers 1854–55. Vol. 45. London: William Ridgway, 1865.

Buck-Morss, Susan. *Hegel, Haiti, and Universal History*. Pittsburgh, PA: University of Pittsburgh Press, 2009.

Busto, Emiliano. *Estadística de la República Mexicana: Estado que guardan la agricultura, indutria, mineria y comercio. Resúmen y análisis de los informes rendidos á la secretaría de hacienda por los agricultores, mineros, industriales y comerciantes de la república y los agentes de Mexico en el exterior, en respuesta a las circulares de l de agosto de 1877*. Vol. 3. Mexico City: Imprenta de Ignacio Cumplido, 1880.

Buzan, Barry, Ole Wæver, and Jaap de Wilde. *Security: A New Framework for Analysis*. Boulder, CO: Lynne Rienner, 1998.

Calargé, Carla, Raphael Dalleo, Luis Duno-Gottberg, and Clevis Headley, eds. *Haiti and the Americas*. Jackson: University Press of Mississippi, 2013.

Camarena Castellanos, Ricardo. *El control inquisitorial del teatro en la Nueva España durante el siglo XVIII*. Mexico City: Instituto Nacional de Bellas Artes, 1995.

Camhaji, Elías. "El pasado esclavista que México halló en el fondo del mar." *El País*, September 17, 2020. https://elpais.com/mexico/2020-09-16/el-pasado-esclavista-que-mexico-hallo-en-el-fondo-del-mar.html.

Cañeque, Alejandro. "Imaging the Spanish Empire: The Visual Construction of Imperial Authority in Habsburg New Spain." *Colonial Latin American Review* 19, no. 1 (2010): 29–68.

Cañeque, Alejandro. *The King's Living Image: The Culture and Politics of Viceregal Power in Colonial Mexico*. New York: Routledge, 2004.
Caplan, Karen D. *Indigenous Citizens: Local Liberalism in Early National Oaxaca and Yucatán*. Stanford, CA: Stanford University Press, 2010.
Carrera, Magali M. *Imagining Identity in New Spain: Race, Lineage, and the Colonial Body in Portraiture and Casta Paintings*. Austin: University of Texas Press, 2003.
Carroll, Noel. *The Philosophy of Horror, or, Paradoxes of the Heart*. New York: Routledge, 1990.
Castellanos, Rosario. *Oficio de tinieblas*. Mexico City: Joaquín Mortiz, 1962.
Castillo Palma, Norma Angélica. *Cholula sociedad mestiza en ciudad india*. Mexico City: Universidad Autónoma Metropolitana, 2001.
Castro Gutiérrez, Felipe. *Nueva ley y nuevo rey: Reformas borbónicas y rebelión popular en Nueva España*. Zamora, Mexico: Colegio de Michoacán, 1996.
Cervantes, Jesusa, and Jorge Carrasco Araizaga. "Premios a quienes custodiaron a Peña-Nieto como candidato." *Revista Proceso*, June 1, 2017. https://www.proceso.com.mx/reportajes/2017/6/1/premios-quienes-custodiaron-pena-como-candidato-185266.html.
Chang, Jason Oliver. *Chino: Anti-Chinese Racism in Mexico, 1880–1940*. Urbana: University of Illinois Press, 2017.
Chasteen, John Charles, and Castro-Klarén, Sara. *Beyond Imagined Communities: Reading and Writing the Nation in Nineteenth-Century Latin America*. Washington, DC: Woodrow Wilson Center Press, 2003.
Chávez Orozco, Luis. *La gestión diplomática del doctor Mora*. Mexico City: Editorial Porrúa, 1970.
Chávez Orozco, Luis. *Un esfuerzo de México por la independencia de Cuba*. Mexico City: Publicaciones de la Secretaria de Relaciones Exteriores, 1930.
Clayton, Daniel. "On the Colonial Genealogy of George Vancouver's Chart of the North-West Coast of North America." *Ecumene* 7, no. 4 (October 2000): 371–401.
Clover, Joshua. *Riot Strike Riot: The New Era of Uprisings*. London: Verso, 2016.
Cohen, Ashley L. "The Global Indies: Reading the Imaginative Geography of British Empire 1763–1871." PhD diss., University of Pennsylvania, 2013.
Colín Huizar, Alberto. "El extractivismo de las zonas económicas especiales." *Tercera Vía*, September 4, 2017. https://terceravia.mx/2017/09/extractivismo-las-zonas-economicas-especiales/.
Colín Huizar, Alberto. "La lucha contra las zonas económicas especiales apenas comienza." *Tercera Vía*, December 13, 2017. https://terceravia.mx/2017/12/la-lucha-contra-las-zonas-economicas-especiales-apenas-comienza/.
Collins, Mary Austin. "Hipólito Villarroel and the Reforms of Charles the Third." Master's thesis, University of California, 1922.
Comay, Rebecca. *Mourning Sickness: Hegel and the French Revolution*. Cultural Memory in the Present. Stanford, CA: Stanford University Press, 2011. Kindle edition.

Comella, Luciano Francisco. *El negro sensible: Melodrama en dos actos.* Cádiz, Spain: Librería de Murguia.
Constitución Federal de los Estados Unidos Mexicanos sancionada y jurada por el Congreso General Constituyente el 5 de febrero de 1857. Mexico City: Imprenta de Ignacio Cumplido, 1857.
Cope, R. Douglas. *The Limits of Racial Domination: Plebeian Society in Colonial Mexico City, 1660–1720.* Madison: University of Wisconsin Press, 1994.
Cortés Campos, Rocío Leticia. *Entre héroes y bárbaros: El periodismo yucateco durante la Guerra de Castas.* Mérida, Mexico: Universidad Autónoma de Yucatán, 2013.
Craib, Raymond. *Cartographic Mexico: A History of State Fixations and Fugitive Landscapes.* Durham, NC: Duke University Press, 2004.
Curcio-Nagy, Linda A. *The Great Festival of Colonial Mexico City: Performing Power and Identity.* Albuquerque: University of New Mexico Press, 2004.
Curran, Andrew S. *The Anatomy of Blackness: Science and Slavery in an Age of Enlightenment.* Baltimore, MD: Johns Hopkins University Press, 2011.
Curran, Andrew S., and Patrick Graille. "The Faces of Eighteenth-Century Monstrosity." *Eighteenth-Century Life* 21, no. 2 (1997): 1–15.
Dabove, Juan Pablo. *Nightmares of the Lettered City: Banditry and Literature in Latin America, 1816–1929.* Pittsburgh, PA: University of Pittsburgh Press, 2007.
Dassow, Laura. *The Passage to Cosmos: Alexander von Humboldt and the Shaping of America.* Chicago: University of Chicago Press, 2009.
Daut, Marlene L. *Tropics of Haiti: Race and the Literary History of the Haitian Revolution in the Atlantic World, 1789–1865.* Liverpool: Liverpool University Press, 2015.
De Vito, Christian Giuseppe. "Convict Labor in the Southern Borderlands of Latin America (ca. 1750s–1910s): Comparative Perspectives." In *On Coerced Labor: Work and Compulsion after Chattel Slavery,* edited by Marcel van der Linden and Magaly Rodríguez García, 98–126. Leiden, Netherlands: Brill, 2016.
De Vito, Christian Giuseppe. "The Spanish Empire: 1500–1898." In *A Global History of Convict and Penal Colonies,* edited by Clare Anderson, 65–95. London: Bloomsbury Academic, 2018.
Deans-Smith, Susan. *Bureaucrats, Planters, and Workers: The Making of the Tobacco Monopoly in Bourbon Mexico.* Austin: University of Texas Press, 1992.
Del Castillo, Severo. *Cecilio Chi.* Mérida, Mexico: Distribuidora de Libros Yucatectos, 1978. First published 1869.
Derrida, Jacques. *The Death Penalty.* Vol 1. Translated by Peggy Kamuf. Chicago: University of Chicago Press, 2014.
Desmond, Lawrence. *Yucatán through Her Eyes: Alice Dixon Le Plongeon, Writer and Expeditionary Photographer.* Albuquerque: University of New Mexico Press, 2009.
Desmond, Lawrence, and Phyllis Mauch Messenger. *Dream of Maya: Augustus and Alice Le Plongeon in Nineteenth-Century Yucatan.* Albuquerque: University of New Mexico Press, 1988.

Diario de los debates del Congreso de la Unión correspondiente al periodo de sesiones extraordinarias y al segundo de las ordinarias del año de 1870 a 1871. Vol. 4. Mexico City: Imprenta del Gobierno en Palacio a cargo de José María Sandoval, 1871.

Dillon, Elizabeth Maddock. *New World Drama: The Performative Commons in the Atlantic World, 1649–1849*. Durham, NC: Duke University Press, 2014.

Dillon, Elizabeth Maddock, and Michael Drexler, eds. *The Haitian Revolution and the Early United States: Histories, Textualities, Geographies*. Philadelphia: University of Pennsylvania Press, 2016.

Dippie, Brian W. *The Vanishing American: White Attitudes and U.S. Indian Policy*. Middletown, CT: Wesleyan University Press, 1982.

Dirección de Colonización e Industria. *Memoria de la dirección de colonización e industria*. Mexico City: Imprenta de Vicente G. Torres, 1850.

Domínguez, Daylet. "Imaginarios antillanos: Humboldt, Haití y la Confederación Africana en las Antillas." *Revista Iberoamericana* 84, no. 262 (2018): 45–63.

Domínguez Michael, Christopher. *Vida de Fray Servando*. Mexico City: Ediciones Era, 2005.

Donahue-Wallace, Kelly. "Abused and Battered: Printed Images and the Female Body in Viceregal New Spain." In *Woman and Art in Early Modern Latin America*, edited by Kellen Kee McIntyre and Richard E. Phillips, 125–147. Leiden, Netherlands: Brill, 2007.

Donahue-Wallace, Kelly. "Ilustrando el terror de rebelión: Los grabados de *La vida de J. J. Dessalines*." In *Arte y crisis en Iberoamérica: Segundas jornadas de historia del arte*, edited by Fernando Guzmán, Gloria Cortés, and Juan Manuel Martínez, 83–91. Santiago, Chile: Ril Editores, 2004.

Donahue-Wallace, Kelly. "Spinning the King: Prints, Imprinting and the Equestrian Portrait of Charles IV." *Print Quarterly* 29, no. 4 (2012): 411–416.

Dosemeci, Mehmet. "Social Movement vs. Social Arrest: The Global Occupations of the 21st Century." *Critique and Humanism Journal* 46 (2016): 191–210.

Draper, Susana. *1968 Mexico: Constellations of Freedom and Democracy*. Durham, NC: Duke University Press, 2018.

Dubois, Laurent. *Avengers of the New World: The Story of the Haitian Revolution*. Cambridge, MA: Harvard University Press, 2004.

Dubroca, Louis. *La vie de J. J. Dessalines, chef de noirs révoltés de Saint-Domingue, avec des notes très détaillées sur l'origine, le caractère, la vie et les atrocités des principaux chefs de noirs, depuis l'insurrection de 1791*. Paris: Chez Dubroca et Rondonneau, 1804.

Ducey, Michael T. "Viven sin ley ni rey: Rebeliones coloniales en Papantla, 1760–1790." In *Procesos rurales e historia regional*, edited by Victoria Chenaut, 125–168. Mexico City: CIESAS, 1996.

Dumond, Don E. *El machete y la cruz: La sublevación de campesinos en Yucatán*. Translated by Luis F. Verano. Mexico City: Universidad Nacional Autónoma de México, 2005.

Dun, James Alexander. *Dangerous Neighbors: Making the Haitian Revolution in Early America*. Philadelphia: University of Pennsylvania Press, 2016.

Edsel, Carlos. "Los jacobinos negros en la insurgencia de los esclavos de la serranía de Coro." In *José Leonardo Chirino y la insurrección de la Serranía de Coro de 1795: Insurrección de libertad o rebelión de independencia*, edited by Luis Cipriano Rodríguez. Proceedings of the Symposium Held in Mérida, Venezuela, on November 16 and 17, 1995. Mérida, Venezuela: Universidad de los Andes, Universidad Central de Venezuela, 1996.

Escalante Gonzalbo, Fernando. *Ciudadanos imaginarios: Memorial de los afanes y desventuras de la virtud y apología del vicio triunfante en la República Mexicana: Tratado de moral pública*. Mexico City: Centro de Estudios Sociológicos, El Colegio de México, 1992.

Escandón, Patricia. "Hipólito Villarroel: Pensamiento ilustrado y autobiografía en las *Enfermedades Políticas*." *Revista de Historia de América* 157 (July–December 2019): 107–128.

Escobar, Manuel. *Verdad reflexa, platica doctrinal sobre los varios sucesos que intervinieron en la ciudad de San Luis Potosí desde el día 10 de mayo hasta el día 6 de octubre del mismo año, en que se ejecutaron los últimos suplicios de los tumultuarios [. . .]*. Mexico City: Imprenta Real del Superior Gobierno por el Br. D. Joseph Antonio de Hogal, Calle de Tiburcio, 1768.

Escobar Ohmstede, Antonio, and Leticia Reina, eds. *Indio, nación y comunidad en el México del siglo XIX*. Mexico City: Centro de Investigaciones y Estudios Superiores en Antropología Social, 1993.

Esdaile, Charles. *Napoleon's Wars: An International History*. New York: Viking, 2007.

Esteva Pulido, Diego. "La tumba del Pacífico: Historia de la colonia penal de las Islas Marías 1905–1939." Master's thesis, Instituto de Investigaciones Dr. José María Luis Mora, 2007.

Estrade, Paul. "Los esclavos yucatecos como sustitutos de los esclavos negros." In *Cuba, la perla de las Antillas: Actas de las I Jornadas sobre "Cuba y su Historia,"* edited by Consuelo Naranjo and Tomás Mallo, 93–108. Madrid: Doce Calles, 1994.

"Extracto de las cartas de Mr. Talleyrand remitidas al secretario de Estados Unidos." *Gazeta de México*, July 9, 1806.

Eyal, Hillel. "Beyond Networks: Transatlantic Immigration and Wealth in Late Colonial Mexico City." *Journal of Latin American Studies* 47, no. 2 (May 2015): 317–348.

Falcón, Romana. *Las rasgaduras de la descolonización: Españoles y mexicanos a mediados del siglo XIX*. Mexico City: El Colegio de México, 1996.

Falcón, Romana. *México descalzo*. Mexico City: Plaza y Janés, 2002.

Farge, Arlette. *The Allure of the Archive*. Translated by Thomas Scott-Railton. New Haven, CT: Yale University Press, 2015.

Farriss, Nancy. *Maya Society under Colonial Rule*. Princeton, NJ: Princeton University Press, 1984.

Ferrer, Ada. "Cuba en la sombra de Haití: Noticias, sociedad y esclavitud." In *El ru-

mor de Haití en Cuba: Temor, raza y rebeldía, 1789–1844, edited by Ma. Dolores González-Ripoll Navarro, 179–231. Madrid: Consejo Superior de Investigaciones Científicas, 2004.
Ferrer, Ada. *Freedom's Mirror: Cuba and Haiti in the Age of Revolution*. New York: Cambridge University Press, 2014.
Ferrer, Ada. "Haiti, Free Soil, and Antislavery in the Revolutionary Atlantic." *American Historical Review* 117, no. 1 (2012): 40–66.
Fields, Gary. *Enclosure: Palestinian Landscapes in a Historic Mirror*. Berkeley: University of California Press, 2017.
Fischer, Sibylle. "Bolívar in Haiti: Republicanism in the Revolutionary Atlantic." In *Haiti and the Americas*, edited by Carla Calargé, Raphael Dalleo, Luis Duno-Gottberg, and Clevis Headley, 25–53. Jackson: University Press of Mississippi, 2013.
Fischer, Sibylle. *Modernity Disavowed: Haiti and the Cultures of Slaves in the Age of Revolution*. Durham, NC: Duke University Press, 2004.
Florescano, Enrique. *Etnia, estado y nación*. Mexico City: Aguilar, 1997.
Foucault, Michel. *Abnormal: Lectures at the Collège de France, 1974–1975*. Edited by Valerio Marchetti and Antonella Salomoni. Translated by Graham Burchell. New York: Picador, 2003.
Foucault, Michel. *The Birth of Biopolitics: Lectures at the Collège de France 1978–1979*. Edited by Arnold Davidson. Translated by Graham Burchell. London: Palgrave Macmillan UK, 2008.
Foucault, Michel. *Discipline and Punish*. Translated by Alan Sheridan. New York: Vintage, 1995.
Foucault, Michel. *"Society Must Be Defended": Lectures at the Collège de France, 1975–1976*. Edited by Mauro Bertani and Alessandro Fontana. Translated by David Macey. New York: Picador, 2003.
Fra Molinero, Baltasar. *La imagen de los negros en el siglo de oro*. Madrid: Siglo XXI Editores, 1995.
Fradinger, Moira. *Binding Violence: Literary Visions of Political Origins*. Stanford, CA: Stanford University Press, 2010.
Fraser, Nancy. "Behind Marx's Hidden Abode." *New Left Review* 86 (March–April 2014): 55–72.
Gabbert, Wolfgang. *Becoming Maya: Ethnicity and Social Inequality in Yucatán since 1500*. Tucson: University of Arizona Press, 2004.
Galemba, Rebecca B. *Contraband Corridor: Making a Living at the Mexico-Guatemala Border*. Stanford, CA: Stanford University Press, 2018.
Gallart y Nocetti, Isaura Elvira. "Las rebeliones populares de 1767 en Nueva España." Undergraduate thesis, Universidad Nacional Autónoma de México, 1981.
Gálvez, José de. *Informe general que en virtud de real orden instruyó y entregó el Excmo. Sr. Marqués de Sonora al Virrey D. Antonio Bucarely y Ursúa con fecha de 31 de diciembre de 1771*. Mexico City: Imprenta de Santiago White, 1867.
Gálvez, José de. *Informe sobre las rebeliones populares de 1767 y otros documentos in-*

éditos. Edited by Felipe Castro Gutiérrez. Mexico City: Universidad Nacional Autónoma de México, Instituto de Investigaciones Históricas, 1990.

Gamio, Manuel. *Forjando Patria*. Mexico City: Editorial Porrúa, 1960.

García Cubas, Antonio. *Atlas geográfico estadístico e histórico de la República Mexicana*. Mexico City: Imprenta de José Mariano Fernández de Lara, 1858.

García Cubas, Antonio. *El libro de mis recuerdos: Narraciones históricas, anecdóticas y de costumbres mexicanas anteriores al actual estado social*. Mexico City: Imprenta de Arturo García Cubas, Hermanos Sucesores, 1904.

García de Icazbalceta, Joaquín. *Vocabulario de mexicanismos*. Mexico City: Tipografía y Litografía "La Europea" de J. Aguilar Vera, 1899.

García Martínez, Cynthia. "Fugas, ventas y otras noticias sobre la población afrodescendiente en el *Diario de México* y la *Gazeta de México*, 1784–1809." Master's thesis, Instituto de Investigaciones Dr. José María Luis Mora, 2016.

Garrigan, Shelley E. *Collecting Mexico: Museums, Monuments, and the Creation of National Identity*. Minneapolis: University of Minnesota Press, 2012.

Geggus, David, ed. *The Impact of the Haitian Revolution in the Atlantic World*. Columbia: University of South Carolina Press, 2001.

Geggus, David. "The Sounds and Echoes of Freedom." In *Beyond Slavery: The Multilayered Legacy of Africans in Latin America and the Caribbean*, edited by Darien J. Davis, 19–36. Lanham, MD: Rowman and Littlefield, 2007.

Geler, Lea. "Categorías raciales en Buenos Aires: Negritud, blanquitud, afrodescendencia y mestizaje en la blanca ciudad capital." *RUNA, Archivo para las ciencias del hombre* 37, no. 1 (July 2016): 71–87.

Geler, Lea. *Andares negros, caminos blancos: Afroporteños, Estado y Nación Argentina a fines del siglo XIX*. Rosario: Prohistoria Ediciones; TEIAA (Universidad de Barcelona), 2010.

Gibson, Charles. *Aztecs under Spanish Rule*. Stanford, CA: Stanford University Press, 1964.

Gil Amate, Virginia. "Hipólito Villarroel: Una mirada ilustrada sobre la ciudad de México." *Tema y variaciones de literatura* 32 (January–June, 2009): 255–287.

Gilmore, Ruth Wilson. "Geografía abolicionista y el problema de la inocencia." *Tabula Rasa*, no. 28 (2018): 57–77. https://doi.org/10.25058/issn.2011-2742.

Gilmore, Ruth Wilson. *Golden Gulag: Prisons, Surplus, Crisis, and Opposition in Globalizing California*. Berkeley: University of California Press, 2007.

Goldberg, David M. *Black and Slave: The Origins and History of the Curse of Ham*. Philadelphia: University of Pennsylvania Press, 2017.

Goldberg, David M. *The Curse of Ham: Race and Slavery in Early Judaism, Christianity and Islam*. Princeton, NJ: Princeton University Press, 2005.

Goldberg, David Theo. *The Racial State*. Malden, MA: Blackwell, 2002.

Gómez Izquierdo, José Jorge. "El movimiento anti-chino en México (1871–1934): Problemas del racismo y del nacionalismo en México durante la Revolución Mexicana." Undergraduate thesis, Universidad Nacional Autónoma de México, 1988.

González Navarro, Moisés. *El porfiriato: La vida social*. Vol. 4 of *Historia Moderna de México*, edited by Daniel Cosío Villegas. Mexico City: Hermes, 1957.

González Navarro, Moisés. *La colonización en México 1877–1910*. Jalapa, Mexico: Universidad Veracruzana, 1960.

González Navarro, Moisés. *Raza y tierra: La guerra de castas y el henequén*. Mexico City: Colegio de México, 1979.

Gordillo, Gastón. "The Savage Outside of White Argentina." In *Rethinking Race in Modern Argentina*, edited by Paulina Alberto and Eduardo Elena, 241–267. Cambridge: Cambridge University Press, 2016.

Gotkowitz, Laura. "Introduction: Racisms of the Present and the Past in Latin America." In *Histories of Race and Racism: The Andes and Mesoamerica from Colonial Times to the Present*, edited by Laura Gotkowitz, 1–56. Durham, NC: Duke University Press, 2011.

Gott, Richard. "Latin America as a White Settler Society." *Bulletin of Latin American Research* 26, no. 2 (2007): 269–289.

Grafenstein, Johanna von. "Jean Jacques Dessalines: Fundador de la nación haitiana." *Secuencia* 5 (May–August 1986): 112–122.

Grafenstein Gareis, Johanna von. *Nueva España en el Circuncaribe, 1779–1808: Revolución, competencia imperial y vínculos intercoloniales*. Mexico City: Universidad Nacional Autónoma de México, 1997.

Granados, Luis Fernando. *En el espejo haitiano: Los indios del Bajío y el colapso del orden colonial en América Latina*. Mexico City: Ediciones Era, 2016.

Greer, Margaret R., Walter Mignolo, and Maureen Quilligan, eds. *Re-Reading the Black Legend: The Discourses of Religious and Racial Difference in the Renaissance Empires*. Chicago: University of Chicago Press, 2007.

Gruzinski, Serge. *Images at War: Mexico from Columbus to Blade Runner (1492–2019)*. Translated by Heather MacLean. Durham, NC: Duke University Press, 2001.

Guenther, Lisa. "An Abolitionism Worthy of the Name: From the Death Penalty to the Prison Industrial Complex." In *Deconstructing the Death Penalty: Derrida's Seminars and the New Abolitionism*, edited by Kelly Oliver and Stephanie M. Straub, 239–258. New York: Fordham University Press, 2018.

Güereca Durán, Raquel. *Milicias indígenas en la Nueva España: Reflexiones del derecho indiano sobre los derechos de guerra*. Mexico City: Universidad Nacional Autónoma de México, Instituto de Investigaciones Jurídicas, 2016.

Guerra, Francois-Xavier. *Modernidad e independencia: Ensayos sobre las revoluciones hispánicas*. Mexico City: Fondo de Cultura Económica, 1992.

"Guerra de castas." *El Monitor Republicano*, March 25, 1849.

"Guerra de castas." *El Universal: Periódico independiente*, December 8, 1848. http://www.hndm.unam.mx.

Guha, Ranajit. "The Prose of Counter-Insurgency." In *Selected Subaltern Studies*, edited by Ranajit Guha and Gayatri Chakravorty Spivak, 45–86. Oxford: Oxford University Press, 1988.

Hale, Charles A. "Jose María Luis Mora and the Structure of Mexican Liberalism." *Hispanic American Historical Review* 45 (1965): 196–227.

Hale, Charles A. *Liberalismo mexicano en la época de Mora*. Mexico City: Siglo XXI Editores, 1999.

Hamill, Hugh M. *The Hidalgo Revolt: Prelude to Mexican Independence*. Gainesville: University of Florida Press, 1966.

Hamnett, Brian. *Roots of Insurgency: Mexican Regions, 1750–1824*. Cambridge: Cambridge University Press, 1986.

Harley, John Brian. "Maps, Knowledge, and Power." In *The Iconography of Landscape: Essays on the Symbolic Representation, Design and Use of Past Environments*, edited by Denis Cosgrove and Stephen Daniels, 277–312. New York: Cambridge University Press, 1988.

Harris, Cheryl L. "Whiteness as Property." *Harvard Law Review* 106, no. 8 (June 1993): 1707–1791.

Hartman, Saidiya. *Scenes of Subjection: Terror, Slavery, and Self-Making in Nineteenth-Century America*. New York: Oxford University Press, 1997.

Hartman, Saidiya. "Venus in Two Acts." *Small Axe* 12, no. 2 (2008): 1–14.

Hartman, Saidiya. *Wayward Lives, Beautiful Experiments: Intimate Histories of Riotous Black Girls, Troublesome Women, and Queer Radicals*. New York: Norton, 2019.

Haslip-Viera, Gabriel. *Crime and Punishment in Late Colonial Mexico City*. Albuquerque: University of New Mexico Press, 1999.

Hernández Souberville, José Armando. *Un rostro de Piedra para el poder: Las nuevas casas reales de San Luis Potosí, 1767–1827*. Mexico City: El Colegio de San Luis y el Colegio de Michoacán, 2013.

Hernández, Tanya Katerí. *Racial Subordination in Latin America: The Role of the State, Customary Law, and the New Civil Rights Response*. Cambridge: Cambridge University Press, 2012.

Hernández, R. Aída, and Shannon Speed. "De Ferguson a Ayotzinapa: Racismo y criminalización de la protesta social." *La Jornada*, December 17, 2014.

Hernández Torres, Yolopattli. "*Enfermedades políticas* de Hipólito Villarroel: Migración, higiene y orden social en la Nueva España ilustrada. (Ensayo crítico)." *Chasqui* 44, no. 1 (2015): 77–90.

Hernández y Dávalos, Juan E., ed. *Colección de documentos para la historia de la guerra de independencia de México de 1808 a 1821*. 6 vols. Mexico City: José María Sandoval, 1877–1882.

Herrejón Peredo, Carlos. *Del sermón al discurso cívico: México, 1760–1834*. Zamora, Mexico: Colegio de Michoacán, 2003.

Hickey, Donald R. "America's Response to the Slave Revolt in Haiti, 1791–1806." *Journal of the Early Republic* 4 (1982): 361–379.

Higuera Bonfil, Antonio. *Quintana Roo entre tiempos*. Chetumal, Mexico: Universidad de Quintana Roo, 1997.

Holt, Thomas. "Marking: Race, Race-Making, and the Writing of History." In

American Historians Interpret the Past, edited by Anthony Molho and Gordon S. Wood, 107–119. Princeton, NJ: Princeton University Press, 1998.
Hu de Hart, Evelyn. *Yaqui Resistance and Survival: The Struggle for Land and Autonomy, 1821–1910*. Madison: University of Wisconsin Press, 1984.
Humboldt, Alexander von. *Political Essay on the Kingdom of New Spain*. Vol. 2. Translated from the French by John Black. New York: I. Riley, 1811.
Hussain, Nasser. *The Jurisprudence of Emergency: Colonialism and the Rule of Law*. Ann Arbor: University of Michigan Press, 2003.
Ibsen, Kristine. "The Hiding Places of My Power: Sebastiana Josefa de la Santísima Trinidad and the Hagiographic Representation of the Body in Colonial Spanish America." *Colonial Latin American Review* 7, no. 2 (1998): 251–270.
Illades, Carlos. "Poblamiento y colonización: Las políticas públicas, 1854–1910." In *México en el siglo XIX*, 134–147. Vol. 3 of *El poblamiento de México: Una visión histórico demográfica*, edited by Consejo Nacional de Población. Mexico City: Secretaría de Gobernación/Consejo Nacional de Población, 1993.
Ince, Onur Ulas. "Primitive Accumulation, New Enclosures, and Global Land Grabs: A Theoretical Intervention." *Rural Sociology* 79, no. 1 (2014): 104–131. https://doi.org/10.1111/ruso.12025.
Instituto Nacional de Antropología e Historia. "Identifica INAH al primer naufragio esclavista de mayas en México." *Boletín* 354 (September 15, 2020). https://www.inah.gob.mx/boletines/9412-identifica-inah-al-primer-naufragio-esclavista-de-mayas-en-mexico.
Irving, "The 1790 Theater Season of the Mexico City Coliseo." *Hispanic Review* 19, no. 2 (1951): 104–120.
Jameson, Fredric. *Valences of the Dialectic*. London: Verso, 2010.
Jenson, Deborah. *Beyond the Slave Narrative: Politics, Sex, and Manuscripts in the Haitian Revolution*. Liverpool: Liverpool University Press, 2011.
Johnson, Ronald Angelo. "Haiti's Connection to Early America: Beyond the Revolution." *History Compass* 16, no. 3 (2018). https://doi.org/10.1111/hic3.12442.
Joseph, Gilbert M. "From Caste War to Class War: The Historiography of Modern Yucatán (c. 1750–1940)." *Hispanic American Historical Review*, no. 65 (1985): 111–134.
Joseph, Gilbert M. *Rediscovering the Past at Mexico's Periphery: Essays on the History of Modern Yucatán*. Tuscaloosa: University of Alabama Press, 1986.
Joseph, Gilbert M. *Revolution from Without: Yucatán, Mexico, and the United States, 1880–1924*. Durham, NC: Duke University Press, 1988.
Joseph, Gilbert M., and Daniel Nugent, eds. *Everyday Forms of State Formation: Revolution and the Negotiation of Rule in Modern Mexico*. Durham, NC: Duke University Press, 1994.
Joseph, Gilbert M., and Jürgen Buchenau. *Mexico's Once and Future Revolution: Social Upheaval and the Challenge of Rule since the Late Nineteenth Century*. Durham, NC: Duke University Press, 2013.
Kahn, Paul W. *Sacred Violence: Torture, Terror, and Sovereignty*. Ann Arbor: University of Michigan Press, 2008.

Kant, Immanuel. *The Conflict of Faculties / Der Streit der Fakultäten*. Translated and with an introduction by Mary J. Gregor. New York: Abaris, 1979.
Katz, Friedrich, ed. *Riot, Rebellion, and Revolution: Rural Social Conflict in Mexico*. Princeton, NJ: Princeton University Press, 1988.
Katzew, Ilona. *Casta Painting: Images of Race in Eighteenth-Century Mexico*. New Haven, CT: Yale University Press, 2004.
Kazanjian, David. *The Brink of Freedom: Improvising Life in the Nineteenth-Century Atlantic World*. Durham, NC: Duke University Press, 2016.
Kazanjian, David. *The Colonizing Trick: National Culture and Imperial Citizenship in Early America*. Minneapolis: University of Minnesota Press, 2003.
Knight, Alan. "Racism, Revolution, and Indigenismo: Mexico, 1910–1940." In *The Idea of Race in Latin America, 1870–1940*, edited by Richard Graham, 71–113. Austin: University of Texas Press, 1990.
Koeninger, Frieda. "*El negro y la blanca*: La censura de una obra abolicionista en Madrid y México." *Dieciocho: Hispanic Enlightenment* 37, no. 1 (Spring 2014): 123–138.
Koeninger, Frieda. "Santos Diez Gonzalez, Civil Censor: Balancing the Theory and Practice of Theater Reform in Madrid, 1788–1804," *Restoration and 18th Century Theatre Research* 29, no. 2 (Winter 2014): 9–26.
Konetzke, Richard, ed. *Colección de documentos para la historia de la formación de Hispanoamérica, 1493–1810*. 3 vols. Madrid: Consejo Superior de Investigaciones Científicas, 1953–1962.
Kuethe, Allan J. *The Spanish Atlantic World in the Eighteenth Century: War and the Bourbon Reforms, 1713–1796*. Cambridge: Cambridge University Press, 2014.
Kwass, Michael. *Privilege and the Politics of Taxation in Eighteenth Century France: Liberté, Egalité, Fiscalité*. Cambridge: Cambridge University Press, 2006.
La cuarta guerra mundial (Subcomandante Insurgente Marcos, Noviembre de 1999) / Símbolos (Eduardo Galeano, Octubre del 2001). Mexico: CCD Defensores de la República - Frente Zapatista de Liberación Nacional, 2001. Pamphlet accessed through Princeton University's Digital Archive of Latin American and Caribbean Ephemera, https://lae.princeton.edu/catalog/f595d292-6b98-46a6-9d6e-916 2457ba288?locale=en#?c=0&m=0&s=0&cv=0&xywh=1345%2C5399%2C3982 %2C3599.
Ladd, Doris M. *The Making of a Strike: Mexican Silver Workers' Struggles in Real del Monte 1766–1775*. Lincoln: University of Nebraska Press, 1988.
Lane, Jill. *Blackface Cuba, 1840–1895*. Philadelphia: University of Pennsylvania Press, 2005.
Lasso, Marixa. *Myths of Harmony: Race and Republicanism during the Age of Revolution in Colombia*. Pittsburgh, PA: University of Pittsburgh Press, 2007.
Lockhart, James. *The Nahuas after the Conquest*. Stanford, CA: Stanford University Press, 1992.
Lomnitz, Claudio. *Deep Mexico, Silent Mexico: An Anthropology of Nationalism*. Minneapolis: University of Minnesota Press, 2001.
Lomnitz, Claudio. *El antisemitismo y la ideología de la Revolución Mexicana*. Translated by Mario Zamudio. Mexico City: Fondo de Cultura Económica, 2012.

Lomnitz, Claudio. "Mexico's Race Problem and the Real Story behind Fox's Faux Pas." *Boston Review*, November–December 2005.

Lomnitz, Claudio. *The Return of Comrade Ricardo Flores Magón*. Brooklyn, NY: Zone Books, 2014.

López de Cancelada, Juan. *Código formado por los negros de la isla de Santo Domingo de la parte francesa hoi estado de Hayti, sancionado por Henrique Cristoval, presidente y generalísimo*. Cádiz, Spain: Quintana, 1810.

López de Cancelada, Juan. *Vida de J. J. Dessalines, Gefe de los negros de Santo Domingo, con notas muy circunstanciadas sobre el origen, carácter, atrocidades de los principales gefes de aquellos rebeldes desde el principio de la insurrección en 1791 traducida del francés por D.M.G.C. año de 1805*. Mexico City: Oficina de Mariano de Zúñiga y Ontíveros, 1806.

López Sarrelangue, Delfina. *La nobleza indígena de Pátzcuaro en la época virreinal*. Morelia: Morevallado, 1999.

Loveman, Brian. *The Constitution of Tyranny: Regimes of Exception in Spanish America*. Pittsburgh, PA: University of Pittsburgh Press, 1993.

Lowe, Lisa. "History Hesitant." *Social Text* 33, no. 4 (December 2015): 85–107. https://doi.org/10.1215/01642472-3315790.

Lowe, Lisa. *The Intimacies of Four Continents*. Durham, NC: Duke University Press, 2015.

Lucena Salmoral, Manuel. *La esclavitud en la América española*. Warsaw: University of Warsaw CESLA, 2002.

Lucena Salmoral, Manuel. *Los códigos negros de la América Española*. Alcalá, Spain: Universidad Alcalá y Ediciones UNESCO, 1996.

Lund, Joshua. *The Mestizo State: Reading Race in Modern Mexico*. Minneapolis: University of Minnesota Press, 2012.

Lund, Joshua. "They Were Not a Barbarous Tribe." *Journal of Latin American Cultural Studies* 12, no. 2 (2003): 171–189.

Lytle Hernández, Kelly. *City of Inmates: Conquest, Rebellion, and the Rise of Human Caging in Los Angeles 1771–1965*. Chapel Hill: University of North Carolina Press, 2017.

Macías Richard, Carlos. *Nueva frontera mexicana: Milicia, burocracia y ocupación territorial en Quintana Roo, 1902–1927*. Mexico City: Consejo Nacional de Ciencia y Tecnología/Universidad de Quintana Roo, 1997.

Mallon, Florencia E. *Peasant and Nation: The Making of Postcolonial Mexico and Peru*. Berkeley: University of California Press, 1995.

Mañón, Manuel. *Historia del teatro principal de México*. Mexico City: Instituto Nacional de Bellas Artes, 2013.

Marichal, Carlos. *Bankruptcy of Empire: Mexican Silver and the Wars between Spain, Britain and France, 1760–1810*. Cambridge: Cambridge University Press, 2007.

Marino, Daniela. "El afán de recaudar y la dificultad en reformar: El tributo indígena en la Nueva España." In *De colonia a nación: Impuestos y política en México, 1750–1860*, edited by Carlos Marichal and Daniela Marino, 61–84. Mexico City: El Colegio de México, 2001.

Martínez, Jennifer. *The Slave Trade and the Origins of International Human Rights Law.* Oxford: Oxford University Press, 2012.

Martínez, María Elena. "The Black Blood of New Spain: Limpieza de Sangre, Racial Violence, and Gendered Power in Early Colonial Mexico." *William and Mary Quarterly* 61, no. 3 (July 2004): 479–520.

Martínez, María Elena. *Genealogical Fictions: Limpieza de Sangre, Religion, and Gender in Colonial Mexico.* Stanford, CA: Stanford University Press, 2008.

Martín Puente, Cristina. "La Historia de Roma en la obra dramática de Ramón de la Cruz y Vicente Rodríguez de Arellano." *Cuadernos de Filología Clásica: Estudios Latinos* 32, no. 2 (2013): 347–360. https://doi.org/10.5209/rev_CFCL.2012.v32.n2.41030.

Marx, Karl. *Capital: A Critique of Political Economy.* Vol. 1. New York: Penguin, 1990.

Mathews, Jennifer P., and John R. Gust. *Sugarcane and Rum: The Bittersweet History of Labor and Life on the Yucatán Peninsula.* Tucson: University of Arizona Press, 2020.

Mbembe, Achille. "Necropolitics." *Public Culture* 15, no. 1 (Winter 2003): 11–40.

McClelland, Ivy Lilian. "The Comellan Conception of Stage-Realism." *Dieciocho: Hispanic Enlightenment* 1–2, no. 16 (1993): 111–117.

McClelland, Ivy Lilian. *Spanish Drama of Pathos 1750–1808.* Vol. 2. Toronto: University of Toronto Press.

Mendoza Vargas, Héctor. "Historia de la geografía en México siglo XIX." Undergraduate thesis, Universidad Nacional Autónoma de México, 1989.

Mendoza Vargas, Héctor. "Las opciones geográficas al inicio del México independiente." In *México a través de los mapas*, edited by Héctor Mendoza Vargas, 89–110. Mexico City: Instituto de Geografía, Universidad Nacional Autónoma de México; Plaza y Valdés Editores, 2000.

Menéndez, Carlos R. *Historia del infame y vergonzoso comercio de indios, vendidos a los esclavistas de Cuba por los políticos yucatecos, desde 1848 hasta 1861: Justificación de la revolución indígena de 1847. Documentos irrefutables que lo comprueban.* Mérida, Mexico: Talleres gráficos de La Revista de Yucatán, 1923.

Menéndez, Carlos R., ed. *Memorias de Don Buenaventura Vivó y la venta de indios yucatecos a Cuba.* Mérida, Mexico: Biblioteca de Historia del "Diario de Yucatán," 1923.

Mier, Fray Servando Teresa de. *Escritos inéditos.* Edited by Josep María Miquel I. Vergés and Hugo Díaz-Thomé. Mexico City: El Colegio de México, 1944.

Mier, Fray Servando Teresa de. *Historia de la revolución.* London: G. Glindon, 1813.

Mier, Fray Servando Teresa de. *Idea de la constitución.* Mexico City: Cuadernos Causa/Centro de Documentación Política, 1977.

"Migración China." *Diario Oficial del Gobierno Supremo de la República.* October 12, 1871.

Miller, Todd. *Empire of Borders: The Expansion of the US Border around the World.* New York: Verso, 2019.

Miller, William. "A Journey from British Honduras to Santa Cruz, Yucatan." *Proceedings of the Royal Geographical Society and Monthly Record of Geography* 11, no. 1 (January 1, 1889): 23–28.
Mills, Charles W. "Race and Global Justice." In *Empire, Race and Global Justice*, edited by Duncan Bell, 94–119. Cambridge: Cambridge University Press, 2019.
Milton, Cynthia E., and Ben Vinson III. "Counting Heads: Race and Non-native Tribute Policy in Colonial Spanish America." *Journal of Colonialism and Colonial History* 3, no. 3 (2002). https://doi.org/10.1353/cch.2002.0056.
Montejano y Aguiñaga, Rafael. *El Valle de Santa Isabel del Armadillo, San Luis Potosí*. San Luis Potosí, Mexico: Imprenta Evolución, 1964.
Mora, Arnulfo. "Amagan con desalojar a campesinos de Infiernillo." *Quadtradín*, February 15, 2014. https://www.quadratin.com.mx/sucesos/Amagan-con-desalojar-campesinos-de-Infiernillo/.
Mora, Mariana. "Ayotzinapa and the Criminalization of Racialized Poverty in La Montaña, Guerrero, Mexico." *Political and Legal Anthropology Review* 40, no. 1 (2017): 67–85. https://doi.org/10.1111/plar.12208.
Mora, Mariana. *Kuxlejal Politics: Indigenous Autonomy, Race, and Decolonizing Research in Zapatista Communities*. Austin: University of Texas Press, 2017.
Mora, Mariana. "La criminalización de la pobreza y los efectos estatales de seguridad neoliberal: Reflexiones desde la Montaña, Guerrero." *Revista de Estudos e Pesquisas sobre as Américas* 7, no. 2 (2013): 174–208. http://ojs.bce.unb.br/index.php/repam/article/view/10027/7340.
Moraña, Mabel, Enrique Dussel, and Carlos A. Jáuregui, eds. *Coloniality at Large: Latin America and the Postcolonial Debate*. Durham, NC: Duke University Press, 2008.
More, Anna. *Baroque Sovereignty: Carlos de Sigüenza y Góngora and the Creole Archive of Colonial Mexico*. Philadelphia: University of Pennsylvania Press, 2013.
Muro, Manuel. *Historia de San Luis Potosí*. Vol. 1. Mexico City: Sociedad Potosina de Estudios Históricos, 1973.
Naranjo Orovio, Consuelo. "La amenaza haitiana un miedo interesado: Poder y fomento de la población blanca en Cuba." In *El Rumor de Haití En Cuba: Temor, Raza y Rebeldía, 1789–1844*, edited by Ma. Dolores González-Ripoll Navarro, 83–177. Madrid: Consejo Superior de Investigaciones Científicas, 2004.
Navarrete Linares, Fernando. *México racista: Una denuncia*. Barcelona: Grijalbo, 2016.
Negri, Antonio. "The Political Monster: Naked Life and Power." In *In Praise of the Common: A Conversation on Philosophy and Politics*, edited by Cesare Casarino and Antonio Negri, 193–218. Minneapolis: University of Minnesota Press, 2008.
Nemser, Daniel. *Infrastructures of Race: Concentration and Biopolitics in Colonial Mexico*. Austin: University of Texas Press, 2017.
Nemser, Daniel. "Primitive Spiritual Accumulation and the Colonial Extraction Economy." *Política Común* 5 (2014). http://dx.doi.org/10.3998/pc.12322227.0005.003.

Nemser, Daniel. "Triangulating Blackness: Mexico City, 1612." *Mexican Studies / Estudios Mexicanos* 33, no. 3 (Fall 2017): 344–366.
Neocleous, Mark, and George Rigakos. "On Pacification: Introduction to the Special Issue." *Socialist Studies/Études Socialistes* 9, no. 2 (2013). https://www.acade mia.edu/12192672/On_Pacification_Introduction_to_the_Special_Issue.
Novelo, Victoria. *Yucatecos en Cuba: Etnografía de una migración.* Mexico City: CIESAS, 2009.
O'Gorman, Edmundo. *La invención de América: Investigación acerca de la estructura histórica del Nuevo Mundo y del sentido de su devenir.* 4th ed. Mexico City: Fondo de Cultura Económica, 2006.
O'Hara, Matthew D., and Andrew B. Fisher, eds. *Imperial Subjects: Race and Identity in Colonial Latin America.* Durham, NC: Duke University Press, 2009.
Ojeda, Jorge Victoria, and Jorge Canto Alcocer. *San Fernando Aké: Microhistoria de una comunidad afroamericana en Yucatán.* Mérida, Mexico: Universidad Autónoma de Yucatán, 2006.
Olavarría y Ferrari, Enrique de. *Reseña histórica del teatro en México.* Vol. 1. Mexico City: La Europea, 1895.
Olund, Eric N. "From Savage Space to Governable Space: The Extension of United States Judicial Sovereignty over Indian Country in the Nineteenth Century." *Cultural Geographies* 9, no. 2 (April 2002): 129–157.
Olveda Legaspi, Jaime. "La abolicion de la esclavitud en Mexico, 1810–1917." *Signos Históricos* 15, no. 29 (2013): 26–27.
Omi, Michael, and Howard Winant. *Racial Formation in the United States.* London: Routledge, 2014.
Ortíz Escamilla, Juan. "Las fuerzas militares y el Proyecto de Estado en México, 1767–1835." In *Cincuenta años de historia en México*, vol. 2, edited by Alicia Hernández Chávez and Manuel Miño Grijalva, 261–282. Mexico City: El Colegio de México, 1991.
Osborne, Peter. *The Politics of Time: Modernity and Avant-Garde.* London: Verso, 1995.
Ota Mishima, María Elena, ed. *Destino México: Un estudio de las migraciones asiáticas a México, siglos XIX y XX.* Mexico City: El Colegio de México, 1997.
O'Toole, Rachel Sarah. *Bound Lives: Africans, Indians, and the Making of Race in Colonial Peru.* Pittsburgh, PA: University of Pittsburgh Press, 2012.
Padilla Ramos, Raquel. *Yucatán, fin del sueño yaqui: El tráfico de los yaquis y el otro triunvirato.* Hermosillo, Mexico: Gobierno del Estado de Sonora, Secretaría de Educación y Cultura, Instituto Sonorense de Cultura, 1995.
Paley, Dawn Marie. "The Tren Maya and the Remaking of Mexico's South." Toward Freedom, February 1, 2020. https://towardfreedom.org/story/the-tren-maya -and-the-remaking-of-mexicos-south-border/.
Palmer, Colin A. *Slaves of the White God: Blacks in Mexico, 1570–1650.* Cambridge, MA: Harvard University Press, 1976.

Paniagua Pérez, Jesús. *La revolución haitiana en la obra de Juan López de Cancelada*. León, Spain: Universidad de León, 2016.
Paso y Troncoso, Francisco del. *Las guerras con las tribus yaqui y mayo de Sonora*. Mexico City: Tipografía del Departamento del Estado Mayor, 1905.
Patch, Robert. *Maya and Spaniard in Yucatan, 1648–1812*. Stanford, CA: Stanford University Press, 1993.
Pérez Estévez, Rosa María. *El problema de los vagos en la España del siglo XVII*. Madrid: Confederación Española de Cajas de Ahorros, 1976.
Pietschmann, Horst. *Las reformas borbónicas y el sistema de intendencias en Nueva España: Un estudio político administrativo*. Mexico City: Fondo de Cultura Económica, 1996.
Popkin, Jeremy D. *You Are All Free: The Haitian Revolution and the Abolition of Slavery*. New York: Cambridge University Press, 2010.
Priestly, Herbert Ingram. *José de Gálvez, Visitor General of New Spain (1765–1771)*. Berkeley: University of California Press, 1912.
Proctor, Frank T., III. *Damned Notions of Liberty: Slavery, Culture, and Power in Colonial México 1640–1769*. Albuquerque: University of New Mexico Press, 2010.
Programa para la seguridad nacional 2014–2018: Una política multidimensional para México en el siglo XXI. Mexico City: Consejo de Seguridad Nacional, Presidencia de la República, 2014.
"Pueblos del Istmo (APOYO): La creación de Zonas Económicas Especiales es la validación de política de despojo." Centro de Medios Libres, March 18, 2017. https://www.centrodemedioslibres.org/2017/03/18/pueblos-del-istmo-apoyo-la-creacion-de-las-zonas-economicas-especiales-es-la-validacion-de-politica-de-despojo/.
Quezada, Sergio. *Los pies de la república*. Mexico City: CIESAS, 1997.
Quijada, Mónica. "From Spain to New Spain: Revisiting the Potestas Populi in Hispanic Political Thought." *Mexican Studies / Estudios Mexicanos* 24, no. 2 (Summer 2008): 185–219.
Quijano, Aníbal. "Coloniality of Power, Eurocentrism, and Latin America." *Nepantla: Views from the South* 1, no. 3 (2000): 533–580.
Quintal Martín, Fidelio. *Correspondencia de la Guerra de Castas: Epistolario documental, 1843–1866*. Mérida, Mexico: Universidad Autónoma de Yucatán, 1992.
Rabasa, José. *Inventing America: Spanish Historiography and the Formation of Eurocentrism*. Norman: University of Oklahoma Press, 1993.
Ramayo Lanz, Teresa. *Los mayas pacíficos de Campeche*. Campeche, Mexico: Universidad Autónoma de Campeche, 1996.
Ramos Smith, Maya, ed. *Censura y teatro novohispano (1539–1822): Ensayos y antología de documentos*. Mexico City: CONACULTA, 1998.
Rappaport, Joanne. *The Disappearing Mestizo: Configuring Difference in the Colonial New Kingdom of Granada*. Durham, NC: Duke University Press, 2014.
Recopilación de leyes de los Reynos de las Indias, mandadas imprimir y publicar por

la Magestad Católica del Rey Don Cárlos II. Nuestro Señor [. . .]. 4th ed. 3 vols. Madrid: La viuda de D. Joaquín Ibarra, 1791.
Reed, Nelson. The Caste War of Yucatán. Rev. ed. Stanford, CA: Stanford University Press, 2001.
Reglamento e instrucción para los presidios que se han de formas en la línea de frontera de la Nueva España resuelto por el rey nuestro señor en cédula de 10 de setiembre de 1772. Mexico City: Oficina de la Águila dirigida por José Ximeno, 1834.
Reina, Leticia. Las rebeliones campesinas en México, 1819–1906. Mexico City: Siglo XXI Editores, 1980.
Restall, Matthew. The Black Middle: Africans, Mayas, and Spaniards in Colonial Yucatán. Stanford, CA: Stanford University Press, 2009.
Restall, Matthew. Maya Conquistador. Boston: Beacon, 1998.
Restall, Matthew. The Maya World. Stanford, CA: Stanford University Press, 1997.
Reyes Palacios, Felipe. "Fernández de Lizardi y la comedia lacrimosa." In Actas del XIV Congreso de la Asociación Internacional de Hispanistas, edited by Isaías Lerner, Robert Nival, and Alejandro Alonso, vol. 4, 581–588. Newark, DE: AIH/Juan de la Cuesta, 2004.
Rodríguez, José Manuel. Cómo deben haberse los vasallos con sus reyes: Plática doctrinal predicada por Joseph Manuel Rodríguez a los terceros de la misma orden. Mexico City: Imprenta Real Superior del Gobierno de Joseph Antonio de Hogal, 1768.
Rodríguez de Arellano, Vicente. El negro y la blanca: Melodrama en dos actos. Madrid: J. Sánchez, 1802.
Rodríguez O., Jaime. We Are Now the True Spaniards. Stanford, CA: Stanford University Press, 2012.
Rodríguez Piña, Javier. Guerra de castas: La venta de indios mayas a Cuba. Mexico City: Consejo Nacional para la Cultura y las Artes, 1990.
Rojas Rodríguez, Julio David. "Trabajo coactivo en Cuba: Inmigración y situación legal de los mayas yucatecos contratados, 1847–1860." Master's thesis, Universidad Iberoamericana (in progress).
Romero Peña, María Mercedes. El teatro de la guerra de independencia. Madrid: Fundación Universitaria Española, 2007.
Rosemblatt, Karin Alejandra. The Science and Politics of Race in Mexico and the United States, 1910–1950. Chapel Hill: University of North Carolina Press, 2018.
Rugeley, Terry. "The Caste War in Guatemala." Saastun: Revista de Cultura Maya, no. 3 (December 1997): 94.
Rugeley, Terry. "The Maya Elites of Nineteenth-Century Yucatán." Ethnohistory 42, no. 3 (Summer 1995): 477–493.
Rugeley, Terry. Maya Wars: Ethnographic Accounts from Nineteenth-Century Yucatán. Norman: University of Oklahoma Press, 2001.
Rugeley, Terry. Of Wonders and Wise Men: Religion and Popular Cultures in Southeast Mexico, 1800–1876. Austin: University of Texas Press, 2001.

Rugeley, Terry. *Rebellion Now and Forever: Mayas, Hispanics, and Caste War Violence in Yucatán, 1800–1880*. Stanford, CA: Stanford University Press, 2009.
Rugeley, Terry. "Rural Popular Violence and the Origins of the Caste War." *The Americas* 53, no. 4 (April 1997): 480.
Rugeley, Terry. *Yucatán's Maya Peasantry and the Origins of the Caste War*. Austin: University of Texas Press, 1996.
Sá Carvalho, Carolina. "How to See a Scar: Humanitarianism and Colonial Iconography in the Putumayo Rubber Boom." *Journal of Latin American Cultural Studies: Travesía* 27, no. 3 (2018): 371–397.
Sabau, Ana. "The Paths of Unfreedom: Indentured Labor from Yucatán to Cuba." *Revista de Estudios Hispánicos* 53, no. 2 (2019): 537–561.
Saldaña-Portillo, María Josefina. "'How Many Mexicans [Is] a Horse Worth?' The League of United Latin American Citizens, Desegregation Cases, and Chicano Historiography." *South Atlantic Quarterly* 107, no. 4 (2008): 809–831.
Saldaña-Portillo, María Josefina. *Indian Given: Racial Geographies across Mexico and the United States*. Durham, NC: Duke University Press, 2016.
Saldaña-Portillo, María Josefina. *The Revolutionary Imagination in the Americas and the Age of Development*. Durham, NC: Duke University Press, 2003.
"Salinas de Gortari—6 de enero 1994." YouTube video. Posted January 27, 2010, by EstrategiaElectoral. Accessed at "Video: El discurso inicial de Salinas frente al EZLN." Aristegui Noticias, January 6, 1994. https://aristeguinoticias.com/3012/mexico/video-el-discurso-inicial-de-salinas-frente-al-ezln/.
Salvatore, Ricardo D., and Carlos Aguirre. "Colonies of Settlement or Places of Banishment and Torment? Penal Colonies and Convict Labour in Latin America, c. 1800–1940." In *Global Convict Labour*, edited by Christian Giuseppe De Vito and Alex Lichtenstein, 273–309. Leiden, Netherlands: Brill, 2015.
Sánchez, Rafael. *Dancing Jacobins: A Venezuelan Genealogy of Latin American Populism*. New York: Fordham University Press, 2016.
Sanders, James E. *The Vanguard of the Atlantic World: Creating Modernity, Nation, and Democracy in Nineteenth-Century Latin America*. Durham, NC: Duke University Press, 2014.
Sarmiento, Domingo F. *Conflicto y armonía de las razas en América*. Buenos Aires: D. Tuñez, 1883.
Sarmiento, Domingo Faustino. *Civilización y barbarie: Vida de Facundo Quiroga*. Santiago, Chile: Imprenta del Progreso, 1845.
Schmitt, Carl. *The Nomos of the Earth in the International Law of the Jus Publicum Europaeum*. Translated by G. L. Ulmen. New York: Telos, 2006.
Schmitt, Carl. *Political Theology: Four Chapters on the Concept of Sovereignty*. Translated by George Schwab. Cambridge, MA: MIT Press, 1985.
Schreffler, Michael. *The Art of Allegiance: Visual Culture and Imperial Power in Baroque New Spain*. University Park: Pennsylvania State University Press, 2007.
Schuller, Kyla. *The Biopolitics of Feeling: Race, Sex, and Science in the Nineteenth Century*. Durham, NC: Duke University Press, 2018.

Scott, James C. *Domination and the Arts of Resistance: Hidden Transcripts.* New Haven, CT: Yale University Press, 1990.

Scott, James C. *Seeing Like a State: How Certain Schemes to Improve the Human Condition Have Failed.* New Haven, CT: Yale University Press, 1998.

Seed, Patricia. *Ceremonies of Possession in Europe's Conquest of the New World, 1492–1640.* Cambridge: Cambridge University Press, 1995.

Serulnikov, Sergio. *Revolution in the Andes: The Age of Tupac Amaru.* Durham, NC: Duke University Press, 2013.

Servin, Elisa, Leticia Reina, and John Tutino, eds. *Cycles of Conflict, Centuries of Change: Crisis, Reform, and Revolution in Mexico.* Durham, NC: Duke University Press, 2007.

Sierra O'Reilly, Justo [José Turrisa, pseud.]. *La hija del judío.* Vol. 2. Jalapa, Mexico: Universidad Veracruzana, 2008.

Sigüenza y Góngora, Carlos de. *Alboroto y motín de México del 8 de junio de 1692.* Edited by Andrés de Pez and Irving A. Leonard. Mexico City: Talleres gráficos del Museo Nacional de Arqueología, Historia y Etnografía, 1932.

Silva, Denise Ferreira da. *Toward a Global Idea of Race.* Minneapolis: University of Minnesota Press, 2007.

Silva Prada, Natalia. *La política de una rebelión: Los indígenas frente al tumulto de 1692 en la Ciudad de México.* Mexico City: El Colegio de México, 2007.

Singh, Nikhil Pal. *Race and America's Long War.* Berkeley: University of California Press, 2017.

Soriano, Kari. "Geografía militar y humana: La Guerra de castas en *Cecilio Chi,* de José Severo del Castillo." In *Entre El Humo y La Niebla: Guerra y Cultura en América Latina,* edited by Javier Uriarte and Felipe Martínez Pinzón, 29–54. Nueva América. Pittsburg, PA: International Institute of Latin American Literature, University of Pittsburg, 2016.

Spell, Jefferson Rea. *The Life and Works of José Joaquín Fernández de Lizardi.* Series in Romantic Languages and Literatures 23. Philadelphia: University of Pennsylvania Press, 1931.

Stein, Barbara H., and Stanley J. Stein. *Apogee of Empire: Spain and New Spain in the Age of Charles III.* Baltimore, MD: Johns Hopkins University Press, 2003.

Stoler, Ann Laura. *Along the Archival Grain: Epistemic Anxieties and Colonial Common Sense.* Princeton, NJ: Princeton University Press, 2009.

Stoler, Ann Laura. *Duress: Imperial Durabilities in Our Times.* Durham, NC: Duke University Press, 2016.

Stoler, Ann Laura. "Imperial Debris: Reflections on Ruins and Ruination." *Cultural Anthropology* 23, no. 2 (2008): 191–219. https://doi.org/10.1111/j.1548-1360.2008.00007.x.

Sue, Christina A. *Land of the Cosmic Race: Race Mixture, Racism, and Blackness in Mexico.* New York: Oxford University Press, 2013.

Sullivan, Paul. "John Carmichael: Life and Design on the Frontier in Central America." *Revista Mexicana del Caribe* 5, no. 10 (2000): 6–88.

Sullivan, Paul. *¿Para qué lucharon los mayas? Vida y muerte de Bernardino Cen*. Quintana Roo, Mexico: Universidad de Quintana Roo, 1998.
Sullivan, Paul. *Unfinished Conversations: Mayas and Foreigners between Two Wars*. New York: Knopf, 1989.
Surwilio, Lisa. *Monsters by Trade: Slave Traffickers in Modern Spanish Literature and Culture*. Stanford, CA: Stanford University Press, 2014.
Taylor, William B. *Drinking, Homicide, and Rebellion in Colonial Mexican Villages*. Stanford, CA: Stanford University Press, 1979. Spanish edition: *Embriaguez, homicidio y rebelión en las poblaciones coloniales mexicanas*. Mexico City: Fondo de Cultura Económica, 1987.
Terreros y Pando, Esteban de. *Diccionario castellano con las voces de ciencias y artes y sus correspondientes en las tres lenguas francesa, latina é italiana*. Vol. 3. Madrid: Viuda de Ibarra, Hijos y Compañía, 1788.
Thompson, Guy P. C. "Bulwarks of Patriotic Liberalism: The National Guard, Philharmonic Corps and Patriotic Juntas in México 1847–88." *Journal of Latin American Studies* 22, no. 1 (March 1990): 31–68.
Thomson, Sinclair. "Sovereignty Disavowed: The Tupac Amaru Revolution in the Atlantic World." *Atlantic Studies* 13, no. 3 (2016): 407–431.
Thomson, Sinclair. *We Alone Will Rule: Native Andean Politics in the Age of Insurgency*. Madison: University of Wisconsin Press, 2002.
Tovar, Pantaleón. *Historia Parlamentaria del cuarto congreso constitucional*. Vol. 1. Mexico City: Imprenta de I. Cumplido, 1872.
Trouillot, Michel-Rolph. *Silencing the Past: Power and the Production of History*. Boston: Beacon, 1995.
Tsing, Anna. *Friction: An Ethnography of Global Connection*. Princeton, NJ: Princeton University Press, 2011.
Turner, John Kenneth. *Barbarous Mexico*. Chicago: Charles H. Kerr, 1910.
Tutino, John. *From Insurrection to Revolution in Mexico: Social Bases of Agrarian Violence, 1750–1940*. Princeton, NJ: Princeton University Press, 1986.
Tutino, John. *Making a New World: Founding Capitalism in the Bajío and Spanish North America*. Durham, NC: Duke University Press, 2011.
Twinam, Ann. *Purchasing Whiteness: Pardos, Mulattos, and the Quest for Social Mobility in the Spanish Indies*. Stanford, CA: Stanford University Press, 2015.
Urías Horcasitas, Beatriz. *Historias secretas del racismo en México, 1920–1950*. Mexico City: Tusquets, 2007.
Valentini, Philipp. "A New and an Ancient Map of Yucatán." *Magazine of American History* 3 (1879): 295–299.
Van Young, Eric. *La crisis del orden colonial: Estructura agraria y rebeliones populares en la Nueva España, 1750–1821*. Mexico City: Alianza Editorial, 1992.
Van Young, Eric. *The Other Rebellion: Popular Violence, Ideology, and the Struggle for Mexican Independence, 1810–1821*. Stanford, CA: Stanford University Press, 2001.
Velázquez, María del Carmen. *El estado de guerra en Nueva España, 1760–1808*. México, Colegio de México, Centro de Estudios Históricos, 1997.

Velázquez Delgado, Graciela. "La ciudadanía en las constituciones mexicanas del siglo XIX: Inclusión y exclusión político-social en la democracia mexicana." *Acta Universitaria* 18, no. 1 (September 2008): 41–49. https://doi.org/10.15174/au.2008.131.

Veracini, Lorenzo. *Settler Colonialism*. London: Palgrave Macmillan, 2010.

Verdesio, Gustavo. "Colonialismo acá y allá: Reflexiones sobre la teoría y la práctica de los estudios coloniales a través de fronteras culturales." *Cuadernos del CILHA* 13, no. 17 (2012): 176–192.

Verdesio, Gustavo. "Endless Dispossession: The Charrua Re-emergence in Uruguay in the Light of Settler Colonialism." *Journal of Settler Colonial Studies* (2020): 1–26. https://doi.org/10.1080/2201473X.2020.1823752.

Verdesio, Gustavo. "Invisible at a Glance: Indigenous Cultures of the Past, Ruins, Archaeological Sites, and Our Regimes of Visibility." In *Ruins of Modernity*, edited by Julia Hell and Andreas Schönle, 339–354. Durham, NC: Duke University Press, 2009.

Verna, Paul. *Petión y Bolivar: Cuarenta años (1790–1830) de relaciones haitianovenezolanas y su aporte a la emancipación de Hispanoamérica*. Caracas: Ministerio de Educación, 1969.

Villalobos González, Martha Herminia. *El bosque sitiado: Asaltos armados, concesiones forestales y estrategias de resistencia durante la Guerra de Castas*. Mexico City: Conaculta/CIESAS/INAH/Porrúa, 2006.

Villa Rojas, Alfonso. *Los elegidos de Dios: Etnografía de los mayas de Quintana Roo*. Mexico City: Instituto Nacional Indigenista, 1978.

Villa Rojas, Alfonso. *The Maya of East-Central Quintana Roo*. Washington, DC: Carnegie Institution, 1943.

Villarroel, Hipólito. *Enfermedades políticas que padece la capital de esta Nueva España*. Mexico City: Porrúa, 1999.

Viñas, David. *Indios, ejército y frontera*. Buenos Aires: Siglo XXI Editores, 1982.

Vinson, Ben, III. "Articulating Space: The Free-Colored Military Establishment in Colonial Mexico for the Conquest to Independence." *Callaloo* 27, no. 1 (Winter 2004): 150–171.

Vinson, Ben, III. *Bearing Arms for His Majesty: The Free-Colored Militia in Colonial Mexico*. Stanford, CA: Stanford University Press, 2003.

Vinson, Ben, III. *Before Mestizaje: The Frontiers of Race and Caste in Colonial Mexico*. Cambridge: Cambridge University Press, 2017.

Vinson, Ben, III. "From Dawn 'til Dusk: Black Labor in Late Colonial Mexico." In *Black Mexico: Race and Society from Colonial to Modern Times*, edited by Ben Vinson III and Matthew Restall, 96–135. Albuquerque: University of New Mexico Press, 2009.

Vinson, Ben, III, and Bobby Vaughn. *Afroméxico: Herramientas para la historia*. Mexico City: Fondo de Cultura Económica, 2004.

Viqueira Albán, Juan Pedro. *¿Relajados o reprimidos? Diversiones públicas y vida so-*

cial en la Ciudad de México durante el Siglo de Las Luces. Mexico City: Fondo de Cultura Económica, 1987.
Virilio, Paul. *Speed and Politics: An Essay on Dromology*. Foreign Agents. New York: Columbia University Press, 1986.
Viveros, Germán. *Manifestaciones teatrales en Nueva España*. Mexico City: Universidad Nacional Autónoma de México, 2005.
Viveros, Germán. *Talía novohispana: Espectáculos, temas y textos teatrales dieciochescos*. Mexico City: Universidad Nacional Autónoma de México, 1996.
Viveros, Germán. *Teatro dieciochesco de Nueva España*. Mexico City: Universidad Nacional Autónoma de México, 1990.
Vivó, Buenaventura. *Memorias de Don Buenaventura Vivó, ministro de Méjico en España durante los años 1853, 1854 y 1855*. Madrid, Spain: M. Rivadeneyra, 1856.
Wang, Jackie. *Carceral Capitalism*. Intervention 21. South Pasadena, CA: Semiotext(e), 2018; distributed by MIT Press.
Warren, Richard. *Vagrants and Citizens: Politics and the Masses in Mexico City from Colony to Republic*. Wilmington, DE: SR Books, 2001.
Weber, David J. *Bárbaros: Spaniards and Their Savages in the Age of Enlightenment*. New Haven, CT: Yale University Press, 2005.
Wells, Allen, and Gilbert M. Joseph. *Summer of Discontent, Seasons of Upheaval: Elite Politics and Rural Insurgency in Yucatán, 1876–1915*. Stanford, CA: Stanford University Press, 1996.
Williams, Gareth. *The Mexican Exception: Sovereignty, Police, and Democracy*. New York: Palgrave Macmillan, 2011.
Williams, Robert A. *The American Indian in Western Legal Thought: The Discourses of Conquest*. Oxford: Oxford University Press, 1992.
Wolfe, Patrick. "Settler Colonialism and the Elimination of the Native." *Journal of Genocide Research* 8, no. 4 (2006): 387–409. https://doi.org/10.1080/14623520601056240.
Wolfe, Patrick. *Traces of History: Elementary Structures of Race*. London: Verso, 2016.
Young, Carol M. "Lizardi's *El negro sensible*." *CLA Journal* 24, no. 3 (March 1981): 369–375.
Yun, Lisa. *The Coolie Speaks: Chinese Indentured Laborers and African Slaves of Cuba*. Philadelphia, PA: Temple University Press, 2008.
Zavala, Lorenzo de. *Ensayo histórico de las revoluciones de México desde 1808 hasta 1830*. Mexico City: Imprenta a cargo de M. N. de la Vega, 1845.
Zavala, Oswaldo. *Los carteles no existen: Narcotráfico y cultura en México*. Barcelona: Malpaso, 2018.
Zea, Leopoldo. *El positivismo en México*. Mexico City: El Colegio de México, 1943.
Zeuske, Michael. "Humboldt y la comparación de las esclavitudes en América." *HiN* 6, no. 11 (2005): 65–89.

Index

Page numbers followed by f indicate illustrations.

Abad y Queipo, Manuel, 105, 107, 109, 123–124
abolition of *casta*, 2, 128
abolition of jails and tribute, 64–66
abolition of slavery: in Caracas, 130; and *El negro y la blanca*, 111, 112; in Haiti, 8, 83, 106, 120, 242n5, 249n8; Alexander von Humboldt on, 251n19; narratives around, 113; and Spanish American republics, 132–133
accretion, 7, 34
Acereto, Agustín, 152, 153–154
Adolphus, Edwin, 179
African laborers, 198, 200, 201
Agamben, Giorgio, 9, 11
Age of Revolution, 10
agriculture: and Caste War, 172, 175; and colonization, 197; and development, 176; and indigenous labor, 143, 162; and peonage system, 194–195; and racial hierarchy, 200; Hipólito Villarroel on, 74–75, 78–79. *See also specific crops*
Alamán, Lucas, 3
Alaniz, José Patricio, 53–54
alboroto, 59–60

Alencastre, Fernando de (Duke of Linares), 72
alliances: between American investors and Mexican elites, 194; and Bajío riots, 39, 54–55, 56, 58–60, 233n75; and Caste War, 155, 158–159, 267n21; and Haiti, 133; and Mexican popular uprisings, 26
Allure of the Archives (Farge), 54
Altamirano Velasco y Flores, Juan de, 238n50
Alto Perú, 1–2
American Magazine, 270–271n4
Anderson, Clare, 157
Andrade, José, 179
anomalous zones, 11, 40, 45, 146–147, 203, 232n42. *See also* legal anomaly; legal exception
anti-Black racism, 125–126
Antochiw, Michel, 180
Apache people, 3
Aranda, Count of, 35
archives: and *capitulaciones*, 60, 65; and cartography, 171; and Caste War, 165; and Cuban theater, 253–254n45; and Haitian Revolution, 107; incompleteness of, 54; and Maya indenture,

140; and race war paradigm, 5; reading against the grain, 107, 127; reading along the grain, 28; reading of, 236n10; of subaltern actors, 26; and Yucatán geography, 177–180
Argentina, 2, 197
Arnold, Channing, 271n7
Article 27 reform, 211
Asian laborers, 140, 196, 198, 199, 200–201, 207, 226n80
assimilation: and Asian workers, 201; and Bourbon Reform, 32; and cartography, 183–184; in *El negro y la blanca*, 114; in *Los misterios de Chan Santa Cruz*, 158–161; and *mestizaje*, 24, 207–208, 211; and repression, 20; and state violence, 14–15; and Zapatista movement, 211–212
Atlantic slave trade, 112, 113, 157
Atlas geográfico estadístico e histórico de la República Mexicana (García Cubas 1858), 168, 171–172
Aureoles, Silvano, 214–215
Ay, Manuel Antonio, 143
Aznar y Pérez, Andrés, 180, 182, 183–184

Bajío rebellion (1810), 105, 109–110, 122
Bajío riots (1767): and *capitulaciones*, 60–64; and colonial structure, 31–32; and José de Gálvez, 21; and mining industry, 10–11; and penality, 16–17; punitive expedition against, 40–41, 42; and race war paradigm, 7–8; and racial boundaries, 34–35; and whiteness, 46–51
Barbachano, Miguel, 147, 149, 151–152, 260n15, 269n43
barbarism: and abolitionism, 133; in *Barbarous Mexico*, 193–195; and Caste War, 155; in *Cecilio Chi*, 175; in *El negro y la blanca*, 114; Alexander von Humboldt on, 109, 146; and legal exception, 16; and Le Plongeon expedition, 178; and pacification, 23; and race war paradigm, 4, 190; and racialization, 20–21; Domingo Faustino Sarmiento on, 1–2; slavery as, 161; and trade in Maya indentured people, 149, 151, 153–154; and US-Mexico border tribes, 3; in *Vida de J. J. Dessalines*, 91–92; Hipólito Villarroel on, 78; and Yaqui deportations, 205–206
Barbarous Mexico (Turner 1908), 193, 194–195, 205–206, 270–271n4
Barradas, Isidro, 132
Barrera, José María, 190
Barrera, Pantaleón, 158, 160, 161
Belize, 23, 143, 155, 159. *See also* British Honduras
Benton, Lauren, 39, 146–147
Berendt, Karl Hermann, 178, 180
Biassou, Georges, 101–102
biopolitics, 157, 214, 224–225n70
Black bodies, 88–89, 129–130
blackface, 116, 253n41
"Black Jacobins" of Haiti, 112
Black Legend, 10, 221n32
Blackness: and barbarism, 92; and class, 225n71; in *El negro sensible*, 117; and *El negro y la blanca*, 114; and impressibility, 91; and Indianness, 110, 121; and metonymic displacements, 20; New Spain's racial histories of, 84; racializing discourses on, 99; and sexuality, 114–115; stereotypes of, 130
Black slaves, 108, 109–110, 115, 130, 133
Bolívar, Simón, 126, 130, 131
Botany Bay penal colony, 157
Bourbon Reform: and Bajío demographics, 229n14; and Bajío riots, 31–32, 54, 64, 66–67; and *capitulaciones*, 62; and inspectors, 228–229n9; and penality, 16–17; and race war paradigm, 7; and racialization, 21–

Bourbon Reform (*continued*)
22; and slavery, 249–250n12; and tribute, 230n25
Boyer, Jean-Pierre, 131–132
Bravo, Ignacio, 187, 269–270n56
Britain, 140, 258–259n5
British Empire, 258–259n5
British Honduras, 170, 178–179, 186, 267n21. *See also* Belize
Bucareli, Antonio María de, 36–39
Bustamente, Carlos María de, 69, 239–240n1

Cádiz, 125, 128–129
Cádiz constitution (1812), 12
Calderón, Felipe, 213
Calleja, Felix, 131
Campeche, 4, 139, 168, 191
Canuto Vela, José, 190
capitalism: and Bajío riots, 31; and cartography, 167–168; and Caste War, 173–174; contradictions in, 263n42; and global interconnection, 86; and Indianness, 36; and monstrosity, 88; and plebeian sectors, 19–20; and racialization, 210; and regime of movement, 174; and special economic zones, 214; and workers, 224–225n70
capital punishment, 148, 149–150, 156, 264n47
capitulaciones, 60–66, 67
Caracas, 123, 130, 255n64
Caribbean region, 89, 145, 146
Carta de Yucatán (Hernández), 180
Carta General de la República Mexicana (García Cubas 1856), 164
Carta General de la República Mexicana (García Cubas 1858), 164, 165f, 166–168
Carta General de la República Mexicana (García Cubas 1863), 168f
cartography, 166–172
Casement, Roger, 271n7

caste (*casta*): abolition of, 2, 19; and Bajío riots, 34–35; and bans on arms and horses, 47; and census, 37; colonial bans on, 47–51; and dress codes, 50; *El Universal* on, 3; José de Gálvez on, 43–44; and gender, 76–77; and geography, 42; and Indianness, 46; Juan López de Cancelada on, 94; paintings by, 101; population distribution of, 250n15; and scientific racism, 24; and theater, 119–120; and tribute, 38; Hipólito Villarroel on, 70, 72–73; and visual codes, 93; and whiteness, 25, 97–98
caste distinctions: fluidity of, 48; and migration, 77; and *policía*, 76; and tribute, 39; and *Vida de J. J. Dessalines*, 93–94; Hipólito Villarroel on, 72–73, 74; and women's bodies, 99; and worker movement, 43–44
Caste War: and cartography, 171, 172, 173, 180, 182–183; and coercive labor, 199; and convict labor, 146, 147; and criollo elites, 164; and deportation, 149; and displaced people, 168–169; and José Pantaleón Domínguez, 15–16; end of, 187; and European settlers, 201; and faithful/unfaithful Indian dichotomy, 176–177; and foreign colonization, 198; Antonio García Cubas on, 267n20; and internal divisions, 267n21; and journalism, 220n14; and labor scarcity, 196; Alice Dixon Le Plongeon on, 178–179; letters by rebel leaders, 188–192; and literary fiction, 158–161; and Maya indenture, 139, 259n7; and militias, 225n72; José María Luis Mora on, 22–23; and race war paradigm, 8, 143; and racial geographies, 166–167; and rebel versus pacified Maya, 154–157; repurposing racial categories, 6; and sugar plantation econ-

omy, 162; surrender agreements, 21; and tribute, 238–239n55; and whiteness, 151–152
caste wars: and José Pantaleón Domínguez, 15–16; indigenous uprisings as, 3–4; and Maya indenture, 141–142; José María Luis Mora on, 260n14; and Yaqui deportations, 202–203
del Castillo, Severo, 177, 182
Catherwood, Frederick, 178
Catholicism, 114, 119
Cecilio Chi (del Castillo 1869), 174–176, 268n34
censorship: of *El negro y la blanca*, 115; Juan López de Cancelada on, 89; and theater, 107, 111, 118–124, 251–252n25, 253–254n45, 254n54
census: and *casta*, 97–98; and coercive labor, 199; and labor, 75–76; and racial makeup, 108, 250n15; Hipólito Villarroel on, 77; and Yaqui deportations, 204
Cerro de San Pedro: and Bajío riots, 53; and *capitulaciones*, 60–64; and San Nicolás, 55–57, 59; siege of, 41, 44; and taxation of resources, 61–62
Cetro, 144, 145
Chang, Jason Oliver, 24
Chan Santa Cruz: Ignacio Bravo's invasion of, 186f, 187; and cartography, 177, 180, 183–184; and creation of Quintana Roo, 269–270n56; Alice Dixon Le Plongeon on, 179; in *Los misterios de Chan Santa Cruz*, 158–159, 265n68; and pleas for justice, 262n23; and travelers, 185
Charles III, 32, 69
Charles IV, 122–123
Charnay, Desiré, 178
Chi, Cecilio, 143
Chiapas, 15–16, 211, 215
Chichanhá, 185
chichiguas, 76–77

Chichimeca people, 55
Chinese laborers, 140, 179, 198, 207, 259n10
Chole people, 209
Christophe, Henri, 101–102, 125, 242–243n6
citizenship: and abstract universal equality, 190; and Haiti, 113; and Indianness, 211; and Maya rebels, 153; and race, 4, 128–129; racialization of, 21; and racial segmentation, 136
civilization: and Caste War, 154; in *Cecilio Chi*, 176–177; and Maya indenture, 141–142, 149, 161; and Mexico's secret mission to Haiti, 133; and racial harmony, 9–10; and racialization, 92; and religion, 114; and whiteness, 151
civil liberties, 12, 13, 223n49
civil rights, 12
class: and Bajío riots, 33; and Blackness, 225n71; and Caste War, 189; and plebeian sectors, 19; and racial differentiation, 219n7; and racial hierarchy, 2; and racialization, 47–48; and tribute, 39
climate, 73, 91, 197
Cob, Francisco, 190
Código formado por los negros de la isla de Santo Domingo (López de Cancelada), 125–126
coercive labor, 7, 21, 162–163, 199, 262n24, 263n42. *See also* Maya indenture
coffee, 194
Colombia, 127–128, 132, 257n26
colonial geography, 61, 73, 129
colonialism: and capitalism, 33; and convict labor, 146–147; and faithful/unfaithful Indian dichotomy, 155–156; and monstrosity, 243n10; and racialization, 219n8; residues of, 209–211; and zones of exception, 222n35

colonization: and convict labor, 194; and economic development, 7; and forced migration, 17; foreign, 195–202, 206–207; and Indianness, 37; meanings of, 271n9; and miscegenation, 24; and whitening, 15–16, 23. *See also* settlers
colonos, 198–201. *See also* settlers
Comanche people, 3
Comay, Rebecca, 86, 87–88
Comella, Luciano Francisco, 115, 116, 117
communal lands, 15, 166, 185, 215
Conflict of Faculties (Kant), 86
Conflicto y armonía de las razas en América (Sarmiento 1883), 1
conservatives: and cartography, 164; and Caste War, 8; on caste wars, 3, 17; and constitution of 1836, 225; and legal exception, 12; and trade in Maya indentured people, 142; and Yucatán, 13–14, 269n43
Constant, Benjamin, 157
convict labor: and Bajío riots, 53; and colonization, 194; and Mexican law, 263n42; and moral reform, 17; and trade in Maya indentured people, 144–148; and Yaqui deportations, 202, 273n33
Corozal, 179
Craib, Raymond B., 167
criminalization: and *casta*, 70, 72; and Maya indenture, 150, 157–158; and national security, 216–217; and Program for National Security, 213; and rebel versus pacified Maya, 156; and social conflict, 14; and Yaqui deportations, 205, 206
criollos: and Bajío riots, 233n75; and Caste War, 143; and *El negro sensible*, 135–136; Alexander von Humboldt on, 250–251n16; as insurgents, 128, 131; and literacy, 93;

Fray Servando Teresa de Mier on, 130; and *peninsulares*, 98; in Saint-Domingue, 105; and tribute, 39; John Tutino on, 56; Hipólito Villarroel on, 72–73; and white privilege, 46–47
critical race studies, 23–24, 25
Croix, Viceroy Marqués de, 32, 35–36, 46, 53
Croquis del teatro de la guerra que actualmente se sostiene en el Estado de Yucatán, 181f
Cruz, Juan de la, 189, 262n23
Cuba: and Chinese laborers, 198, 259n10; and Haitian Revolution, 242n15, 250n13; and Mexico, 257n24; and Spanish American republics, 132–133; and theater, 253–254n45; and trade in Maya indentured people, 139–140, 144–145, 147–154, 162–163, 223n48, 258–259n5, 259n7; and Yucatán Caste War, 23; and Yucatán mutinies, 13
Cuevas Gutiérrez, Gustavo, 212
cultural appropriation, 211

death penalty, 148, 149–150, 156, 264n47
debt peons. *See* coercive labor
Declaration of the Rights of Man and of the Citizen (1789), 112
de la Cruz, Atanasio, 55–57
Del Castillo, Severo, 172–176
democracy, 12, 127, 150–151, 161
deportation: and Miguel Barbachano, 149–150, 151; and Caste War, 147; and José Pantaleón Domínguez, 15; and international law, 148, 154; of "vagrants," 53; of Yaqui people to Yucatán, 202–207, 273n32. *See also* Maya indenture
Derrida, Jacques, 150–151
desertion, 169, 267n18

INDEX { 307 }

Dessalines, Jean Jacques, 100f, 103f; coronation speech of, 83, 120; Juan López de Cancelada on, 101–102; mischaracterization of, 91; and Napoleon, 242–243n6
developmentalist discourse, 211
De Vito, Christian G., 146
Díaz, Porfirio, 186–187, 194, 195–202, 205, 269–270n56, 270–271n4, 271n5
Díaz de la Vega, Rómulo, 180, 269n43
Dillon, Elizabeth Maddock, 111
Direction of Colonization and Industry, 2–3, 219n9
displacement: and Bourbon Reform, 16–17; and Caste War, 151; and economic development, 7; and empire, 242n4; in literary fiction, 161; and Maya rebel manifesto, 188–189; and productivity, 78–79
Dolores, Guanajuato, 105
domestic workers, 76–77
Domínguez, José Pantaleón, 15–16, 17
Donahue-Wallace, Kelly, 99, 101–102
Dondé, Manuel, 196, 197–199
dress codes, 33, 48, 50–51
Drinking, Homicide, and Rebellion (Taylor), 58
Dubroca, Louis, 90–91, 93, 94, 101, 241–242n1
due process, 147

economic development, 7, 9–10, 15, 167, 213–214
El Arcoiris, 4
El Constitucional, 162
El Fénix, 171
El Imparcial, 270–271n4
El Monitor Republicano, 4
El negro sensible (Comella), 115–118, 119–120, 121–122, 134, 254n52
El negro sensible (Lizardi), 134–136
El negro y la blanca (Rodríguez de Arellano), 111–112, 113–115, 117–118, 121

El Porvenir (The Future), 207–208
El Universal, 3
enclosure, 166, 177, 210, 214
En el espejo haitiano (Granados), 109–110
energy infrastructures, 212–213
Enfermedades políticas que padece la capital de esta Nueva España (Villarroel), 69–79, 239–240n1
Enlightenment, 84–85, 112, 114
equality: in *El negro sensible*, 135; and fear of race war, 136; and Haitian Revolution, 84, 112; and independence, 127–128; and Maya rebels, 136, 190–191; and racial difference, 6; and slavery, 117
Escobar, Manuel, 34–36, 48, 49–50
Espita parish, 187
Estado Mayor Presidencial, 212
eugenic theories, 24, 88, 207

Facundo o civilización y barbarie (Sarmiento 1845), 1, 268n36
fagina workers, 172–173, 174
Farge, Arlette, 54
Federal Commission of Electricity (Comisión Federal de Electricidad; CFE), 212
Ferdinand VII, 125, 131–132, 254n54
Ferrand, Jean-Louis, 254n54
Fischer, Sibylle, 107, 126–127
Flores Magón brothers, 271n5
Foucault, Michel, 14, 224–225n70, 243n10
Fradinger, Moira, 113
France: and abolition of slavery, 112; and Haiti, 243n10; and Maya indenture, 140; and moral translation, 86–88; and Napoleonic Wars, 125; and Spanish support of Haiti, 248n4; and state of siege, 222n44; and United States, 97; and whiteness, 101
François, Jean, 248n4

freedom: and Bajío riots, 54; burdened individuality of, 223–224n58; and *capitulaciones*, 61, 63–64, 65; and constitutional rights, 13; and criollo elites, 135–136; and Haitian Revolution, 102; Saidiya Hartman on, 117; of mobility, 46; as privilege, 90–91; and racial difference, 6; and tribute, 66
free mulattos, 31–32, 61–62, 108
French Revolution, 85–86, 87, 243n10, 243n12
French-Spanish alliance, 84
Frost, Frederick J. Tabor, 271n7
fugitivity, 169, 172, 175–176, 177, 179–180, 183, 187, 188

Gaceta de Madrid, 113
gachupines, 55, 56–57, 59–60, 64–65, 66
Gálvez, Bernardo de, 118
Gálvez, José de: and Bajío riots, 17–18, 21, 33, 51–52; and Bourbon Reform, 32, 66–67, 228–229n9; and Cerro de San Pedro siege, 54; and Guanajuato siege, 41–42; and militarization, 71; on mobility of racialized bodies, 70, 232n48; and plebeian sectors, 35; on racial aspect of riots, 57; and spatial interventions, 43–47; on tribute, 36–40; and vanishing Indian trope, 230–231n26
Gálvez, Mariano, 2–3
Garay, Antonio, 2–3
García Cubas, Antonio, 164–168, 169, 170–172, 177, 180, 182, 267n20
García Morales, José, 196, 197–199
García Peña, Ángel, 203–204
garrison reforms, 78–79
Gazeta de México, 83, 89, 93, 95, 97, 249n8, 254n54
gender: in *El negro sensible*, 117; and equality, 112; and migration, 76–77;

and race war, 98–99; and racial repression, 49–51; and trade in Maya indentured people, 23, 142; and whiteness, 95, 101; and Yaqui deportations, 203–204
global white supremacy, 95
Gómez Farías, Valentín, 265–266n1
Gordillo, Gastón, 25–26
governmentality: and Bajío rebellion, 122; and Bajío riots, 57–58; and Caste War, 155–156; and mobility, 70; and penal labor, 157; and plebeian sectors, 18; and *policía*, 71; and power, 41; and racial distinctions, 19, 52, 93; and racialization, 8; and sovereignty, 224–225n70; and spatial interventions, 45; and theater, 110–111; and tribute, 63, 231n36
Granados, Luis Fernando, 109–110
Guanajuato, 41–42, 44, 52, 105
Guaraní uprisings, 1–2
Guenther, Lisa, 150–151
"Guerra de Reforma" (1858–1861), 12–13
Guerrero, 215
Guerrero, Vicente, 131–132
Gutiérrez de Lara, Lázaro, 194, 271n5
Gypsies, 72

hacienda system, 143
hairstyles, 234n84
Haiti: boycotts of, 242n5; constitution of (1805), 83, 84, 120; constitution of (1807), 125; and criollo insurgents, 126–127, 131–132, 133–134; and Francisco Xavier Mina expedition, 255–256n2; and monstrosity, 88–89, 243n10
Haitian Revolution: Manuel Abad y Queipo on, 105–106; and Blackness, 127; Luis Fernando Granados on, 109–110; Alexander von Humboldt on, 251n19; Juan López de Cancelada on, 83–91, 92–95, 97–98, 125–

126; and New Spain colonial authorities, 10–11; and race war paradigm, 7–8; and racial fear, 221n26; Spanish press on, 113; and visual codes, 101–102; and whiteness, 25
Halachó, Yucatán, 144
Ham, curse of, 48–49
Hartman, Saidiya, 117
Havana: and convict transportation, 145; and international relations, 132; in *Los misterios de Chan Santa Cruz*, 159–160; and master-slave relations, 122–123; and trade in Maya indentured people, 139, 144, 146, 148; and "vagrant" deportation, 53, 79
Hecelchakán, 148–150
Heller, Karl, 178
henequen: and Caste War, 196; and coercive labor, 193; and Porfirio Díaz, 187; and global capitalist system, 11; and trade in Maya indentured people, 158, 162; John Kenneth Turner on, 193, 194–195; and Yaqui deportations, 202, 203
Hernández, Manuel, 180
Histoire de Louis Anniaba: Rois D'Essenie en Afrique sur la Côte de Guinée (Anonymous 1740), 112
Hübbe, Juan, 180, 182, 183–184
humanitarianism, 141, 143, 148–154, 161, 162, 260n12
human trafficking, 112, 114, 163, 259n8. See also Maya indenture
Humboldt, Alexander von, 108–109, 145–146, 250n15, 250–251n16, 251n19, 268n27

"Idea de la constitución" (Mier), 130
idleness, 44, 71, 72–73, 74–75
images, 93–94, 98–99, 101–102, 126, 178, 185, 245n35
immigration, 23, 197, 199–200, 260n14
impressibility, 244n24, 245n34

Ince, Onur Ilas, 33
indenture. *See* coercive labor; Maya indenture
Independencia (ship), 186
Indian neighborhoods, 45–46
Indianness: and Bajío riots, 46–47; and Blackness, 110, 121; and colonial structure, 36; and dress codes, 50–51; and legal exception, 15–16; and Maya indenture, 142; and metonymic displacements, 20
Indians: and *alboroto*, 59–60; and hairstyles, 234n84; and plebeian sectors, 35–36; and tribute, 36–39; and Hipólito Villarroel, 240n5; Hipólito Villarroel on, 78–79; and weapons ban, 234n80
Indian subjectivity, 216
indigenous activist groups, 213, 215, 216
indigenous labor, 142, 204
indigenous populations, 36–37, 143, 156, 215, 258–259n15, 260n14, 276n28. *See also specific peoples*
indigenous uprisings, 3–4, 209–211
indios vagos, 31–32, 62, 109–110
industrial economy, 74, 75
Informe sobre las rebeliones populares de 1767 y otros documentos inéditos (Gálvez), 32, 41–42
Inquisition, 107, 111, 115, 118, 253–254n45, 254n54
Institutional Revolutionary Party (Partido Revolucionario Institucional; PRI), 209–211
"Instructive Edict" (Abad y Queipo), 123–124
insurgent textualities, 54–59
intendencias, 69, 240n2
international law, 148–154
investigative journalists, 194
Irigoyen, Liberio, 178
Islam, 119
Isthmus of Tehuantepec, 213, 216

jails, 64–66
Jamaica, 85, 89
James, C. L. R., 112
Jameson, Fredric, 121
Jesuits, expulsion of, 31, 59, 68
Juárez, Benito, 12–13, 152, 161, 174, 186

Kant, Immanuel, 86, 87–88, 243n12
Kaplan, Caren, 21
Karte der Halbinsel Yucatan (Hübbe and Aznar 1879), 183f
Katz, Friedrich, 26
Kazanjian, David, 6, 61, 189, 190
Koeninger, Frieda, 114

La Acordada, 146
labor conditions, 108, 194, 210, 271n7
labor relations, 76–77, 195, 263n37
labor scarcity, 142, 193, 195–196, 199
Lacandon Jungle, 209
La Cruz, Atanasio de, 59, 60
La guerra de razas en el año de 1977 (Anonymous), 207–208
land distribution: and Article 27 reform, 211; and Bajío riots, 33, 40; and *capitulaciones*, 62; and Caste War, 143, 162; and maps, 166; and Maya indenture, 158; and Maya rebels, 190–191; and Program for National Security, 214; and racialization, 42; and ranchers, 45; and special economic zones, 213; and Yaqui deportations, 202–203
La Opinión, 207
La Rea, José Simón de, 83, 93
Las Garantías Sociales, 148–150
Las guerras contra las tribus Yaqui y Mayo del Estado de Sonora (Paso y Troncoso 1905), 203–204
Lasso, Marixa, 127–128
Laws of Indies, 44, 47
Lázaro Cárdenas, 214–215
Le droit des gens, ou Principes de la loi naturelle, appliqués à la conduite et aux affaires des nations et des souverains (Vattel 1758), 153
legal anomaly, 76, 140, 147, 214. *See also* anomalous zones
legal exception: anxieties surrounding, 223n49; and convict labor, 146; and Mexico's 1857 constitution, 222n44; and pacification, 212–213; and plebeian sectors, 20; and race war paradigm, 11–16; and rhetoric of race war, 21–22; and securitization, 216–217. *See also* anomalous zones
León, Juan José de, 268n27
Le Plongeon, Alice Dixon, 178, 185
Le Plongeon, Augustus, 178, 185
Les mystères de Paris (Sué 1842–1843), 158
liberalism: and conservative mutinies of 1867, 13; and *El negro sensible*, 135; in *Los misterios de Chan Santa Cruz*, 160–161; and trade in Maya indentured people, 142, 156, 157, 163; and whiteness, 25
liberalization, 210
licentiousness, 70, 72, 99, 101
literacy, 93
Lizardi, José Joaquín Fernández de, 134–136
López de Cancelada, Juan: *Código formado por los negros de la isla de Santo Domingo*, 125–126; and Napoleonic project, 242–243n6; on New Spain, 129; *Vida de J. J. Dessalines*, 83–91, 92–95, 97–98, 101–102, 105–106, 117, 120
López de Santa Anna, Antonio, 222n45, 260n14
López López, Manuel, 96f, 100f, 103f; and coded images, 94, 99, 101, 114; renown of, 83, 93
López Obrador, Andrés Manuel, 191, 216

INDEX { 311 }

"Los amantes de la felicidad yucateca," 152–154, 156–157
Los misterios de Chan Santa Cruz (Barrera 1864), 158–161
Louverture, Toussaint, 91–92, 101–102
Loveman, Brian, 12
Lund, Joshua, 42

Mallon, Florencia, 26
Mame people, 209
Mann, Mary, 1
Mapa militar de la Península de Yucatán (approx. 1865), 174f
Mapa militar de pueblos en la Zona Rebelde Península de Yucatán (1865), 173f
maquiladoras, 214
marriage: among enslaved people, 122; in *El negro y la blanca*, 114–115; payments for, 190; and racial laws, 99, 101; and tribute, 50–51. See also miscegenation
martial law, 12–14
Martínez, María Elena, 48–49, 99
Maximilian of Habsburg, 13, 169, 172, 197
Maya indenture: and convict labor, 194; diplomatic discussion surrounding, 223n48; as legal anomaly, 144–148; and literary fiction, 159–160, 264n68; and Antonio López de Santa Anna, 260n14; and Mexican history, 139; public debate over, 140–143, 149–150, 151–154, 156–158, 161–163; and racialization, 151; stages of, 258–259n5. See also coercive labor; deportation; human trafficking
Maya peasants, 172–173
Maya rebels: and capital punishment, 150; and cartography, 180, 185; categorization of, 264n57; and citizenship, 153; and indenture, 139–140; and Benito Juárez administration, 161–162; letters by, 188–192; and Maya indenture, 149; and pacified Maya groups, 154–157; repurposing racial categories, 6; surveillance of, 186
Mayo people, 202–203
Mazocoba massacre, 204
Mérida, 143
mestizaje: and assimilation, 207–208, 211; and Mexican state, 24; pillars of, 226n80; and race war paradigm, 274n3; and racial differentiation, 219n7; as racial ideology, 2
metonymic displacements of race, 20, 36, 225n71
Mexican-American War (1846–1848), 22
Mexican constitution (1857), 12–13
Mexican Republic: and cartography, 164, 167; and Caste War, 8; and convict labor, 194; and *El negro sensible*, 136; and plantation economies, 193; and trade in Maya indentured people, 142. See also Mexico
Mexican Revolution, 209–210, 211, 274n3
Mexican Society for Geography and Statistics (Sociedad Mexicana de Geografía y Estadística; SMGE), 164, 171, 265–266n1
Mexico, 165f; and Colombia, 257n26; and colonization, 196–198; constitution of (1836), 225n73; constitution of (1857), 150, 199, 225n73, 263n42; and convict labor, 147; and Cuba, 257n24; and Porfirio Díaz, 195; and Haitian Revolution, 106–107, 123–124; independence of, 127; and Benito Juárez administration, 161; and legal exception, 11–16; and Maya indenture, 139–140, 148–154; and penality, 16–17; production of race in, 151; and racial conflict, 1–2; and racial equality discourse, 128; and se-

Mexico (*continued*)
cret mission to Haiti, 132, 133; US invasion of (1846–1848), 164. *See also* Mexican Republic
Mexico City: and Haitian Revolution, 92; and Maya indenture, 147; and riots of 1692, 18, 46, 234n84; and theater, 254n51; and theater regulations, 118–119; Hipólito Villarroel on, 74
Michoacán, 214–215
Mier, Fray Servando Teresa de, 128–131
Migangos, José Antonio, 144, 260n14
migrant women, 76–77
migration: and gender, 76–77; and Maya indenture, 157–158; as punishment, 17, 141; and tribute, 38; Hipólito Villarroel on, 70–71, 74, 78–79; and whitening, 23
militarization: and Bajío riots, 31, 35, 52, 71; and Bourbon army, 224n62; and convict labor, 146–147; of oil and energy infrastructure, 212–213; and passports, 155; and race war paradigm, 17–18
militias: and Bajío riots, 21, 32; and bans on Indian power, 47–48; and Bourbon Reform, 17; and Caste War, 225n72; and free Blacks and mulattos, 17; and ranchers, 44–45
Miller, William, 183–185
Mills, Charles W., 95
Milton, Cynthia, 50–51
Mina, Francisco Xavier, 131, 255–256n2
mining: and Bajío riots, 8, 17, 21, 31; and *capitulaciones*, 61–63; and forced migration, 78–79; José de Gálvez on, 43–44, 71; and New Spain's economy, 11, 52, 108; and racial difference, 33; and tribute, 37; and white colonization, 198; and worker movement, 41, 77, 232n48; and Yaqui deportations, 203–204
miscegenation: Manuel Escobar on, 49–50; José María Luis Mora on, 22, 23, 24, 260n14; prohibitions on, 129; and whitening, 197. *See also* marriage
mobility: and Bajío riots, 41; and Caste War, 154–155; racialized regulation of, 65; and tribute, 38; and vagabondage, 44; Hipólito Villarroel on, 70, 73–74; and whiteness, 46; and Yaqui deportations, 204
modernity: and capitalism, 174; in *Cecilio Chi*, 175–176; Rebecca Comay on, 244n15; and *El negro y la blanca*, 113; and Haitian Revolution, 244n16; and revolutions in France and Haiti, 87–88; and slavery, 135, 161; and trade in Maya indentured people, 163; and violence, 113
Molina, Olegario, 202
monstrosity: and capitalism, 88; and Enlightenment philosophy, 84–85; Michel Foucault on, 243n10; and Haitian Revolution, 101–102, 107; and race wars, 104; and racist rhetoric, 83–84
Mora, Francisco, 45
Mora, José María Luis, 22–24, 197, 260n14
Mora, Mariana, 215
morality, 86, 87, 114, 117, 142–143
moral translation, 87
More, Anna, 46
Mourning Sickness (Comay), 86
Múuch' Xíinbal, 191–192

Napoleon [Bonaparte], 252n29
Napoleonic Wars, 84, 110, 120–121, 125, 248n4
National Guard, 155, 225n72
national security, 14, 22, 210, 213–214, 216–217
natural resources, 215
Negri, Antonio, 88

Nemser, Daniel, 18, 19, 42
neoliberalism, 209–210, 211
New Granada, 50–51
New Orleans, 146
New Spain: and Bajío riots, 31–32, 56; and convict labor, 145–146; and crisis of sovereignty, 122; and Haitian Revolution, 94, 105–106, 123–124, 244n23; Alexander von Humboldt on, 109; and racial boundaries, 34–36; and racialization, 9; and relocation of convert Indians, 56; and slavery, 108; and tax, 231n40; and theater, 118–124; and transatlantic slave trade, 95; and tribute, 37–39, 51–52; and *Vida de J. J. Dessalines*, 93–94; Hipólito Villarroel on, 69–79; and weapons ban, 67–68; and whiteness, 97–98
newspapers: and Caste War, 158, 188; and elite anxieties, 4; and Haitian Revolution, 107; and humanitarianism, 260n12; and Alice Dixon Le Plongeon, 178; as primary source, 27; and race war paradigm, 190; and trade in Maya indentured people, 140; and Yaqui deportations, 205
Nigra, Santiago, 171, 172
Novelo, Juan María, 185
Nuevo León, 55

Oaxaca, 215
Ocampo, Melchor, 161, 162
Omi, Michael, 58
Onis, Luis, 131
Opata, 202
Oportunidades (now Prospera), 215–216
organized crime, 210
Orosio, Antonio, 53–54
Orozco y Berra, Manuel, 180
Ortega, Santiago, 238n50
Ortiz, Severiano, 64

Other Rebellion (Van Young 2001), 26
Otomí people, 55

pacification: and *capitulaciones*, 58; and Caste War, 23; and coercive labor, 202; and convict labor, 146; and development, 212–217; José Pantaleón Domínguez on, 15; *El Universal* on, 3; José de Gálvez's methods for, 32–34; and legal exception, 12; and Maya indenture, 145, 161; and race war paradigm, 7, 210–211; and racial geographies, 177; and rebel versus pacified Maya, 154–157; and rebel Yaqui people, 204–206; and settlements, 196; subjects of, 21
pactism, 67, 239n58
Paniagua Pérez, Jesús, 93
Partido Liberal Mexicano, 271n5
Paso y Troncoso, Francisco del, 203–204
Pat, José Isaac, 190
Pátzcuaro, 52
Peasant and Nation (Mallon 1995), 26
Pemex, 212
Peña Nieto, Enrique, 212, 213, 215
peninsulares, 39, 73, 98
peonage system, 194
Peraza, Martín Francisco, 148–150
peripeteia, 120–122
peripheral zones, 198–199
Perú, 1–2, 109, 198
Pétion, Alexandre, 126
Pétion, Alexandre Sabès, 131
Peto, 172, 173, 177, 187
Pima, 202
Plano de Yucatán (Nigra 1848), 171f
plebe, 18–20, 33, 35–38, 72, 74, 107, 131
plebeian sectors, 18–20, 233n75
plural universality, 6, 190
policía, 53, 71, 76, 240n11
Political Essay on the Kingdom of New Spain (Humboldt), 108–109, 145–146
political geography, 1–2, 75–76, 190–191

Polvérel, Étienne, 112–113
Poot, Cresencio, 158
popular sovereignty, 150–151
Porfiriato, 7, 24, 186, 219n7, 271n9
postcolonialism, 8, 24, 134, 219n8
poverty, 4, 72, 211, 213–214, 216
predatory economics, 64–65, 66
Principes de politiques applicables à tous les gouvernments representatifs (Constant 1815), 157
printing press, 84, 92–93
prisons, 5, 65
privatization, 210
profit: and Bajío riots, 16–17; and coercive labor, 193; and forced migration, 142, 151, 157; José de Gálvez on, 71; and mercantilism, 231n33; and racial conflict, 10–11; and racial difference, 33; and SEZ program, 215–216; and silver mining, 108; and state violence, 47, 51–52; and tribute, 37–39; and unemployment, 75
Program for National Security (PNS), 213–216
public security, 214–215
Puerto Rico, 254n54

Quichua, 1–2
Quintana Roo, 187

race: and census, 250n15; and class, 189; and coercive labor, 193–194; in colonial and postcolonial periods, 134; and Haitian Revolution, 106–107; production of, 57–58; as social construct, 6; and sovereignty, 150–151; and tribute, 50–51
race war: and assimilation, 201; and Direction of Colonization and Industry, 2–3; fear of, 88, 126, 128, 136; Alexander von Humboldt on, 108–109; language of, 1; and legal exception, 11–16; Fray Servando Teresa de Mier on, 128–131; and monstrosity, 85; and racial democracy, 127–128; and whiteness, 95
race war paradigm: and Caste War, 143; flashpoints of, 7–9; and global capitalist system, 10–11; and international affairs, 133–134; language of, 4–5; and Maya indenture, 140; and *mestizaje*, 274n3; and militarization, 17–18; and neoliberalism, 209–211; plasticity of, 71; and racial stratification, 19–20; and republican rule, 15–16; and securitization, 216–217; and special economic zones, 215–216; and universal equality, 190; and *Vida de J. J. Dessalines*, 94; and Yaqui deportations, 203
racial categories, 6, 37, 70, 97–98, 187–188, 240n12
racial conflict: and conservative mutinies of 1867, 14; framing of, 11–12; and New Spain colonial authorities, 10–11; and penality, 16–17; and rule of law, 15; Sarmiento on, 1–2; Hipólito Villarroel on, 74, 77–79
racial democracy, 127–128
racial discourse, 211, 216
racial exclusion, 24
racial fear, 130–131, 176, 198, 221n26
racial formation, 242n4
racial geography, 62, 77, 198–200, 215–216, 238n35
racial harmony, 9–10, 106, 110, 120, 221n31
racial hierarchy, 2, 50, 200
racial inclusion, 24
racialization: and accretion, 7; and Bajío riots, 32–33; of Black male subjectivity, 117; and church records, 187; and civilization, 92; and class, 47–48; discourse of, 206–207; and forced labor, 162–163; gradated burdens of, 21–22; and history, 6; of

horror, 88; and immigration, 199–200; and inequality, 109; and labor, 75–76, 198–199; and legal decrees, 234n80; in Alice Dixon Le Plongeon's articles, 179; and Maya indenture, 140; Maya rebels' challenges to, 189; and *mestizaje*, 274n3; and metonymic displacements, 20; and national security, 216–217; and neoliberalism, 210; and public versus private sphere, 275n7; and race riots, 229n12; and rhetoric, 5; and spatial interventions, 42; and special economic zones, 215–216; and stereotypes, 184–185; and tribute, 38, 39; John Kenneth Turner on, 194–195; and whiteness, 25; and worker movement, 43–44; and Yaqui deportations, 205
racializing discourses, 134
racial regimes, 6
racial state, 218–219n6
racial stratification, 18–19
racial uprisings: elite fear of, 6–7; framing of, 13–14; military campaigns against, 3; José María Luis Mora on, 22–23
racism, 83–84, 128, 226n80, 237n28, 275n7
radical abolitionism, 150–151
railroads, 193
Rean, Pastora, 158
rebel archive, 5–6, 54–55, 191
rebellions: Lucas Alamán on, 18; in Bajío (1810), 107; and cartography, 164; and colonial governmentality, 110; conceptualized as race wars, 4–5; and conservative mutinies of 1867, 13; José de Gálvez's repression of, 21, 32, 41–42, 229n10; and Haiti, 131; and indigenous populations, 260n14; and methodology, 26–28; and metonymic displacements of race, 20;

and monstrosity, 89; and public opinion, 3; suppression of, 14; William B. Taylor on, 58; and tribute, 39; and viscerality, 237n20; and Yaqui deportations, 203; in Yucatán (*see* Caste War)
Regeneración, 205, 206
Regil Peón, Pedro de, 196, 197–199
regime of movement, 173–174
regimes of visibility, 184
Reglamento u Ordenanzas de Teatros, 118–119
Reglas de Policía y Buen Gobierno, 53
rent, 45, 62, 63
repúblicas de españoles, 31–32
repúblicas de indios, 31–32, 55, 233n74
revolutions, 67, 85–87, 106, 110, 112
rhetoric: and coded images, 101; of criminality, 43–44, 71–72; of exception, 15; of monstrosity, 83–84; moralizing, 79; and pacification, 7; of race war, 211–212; and race war paradigm, 9; of racial conflict, 4–5, 14, 21–22; of racial fear, 27–28; of racial harmony, 10
Rocafuerte, Vicente, 132–133
Rodríguez, José Manuel, 67–68
Rodríguez de Arellano, Vicente, 111, 112
Romero Ancona, Manuel, 195
Rugeley, Terry, 139
rule of law, 11, 14–15

Saban, 177
Sacalaca, 177
Saint-Domingue: Manuel Abad y Queipo on, 105, 123–124; contrasted with New Spain, 84, 94–95, 108; and emancipation, 113; and fear of race war, 128–129; and freedom, 90–91; and horror, 87; and monstrosity, 85; and visual codes, 102; and whiteness, 97–98

Saldaña-Portillo, María Josefina, 155–156, 176
Salinas de Gortari, Carlos, 209–212
Sanders, James E., 133
San Fernando Aké, 248n4
San Luis de la Paz, 59
San Luis Potosí: and Bajío riots, 46; and *capitulaciones*, 60–64; Manuel Escobar's sermon to, 34–36, 48; and Indianness, 45; and "obsequios" to Ferdinand VII, 254n54; and rioters' demands, 53–54; and tribute, 52
San Nicolás de Armadillo, 55–57, 59
San Pedro de Guadalcázar, 64, 238n50
Santa Elena, 197
Santo Domingo, 254n54
Sarmiento, Domingo Faustino, 1–2, 268n36
scholastic pactism, 67
Schuller, Kyla, 90
scientific racism, 24
Search for Sovereignty (Benton), 39
secession, 142
Secretary of Development, Colonization, and Industry, 195
securitization, 216–217
segregation, 46, 129, 241n19
Sel, Apolinar, 190
serranos, 53, 56
settler colonialism, 2, 218n4, 229–230n24
settlers, 15–16, 23, 155, 165–166, 170, 197, 267n21. *See also* colonization; *colonos*
Seven Years' War (1756–1763), 31
sexual violence, 99, 114
Sierra Gorda, 3–4, 17–18, 164
Sigüenza y Góngora, Carlos de, 18, 46
silver, 31–32, 37, 41, 63, 108
Sisal, 139, 146
slavery: and Bourbon Reform, 249–250n12; and Charles IV's decree (1789), 122–123; and Cuba, 132–133; and "curse of Ham," 48; in *El negro sensible*, 115–118, 135; and *El negro y la blanca*, 112; and Haitian Revolution, 89, 113, 242n5; Alexander von Humboldt on, 108–109; and indenture, 258–259n5; and Maya indenture, 140–141, 161; and peonage system, 194; and racial conflict, 2; and Guadalupe Victoria's conciliatory order, 134
social hygiene, 70, 79
social reproduction, 61, 62, 64, 111, 204
Soliman II (Favart), 112
Sommer, Doris, 175
Sonora, 202–206
Sonthonax, Léger-Félicité, 112–113
Sotillo, Soto, Soto Mayor (Villergas 1845), 160
sovereignty: and *capitulaciones*, 63; and pactism, 239n58; partial, 221–222n33; and racialization, 150–151; José Manuel Rodríguez on, 67–68; and tribute, 39–40; and whiteness, 153
Spain: and Black Legend, 10, 129; and Bourbon Reform, 33; and convict labor, 145–147; and criollo insurgents, 128; and curse of Ham, 49; and *El negro y la blanca*, 113–114; and Gypsies, 72; and Haiti, 125–126, 131, 242–243n6, 248n4, 252n31; imperial army of, 17, 31; and imperial reproduction, 101; legal system of, 146–147; and Maya indenture, 140; and mining industry, 52; and Napoleonic Wars, 125; Napoleon's invasion of, 120, 239n58; and racialization, 36; and racialized legal decrees, 234n80; and Santo Domingo, 254n54; and sovereignty, 39–40; and trade in Maya indentured people, 140; and tribute, 38–39, 68
Spanish Empire: and censorship, 119; and convict labor, 145–147; and cri-

sis of sovereignty, 122; and Haiti, 132; and Haitian Revolution, 107; and mining industry, 11; and Napoleon's 1808 invasion, 120–121; and penality, 16–17; racialized structure of, 98–99; and slavery, 249–250n12
spatiality, 33, 42, 72–73, 188–191
special economic zones (SEZ), 213–216
spectators, 118–119
State of Exception (Agamben), 11
Stephens, John Lloyd, 178
stereotypes, 184–185
Stoler, Ann Laura, 28
Suárez y Navarro, Juan, 161
subaltern studies, 26
Subcomandante Marcos, 217
Sue, Christina A., 24
Sué, Eugène, 158
sugar industry: and Caste War, 143, 144, 162, 168–169; and Chinese laborers, 179; in Cuba, 242n5; in *El negro sensible*, 115, 116; and henequen, 11; in *Los misterios de Chan Santa Cruz*, 160; in Saint-Domingue, 108; and trade in Maya indentured people, 140

Talleyrand, Charles Maurice de, 95, 98
Tamaulipas, 132
Tampico, 139, 146
taxation: and Bajío riots, 21, 57–58, 63; and *capitulaciones*, 61, 63, 65–66; and Caste War, 143; and colonization, 196; José de Gálvez on, 41, 51–52, 71; and migration, 70; José María Luis Mora on, 23; and New Spain, 231n40; as punishment, 236n8; and racial conflict, 5; racialized exaction of, 143; of resources, 61; José Manuel Rodríguez on, 68; and San Pedro de Guadalcázar riot, 65
Taylor, William B., 58, 65
Tekax, 149, 172, 173, 187, 190

theater, 110–111, 114–115, 118–124
Tihosuco, 173, 177
Tizimín, 148–150
Tlaxcalilla, 40, 44
Tlaxcaltecans, 234n80
tobacco, 194, 195
Tojolabal people, 209
Torres, Luis E., 202
Torres, Nicolás Fernando de, 55
torrid zones, 73
transatlantic slave trade, 95, 249–250n12, 252n28, 258–259n15
transnational capital, 210
Tren Maya, 191–192
tribute: and Bajío rebellion, 110; and Bajío riots, 31–32, 51–52, 58; and Bourbon Reform, 230n25; and Caste War, 143; and colonial governmentality, 231n36; and dress codes, 50–51; and José de Gálvez, 33; José de Gálvez on, 36–39; indigenous exemptions from, 55; and racial conflict, 5; racializating nature of, 63–64; and San Pedro de Guadalcázar riot, 66; and sovereignty, 40; and spatial interventions, 43–44; and Hipólito Villarroel, 240n5; Hipólito Villarroel on, 76
Trouillot, Michel-Rolph, 102
tumultos, 31, 58, 65
Tunkás, 158
Tupac Amaru rebellion, 109
Turner, John Kenneth, 193, 202, 205–206, 271n7
Tutino, John, 31, 56
Tzeltal people, 209
Tzotzil people, 209
Tzuc, José María, 185

Uc, Pedro, 191
Uh, Pantaleón, 190
underdevelopment, 216
unemployment, 71–73, 74

Unión, 139, 259n7
United States: and *Barbarous Mexico*, 194–195; and Caste War refugees, 168; and emancipation, 223–224n58; and Haiti, 97; Alexander von Humboldt on, 109; invasion of Mexico (1846–1848), 164; and Mexican-American War (1846–1848), 22; and penitentiary reform, 263n42; and settler practices, 197; and slavery, 161
Uresti, Joseph Ignacio de, 53
US-Mexico border, 3

vagrants, 32, 53
Valdés Murguía y Saldaña, Manuel Antonio, 255n66
Valentini, Philipp, 182
Valladolid, 148–150, 172, 173, 187
Valle Nacional, 193
vanishing Indian trope, 34, 37, 229–230n24, 230–231n26
Van Young, Eric, 26
Vattel, Emmerich de, 153
Veracruz, 139, 146, 215
Vías de comunicación y movimiento marítimo (García Cubas 1885), 169–170, 170f
Victoria, Guadalupe, 134
Vida de J. J. Dessalines (López de Cancelada): and audience, 89–90; and author's support for Napoleonic project, 242–243n6; and barbarism discourse, 92; coded images in, 93–94, 96f, 100f, 101–102, 103f; and *Código formado por los negros de la isla de Santo Domingo*, 125; and Louis Dubroca, 241–242n1; and Haiti–New Spain communication, 244n23; and monstrosity, 87–88, 104, 242n4; and theatrical metaphor, 83; and whiteness, 97–98; and Felipe Zúñiga y Ontiveros, 255n66
Villalobos, Joaquín, 152

Villarroel, Hipólito, 69–79, 239–240n1, 240n5
Villergas, Juan Martínez, 160
Vinson, Ben, 50–51
visual codes, 101–102, 245n35
Vivó, Buenaventura, 144–145
Voz de la patria, 69

wages, 210
water, 44–45, 61, 202
weapons ban, 53, 57, 68, 234n80
Western eugenic philosophy, 88
whiteness: construction of, 25–26; fragility of, 197; and individual liberties, 200–201; and legal exception, 214; and Maya indenture, 151–152; and *mestizaje*, 207–208; and New Spain's elites, 84; and property, 226n83; protection of, 46–51; shared structures of, 94–95, 97–98; and sovereignty, 153
whitening, 17, 114, 197
white women's bodies, 99, 101
Winant, Howard, 58
Wolfe, Patrick, 6
women's bodies, 51, 76–77, 99, 246–247n55
workers, 199–200

Yam, Calixto, 190
Yam, Juan Justo, 190
Yaqui people, 202–207, 273n32
Yucatán: and *Carta General*, 164–165, 166–168, 166f; and cartography, 171–172, 180, 185–186; and Caste War, 8, 143; in *Cecilio Chi*, 174–176; and conservatives, 13, 269n43; and foreign colonization, 195–202; and foreign visitors' accounts, 178–179; and henequen economy, 11, 193; indigenous population of, 260n15; indigenous uprisings in, 3–4, 22–23, 141; and Maya indenture, 139; produc-

tion of race in, 151; and racial hierarchy, 199–200; rail projects in, 216; and rebel manifesto, 188–189; reports of abuses in, 271n7; and special economic zones, 215; and statehood, 142; and trade in Maya indentured people, 260n14; and whiteness, 152–153; and Yaqui deportations, 202–207, 273n32

Zaïre (Voltaire), 112
Zangroniz Hermanos y Compañía, 139

Zapatista Army of National Liberation (Ejército Zapatista de Liberación Nacional; EZLN), 209–212
Zaragoza (ship), 186
Zarco, Francisco, 161
Zavala, Lorenzo de, 133
Zoque people, 209
Zúñiga y Ontiveros, Felipe, 122, 123, 255n66

www.ingramcontent.com/pod-product-compliance
Lightning Source LLC
Chambersburg PA
CBHW020727300425
25857CB00003B/18